NEW INSCRIPTIONS AND SEALS RELATING TO THE BIBLICAL WORLD

Society of Biblical Literature

Archaeology and Biblical Studies

Tammi Schneider, Editor

Number 19

New Inscriptions and Seals
Relating to the Biblical World

NEW INSCRIPTIONS AND SEALS RELATING TO THE BIBLICAL WORLD

edited by

Meir Lubetski

and

Edith Lubetski

Society of Biblical Literature
Atlanta, Georgia

NEW INSCRIPTIONS AND SEALS RELATING TO THE BIBLICAL WORLD

Copyright © 2012 by the Society of Biblical Literature

All rights reserved. No part of this work may be reproduced or transmitted in any form or by any means, electronic or mechanical, including photocopying and recording, or by means of any information storage or retrieval system, except as may be expressly permitted by the 1976 Copyright Act or in writing from the publisher. Requests for permission should be addressed in writing to the Rights and Permissions Office, Society of Biblical Literature, 825 Houston Mill Road, Atlanta, GA 30329 USA.

Library of Congress Cataloging-in-Publication Data

Lubetski, Meir.
  New inscriptions and seals relating to the biblical world / by Meir Lubetski.
    p. cm. — (Society of Biblical Literature archaeology and biblical studies ; no. 19)
  Includes bibliographical references and index.
  ISBN 978-1-58983-556-6 (paper binding : acid-free paper) — ISBN 978-1-58983-557-3 (electronic format)
  1. Inscriptions, Hebrew—Israel. 2. Inscriptions, Hebrew—Palestine. 3. Seals (Numismatics)—Israel. 4. Seals (Numismatics)—Palestine. 5. Jewish seals (Numismatics) 6. Israel—Antiquities. 7. Palestine—Antiquities. 8. Bible—Antiquities. I. Society of Biblical Literature. II. Title.
  PJ5034.8.I8L83 2012
  492—dc23
                            2012022075

Printed on acid-free, recycled paper conforming to ANSI/NISO Z39.48-1992 (R1997) and ISO 9706:1994 standards for paper permanence.

To our dearest children and grandchildren, whose worth is far more than rubies,

                        Saul and Rebecca Lubetski
                                Mia Leora
                              Yitshak Emanuel
                              Raphael Yishayahu

                            Uriel and Shani Lubetski
                                     Yaakov
                                    Yehudah
                                      Dovid

                            Leah and Ari Feldman
                                  Talia Sarah
                                Ilan Yehudah
                                  Atara Baila
                                  Aliza Tamar

May God bless you with long life filled with good deeds, health and wealth;
May all your endeavors succeed and your heartfelt wishes be fulfilled for good.

Participants of the European Association of Biblical Studies conference, Lisbon, 2008. Sitting, from left to right: André Lemaire, W. G. Lambert (deceased), Kathleen Abraham, Shlomo Moussaieff. Standing: Robert Deutsch, Martin Heide, Chaim Cohen, Alan Millard, Peter Van der Veen, Meir Lubetski.

Contents

Foreword		ix
Acknowledgments		xv
Abbreviations		xvii
1.	From the Origin of the Alphabet to the Tenth Century B.C.E.: New Documents and New Directions ANDRÉ LEMAIRE	1
2.	Gedaliah's Seal Material Revisited: Some Preliminary Notes on New Evidence from the City of David PETER VAN DER VEEN	21
3.	Sixteen Strong Identifications of Biblical Persons (Plus Nine Other Identifications) in Authentic Northwest Semitic Inscriptions from before 539 B.C.E. LAWRENCE J. MYKYTIUK	35
4.	Six Hebrew Fiscal Bullae from the Time of Hezekiah ROBERT DEUTSCH	59
5.	*Dml*': A Seal from the Moussaieff Collection MEIR LUBETSKI	69
6.	Who Was *Bat Pharaoh*, the Daughter of Pharaoh? CLAIRE GOTTLIEB	83
7.	New Perspectives on the Trade between Judah and South Arabia ANDRÉ LEMAIRE	93
8.	A Unique Bilingual and Biliteral Artifact from the Time of Nebuchadnezzar II in the Moussaieff Private Collection KATHLEEN ABRAHAM	111
9.	Bricks and Brick Stamps in the Moussaieff Private Collection KATHLEEN ABRAHAM	129

10.	A Babylonian Boundary Stone in the Moussaieff Collection W. G. Lambert†	137
11.	A New Inscribed Palmyrene Stone Bowl from the Moussaieff Collection André Lemaire	147
12.	Mandaic Magic Bowls in the Moussaieff Collection: A Preliminary Survey Matthew Morgenstern	157
13.	Katuwas and the Masoretic Text of Kings: Cultural Connections between Carchemish and Israel Richard S. Hess	171
14.	Hebrew Seals, Stamps, and Statistics: How Can Fakes Be Found? Alan Millard	183
15.	The Moabitica and Their Aftermath: How to Handle a Forgery Affair with an International Impact Martin Heide	193
16.	Biblical Hebrew Philology in Light of the Last Three Lines of the Yeho'ash Royal Building Inscription (YI: lines 14–16) Chaim Cohen	243
17.	Dr. Shlomo Moussaieff's View of the Nerva Coin Meir Lubetski	277
18.	A Teacher, A Colleague, A Friend: Wilfred G. Lambert, 1926–2011 Meir Lubetski	283

Subject Index	287
Index of Sources	295
Index of Authors	307

Foreword

It was not so long ago, from the perspective of history, that men were blissfully unaware of buried treasures telling tales of ancient civilizations. People had only a vague notion of the large number of cultures that had slipped into obscurity but had left an immutable impact on future generations. As the number of archaeological digs multiplies, the seal, the cuneiform tablet, the papyrus scroll, the stone stele, the ostraca, and even a crude ceramic, each provide an eye-opening glimpse into the days of yore.

Our volume continues the tradition of *New Seals and Inscriptions, Hebrew, Idumean and Cuneiform*[1] by publishing the papers of eminent scholars originally presented at conferences of the International Meetings of the Society of Biblical Literature (Vienna, 2007; Rome, 2009) and the European Association of Biblical Studies (Lisbon, 2008). The majority of the papers focus on the analysis of archaeological material from Dr. Shlomo Moussaieff's outstanding collection and the conclusions of the scholars broaden and deepen our understanding of the biblical epoch.

Varied as they are, the articles signal fresh approaches to the study of ancient artifacts. A standard model is challenged by other alternatives and a multifaceted paradigm slowly replaces the existing one. There is recognition of the limitations of sole paleographic examination for determining the era and the classification of ostraca and seals. Nevertheless, this does not diminish the salient importance of studies on philology, onomastics, and paleography, fields that continue to be cornerstones of research. Indeed, a number of papers on these topics appear in this volume. For example, André Lemaire provides a fresh outlook on the origin of the alphabet from new texts, and Peter van der Veen analyzes a famous biblical figure whose name appears on extra-biblical seals.

Lawrence Mykytiuk identifies many biblical figures from inscriptions that were found in registered archaeological excavations. The compatibility between

---

1. Meir Lubetski, ed., *New Seals and Inscriptions, Hebrew, Idemean and Cuneiform* (Sheffield: Sheffield Phoenix, 2007).

the person's function and position as described in the inscriptions and in the Bible adds veracity not only to the narrative of the biblical text but also to the authenticity of the inscriptions.

After many decades of the primacy of linguistics in the field, this book indicates the almost universal growth of interest in the glyptic. Iconic art as a factor in understanding cultural motifs in the literature of the Bible is gaining ground. The growth in the number of iconic and aniconic seals unearthed seems to reveal a rising group of officials eager to have a clearly recognizable symbol of authority with or without aesthetic qualities. Moreover, the elaborate engraving reveals use by the elite echelons who engaged professional seal cutters to adapt designs from a universal glyptic repertory.

Robert Deutsch interprets six bullae from the late Judean Monarchical period. Four of the bullae are aniconic while the other two are iconic depicting Egyptian iconography. The seal impressions are used as "fiscal bullae" in King Hezekiah's taxation system. They include names of biblical towns heretofore unknown to us from collateral sources.

Meir Lubetski's article suggests that the name on a Hebrew seal from Dr. Moussaieff's treasure trove is Egyptian-inspired and that the seal cutter ornamented the seal with meaningful Egyptian iconography. The religious symbols on the seal provide divine protection to the owner and give it amuletic power as well.

There is a growing recognition that Israel's southwestern neighbor, Egypt, is at least as important as Mesopotamia in understanding the Bible. Claire Gottlieb illuminates the specific meaning of *Bat Pharaoh* by drawing upon the Egyptian language and comparing it to similar Egyptian and biblical titles.

Continuing to look in a southern direction, André Lemaire's explanation of a Sabean inscription suggests the possible commercial ties between the kingdom of Judah and that of the South Arabia. The spread of international trade testifies to a shift from an autarchy and a *politeia*, to a centralized administration relying on a commercial fleet purchasing imported luxury goods to supply the needs of an emerging wealthy customer class. It appears to be a hypothesis that suits some biblical accounts.

New cuneiform tablets from the Moussaieff collection are most instructive. For example, Kathleen Abraham's translation and interpretation of a Mesopotamian artifact provides us with the spectacular multilingual knowledge of the Babylonian administration during the time of Nebuchadnezzar II. The same author discusses two royal inscriptions, one that honors King Nebuchadnezzar II for restoring the Temple of Shamash in Larsa, and the other inscribed on a printing block that was used to label the bricks for the construction of the Temple of Inanna/Ishtar in Adab. W. G. Lambert[†] deciphers a unique legal boundary-stone document. This boundary stone was cut to resemble a clay tablet. King

Adad-apla-iddina, eighth king of the Second Isin Dynasty (ca. 1069 B.C.E.), in his generosity, gives a piece of land in perpetuity to a named person, the king's exorcist. The boundary stone includes a sketched map of the land with marked borders.

The variety of artifacts in Moussaieff's storehouse opens the window to additional fields of inquiry. The Palmyrene stone bowl from the Seleucid era, ca. 155 C.E. that Lemaire describes is in that category. Scholars believe that such vessels were used by the upper classes in connection with excessive drinking. He ties it in with the biblical *marzeaḥ* that is attested later in Palmyra. Indeed, the Bible describes *marzeaḥ* as loathsome, something that should be avoided (Amos 6:7). I might add that the rabbis of the first and second centuries C.E. linked the *marzeaḥ* practices with an orgiastic banquet of the *maiumas*, consisting of wine, women, and song.[2]

Dr. Moussaieff has a significant number of magic texts written in Mandaic or the so-called Manichaean Syriac script. Matthew Morgenstern presents a preliminary survey of the magic texts and offers insights to direct future studies. The texts were written in different scripts, and possibly came from varied religious groups. Those in Aramaic were a product of Jews, in Syriac the work of Christians, and Mandaic was produced by the Mandaean Gnostic community.

Richard Hess tackles a new area laden with potential.[3] He finds parallels and similarities between a Luwian inscription from Carchemish and the Masoretic text of Kings. Indeed, Billie Jean Collins confirms: "The resumption of archaeological fieldwork [in that region] ... is affording us a much clearer view in a period that was key to the development, among other things, of the Israelite state."[4]

Examining archaeological items housed in private collections has not only expanded our vistas in understanding the ancient world, but has also opened a Pandora's box of issues dealing with unprovenanced items. The problems are often more difficult to solve than deciphering the artifact. The world of academia is currently grappling with the reliability of the artifacts discovered in unauthor-

---

2. *Sipre Numbers* 131; *Lev. Rab.* 5:3. Biblical *marzeaḥ* is anticipated in Ebla texts as a religious institution. *Ugula mar-za-u₉* is *sorvegliante festa*. Alfonso Archi, *Testi Amministrativi: Assegnazioni Di Tessuti (archivio L. 2769)* (ARET 1; Rome: Missione archeologica italiana in Siria, 1985), 3:rev. xi:3. We also find the phrase *mar-za-u₉ en*. Pettinato assumes this to be a specific festival day or a fixed sacrifice day of the *en*, ruler. Dietz Otto Edzard, *Verwaltungstexte Verschiedenene Inhalts (archivio L. 2769)* (ARET 2; Rome: Missione archeologica italiana in Siria, 1985), 5:rev. x: 6–7. See *mar-za-u₉, ARET* 2, 133. The employee has the title of *lú*, man of, *mar-za u₉* (*ARET* 2: 5: rev.x:12–13).

3. See *Near Eastern Archaeology* 72 (December 2009). The entire issue features the Neo-Hittites in the region of Karatepe, Malatya, Karkamish, and Zincirli.

4. Billie Jean Collins, "From the Editor," ibid.: 2.

ized archaeological excavations or bought on the antiquity markets. Scholars tend to split into two opposing camps. While one group maintains that archaeological items coming from unprovenanced sites should be ignored because of possible fraud, the other group regards this approach as irresponsible and a disservice to the field. Ancient Near Eastern scholarship is suffering from the needless division into two branches.

The debate about art forgery is not novel. Almost eight decades ago, Cyrus H. Gordon discussed the issue of probable well-copied fakes, nonetheless he included them in the registry of his deciphered seals with a warning that some might be imitations.[5] He was aware that forgeries in art are an old practice, as old as humanity itself. However, copying and imitating is a needed step in the procedure of pupils acquiring the skills from a master artist in antiquity. Accordingly, scholars should not automatically disqualify objects. He wrote:

> The scholar should not take it upon himself to decide with finality that such and such monument is a modern imitation without value, for a peculiar seal may belong to a little known or totally unknown category and it may be only a matter of time until the suspected seal will prove to be a genuine with copious analogues.[6]

Years later, Joseph Naveh noted that a great portion of Hebrew pre-exilic seals came from unauthorized archaeological excavations. Unfortunately, there is no record of where the lion's share of the seals were found and many were purchased from antiquity dealers. That did not stop Nahman Avigad from deciphering, describing, and publishing the artifacts and it did not elicit an objection from Naveh who maintained that, "The avoidance of publishing seals bought on the market cannot serve as a remedy for the looting of ancient objects."[7] Furthermore, limiting examination of artifacts from authorized digs only would stunt epigraphic and numismatic research, art history of the ancient era, post-exilic research, even the Dead Sea Scrolls investigation.[8] Like his predecessor Cyrus H.

---

5. Cyrus H. Gordon, "Western Asiatic Seals in the Walters Art Gallery," *Iraq* 6 (Spring 1939): 3–34. For example, p. 34, #125–27; See also plate XV; p. 23 #64, plate VIII.

6. Ibid., 5. Gordon mentioned to his students the case of Agoracritus, a sculptor and a student of Phidias. The master teacher loaned his name to a statue that, in fact, was made by his favorite student, Pausanias (I.33.3), however, ascribes the statue to Phidias, the master teacher. See also "Agoracritus," in Simon Hornblower and Antony Spawforth, *The Oxford Classical Dictionary* (Oxford: Oxford University Press, 1996), 43.

7. Joseph Naveh, "Introduction," in André Lemaire, Nahman Avigad, and Michael Heltzer, *West Semitic Seals: Eighth–Sixth Centuries BCE* (Haifa: University of Haifa, 2000), 10.

8. Ibid.

Gordon, Naveh acknowledged the real risks inherent in passing a verdict on an archaeological piece. During the final years of the former century, he advised:

> Pedantic scholars argue with some justice that material not derived from an archeological excavation may be forged. Nowadays, however, specialists in various fields have better means of telling an authentic object from a forgery.... Suspicion alone, however, cannot disqualify a seal. Whoever claims that a certain seal is a forgery bears the burden of proof.[9]

Does statistical evidence help determine what is a forgery? Alan Millard questions the validity of determining forgeries in unprovenanced material on statistical evidence alone. Millard's analysis is rooted not only on statistics, but rests more on the competence of a scholar to interpret the finds. In the field of sorting out the fake items, an experienced eye is still a major asset, as no tool, mechanical device, or chemical substance exists that is capable of identifying a forgery definitively. His conclusion is that "statistics cannot yet answer the question of authenticity; that will remain dependent upon the experienced eye."[10] That seems to be fair advice without quibble.

Even if we identify objects as forgeries do they still have value? Jean J. Fiechter, a Swiss born historian and author of the volume, *Fake Egyptian Artifacts*, concludes that while a fake is an enemy of the historian there is still value to it. The author says,

> Forgery production is incontestably an integral part of the contemporary world's dialog with the Ancients.... As for the finest fakes, once unmasked there is no harm in admiring their aesthetic qualities ... as modern works by contemporary artists looking toward the past. For, as the restorer of antiquities Vincent Diniacopoulos advised the young expert Jean Roudillon: "If you encounter a masterpiece, even a fake one, do not destroy it, as masterpieces are few and far between."[11]

No doubt it is a novel approach to reflect upon and weigh carefully. With this in mind, I call attention to the thorough examination of Moabitica by Martin Heide. The author sets forth guidelines for dealing with suspicious artifacts.

One of the most controversial artifacts to be dealt with recently is the Yeho'ash Inscription.[12] If genuine, the text would have been the first royal Judean monar-

---

9. Ibid., 11.
10. See Millard's article in this volume.
11. Jean-Jacques Fiechter, *Egyptian Fakes* (Paris: Flammarion, 2009), 245.
12. See a discussion of this subject in Hershel Shanks, *Freeing the Dead Sea Scrolls*

chic inscription ever unearthed. However, many respected philologians consider it a forgery. Chaim Cohen, in the current article that completes his analysis of the inscription,[13] emphasizes that he does not know whether or not the inscription is authentic, yet, as of now, it cannot be proven, philologically, a forgery. He adds that if it turns out to be a fake then it is the work of a brilliant Hebrew forger familiar with infrequent Hebrew formations. Cohen's salient arguments merit serious deliberation.

This volume includes another topic of controversy. Shlomo Moussaieff discusses the humiliating tax, *fiscus Iudaicus*, levied on the Jewish population of the Roman Empire. Did the coin promulgated by Nerva indicate that indeed this tax was rescinded? If so, who influenced Nerva's decision?

Seeking the truth is an ongoing activity. Year by year, archaeology reveals fresh major finds that help fill the void in our knowledge of the past.[14] Some have been deciphered and others remain to be examined and published. Rabbi Tarfon the Sage taught his disciples: "It is not for thee to complete the task, yet neither art thou free to desist therefrom" (Ethics of the Fathers 2:21). There is a great deal to learn from our ancestors and it is a worthwhile endeavor to persist in uncovering where we come from in order to better know who we have become. Nearly two thousand years ago Cicero, the great Roman orator observed:

> Nescire autem quid ante quam natus sis acciderit, id est semper esse puerum. Quid enim est aetas hominis, nisi ea memoria rerum veterum cum superiorum aetate contexitur?

> To be ignorant of what occurred before you were born is to remain always a child. For what is the worth of human life, unless it be woven into the life of our ancestors by the records of history? (*De oratore*, XXXIV)

An insight that is neither "dimmed with time nor is its vigor abated."

---

and Other Adventures of an Archaeology Outsider (New York: Continuum, 2010), 193–202, 224–27.

13. Part one is published in Lubetski, ed., *New Seals and Inscriptions*, 222–84.

14. The current major interest of history and archaeology in Mesopotamia is the antecedents of cities. "Our real focus now should not be on the Uruk period but the Ubaid," according to Professor Richard L. Zettler on the importance of the recent excavations conducted by the University of Chicago Oriental Institute. John N. Wilford, "In Syria, a Prologue for Cities," *New York Times* (6 April 2010), D1, 4. It is interesting to note that eight decades ago, Cyrus H. Gordon, then a young archaeologist in Iraq, already predicted the importance of Ubaid. Cyrus H. Gordon, "Buried Cultures of the Near East-1," *Asia* (January 1936): 28.

Acknowledgments

The completion of a second volume presenting some of the many treasures in Dr. Shlomo Moussaieff's collection is very exciting. The findings of an exceptional group of scholars underscores the role of archaeological evidence in reconstructing the legacy of antiquity, especially that of the biblical world.

In the course of unlocking the bars to enter the world of those who have long died, I have accumulated several debts of gratitude. First and foremost I wish to recognize the enormous contribution of Dr. Shlomo Moussaieff who responded favorably to the idea of sponsoring the lectures and later on to publishing the material and providing support for the project. Kudos to his family, his wife Aliza and his daughters, who have always encouraged him in his endeavors and have fostered the cause of disseminating the understanding of the biblical world among the broader community.

The PSC-CUNY Research Foundation supported my research. The Littauer Foundation, headed by Dr. Robert D. Frost, was most generous in supporting this scholarly pursuit, and has provided assistance for previous endeavors. Prof. Jeffrey Peck, Dean of the Weissman School of Liberal Arts and Sciences approved my request for Reassigned Time and Professor Elena Martinez, Chair of the Department of Modern Languages and Comparative Literature at Baruch College, City University of New York, limited the number of classes that I had to teach. Sincere appreciation to the libraries of Baruch College and Yeshiva University for their expert and gracious assistance.

I benefitted from the warm receptiveness of Philip Davies, Lester Grabbe, and staff of the European Association of Biblical Studies to hosting our session in Lisbon.

Special thanks are due to the Society of Biblical Literature that agreed to include a unit on epigraphical and paleographical material relating to the Bible. It was a privilege to work with Professors Kent Harold Richards, Matthew Collins, Charles Haws and the capable Executive Assistant, Trista Krock, whose experience and expertise made the meetings a great success.

The editors of SBL are to be commended for adding this volume to their list of publications. Professor Tammi Schneider, editor of Archaeology and Biblical

Studies and Bob Buller, Editorial Director must be thanked for their consent—indeed their willingness—to include this work in the much esteemed SBL series. I do not know of another organization that has contributed more to biblical studies and the ancillary literature than SBL.

This volume would not have seen light if not for my colleague Dr. Claire Gottlieb, a former classmate at New York University in the doctoral and post-doctoral courses of our revered teacher, Cyrus H. Gordon. Friends for over forty years, I know her to be generous, unselfish, and loyal. A business partner with her husband Milton, she is dedicated and hard-working. Claire, the academician, considers humanistic scholarship as a rewarding way of life. She always enjoys the stimulation of the interchange of ideas and fresh knowledge constantly attracts her attention. With typical enthusiasm, she generously responded to the need to read the papers and offer her wise counsel and corrections. With her critical eye, Dr. Gottlieb did a superb job. I am truly grateful for her sound judgment and talented editorial skills. Claire's eagerness always reminds me of Tennyson's hero in *Idylls of the King*… "strong in will, to strive, to seek to find and not to yield."

I would also like to acknowledge the assistance of Shmuel Ormianer, a graphic artist par excellence, who can find solutions to the most challenging problems. I also thank Duncan Burns, who was of enormous help in preparing this work for submission to the publisher. It has been a privilege and a pleasure to work with a remarkable editor, Billie Jean Collins in the production of this current volume. Her clear and concise guidance provided coherence to this manuscript and her patience with the resolution of issues was deeply appreciated.

My children have always supported me in my endeavors and for that I am deeply grateful. Specifically I would like to thank: Rebecca and Saul Lubetski for giving me the book, *Egyptian Fakes*, from which I was able to draw upon for this volume; Shani and Uriel Lubetski for their computer expertise; Leah and Ari Feldman for serving as the outpost in London to collect material for me and expedite its delivery; Leah for her invaluable help with the subject index.

My wife and co-editor, Edith, deserves special recognition. She has been the unseen force in assisting me with all the tasks concerning this volume. Her patient and unstinting encouragement have been indispensible.

Finally, to all those who have had a share in the many aspects of this work I cannot find a better way of wishing them well than invoking the blessing of Rabban Gamliel, the son of Rabbi Judah the Prince:

All who exert themselves for the community …
their forefathers aid them
and their righteousness endures forever. (*Ethics of the Father* 2:2).

Meir Lubetski

Abbreviations

A	Aleppo Codex
AASOR	The Annual of the American Schools of Oriental Research
ÄAT	Ägypten und Altes Testament
AB	Anchor Bible
AfO	*Archiv für Orientforschung*
AHw	*Akkadisches Handwörterbuch*. W. von Soden. 3 vols. Wiesbaden, 1965–1981
Akk.	Akkadian
ALASP	Abhandlungen zur Literatur Alt-Syrien-Palästinas
AnOr	Analecta orientalia
ANRW	*Aufstieg und Niedergang der römischen Welt: Geschichte und Kultur Roms im Spiegel der neueren Forschung*. Edited by H. Temporini and W. Haase. Berlin, 1972–
A.0.	A = Assyrian Periods; 0 = Dynasty Inapplicable (RIMA 3:xiii)
AOAT	Alter Orient und Altes Testament
ANET	*Ancient Near Eastern Texts Relating to the Old Testament*. Edited by J. B. Pritchard. 3d ed. Princeton, 1969
Aram.	Aramaic
AS	*Aramaic Studies*
AuOrSup	Aula Orientalis Supplementa
AUSS	*Andrews University Seminary Studies*
b. ^cAbod. Zar.	Abodah Zarah
b. Giṭ	Giṭṭin
B	Bulla (City of David)
BA	Biblical Aramaic
BA	*Biblical Archaeologist*
BAH	Bibliothèque archéologique et historique
BAR	*Biblical and Archaeological Review*
BASOR	*Bulletin of the American Schools of Oriental Research*
BDB	Brown, F., S. R. Driver, and C. A. Briggs. *Hebrew and English Lexicon of the Old Testament*. Oxford, 1906

BH	Biblical Hebrew
BHS	*Biblia Hebraica Stuttgartensia.* Edited by K. Elliger and W. Rudolph. Stuttgart, 1983
BN	*Biblische Notizen*
BO	*Bibliotheca orientalis*
BSOAS	*Bulletin of the School of Oriental and African Studies*
BZ	*Biblische Zeitschrift*
BZAW	Beiheft zur Zeitschrift für die alttestamentliche Wissenschaft
CAD	*The Assyrian Dictionary of the Oriental Institute of the University of Chicago.* Chicago, 1956–2010
CDA	*A Concise Dictionary of Akkadian.* J. Black et al. 2d ed. Wiesbaden, 2000
CDOG	Colloquien der Deutschen Orient-Gesellschaft
COS	*The Context of Scripture.* Edited by W. W. Hallo. 3 vols. Leiden, 1997–2002
CPJ 2	*Corpus papyrorum judaicorum.* Vol. 2. Edited by V. Tcherikover. Cambridge, 1960.
CPJ 3	*Corpus papyrorum judaicorum.* Vol 3. Edited by V. Tcherikover. Cambridge, 1964
CUSAS	Cornell University Studies in Assyriology and Sumerology
DBH	*A Dictionary of Biblical Hebrew.* M. Z. Kaddari. Ramat-Gan, 2006 (in Hebrew)
DCH	*The Dictionary of Classical Hebrew.* Edited by D. J. A. Clines. Sheffield, 1993–.
Deut. Rab.	*Deuteronomy Rabbah*
DNSWI	*Dictionary of the North-West Semitic Inscriptions.* J. Hoftijzer and K. Jongeling. 2 vols. Leiden, 1995
DOM	*Domitianus*
EABS	European Association of Biblical Studies
ErIsr	*Eretz-Israel*
GBS	Guides to Biblical Scholarship
GKC	*Gesenius' Hebrew Grammar.* Edited by E. Kautzsch. Translated by A. E. Cowley. 2nd ed. Oxford, 1910.
HALOT	Koehler, L., W. Baumgartner, and J. J. Stamm. *The Hebrew and Aramaic Lexicon of the Old Testament.* Translated and edited under the supervision of M. E. J. Richardson. 4 vols. Leiden, 1994–2000
HCOT	Historical Commentary on the Old Testament
Heb.	Hebrew
HSM	Harvard Semitic Monographs

HSS	Harvard Semitic Studies
HTS	Harvard Theological Studies
HUCA	*Hebrew Union College Annual*
IBP	*Identifying Biblical Persons in Northwest Semitic Inscriptions of 1200–539 B.C.E.* Lawrence J. Mykytiuk. SBL Academia Biblica 12. Atlanta, 2004
ICC	International Critical Commentary
ID	identification
IEJ	*Israel Exploration Journal*
ISBE	*International Standard Bible Encyclopedia*. Edited by Geoffrey W. Bromiley. Fully rev. ed. 4 vols. Grand Rapids, 1979–1988
JANES	*Journal of the Ancient Near Eastern Society*
JAOS	*Journal of the American Oriental Society*
JCS	*Journal of Cuneiform Studies*
JBL	*Journal of Biblical Literature*
JEOL	*Jaarbericht ex Oriente Lux*
JNES	*Journal of Near Eastern Studies*
JPS	Jewish Publication Society
JQR	*Jewish Quarterly Review*
JSOT	*Journal for the Study of the Old Testament*
JSOTSup	Journal for the Study of the Old Testament: Supplement Series
JSS	*Journal of Semitic Studies*
KAI	*Kanaanäische und aramäische Inschriften*. H. Donner and W. Röllig. 2d ed. Wiesbaden, 1966–1969
KTU²	*Die keilalphabetischen Texte aus Ugarit*. Edited by M. Dietrich, O. Loretz, and J. Sanmartín. AOAT 24/1. Neukirchen–Vluyn, 1976. 2nd enl. ed. of *KTU: The Cuneiform Alphabetic Texts from Ugarit, Ras Ibn Hani, and Other Places*. Edited by M. Dietrich, O. Loretz, and J. Sanmartín. Münster, 1995 (= *CTU*)
L	Leningrad Codex
LAPO	*Littératures anciennes du Proche-Orient*
Lev. Rab.	*Leviticus Rabbah*
LXX	Septuagint
m. ʿErub	*Mishnah ʿErubin*
MDOG	*Mitteilungen der Deutschen Orient-Gesellschaft*
MO	Moussaieff Ostracon
MT	Masoretic Text
NABU	*Nouvelles assyriologiques breves et utilitaires*
NB	Neo-Babylonian

Nbk	*Inschriften von Nabuchodonosor, König von Babylon (604–561 v. Chr.)* (Babylonische Texte). J. N. Strassmaier. Leipzig, 1889
NEA	*Near Eastern Archaeology*
NF	neue Folge
NJPS	*Tanakh—The Holy Scriptures: The New Jewish Publication Society Translation.* Philadelphia, 1985
NS	New Series
OB	Old Babylonian
OIP	Oriental Institute Publications
OBO	Orbis biblicus et orientalis
OLA	Orientalia Lovaniensia Analecta
Or	*Orientalia*
OTL	Old Testament Library
PEQ	*Palestine Exploration Quarterly*
PEQS	*Palestine Exploration Quarterly Statement*
Phoe.	Phoenician
PIHANS	Publications de l'Institut historique-archéologique néerlands de Stamboul
PSE B-Word	Poetic Semantically Equivalent B-Word
r.	reigned
RA	*Revue d'assyriologie et d'archéologie orientale*
RB	*Revue biblique*
RefR	*Reformed Review*
RH	Rabbinic Hebrew
RlA	*Reallexikon der Assyriologie.* Edited by Erich Ebeling et al. Berlin, 1928–
RIMA	Royal Inscriptions of Mesopotamia. Assyrian Periods
RIME 2	D. R. Frayne, *The Royal Inscriptions of Mesopotamia. Early Periods Volume 2: Sargonic and Gutian Periods (2334–2113 BC).* Toronto
SAA	State Archives of Assyria
SAAS	State Archives of Assyria Studies
SAWW	Österreichische Akademie der Wissenschaften, philosophisch-historische Klasse, Sitzungsberichte
SEE-J	*Scandinavian Evangelical E-Journal*
SBLDS	Society of Biblical Literature Dissertation Series
Sem	*Semitica*
SEL	*Studi epigrafici e linguistici*
SHANE	Studies in the History of the Ancient Near East
SJOT	*Scandinavian Journal of the Old Testament*

TA	*Tel Aviv*
TDOT	*Theological Dictionary of the Old Testament.* Edited by G. J. Botterweck et al. 15 vols. Grand Rapids, 1974–2006
TLOT	*Theological Lexicon of the Old Testament.* Edited by E. Jenni et al. 3 vols. Peabody, 1997
TUAT	*Texte aus der Umwelt des Alten Testaments*
UET VII	*Ur Excavation Texts: 7.* O. R. Gurney. London: British Museum Publications Ltd for the British Museum, and the University Museum, University of Pennsylvania, 1974
Ug.	Ugaritic
UF	*Ugarit-Forschungen*
UNP	*Ugaritic Narrative Poetry.* Edited by S. B. Parker. Atlanta, 1997
UT	*Ugaritic Textbook.* C. H. Gordon. AnOr 38. Rome, 1998
VAB	Vorderasiatische Bibliothek
VTSup	Vetus Testamentum Supplements
WSS	*Corpus of West Semitic Stamp Seals.* N. Avigad and B. Sass. Jerusalem: The Israel Academy of Sciences and Humanities, 1997
y. Ber.	Jerusalem Talmud Berakhot
y. Mo'ed Qat.	Jerusalem Talmud Mo'ed Qatan
YI	Yeho'ash Inscription
ZA	*Zeitschrift für Assyriologie*
ZAH	*Zeitschrift für Althebräistik*
ZDMG	*Zeitschrift der deutschen morgenländischen Gesellschaft*
ZDPV	*Zeitschrift des Deutschen Palästina-Vereins*
ZfA	*Zeitschrift für Assyriologie*

Chapter One
From the Origin of the Alphabet to the Tenth Century b.c.e.: New Documents and New Directions

André Lemaire

During the past five years, several new studies and documents have tried to change the way we understand the inception of the origins of alphabetic writing before the tenth century B.C.E. In the first part of this communication, we will discuss the publications of these new studies, taking into account new documents mentioned in part 2. Finally, in part 3, we will add new unpublished inscriptions.

New Studies

Besides various *status quaestionis* on the diffusion of the alphabet around the Mediterranean Sea, and a few studies of its origins in Egyptian Scripts, as well as general considerations of the use of the alphabet at the turn of the first millennium B.C.E.,[1] it is now necessary to mention two studies by Benjamin Sass presenting a new and revolutionary working hypothesis.

---

1. Diffusion: Juan-Pablo Vita, "Alfabetos lineal y cuneiforme: relaciones en el II milenio A.C.," in *Actas del III congreso espanol de antiguo oriente próximo, Huelva, del 30 de Septiembre al 3 de Octubre de 2003, Huelva Arqueologica* 20 (2004): 11–39; André Lemaire, "La diffusion de l'alphabet dans le bassin méditerranéen," in *Langues et écritures de la Méditerranée* (ed. Rina Viers; Paris/Nice: Karthala/Alphabets, 2006), 199–227; José Àngel Zamora Lopez, "Les utilisations de l'alphabet lors du IIe millénaire av. J.C. et le développement de l'épigraphie alphabétique: une approche de la documentation ougaritique en dehors des tablettes (II)," in *Šapal tibnim mû illakū. Studies Presented to Joaquin Sanmartin on the Occasion of His 65th Birthday* (ed. Gregorio del Olmo Lete et al.; AuOrSup 22; Barcelona: AUSA, 2006), 491–528; Ryan Byrne, "The Refuge of Scribalism in Iron I Palestine," *BASOR* 345 (2007): 1–30; André Lemaire, "La diffusion des

The first one is a paper that proposes to lower the date of the first alphabetic writing to the thirteenth century B.C.E. This new dating is surprising since, twenty years ago the same author proposed to date it to about 2000 B.C.E.[2] Actually, as emphasized by Alan Millard, one may agree that "there is no evidence for placing the origin of the cuneiform alphabet earlier than the thirteenth century B.C.E."[3] However it is clear that this cuneiform script is only an adaptation of a linear alphabet to cuneiform writing on clay tablets.[4] Furthermore, this new hypothesis does not take into account the existence of a few Palestinian fragmentary alphabetic inscriptions from the Middle Bronze age.[5] B. Sass himself recognizes that it is a feeble point[6] in this new but unconvincing hypothesis. Finally, although difficult to date and to interpret, one has to take into account the discovery of the Wadi el-Hôl inscriptions[7] that seem to favor a date "somewhere near the beginning of the second millennium B.C.E."[8]

Another new revolutionary working hypothesis was published in Sass's book *The Alphabet at the Turn of the Millennium*. His main objective is to lower the date

---

écritures alphabétiques (*ca* 1700–500 av. n. è.)," *Diogène* (Revue trimestrielle publiée sous les auspices du Conseil international de la philosophie et des sciences humaines et avec l'aide de l'UNESCO) 218 (April 2007), 52–70 = "The Spread of Alphabetic Scripts (c. 1700–500 BCE)," *Diogenes* 218 (55/2) (2008): 45–58.

Origin: Gordon J. Hamilton, *The Origins of the West Semitic Alphabet in Egyptian Scripts* (The Catholic Biblical Quarterly Monograph Series 40; Washington, D.C.: The Catholic Biblical Association of America, 2006); Orly Goldwasser, "Canaanites reading Hieroglyphs. Horus is Hathor?—The Invention of the Alphabet in Sinai," *Ägypten und Levante* 16 (2006): 121–60.

Use: Seth L. Sanders, "What was the Alphabet for? The Rise of Written Vernaculars and the Making of Israelite National Literature," *Maarav* 11 (2004): 25–56.

2. Benjamin Sass, *The Genesis of the Alphabet and Its Development in the Second Millennium B.C.* (ÄAT 13; Wiesbaden: Harrassowitz, 1988), 135–44; idem, "The Egyptian Middle Kingdom System for Writing Foreign Names and the West-Semitic Alphabet," in *Yigael Yadin Memorial Volume* (ed. Amnon Ben-Tor et alii; Eretz-Israel 20; Jerusalem: Israel Exploration Society, 1989), 44–50 et 195*.

3. Alan Millard, "Alphabetic Writing, Cuneiform and Linear, Reconsidered," *Maarav* 14 (2007): 83–93.

4. Ibid., 86–87.

5. See André Lemaire, "Les 'Hyksos' et les débuts de l'écriture alphabétique au Proche-Orient," in *Des signes pictographiques à l'alphabet* (ed. Rina Viers; Paris/Nice: Karthala/Alphabets, 2000), 103–33, esp. 112–13.

6. Benjamin Sass, "The Genesis of the Alphabet and Its Development in the Second Millennium B.C. Twenty Years Later," *De Kêmi à Birît Nâri* (Paris) 2 (2004/5): 147–66, esp. 156.

7. John Coleman Darnell et al., *Two Early Alphabetic Inscriptions from the Wadi el-Hôl: New Evidence for the Origin of the Alphabet from the Western Desert of Egypt* (AASOR 59; Boston: ASOR, 2005), 63–124.

8. Millard, "Alphabetic Writing," 87.

of the Byblus inscriptions, usually ascribed to the tenth century, to the ninth or even beginning of the eighth century B.C.E., while dating the genesis of the Arabian alphabet to the ninth century B.C.E.[9] and the adoption of alphabetic writing by the Greeks and Phrygians to ca. 825–750 B.C.E.[10]

Without discussing these last two working hypotheses in detail, one must say that the first one—concerning the dating of the Byblian inscriptions—does not seem very convincing. To push them back to the nine–eighth centuries B.C.E., B. Sass is obliged to claim that all of them are archaizing[11] and that "the earliest historically dated monumental inscriptions ... belong to the second half or last third of the ninth century."[12] The first argument is clearly unlikely and the second does not take into account the dating, proposed by W. F. Albright in 1947,[13] of the Abibaal and Elibaal inscriptions to be contemporaneous with the reigns of the pharaohs Sheshonq I and Osorkon I.[14] Now, after rediscovering the Abibaal inscription in the Berlin *Vorderasiatisches Museum*, and thanks to the publication of an Akkadian tablet found in Ugarit,[15] I have shown that the Abibaal and Elibaal inscriptions are not only contemporaneous with the pharaohs Sheshonq I and Osorkon I but also should be dated to the beginning of their reigns.[16] Furthermore, these inscriptions reveal that, during the tenth century B.C.E., the Levant was still under a strong political and cultural Egyptian influence and this may explain several aspects of Solomon's reign as presented in 1 Kgs 3–11.[17]

---

9. Compare Frank Moore Cross, *Leaves from an Epigrapher's Notebook* (HSS 51; Winona Lake, Ind.: Eisenbrauns, 2003), 325.

10. Benjamin Sass, *The Alphabet at the Turn of the Millennium: The West Semitic Alphabet ca. 1150–850 BCE: The Antiquity of the Arabian, Greek and Phrygian Alphabets* (Tel Aviv Occasional Publications 4; Tel Aviv: Emery and Claire Yass Publications in Archaeology, 2005), 150–51.

11. Ibid., 49.

12. Ibid., 55.

13. W. F. Albright, "The Phoenician Inscriptions of the Tenth Century B.C. from Byblus," *JAOS* 67 (1947): 153–60, esp. 153.

14. Sass, *The Alphabet*, 70.

15. Sylvie Lackenbacher, "2. Une lettre d'Égypte," in *Études ougaritiques I, Travaux 1985–1995* (ed. Marguerite Yon and Daniel Arnaud; Ras-Shamra-Ougarit 14; Paris: Éditions Recherche sur les Civilisations, 2001), 239–48.

16. See André Lemaire, "La datation des rois de Byblos Abibaal et Elibaal et les relations entre l'Égypte et le Levant au Xe s. av. n. è.," *Comptes rendus de l'Académie des Inscriptions et Belles-Lettres* (2006): 1697–716. See also Christopher A. Rollston, "The Dating of the Early Royal Byblian Phoenician Inscriptions: A Response to Benjamin Sass," *Maarav* 15 (2008): 57–93.

17. Lemaire, "La datation des rois de Byblos," 1712–15.

Recently Published Documents

Among the newly published documents, one must mention first the graffiti from Wadi el-Ḥôl, in Upper Egypt.[18] Actually these two graffiti remain enigmatic since no one has succeeded in proposing a consistent translation and, therefore, their alphabetic character is not certain. Furthermore, the dating of these rock graffiti, proposed as the early-second millennium, can only be approximate. Yet they seem to confirm the Egyptian origin of the alphabet and a dating in the early-second millennium B.C.E.

The approximate dating of the Kefar Veradim inscribed bronze bowl in the tenth century B.C.E. seems to be clearly indicated by the archaeological context[19] and by the shape of the letters, as explained by Yardenna Alexandre.[20]

More southward,[21] two incised inscriptions should be mentioned. One is a possible Philistine personal name on a shard found in Tell eṣ-Ṣafi/Gath.[22] According to Aaron Maeir, the archaeological dating is "from the late eleventh until the first half of the ninth century B.C.E. according to the modified conventional chronology,"[23] with a possible connection to "non-Semitic names, known from the Greek or Anatolian onomastica."[24] Frank Moore Cross disagreed with the preliminary reading and dating since the shape of the letters does not fit what we

---

18. See Stefan J. Wimmer and S. Wimmer-Dweikat, "The Alphabet from Wadi el-Hôl," *Göttingen Miszellen* 180 (2001): 107–11; Darnell et al., *Two Early Alphabetic Inscriptions from the Wadi el-Ḥôl*, 63–124.

19. Yardenna Alexandre, "The Iron Age Assemblage from Cave 3 at Kefar Veradim," in *Eretz Zafon: Studies in Galilean Archaeology* (ed. Zvi Gal; Jerusalem: Israel Antiquities Authority, 2002), 53–63.

20. Yardenna Alexandre, "A Fluted Bronze Bowl with a Canaanite–Early Phoenician Inscription from Kefar Veradim," in *Eretz Zafon: Studies in Galilean Archaeology*, 65–74; eadem, "A Canaanite–Early Phoenician Inscribed Bronze Bowl in an Iron Age IIA-B Burial Cave at Kefar Veradim, Northern Israel," *Maarav* 13 (2006): 7–41.

21. Although published in 2003, one could also mention a fragmentary incision after firing on the body of a storage jar found in Tel Rehov and probably to be dated in the tenth century B.C.E. See Amihai Mazar, "Three 10th–9th Century B.C.E. Inscriptions from *Tēl Reḥōv*," in Saxa Loquentur, *Studien zur Archäologie Palästinas/Israels. Festschrift für Volkmar Fritz* (ed. Cornelis G. Den Hartog, Ulrich Hübner, Stefan Münger; AOAT 302; Münster: Ugarit Verlag, 2003), 171–84, esp. 172–74. One can hesitate between two uncertain readings: LNḤM or, perhaps better, LNMŠ.

22. Aren M. Maeir, Stefan J. Wimmer, Alexander Zukerman, and Aaron Demsky, "A Late Iron Age I / Early Iron Age II Old Canaanite Inscriptions from Tell es-Sâfi/Gath, Israel: Palaeography, Dating, and Historical-Cultural Significance," *BASOR* 351 (2008): 39–71.

23. Ibid., 48.

24. Ibid., 58, 62.

know so far about tenth-century letters.[25] Actually the shape of the letters seems closer to those in the Izbet Ṣartah ostracon (eleventh century B.C.E.?) but the shard itself looks more tenth century!

About 8 kilometers south-southwest of Tel eṣ-Ṣafi/Gath, an abecedary engraved on a big stone was found during the excavations of Tell Zayit. It has been dated from the mid-tenth century B.C.E. and connected with the Judaean Shephelah by the *editio princeps*.[26] Yet several letters (e.g., *mem* and *nun*) look "surprisingly advanced"[27] and the palaeography is slightly more developed than that in the Gezer tablet. A date in the second half of the tenth or at the beginning of the ninth century B.C.E. looks more likely.[28] Furthermore, if this site, 7 kilometers from Lachish, was connected with the Judaean Shephelah at the end of the eighth century as shown by LMLK and so-called private seal impressions,[29] during the tenth and the beginning of the ninth century B.C.E., it was more probably connected with the Philistine city of Gath. Thus, it is probably a Philistian[30] rather than a Hebrew inscription.

In 2008, the excavations of Khirbet Qeiyafa, in the Judean Shephelah close to the Vale of Elah, under the direction of Yosef Garfinkel and Saar Ganor discovered an ostracon written with ink and announced it to be dated to around 1000 B.C.E. It was quickly published[31] and immediately commented on by several

---

25. Frank Moore Cross and Lawrence E. Stager, "Cypro-Minoan Inscriptions Found in Ashkelon," *IEJ* 56 (2006): 129–59, esp. 151–52.

26. Ron E. Tappy, P. Kyle McCarter, Marilyn J. Lundberg, and Bruce Zuckerman, "An Abecedary of the Mid-Tenth Century B.C.E. from the Judaean Shephelah," *BASOR* 344 (2006): 5–46.

27. Ibid., 36.

28. This palaeograhical dating is independent from the viewpoint of Israel Finkelstein, Benjamin Sass and Lily Singer-Avitz ("Writing in Iron IIA Philistia in the Light of the Tēl Zayit/Zētā Abecedary," *ZDPV* 124 (2008): 1–14) who propose "second half of the 9th century B.C.E."

29. Ibid., 9.

30. For a provisory list of Philistian inscriptions, see André Lemaire, "Phénicien et Philistien: paléographie et dialectologie," in *Actas del IV congreso internacional de studios fenicios y punicos I* (ed. Maria Eugenia Aubet and Manuela Barthélemy; Cadiz: Servicio de Publicaciones, 2000), 243–49.

31. Haggai Misgav, Yosef Garfinel, and Saar Ganor, "The Khirbet Qeiyafa Ostracon," in *New Studies in the Archaeology of Jerusalem and Its Region* (ed. D. Amit, G. D. Stiebel and O. Peleg-Barkat; Jerusalem: Israel Antiquities Authority and the Institute of Archaeology, the Hebrew University of Jerusalem, 2009), 111–23 (Hb).

scholars,[32] with a tentative translation by Gershon Galil[33] and a word of caution by Christopher Rollston.[34] Though suggestive, Galil's reading and translation do not appear to fit all the traces of ink. The palaeographical date of the ostracon appears to be eleventh century rather than tenth century. From its location, this ostracon is probably connected with Philistia (Tell eṣ-Ṣafi/Gath) rather than with Judah (Jerusalem).[35]

During the past four years, five new inscribed arrowheads from approximately the eleventh century B.C.E. have also been published; one by myself[36] and four by Josette Elayi.[37] A sixth one has been presented at the sixth International Congress of Phoenician and Punic Studies in Lisbon, in 2005.[38] Six other ones have just been presented by Gaby Abou Samra at the seventh International Congress of Phoenician and Punic Studies, Hamamet, November 10–14, 2009, thus it appears that we now know of 66[39] inscribed arrowheads. Most of them, if not all, were apparently found in Lebanon and should to be dated in the eleventh or very beginning of the tenth century B.C.E.

---

32. Ada Yardeni, Aaron Demsky, and Shmuel Ahituv, *New Studies in the Archaeology of Jerusalem and Its Region*, 126–32. See also Haggai Misgav, Yosef Garfinkel and Saar Ganor "The Khirbet Qeiyafa Ostracon," and Ada Yardeni, Greg Bearman and William A. Christens-Berry, in *Khirbet Qeiyafa I. Excavation Report 2007–2008* (ed. Yosef Garfinkel and Saar Ganor; Jerusalem: IES and Institute of Archaeology, 2010), ch. 14 and 14A, 243–70. See also http://qeiyafa.huji.ac.il/ostracon.asp.

33. See http://wordpress.haifa.ac.il.

34. See http://www.rollstonepigraphy.com/?p=56.

35. Gath is only ca. 10 km from Khirbet Qeiyafa while Jerusalem is ca. 30 km.

36. "Nouveau roi dans une inscription proto-phénicienne?" in *Atti del V congresso internazionale di studi fenici et punici, Marsala-Palermo 2–8 ottobre 2000* (ed. Antonella Spano Giamellaro; Palermo: Universita degli Studi di Palermo, 2005), 43–46.

37. Josette Elayi, "Four New Inscribed Phoenician Arrowheads," *SEL* 22 (2005): 35–45.

38. See André Lemaire, "Nouvelles inscriptions phéniciennes sur bronze," to be published in *6° Congresso Internacional de Estudos Fenicio Punicos* (ed. Anna Maria Arruda; Lisbon) with the reading ḤṢ BŠʾ / BN WLʿ.

39. Elayi, "Four New Inscribed Phoenician Arrowheads," 35 gets the number "61" but the same arrowhead is numbered XVI and XIX in Robert Deutsch and Michael Heltzer, *West Semitic Epigraphic News of the 1st Millennium BCE* (Tel Aviv: Archaeological Center Publications, 1999), 15.

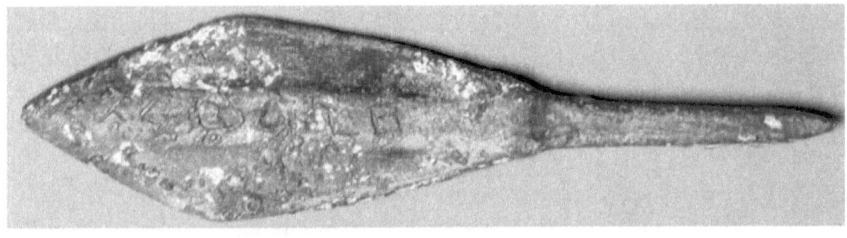

Fig. 1. Arrowhead recto (top) and verso (bottom).
6.8 cm (blade 4.5 cm) long by 1.7 cm wide.

New Documents

Among the new documents, we should like to publish[40] three new proto-Phoenician arrowheads and two Canaanite inscriptions on axes.

The first inscribed arrowhead belongs to the collection of S. Moussaieff (fig. 1). One may propose the reading:

1. ḤṢ.B<N?>ʿNT
2. BN YDN.
1. Arrow of *Be(n)ʿanat*
2. Son of Yadi*n*.

The reading of the middle of the first line and of the end of the second line remains very uncertain. In the middle of line 1, B is probable but seems to be immediately followed by a ʿayin. Is this another case of B for BN as in several old Byblian inscriptions?[41] The name Be(n)ʿanat, "fils de ʿAnat," is already attested

---

40. The first two inscribed arrowheads belong to the Moussaieff collection and I thank him for allowing me to study them. I only know the third one from a good photo. The last two inscriptions were seen on the antiquities market of Jerusalem several years ago. These five non-provenanced inscriptions are published with the usual reservations.

41. See Johannes Friedrich, Wolfgang Röllig, and Maria Giulia Amadasi Guzzo, *Phönizisch-punische Grammatik* (Analecta Orientalia 55; Rome: Pontificio Istituto Biblico, 1999), § 92b, 99b.

on several arrowheads (n. V, VIII,[42] XI, XXXI) as well as in the Bible (Judg 3:31; 5:6) where it has been generally interpreted as the patronym ('Anat) of Shamgar but "Ben'anat" appears clearly as a name on a palaeo-Hebrew seal published by Avigad.[43] This name seems to fit the name of a warrior since 'Anat was a warrior goddess.[44]

On the other side of the arrow, the last two signs could be a *nun* followed by a word divider. The patronym YDN would be new among the onomastics of the arrowheads but it is well attested in Ugaritic[45] and can be compared to 'LYDN on an Ammonite seal (WSS n° 898) as well as YDNYHW in palaeo-Hebrew epigraphy.[46]

The second inscribed arrowhead is a little longer: length 7.5 cm, blade 1.8 cm, width 1.6 cm (fig. 2). The bronze was apparently corroded and later cleaned too much. One may propose to read:

1. ḤṢ TRKRŠYN
2. B[N] '/.D/RL/KT
1. Arrow of Tarkurashyan
2. So[n of] Adalat

---

42. This arrowhead is palimpsest and the first inscription should possibly be read ḤṢ BN'NT BN ZKRB'L. See partly Frank Moore Cross, "The Origin and Early Evolution of the Alphabet," in *E. L. Sukenik Memorial Volume* (ed. N. Avigad et al.; Eretz-Israel 8; Jerusalem: Israel Exploration Society, 1967), 8*–24*, esp. 20*); Emile Puech, "Origine de l'alphabet. Documents en alphabet linéaire et cunéiforme du IIᵉ millénaire," *RB* 93 (1986): 161–213, esp. 164 n. 7; idem, "Les pointes de flèches inscrites de la fin du IIᵉ millénaire en Phénicie et Canaan," in *Actas del IV congreso internacional de estudios fenicios y punicos* I (ed. Aubet and Barthélemy; Cadiz, 2000), 251–69, esp. 252, no. 9.

43. Nahman Avigad, "Two Seals of Women and Other Hebrew Seals," in *Yigael Yadin Memorial Volume* (ed. Amnon Ben-Tor et al.; Eretz-Israel 20; Jerusalem: Israel Exploration Society, 1989), 90–96, esp. 95 no. 16; Nahman Avigad and Benjamin Sass, *Corpus of West Semitic Stamp Seals* (Jerusalem: Israel Exploration Society, 1997), no. 346; Nahman Avigad, Michael Heltzer, and André Lemaire, *West Semitic Seals, Eighth–Sixth Centuries BCE* (The Reuben and Edith Hecht Museum Collection B; Haifa: University of Haifa, 2000), no. 76.

44. See Michael Heltzer, "Ben-'Anat and Samgar Ben-'Anat," *Al-happereq* 8 (1994): 46–49 (Hb); idem, "Comments on the Rise of Secondary States in the Iron Age Levant," *JESHO* 46 (2003): 525–28, esp. 526.

45. See Frauke Gröndahl, *Die Personennamen der Texte aus Ugarit* (Studia Pöhl 1; Rome: Päpstliches Bibelinstitut, 1967), 123, 391.

46. See Graham I. Davies, *Ancient Hebrew Inscriptions: Corpus and Concordance* (2 vols.; Cambridge: Cambridge University Press, 1991, 2004), 1:363; 2:162. See also YDNYH at Elephantine: Walter Kornfeld, *Onomastica Aramaica aus Ägypten* (Österreichische Akademie der Wissenschaften, philosophisch-historische Klasse, Sitzungsberichte, 333. Band; Wien: Verlag der österreichischen Akademie der Wissenschaften, 1978), 52.

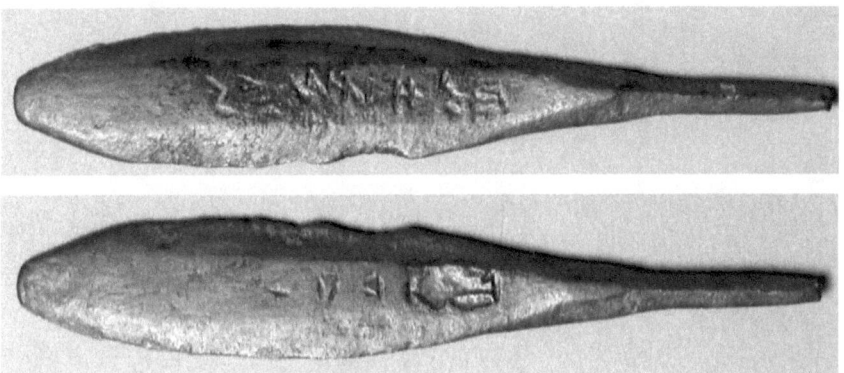

Fig. 2. Recto (top) and verso (bottom).

Though the letters of the recto—except for the last two—are a little overcrowded, the reading seems certain. The examination of the arrow itself makes clear that the second and fourth letters of the name are *resh*. The name TRKRŠYN does not appear Semitic and is probably Luwian. The first element is the theonym TRK, Tarku/Tarḫu(nt), the name of the great storm god of the Luwians. The interpretation of the second element remains uncertain.

The reading of the verso is very uncertain. At the beginning, B is fragmentary but probable. It was probably followed by a *nun* that disappeared in the lacuna. The following vertical stroke might be a separation stroke or possibly the left vertical stroke of an *aleph*. The following letter is probably a *dalet* but a *resh* is not completely impossible. The penultimate may be a *lamed* but a *kaph*, with an eroded left stroke, is not impossible. The last letter looks like a small eroded *taw* with the same shape as the *taw* of line 1. The uncertain name ʾDLT may be new but it might be compared to the possible Anatolian name ʾDLYN[47] (or ʾDLDN[48]) in the papyrus Bauer-Meissner. Thus the name of the owner of this arrowhead might indicate a Luwian/Neo-Hittite origin.

Examining the picture (fig. 3), it is possible to read the third inscribed arrowhead:

1. ḤṢ ŠPṬ
2. BN BʿLʾ

---

47. Ibid., 113.
48. See Bezalel Porten and Ada Yardeni, *Textbook of Aramaic Documents from Ancient Egypt 2. Contracts* (Winona Lake, Ind.: Eisenbrauns, 1989), 12.

Fig 3. Arrowhead recto (top) and detail of the inscription (bottom).

1. Arrow of Shaphat
2. son of Ba'alâ

The name of the owner of this arrowhead (fig. 4) is a well-known Semitic name meaning God "judged/governed." This hypocoristic name is known on other arrowheads (nos XXI, XXVI, XXVIII[49]) and is also very well attested as being both a Phoenician and a Punic name,[50] and is found several times in palaeo-Hebrew epigraphy[51] and in the Bible (Num 13:5; 1 Chr 3:22; 5:12; 27:29), especially as the patronym of the prophet Elisha (1 Kgs 19:16, 19; 2 Kgs 3:11; 6:31).

---

49. However one might hesitate between ŠPṬ and ŠLṬ for no. XXI and XXVI, and no. XXVIII was declared "spurious" by Frank Moore Cross, "The Arrow of Suwar, Retainer of 'Abday," in *Joseph Aviram Volume* (ed. Avraham Biran et al.; Eretz-Israel 25; Jerusalem: Israel Exploration Society, 1996), 9*–17*, esp. 15* = *Leaves from an Epigrapher's Notebook*, 195–202, esp. 199–200, 202.

50. See Frank L. Benz, *Personal Names in the Phoenician and Punic Inscriptions* (Studia Pohl 8; Rome: Biblical Institute Press, 1972), 182–84.

51. See Davies, *Ancient Hebrew Inscriptions*, 1:504, 2:222.

Fig 4. Arrowhead verso (top) and detail of the inscription (bottom).

On the verso, the patronym BʿLʾ is attested on another arrowhead (no XIV), as well as in the Hebrew Samaria ostraca (1,7; 3,3; 27,3; 28,3; 31a,3),[52] probably as a farmer. It is also attested on a Moabite or Hebrew seal (WSS 1131).

The decorated and inscribed bronze axe in fig. 5 is 15.5 cm long, 6.1 cm wide and weigh 310 g. Such an axe is difficult to date even though a few parallels can be mentioned.[53] It presents two different signs/symbols on both sides.

On one side, two signs look like two Canaanite letters. The first sign is an irregular quadrangular sign, incised between a rectangular sign and a triangle. This sign looks like a primitive *beth* that represents a rectangular house. This sign can be compared to a similar *beth* incised on a Gezer shard and found on Proto-Sinaitic inscriptions nos. 350–357, 359–361, 364–365, 374–376. The second sign, clearly incised, represents a fish with head and a superior and mainly inferior fin, as well as a tail. A similar sign is found in Proto-Sinaitic inscriptions nos 346, 352,

---

52. See, for example, André Lemaire, *Inscriptions hébraïques I. Les ostraca* (LAPO 9; Paris: Cerf, 1977), 50.

53. See Jean Deshayes, *Les outils de bronze de l'Indus au Danube (IVᵉ au IIᵉ millénaire)* (Paris, 1960), 113–31: "Chapitre V. Lames à moignons."

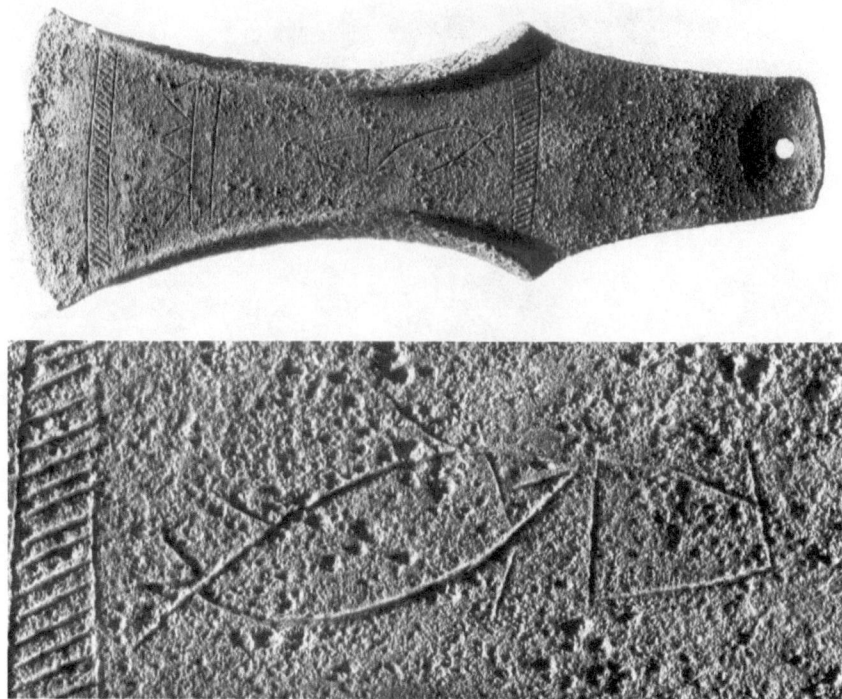

Fig. 5. Bronze axe (top) with detail of two inscribed Canaanite letters (bottom).

357, 358, 375, 376.[54] Unfortunately epigraphers are divided as to the meaning of this fish sign:

1. Most of the epigraphers, including William Foxwell Albright in 1948, and recently Emile Puech,[55] identify this sign with the letter *samek*/S, since a fish is called *samak* in Arabic.

---

54. See Sass, *The Genesis of the Alphabet*, 114.
55. W. F. Albright, "The Early Alphabetic Inscriptions from Sinai and Their Decipherment," *BASOR* 110 (1948): 6–22. Emile Puech, "Quelques remarques sur l'alphabet au deuxième millénaire," in *Atti del I congresso internazionale di studi fenici e punici, Roma 5–10 Novembre 1979*, II (Rome: Consiglio Nazionale delle Ricerche, 1983), 563–81, esp. 566, 579, 580; "Origine de l'alphabet," *RB* 93 (1986): 161–213, esp. 191; "Note sur quatre inscriptions protosinaïtiques," *RB* 109 (2002): 5–39, esp. 14: "le poisson doit logiquement d'abord être lu *samek* comme son nom l'indique, puisque le *dalet* est représenté ailleurs par le battant de porte avec ses gonds, *dalt*."

Fig. 6. Bronze axe verso with triangular signs.

2. Frank Moore Cross, William Foxwell Albright (1967), Joseph Naveh, and Benjamin Sass[56] think that this sign was originally called *dag/digg*, "fish." We do not have any indication of the change of appellation of this sign and Benjamin Sass himself notes: "even though the identification of the Proto-Sinaitic fish sign as *dalet* seems very reasonable, it must be noted that it is not completely certain."

If we adopt the first interpretation that is consistent with what we know about the ancient appellations of the letters, this inscription is to be read: BS, "Bes or Besi," probably a hypocoristicon of the Egyptian god Bes, who is also well known in the Levant. In this context, one could also compare it to the names BS' and BSH attested in Aramaic from Egypt,[57] as well as to the Greek transcriptions *Basou, Bassos*.[58] Alternatively but less likely, it could also be compared to similar North Arabic names.[59]

---

56. Cross, "The Origin and Early Evolution of the Alphabet," esp. 15*–17*. W. F. Albright, *The Proto-Sinaitic Inscriptions and Their Decipherment* (HTS 22; Cambridg, Mass.: Harvard University Press, 1969), esp. fig. 1. Joseph Naveh, *Early History of the Alphabet* (2nd ed.; Jerusalem/Leiden: Magnes, Hebrew University/Brill, 1987), 25. Sass, *The Genesis of the Alphabet*, 113–14, 126.

57. See Kornfeld, *Onomastica Aramaica aus Ägypten* (Wien, 1978), 79. See also the Biblical Hebrew names BSY in Ezra 2:49 and Neh 7:52, as well as Davies, *Ancient Hebrew Inscriptions*, 316; idem, II, 146.

58. See Heinz Wuthnow, *Die semitischen Menschennamen in griechischen Inschriften und Papyri des Vorderer Orients* (Leipzig: Dietrich, 1930), 34.

59. See G. Lancaster Harding, *An Index and Concordance of Pre-Islamic Arabian Names and Inscriptions* (Toronto: University of Toronto Press, 1971), 105: BS, BS', BS'L.

If we adopt Albright's interpretation, one could read these two letters as BD, "Bed/Bod," perhaps a hypocoristicon meaning that the child is "in the hand of" the deity, that is to say belongs to the deity.[60]

On the other side (fig. 6), it seems possible to identify two geometric triangular signs. The right one presents two superposed triangles and looks like a proto-Arabic M. The left one appears to be a big triangle turning leftward with a median vertical stroke parallel to the vertical right one. Such a sign is very difficult to interpret. As a guess, one could compare it to a sign appearing in a proto-Arabic Ur inscription, line 2, last letter on the right,[61] as well in the proto-Arabic seals of Anah and Ward 1211.[62] The Ur sign is interpreted by B. Sass as a *dalet/dal*.[63] One could therefore tentatively read DM or MD[64] in a kind of proto-Arabic writing. Needless to say, such an interpretation is very tentative since this inscription is unfortunately unprovenanced and also especially because, so far, we do not have any clear proto-Arabic inscriptions from the second millennium B.C.E.[65]

As mentioned above, such an axe is very difficult to date. If the interpretation of the first inscription is justified, the shape of these two signs, especially the fish, would be similar to the palaeography of the Proto-Sinaitic inscriptions. Unfortunately their date is disputed and very approximate. We might very tentatively propose a provisory date of about the middle of the second millennium B.C.E.

Another bronze axe (length 18.3 cm; width 3.4–5 cm and weight 308 g; fig. 7), without any decoration and in a simpler style, presents three signs engraved in the butt. The left sign represents schematically the palm of a hand with fingers upwards. This sign is attested on the Gezer shard and in the Proto-Sinaitic

---

60. See Gröndahl, *Die Personennamen der Texte aus Ugarit*, 118, 380; Benz, *Personal Names in the Phoenician and Punic Inscriptions*, 74–88, 283–86; Davies, *Ancient Hebrew Inscriptions*, 301–2; idem, II, 139.

61. See Naveh, *Early History of the Alphabet*, 44

62. See Benjamin Sass, *Studia alphabetica: On the Origin and Early History of the Northwest Semitic South Semitic and Greek Alphabets* (OBO 102; Freiburg/Göttingen: Universitätsverlag/ Vandenhoeck & Ruprecht, 1991), chart 1, n. 20 and 32.

63. Ibid., 40 and fig. 12, 13

64. For a possible MD(D) in Ugaritic names, see Gröndahl, *Die Personennamen der Texte aus Ugarit*, 156, 342, 399.

65. For uncertain conjectural propositions, see François Bron, "Vestiges de l'écriture sud-sémitique dans le Croissant Fertile," in *Présence arabe dans le Croissant Fertile avant l'Hégire* (ed. Hélène Lozachmeur; Paris: Éditions Recherche sur les Civilisations, 1995), 81–91, esp. 81–83; idem, "Les écritures sud-sémitiques: origine et diffusion," in *Langues et écritures de la Méditerranée*, 183–97; Lemaire, "La diffusion de l'alphabet dans le bassin méditerranéen," esp. 203–6.

Fig. 7. Bronze axe (top) with detail of three inscribed Canaanite letters (bottom).

inscriptions. It is very probably the Canaanite letter K, since a palm of hand is called *kaph* in West-Semitic.[66]

The middle sign contains five parallel vertical strokes above a horizontal line and below a double line of 5 points. This sign does not seem to have been identified as yet in the Canaanite inscriptions. The design calls to mind a fence, a kind of barrier (probably *ḥēyṭ* in West Semitic).[67] It is probably the letter Ḥ.[68]

---

66. See Sass, *The Genesis of the Alphabet*, 122–23.
67. See Frank Moore Cross and Thomas O. Lambdin, "A Ugaritic Abecedary and the Origins of the Proto-Canaanite Alphabet," *BASOR* 160 (1960): 21–26, esp. 26.
68. See Cross, "The Origin and Early Evolution of the Alphabet," esp. 24*.

Actually if it is turned clockwise about 90°,[69] this sign is somehow similar to the later Canaanite and Proto-Phoenician letter ḥ. This new shape probably suggests the solution to the difficulty mentioned by B. Sass, because untill now, all the Proto-Sinaitic exemplars of this letter were horizontal (cf. clearly no. 362)[70] and not vertical.[71]

The right sign is a kind of capital L drawn with a double line. This sign is attested in Proto-Sinaitic inscriptions nos 353, 355, 357[72] but its interpretation is still being discussed. B. Sass proposes to see it as a *pê*[73] while Émile Puech thinks of a *gimel*,[74] connecting it to the Egyptian sign of the boomerang.[75]

According to the two possible orientations of reading (right or left), one can therefore propose four different readings:

KḤP
KḤG
PḤK
GḤK

The three letters word is probably the name of the axe owner but none of the possible readings indicate an obvious West Semitic personal name.

As a guess, one could adopt the reading PḤK and think of a Hurrite or Hittite personal name in *puḫi-* or *piḫa-* as attested in Nuzi[76] or Ugarit.[77] Alternatively,

---

69. See the Proto-Sinaitic inscription no 362: Sass, *Genesis of the Alphabet*, 117–20.
70. See, for example, Cross, "The Origin and Early Evolution of the Alphabet," 15*–17*.
71. See Sass, *Genesis of the Alphabet*, 118.
72. See Émile Puech, "Notes sur quatre inscriptions proto-sinaïtiques," *RB* 109 (2002): 5–39, esp. 12, fig. 2.
73. See Sass, *Genesis of the Alphabet*, 128.
74. Actually the Canaanite letters *gimel* and *pê* present shapes similar enough (ibid., 128), especially in the Izbet-Sartah abecedary. One notes also that the *pê* of the Qubur el-Walaydah inscription (Frank Moore Cross, "Newly Found Inscriptions in Old Canaanite and Early Phoenician Script," *BASOR* 238 [1980], 1–20, esp. 3; Naveh, *Early History of the Alphabet*, 36) presents the same shape as this axe sign but upside down.
75. See Puech, "Quelques remarques sur l'alphabet du deuxième millénaire," in *Atti del I congresso internazionale di studi fenici e punici*, 563–81, esp. 579; idem, "Notes," 34. For this interpretation of *gaml*, see already Cross and Lambdin, "A Ugaritic Abecedary," 25.
76. See Ignace J. Gelb et al., *Nuzi Personal Names* (OIP 57; Chicago: University of Chicago Press, 1943), 115–17, 246.
77. See Gröndahl, *Die Personennamen der Texte aus Ugarit*, 287.

one could compare it with the Safaitic name FḤK, which is unfortunately difficult to explain.[78]

The shape of the axe does not suggest any precise dating. The shape of the three signs seems close from the original pictograph. One could therefore consider a Middle Bronze dating, perhaps about the seventeenth century B.C.E. However, since this axe is unprovenanced, its dating can only be conjectural and very tentative.

Thus, although there are many uncertainties, reinforced by the fact that they are unprovenanced, these last two short inscriptions might throw some light on the development of the alphabet in the second millennium B.C.E. while the three new inscribed arrowheads present further evidence for the use of alphabetic writing in the Levant around 1000 B.C.E.

Bibliography

Albright, William Foxwell. "The Early Alphabetic Inscriptions from Sinai and their Decipherment." *BASOR* 110 (1948): 6–22.

———. "The Phoenician Inscriptions of the Tenth Century B.C. from Byblus." *JAOS* 67 (1947): 153–60.

———. *The Proto-Sinaitic Inscriptions and Their Decipherment*. HTS 22. Cambridge: Harvard University Press, 1969.

Alexandre, Yardenna. "A Canaanite–Early Phoenician Inscribed Bronze Bowl in an Iron Age IIA–B Burial Cave at Kefar Veradim, Northern Israel." *Maarav* 13 (2006): 7–41.

———. "A Fluted Bronze Bowl with a Canaanite—Early Phonician Inscriptions from Kefar Veradim." Pages 65–74 in *Eretz Zafon: Studies in Galilean Archaeology*. Edited by Z. Gal. Jerusalem: Israel Antiquities Authority, 2002.

———. "The Iron Age Assemblage from Cave 3 at Kefar Veradim." Pages 53–63 in *Eretz Zafon: Studies in Galilean Archaeology*. Edited by Z. Gal. Jerusalem: Israel Antiquities Authority, 2002.

Avigad, Nahman. "Two Seals of Women and Other Hebrew Seals." Pages 90–96 in *Yigael Yadin Memorial Volume*. Edited by Amnon Ben-Tor et al. Eretz-Israel 20. Jerusalem: Israel Exploration Society, 1989.

Avigad, Nahman, and Sass, Benjamin. *Corpus of West Semitic Stamp Seals*. Jerusalem: Israel Exploration Society, 1997.

———, Michael Heltzer, and André Lemaire. *West Semitic Seals, Eighth–Sixth Centuries BCE*. The Reuben and Edith Hecht Museum Collection B. Haifa: University of Haifa, 2000.

Benz, Frank L. *Personal Names in the Phoenician and Punic Inscriptions*. Studia Pohl 8. Rome: Biblical Institute, 1972.

---

78. See Harding, *An Index and Concordance of Pre-Islamic Arabian Names and Inscriptions*, 463.

Bron, François. "Les écritures sud-sémitiques: origine et diffusion." Pages 183–97 in *Langues et écritures de la Méditerranée*. Edited by Rina Viers. Paris/Nice: Karthala/Alphabets, 2006.

———. "Vestiges de l'écriture sud-sémitique dans le Croissant Fertile." Pages 81–91 in *Présence Arabe dans le Croissant Fertile avant l'hégire*. Edited by Hélène Lozachmeur. Paris: Éditions Recherche sur les Civilisations, 1995.

Byrne, Ryan. "The Refuge of Scribalism in Iron I Palestine," *BASOR* 345 (2007): 1–30.

Cross, Frank Moore. "The Arrow of Suwar, Retainer of 'Abday." Pages 9*–17* in *Joseph Aviram Volume*. Edited by Avraham Biran et al. Eretz-Israel 25. Jerusalem: Israel Exploration Society, 1996 = pages 195–202 in *Leaves from an Epigrapher's Notebook*. Winona Lake, Ind.: Eisenbrauns, 2003.

———. *Leaves from an Epigrapher's Notebook*. HSS 51. Winona Lake: Eisenbrauns, 2003.

———. "Newly Found Inscriptions in Old Canaanite and Early Phoenician Script." *BASOR* 238 (1980): 1–20.

———. "The Origin and Early Evolution of the Alphabet." Pages 8*–24* in *E. L. Sukenik Memorial Volume*. Edited by N. Avigad et al. Eretz-Israel 8. Jerusalem: Israel Exploration Society, 1967.

Cross, Frank Moore, and Lawrence E. Stager. "Cypro-Minoan Inscriptions Found in Ashkelon." *IEJ* 56 (2006): 129–59.

———, and Thomas O. Lambdin. "A Ugaritic Abecedary and the Origins of the Proto-Canaanite Alphabet." *BASOR* 160 (1960): 21–26.

Darnell, John Coleman et al. *Two Early Alphabetic Inscriptions from the Wadi el-Hôl: New Evidence for the Origin of the Alphabet from the Western Desert of Egypt*. AASOR 59. Boston: American Schools of Oriental Research, 2005.

Davies, Graham I. *Ancient Hebrew Inscriptions. Corpus and Concordance*. 2 vols. Cambridge: Cambridge University Press, 1991, 2004.

Deshayes, Jean. *Les outils de bronze de l'Indus au Danube (IVe au IIe millénaire)*. Paris, 1960.

Deutsch, Robert, and Michael Heltzer. *West Semitic Epigraphic News of the 1st Millennium BCE*. Tel Aviv: Archaeological Center Publications, 1999.

Elayi, Josette. "Four New Inscribed Phoenician Arrowheads." *SEL* 22 (2005): 35–45.

Finkelstein, Israel, Benjamin Sass, and Lily Singer-Avitz. "Writing in Iron IIA Philistia in the Light of the Tēl Zayit/Zētā Abecedary." *ZDPV* 124 (2008): 1–14.

Friedrich, Johannes, Wolfgang Röllig, and Maria Giulia Amadasi Guzzo. *Phönizisch-punische Grammatik*. Analecta Orientalia 55. Rome: Pontificio Istituto Biblico, 1999.

Gelb, Ignace J. *Nuzi Personal Names*. OIP 57. Chicago: University of Chicago Press, 1943.

Goldwasser, Orly. "Canaanites Reading Hieroglyphs. Horus is Hathor?—The Invention of the Alphabet in Sinai." *Ägypten und Levante* 16 (2006): 121–60.

Gröndahl, Frauke. *Die Personennamen der Texte aus Ugarit*. Studia Pohl 1. Rome: Päpstliches Bibelinstitut, 1967.

Hamilton, Gordon J. *The Origins of the West Semitic Alphabet in Egyptian Scripts*. The CBQ Monograph Series 40. Washington, D.C.: The Catholic Biblical Association of America, 2006.

Harding, G. Lancaster. *An Index and Concordance of Pre-Islamic Arabian Names and Inscriptions*. Toronto: University of Toronto, 1971.

Heltzer, Michael. "Ben-'Anat and Samgar, Ben-'Anat." *'Al-happereq* 8 (1994): 46–49.

———. "Comments on the Rise of Secondary States in the Iron Age Levant." *JESHO* 46 (2003): 525-28.
Kornfeld, Walter. *Onomastica Aramaica aus Ägypten*. Österreichische Akademie der Wissenschaften, philosophisch-historische Klasse, Sitzungsberichte, 333. Band. Wien: Verlag der österreischichen Akademie der Wissenschaften, 1978.
Lackenbacher, Sylvie. "2. Une lettre d'Égypte." Pages 239-48 in *Études ougaritiques I. Travaux 1985-1995*. Edited by Marguerite Yon and Daniel Arnaud. Ras-Shamra-Ougarit 14. Paris: Éditions Recherche sur les Civilisations, 2001.
Lemaire, André. *Inscriptions hébraïques I. Les ostraca*. LAPO 9. Paris: Cerf, 1977.
———. "La datation des rois de Byblos Abibaal et Élibaal et les relations entre l'Égypte et le Levant au Xe s. av. n. è." *Comptes rendus de l'Académie des Inscriptions et Belles-Lettres* (2006): 1697-716.
———. "La diffusion de l'alphabet dans le bassin méditerranéen." Pages 199-227 in *Langues et écritures de la Méditerranée*. Edited by Rina Viers. Paris/Nice: Karthala/Alphabets, 2006.
———. "La diffusion des écritures alphabétiques (*ca* 1700-500 av. n. è.)." *Diogène* (Revue trimestrielle publiée sous les auspices du Conseil international de la philosophie et des sciences humaines et avec l'aide de l'UNESCO) 218 (April 2007): 52-70 = "The Spread of Alphabetic Scripts (c. 1700-500 BCE)," *Diogenes* 218 (55/2) (2008): 45-58.
———. "Les 'Hyksos' et les débuts de l'écriture alphabétique au Proche-Orient." Pages 103-33 in *Des signes pictographiques à l'alphabet*. Edited by Rina Viers. Paris/Nice: Karthala/Alphabets, 2000.
———. "Nouveau roi dans une inscription proto-phénicienne?" Pages 43-46 in *Atti del V Congresso internazionale di studi fenici e punici, Marsala-Palermo 2-8 ottobre 2000*. Edited by Antonella Spano Giamellaro. Palermo: Universita degli Studi di Palermo, 2005.
———. "Nouvelles inscriptions phéniciennes sur bronze." To be published in *6° Congresso Internacional de Estudios Fenicios Punicos*. Edited by Anna Maria Arruda. Lisbon.
———. "Phénicien et Philistien: paléographie et dialectologie." Pages 243-49 in *Actas del IV congreso internacional de estudios fenicios y punicos I*. Edited by Maria Eugenia Aubet and Manuela Barthélemy. Cadiz: Servicio de Publicaciones, 2000.
Maeir, Aren M. et al. "A Late Iron Age I / Early Iron Age II Old Canaanite Inscription from Tell es-Sâfi/Gath, Israel: Palaeography, Dating, and Historical-Cultural Significance." *BASOR* 351 (2008): 39-71.
Mazar, Amihai. "Three 10th-9th Century B.C.E. Inscriptions from Tēl Reḥōv." Pages 171-84 in Saxa Loquentur. *Studien zur Archäologie Palästinas/Israels. Festschrift für Volkmar Fritz*. Edited by Cornelis G. den Hartog, Ulrich Hübner, and Stefan Münger. AOAT 302. Münster: Ugarit Verlag, 2003.
Millard, Alan. "Alphabetic Writing, Cuneiform and Linear, Reconsidered." *Maarav* 14 (2007): 83-93.
Naveh, Joseph. *Early History of the Alphabet*. 2nd ed. Jerusalem/Leiden: Magnes Press, Hebrew University/Brill, 1987.
Porten, Bezalel, and Ada Yardeni. *Textbook of Aramaic Documents from Ancient Egypt 2. Contracts*. Winona Lake, Ind.: Eisenbrauns, 1989.
Puech, Émile. "Quelques remarques sur l'alphabet au deuxième millénaire." Pages 563-81 in *Atti del I congresso internazionale di studi fenici e punici, Roma 5-10 Novembre 1979. II*. Rome: Consiglio Nazionale delle Ricerche, 1983.

———. "Origine de l'alphabet. Documents en alphabet linéaire et cunéiforme du IIe millénaire." *RB* 93 (1986): 161–213.

———. "Les pointes de flèches inscrites de la fin du IIe millénaire en Phénicie et Canaan." Pages 251–69 in *Actas del IV congreso internacional de estudios fenicios y punicos I*. Edited by Aubet and Barthélemy. Cadiz, 2000.

———. "Note sur quatre inscriptions protosinaïtiques." *RB* 109 (2002): 5–39.

Rollston, Christopher A. "The Dating of the Early Royal Byblian Phoenician Inscriptions: A Response to Benjamin Sass." *Maarav* 15 (2008): 57–93.

Sanders, Seth L. "What Was the Alphabet for? The Rise of Written Vernaculars and the Making of Israelite National Literature." *Maarav* 11 (2004): 25–56.

Sass, Benjamin. *The Alphabet at the Turn of the Millennium: The West Semitic Alphabet ca. 1150–850 BCE: The Antiquity of the Arabian, Greek and Phrygian Alphabets*. Tel Aviv Occasional Publications 4. Tel Aviv: Emery and Claire Yass Publications in Archaeology, 2005.

———. "The Egyptian Middle Kingdom System for Writing Foreign Names and the West-Semitic Alphabet." Pages 44–50, 195* in *Yigael Yadin Memorial Volume*. Edited by Amnon Ben-Tor et al. Eretz-Israel 20. Jerusalem: Israel Exploration Society, 1989.

———. *The Genesis of the Alphabet and Its Development in the Second Millennium B.C.* ÄAT 13. Wiesbaden: Harrassowitz, 1988.

———. "The Genesis of the Alphabet and Its Development in the Second Millennium B.C. Twenty Years Later." *De Kêmi à Birit Nâri* (Paris) 2 (2004/5): 147–66.

———. *Studia alphabetica. On the Origin and Early History of the Northwest Semitic, South Semitic and Greek Alphabets*. OBO 102. Fribourg/Göttingen: Universitätsverlag/Vandenhoeck & Ruprecht, 1991.

Tappy, Ron E. et al. "An Abecedary of the Mid-Tenth Century B.C.E. from the Judaean Shephelah." *BASOR* 344 (2006): 5–46.

Vita, Juan-Pablo. "Alfabetos lineal y cuneiforme: relaciones en el II milenio A.C." *Actas del III congreso español de antiquo oriente próximo. Huelva, del 30 de Septiembre al 3 de Octubre de 2003*. *Huelva Arqueologica* 20 (2004): 11–39.

Wimmer, Stefan J., and S. Wimmer-Dweikat. "The Alphabet from Wadi el-Hôl." *Göttingen Miszellen* 180 (2001): 107–11.

Wuthnow, Heinz. *Die semitischen Menschennamen in griechischen Inschriften und Papyri des Vorderer Orients*. Leipzig: Dietrich, 1930.

Zamora Lopez, José Àngel. "Les utilisations de l'alphabet lors du IIe millénaire av. J.-C. et le développement de l'épigraphie alphabétique: une approche de la documentation ougaritique en dehors des tablettes (II)." Pages 491–528 in *Šapal tibnim mû illakû. Studies Presented to Joaquin Sanmartin on the Occasion of His 65th Birthday*. Edited by Gregorio del Olmo Lete et al. Aula Orientalis Supplementa 22. Barcelona: AUSA, 2006.

Chapter Two
Gedaliah's Seal Material Revisited:
Some Preliminary Notes on New Evidence from the City of David

*Peter van der Veen**

In a previous article on "Gedaliah ben Ahiqam" I discussed the question of identity of a high-ranking court official named Gedalyahu (variously described as *šr 'lhbyt* and *'bd hmlk* on provenanced and unprovenanced bullae).[1] I suggested that the person involved may be one and the same as Gedalyahu ben Ahiqam, who was appointed governor over Judah by the Neo-Babylonians after the fall of Jerusalem in 586 B.C.E. Alternatively, an equation with a like-named minister of King Zedekiah—Gedalyahu ben Pashhur—was also considered possible as a second option, a possibility that had previously been proposed by Bob Becking.[2]

---

* I wish to thank Dr John J. Bimson and Mr. Peter J. James for checking the English text of this article and for making helpful suggestions.

1. Peter G. van der Veen, "Gedaliah ben Ahiqam in the Light of Epigraphic Evidence (A Response to Bob Becking)," in *New Seals and Inscriptions, Hebrew, Idumean and Cuneiform* (ed. Meir Lubetski; Sheffield: Sheffield Phoenix, 2007), 55–70.
A provenanced but unstratified bulla of Gedalyahu *šr 'lhbyt* was found in 1935 at Lachish. Based solely on palaeographic grounds and on close comparison with similar provenanced and stratified seals and bullae from contemporary sites in Judah, this bulla can be safely attributed to Lachish Stratum II. Two other bullae naming a Gedalyahu *'bd hmlk* are unprovenanced and belong to the private collections of Dr. Shlomo Moussaieff and Mr. Yoav Sasson. See van der Veen, ibid., 55–58.

2. See ibid., 62. It must be emphasized that the more general arguments I presented concerning the political role played by Gedalyahu ben Ahiqam and the reliability of the biblical accounts about this individual remain unaltered. Although Becking refers regularly to the work of this author in his recent book, his comments have not convinced him. See his *From David to Gedaliah: The Book of Kings as Story and History* (OBO 228; Fribourg: Universitäts Verlag Freiburg Schweiz, 2007).

Based on the recent discovery of a new "Gedalyahu bulla" from the City of David by Eilat Mazar in 2007 and a close comparison of its palaeographic traits with those of the previously known "Gedaliah bullae" by this author, it now seems likely that their name bearer could have been our second candidate Gedalyahu ben Pashhur.[3] But this study also provided evidence for another hitherto unnoticed area of interest. Namely, it appeared to shed light on the person(s), who was/were in charge of engraving the names of the ministers in Jerusalem into the official stone seals during the last years of the Judahite monarchy. For could it be that only one single seal engraver or else a very small group of seal engravers working closely together was responsible for the production of the official seals of the most influential men of the day? In this article the author will begin looking at these intriguing questions, which, however, will need further study.

The Seal Impression of Gedalyahu ben Pashhur

During her recent excavations in area G near the summit of the City of David (and directly north of the so-called Stepped Stone Structure or Millo), Eilat Mazar discovered a large deposit of finds ranging from the late Judahite monarchy down to the early Persian periods. In addition to many bronze and iron arrowheads, late Judahite anthropomorphic and zoomorphic figurines, as well as inscribed Judahite weights, literally "dozens of bullae and fragments thereof" were retrieved from the sealed soil underneath the northern tower, which she dates to the time of Nehemiah (ca. 445 B.C.E.).[4] One complete bulla reads: "*lgdlyhw // bn pšḥwr*" (fig. 1). The inscription is enclosed by what appears to be a single border line and is separated by a double field divider. Both lines of text are terminated by a decorative dot, a feature attested on other late Iron Age seal impressions as well.[5] Although the inscription is somewhat blurred by scratches in the center

---

3. Eilat Mazar, *The Palace of King David: Excavations at the Summit of the City of David: Preliminary Report of Seasons 2005–2007* (Jerusalem: Shoham Academic Research and Publication, 2009), 66–71.

4. Ibid., 68 and personal communication with Mazar in August 2009. Several finds from the soil underneath the tower appear to support her dating of that structure: the late Iron Age figurines and inscribed weights, the many arrow heads relating to the Neo-Babylonian destruction, bullae impressed by Neo-Babylonian stamp seals and wedged-impressed pottery is all clearly datable to the period before the Persian occupation. While some of the pottery retrieved from underneath the tower appears to date its construction to the early Persian period (e.g., the carrot-shaped bottles and small cosmetic juglets) no evidence has been found so far that would suggest a date later than the mid to late Persian period.

5. See for instance Yair Shoham, "Hebrew Bullae," *Qedem* 41 (2000): no. B2; Robert Deutsch,

Fig. 1. The Gedalyahu ben Pashhur bulla from the City of David. Photo by Gabi Laron, Institute of Archaeology, Hebrew University; reproduced courtesy of Eilat Mazar.

Fig. 2. The Yehukal ben Shelemyahu ben Shobai bulla from the City of David. Photo by Gabi Laron, Institute of Archaeology, Hebrew University; reproduced courtesy of Eilat Mazar.

that intersect the field divider and the letters *yod* in the top line and *pe* and *šin* in the bottom line, close inspection of a good photograph kindly supplied by Eilat Mazar makes clear that her suggested reading is indeed justified.[6] Mazar's reading "leGedalyahu ben Pashhur" is therefore sound. An individual with the same name and patronymic served as minister at the court of King Zedekiah (Jer 38:1). Already during Mazar's 2005 excavation season another bulla (that of "Yehukal, the son of Shelemyahu, the son of Shobai"; fig. 2) was discovered nearby within the outer walls of the Large Stone Structure, an important administrative building from the Judahite monarchy period.[7] This person too is probably to be identified with a high-ranking official in the court of Zedekiah (Jer 37:3 and 38:1). The find spots of both bullae, as well as the stratigraphic position of the Gedalyahu son of Pashhur bulla in the destruction debris of the Neo-Babylonian conquest of Jerusalem, further support these equations.[8]

Palaeographic Affinities between the Gedalyahu Bullae

The palaeographic traits of the letters of the Gedalyahu ben Pashhur bulla from the City of David (below: City of David bulla) not only indicate a date near the end of the period of the Judahite monarchy,[9] they also reveal strong similarities

---

Messages from the Past: Hebrew Bullae from the Time of Isaiah through the Destruction of the First Temple (Tel Aviv: Archaeological Center Publications, 1999), 92, no. 25. This feature is also found at the end of line 2 of the S. Moussaieff bulla described in detail below (see fig. 4 in this article). Also see *WSS* no. 293 (from Beth Shemesh) and *WSS* no. 326 (from Ketef Hinnom).

6. Although at first glance the reading of *pe* in the bottom line appeared uncertain to me, the photograph showed clearly that the oblique line for the head of *pe* was thicker than the damages caused in the central area and could therefore be clearly distinguished.

7. Unlike Israel Finkelstein et al. ("Has King David's Palace in Jerusalem Been Found?," *Tel Aviv* 34 [2007]: 142–64) I agree with Eilat Mazar that the Large Stone Structure was built during the period of the United Monarchy. Unlike Mazar (who dates its construction to the Iron Age I–II transition), I prefer a date nearer the beginning of Iron Age I in accordance with the date of the Stepped Stone Structure nearby. See Peter J. James and Peter G. van der Veen, "Geschichtsbild in Scherben?," *Spektrum der Wissenschaft* (December 2008): 88–93.

8. I have likewise argued that the bullae of Gemaryahu [b]en Shaphan and Azaryahu ben Hilqiahu found by Yigal Shiloh's team in 1982 in the destruction debris of the "House of the Bullae" in Area G support their equation with the like-named contemporaries of the prophet Jeremiah (Jer 36:10; 1 Chr 5:39, 6:13–14). See Peter G. van der Veen, *The Final Phase of Iron Age IIC and the Babylonian Conquest: A Reassessment with Special Emphasis on Names and Bureaucratic Titles on Provenanced Seals and Bullae from Israel and Jordan* (Ph.D. diss., University of Bristol, 2005; forthcoming in the AOAT series published by Ugarit Verlag), 100–127. Also see van der Veen, "Gedaliah ben Ahiqam," 62–65.

9. For a detailed discussion of late Iron Age palaeographic traits on seals and bullae see

Fig. 3. The Gedalyahu 'šr 'lhbyt bulla from Lachish (Photo courtesy of the Wellcome Library, London).

Fig. 4. The Gedalyahu 'bd hmlk bulla from the S. Moussaieff collection (Photo: R. Wiskin, Courtesy of Dr. Shlomo Moussaieff).

van der Veen: *The Final Phase*. Also see Andrew G. Vaughn, "Palaeographic Dating of Judaean Seals and Its Significance for Biblical Research," *BASOR* 313 (1999): 43–64. My palaeographic analysis agrees with that of Vaughn and corroborates his work in almost every detail, while it deviates from that of Robert Deutsch. Both Vaughn and I commence solely with the provenanced epigraphic material as a source for comparison. In my Ph.D. thesis I have also placed the emphasis on other chronological evidence that may serve as an independent yardstick for epigraphic dating: the study of the primary archaeological loci (if firmly established), the study of comparative seal material from contemporary sites and contexts, of other finds uncovered in the near vicinity of the seal material (e.g., diagnostic pottery types and small finds). As palaeographic developments hardly ever occurred at the same pace and regularity in all places and at all times, a too rigid dependency on palaeographic traits alone can be very misleading. A good example of this is Deutsch's recent reattribution of both the provenanced and unprovenanced Shebnayahu 'bd hmlk bullae to the time of Hezekiah instead of to the (later) period of Lachish Stratum II (around 600 B.C.E.) in which the provenanced bulla was found. See Robert Deutsch, "Tracking Down Shebnayahu, Servant of the King: How an Antiquities Market Find Solved a 42-Year-Old Excavation Puzzle," *BAR* 35 (2009): 45–49, 67. By basing his dates primarily on his own comprehension of the palaeographic traits of the *unprovenanced* bulla rather than on the archaeological context of the *provenanced* specimen, his new date contradicts with the available evidence (not just with the *late* letter forms of *he* and *nun*). For instance, his re-attribution of the juglet (which originally contained the Lachish bullae) to the Lachish Stratum III horizon disagrees with the current understanding of this *later* Iron Age IIC cylindrical juglet (Deutsch, "Tracking Down Shebnayahu," 67 n. 7). As a matter of fact, the Lachish II juglet contains a more flaring and elongated body and has a narrower everted neck than its stockier Lachish III precursor. While the latter continued to be produced until the end of the Iron Age the former only came into existence during the seventh century B.C.E. and experienced its heyday within the Lachish II horizon (it is for instance found in City of David

with letters found on the provenanced Gedalyahu *šr 'lhbyt* bulla from Lachish (below: Lachish bulla, see fig. 3) and the two unprovenanced Gedalyahu *'bd hmlk* seal impressions from the Shlomo Moussaieff (below: Moussaieff bulla, see fig. 4) and Yoav Sasson (below: Sasson bulla[10]) private collections respectively.

The following traits are indicative of a *late* date towards the end of the Iron Age IIC period:

- The top horizontal bar of *he* continues to the right of the vertical stem (this applies to all four relevant Gedalyahu bullae). An additional characteristic typical of late Iron Age IIC *he*-forms is the squeezed position of its horizontal bars. Moreover, the left tip of the lowest horizontal bar often bends upwards. These features can be recognized nicely on the City of David bulla. They are also seen especially in the second register of the Lachish bulla (= WSS 405)[11] as well as on the Moussaieff[12] and Sasson bullae (= WSS 409).[13]

- The letter *waw* reflects seventh–sixth century B.C.E. characteristics. Although *waw* is largely "intermediate, nondistinctive"[14] in the second register of the City of David bulla, its distinctive late, elegantly curved head in the first register finds close parallels on seals and bullae from other Iron Age IIC sites for instance on the House of the Bullae seal impressions discovered by Yigal Shiloh in area G of the City of David.[15]

Stratum 10B, in Tel Arad Stratum VII–VI and Tel Ira Stratum VI). See Liorah Freud, "Pottery," in *Tel 'Ira: A Stronghold in the Biblical Negev* (ed. Itzhaq Beit-Arieh; Tel Aviv: Emery ad Claire Sass Publications in Archaeology, 1999), e.g. 219–20; 281 fig. 6.100:17–19. Also Orna Zimhoni, "The Pottery of Levels III and II," in *The Renewed Archaeological Excavations at Lachish (1973–1994)* (ed. David Ussishkin; vol. 4, Tel Aviv: Emery and Claire Sass Publications in Archaeology, 2004), 1884 fig. 26.53:2–3. The evidence clearly points to ca. 600 B.C.E. for both Shebnayahu bullae, a view shared by Vaughn (personal communication, May/August 2009). The archaeological context and the palaeography of the bullae from the City of David (both from the Yigal Shiloh and Eilat Mazar excavations) are consistent with this chronology.

10. No other photo of the Yoav Sasson bulla than the one found in WSS 409 was made available to the author in time and could therefore not be reproduced here.

11. This is especially the case with *he* in the lower register. The horizontals of both *hes* on this bulla are admittedly less squeezed and bent than on the other Gedalyahu seal impressions.

12. Robert Deutsch, *Messages from the Past*, 72–73 no. 8. Here this feature can be recognized in both *hes* both in the top and bottom registers. I was able to study this bulla in February 2002 thanks to the great hospitality of Dr. Shlomo Moussaieff.

13. Here it is especially clear with the letter *he* depicted in the lower register.

14. Following the terminology used by Vaughn, "Palaeographic Dating," 53 with table 6.

15. See Shoham, "Hebrew Bullae," especially B9, B29, B30, B31, B36.

It can also be seen on the Moussaieff bulla and perhaps on the Lachish bulla as well.[16]

- Another diagnostic letter that is unfortunately only found on the City of David bulla is the letter *nun*. The lower left vertical stroke of its head continues beyond its lower horizontal bar and this trait finds many good parallels among the provenanced late Iron Age IIC seal material from ancient Judah.[17]

The striking affinities between the relevant Gedalyahu bullae can especially be seen with the following letters:

a) A long square-legged lamed.

Although this type of *lamed* finds many parallels on seals from the late-eighth till the early-sixth centuries B.C.E., it is not so widely represented among the House of the Bullae seal impressions from the City of David.[18] But even though the use of this *lamed* is widespread, its consistent use on *all* four Gedalyahu bullae deserves attention and may be significant. Its stem always intersects with the upper border line (when found in the top register) or with the field divider above it (when found in the bottom register). Its base is virtually flat and its right vertical stroke is approximately parallel with the stance of its long oblique stem.[19]

b) A dalet *with an indented "nose" and an up-curved right tip.*

Although a *dalet* with a long oblique top stroke which extends beyond the vertical shaft on the right, finds good parallels among the seal material in the period between the late-eighth and sixth centuries B.C.E., two particularities stand out that deserve closer attention:

1) The left lower angle of the head of *dalet* seems to be indented (its left oblique stroke is bent). This is especially obvious on the City of David and

---

16. On the Moussaieff bulla the *waw* is very distinctive indeed, while on the Lachish specimen one cannot be absolutely certain as the letter is found near the upper left edge and the original bulla cannot be checked anymore as its present location is unknown.

17. Concerning this issue also see Vaughn, "Palaeographic Dating," 55 with table 7.

18. See Shoham, "Hebrew Bullae," 52 fig. 1 (only B20–21). This chart is however not completely correct. The base of the possessive *lamed* on the Gemaryahu ben Shaphan bulla (B2) is much squarer on my high resolution photographs of this bulla than has been represented in the chart. The same appears to be the case with B7, B27 and possibly with B35.

19. The *lamed* in the bottom register of the Moussaieff bulla may seem to be an exception to this rule (as its base looks somewhat rounder). This, however, is more apparent than real. Close inspection of the relevant letter has revealed that here too the base of *lamed* is approximately square.

Lachish bullae, while it is less clear on the Moussaieff and Sasson specimens.[20] While it doesn't have any obvious parallels among the "House of the Bullae" seal impressions (from Area G), this feature is also found on the beautifully carved Yaazanyahu ʿ*bd hmlk* seal from Tell en-Nasbeh, which can also be dated to the final years of the Judahite Monarchy.[21]

2) Another striking feature is the undulating shape of the extension of the top stroke of the head of *dalet*, which continues to the right of the vertical stem. Although this feature is perhaps less obvious on the City of David bulla (due to the thinness of the extension), I was able to see it clearly on the high resolution photograph provided by Eilat Mazar.[22]

Both traits are especially obvious on the Lachish and Sasson bullae where the up-curved tip on the right can be recognized especially well. This feature cannot be seen, however, on the Moussaieff bulla as the *dalet* in the first register is damaged by a crack in the clay. The *dalet* in the second register definitely lacks this extension. A modest up-curved tip may perhaps also be seen on the above-mentioned official Yaazanyahu seal.

c) A "squashed" yod.

Most of the Gedalyahu bullae contain *yods* whose horizontal bars create a rather squashed effect. Although this feature again is not unparalleled (for instance several of the House of the Bullae seal impressions contain this feature[23]) its occurrence on at least three of the Gedalyahu bullae again deserves attention. The two left horizontal bars of this type of *yod* are pressed together. This is especially clear on the City of David and Lachish bullae[24] as well as on the Moussaieff

---

20. Both *dalets* in the first register of the Gedalyahu ben Pashhur and Gedalyahu šrʿlhbyt bullae have a rather blunt nose, a feature that may be recognized in the first register on the Y. Sasson specimen as well (= WSS 409). But as I did not have access to the Sasson bulla itself or even to a good photograph, this issue could not be verified. The oblique left stroke of the head of *dalet* in the lower register of the Moussaieff bulla is also slightly bent, but on the whole it is not as distinct as on the City of David and Lachish specimens.

21. See WSS 8; Van der Veen, *The Final Phase*, 1–26.

22. I was unable to investigate the original bulla. Even so, the high resolution image of this impression sufficiently revealed this trait.

23. E.g., Shoham, "Hebrew Bullae," B7, B15, B17?, B20–21, B23, B25, B33, B37.

24. On the Gedalyahu ben Pashhur bulla this feature is especially clear. The top horizontal is curved and pressed towards the up-curved second horizontal stroke. On the Lachish specimen the top horizontal bar of the first *yod* in the top register is also slightly curved, but its second horizontal is definitely straight and was carved only roughly parallel to the top one. The form of *yod* in the bottom register is again more obvious, as the top stroke here is slightly indented and is engraved closer to the second stroke.

bulla, while the *yods* on the City of David and Moussaieff bullae are so close that one can describe them as virtually identical.[25]

d) *A "squashed" he with an extended top horizontal stroke.*

This issue has already been discussed above as has been described as a diagnostic palaeographic trait of *late* Iron Age IIC Judahite seals. It is found on all four Gedalyahu bullae. The *hes* on the City of David and Moussaieff bullae are again virtually identical.

An additional feature that adds weight to the affinities described above is the use of the decorative terminal dot at the end of both registers on the City of David bulla and at the end of the bottom register on the Moussaieff bulla.

Strong Affinities or Evidence of a Single Hand?

As can be seen in Table 1, the letters carved on all four Gedalyahu bullae indeed show striking similarities. Although there are some slight differences also (which may be more apparent than real[26]), in general the letters reveal an almost consistent identical handwriting. This becomes especially clear when one looks at the way the name Gedalyahu itself has been written, where most of the above affinities occur together. How could this consistency in style be explained? Is it mere coincidence? Perhaps it is. But the question must be asked if the consistent application of several letters, sometimes with quite distinct features, may not actually have derived from the hand of one seal engraver, who could have been responsible for the production of all four seals. Alternatively these seals may have been produced by a small group of seal engravers, who belonged to the same school or guild and who wrote approximately with the same handwriting. It was noted that the same features could also be recognized on the seal of Yaazanyahu *'bd hmlk* from Tell en-Nasbeh (see Table 1) who may have been one

---

25. The top horizontal line of *yod* on the Sasson bulla is also curved but it seems to be further away from the second left horizontal stroke. Hopefully future study of the original bulla may help to clarify this point.

26. It is always important to remember that we are talking about very small pieces of clay, whose impressions hardly ever exceed 1×1 cm in size. The individual letters are so small that its features can often only be clearly recognized under strong magnification. Its individual palaeographic traits, which are still smaller than the whole letter, are so tiny that a scribe or engraver could hardly be blamed for not having *always* executed the same letters into stone (also, e.g., in bone and bronze) in precisely the same manner! Notably, the affinities of the letters as described above must therefore be considered to be even more striking than one may have thought at first glance.

Letter	City of David bulla	Lachish bulla	Moussaieff bulla	Sasson bulla	Yehukal bulla	Yaazanyahu seal
dalet	ᐊ	ᐊ	ᐊ ᐊ	ᐊ ᐊ		ᐊ
he	ᐊ ᐊ	ᐊ ᐊ	ᐊ ᐊ	ᐊ	ᐊ ᐊ	ᐊ ᐊ
waw	↑ ↑	↑	↑	↑	↑	↑
yod	⋛	⋛	⋛	⋛	⋛ ⋛ ⋛	⋛ ⋛ ⋛
lamed	⌐ ⌐	⌐ ⌐ ⌐	⌐ ⌐ ⌐	⌐ ⌐ ⌐ ⌐	⌐ ⌐ ⌐	⌐
nun	∫					

Table 1. The late Iron Age diagnostic letters *he*, *waw*, *nun* and the letters that reveal strong affinities on the seals and bullae discussed.

and the same as the army commander who joined forces with Gedalyahu the son of Ahiqam at Mizpah after the Fall of Jerusalem in 586 B.C.E. (2 Kgs 25:23; Jer 40:8). He too must have served King Zedekiah before the exile and it is therefore possible that his seal was also produced by the same person or guild working for the most prominent personalities within the kingdom of Judah. The same can be said about yet another bulla that was recently discovered by Eilat Mazar at the City of David and to which I also referred above (with the inscription "Yehukal the son of Shelemyahu the son of Shobai"). Here too the individual letters once more reveal close affinities with those of the Gedalyahu bullae (again see Table 1). And again this official served king Zedekiah alongside Gedalyahu ben Passhur according to the biblical narrative. The question therefore appears to be a legitimate one: where all these seals produced by the same hand or by a small group of men working closely together within the same school or guild?

Conclusions

This brings us back to our original question of the identity of all four Gedalyahus referred to on the seal impressions discussed above. One of them can now be positively identified as the son of Pashhur due to the recent discovery of his bulla by Eilat Mazar at the City of David. He served as minister during the reign of Zedekiah according to the biblical text of the book of Jeremiah. But was he also the owner of the seals that impressed the other three bullae? Perhaps the most striking stylistic affinities can be found on the City of David and Moussaieff bullae and it may be proposed that both had belonged to the same minister Gedalyahu the son of Pashhur. Indeed, I prefer to think that *all four* bullae could have belonged to the same individual, simply because the stylistic affinities between *all four* bullae are very striking indeed.[27] The final proof for this, however, will have to await further evidence from archaeology.

---

27. Even so, it cannot categorically be ruled out that another Gedalyahu had served at the court of Zedekiah alongside Gedalyahu the son of Pashhur. Hence some of the bullae could also have belonged to him. Indeed, as I have argued elsewhere, it seems likely that Gedalyahu the son of Ahiqam had been in office in Jerusalem before he was appointed governor by the Babylonians at Mizpah in 586 B.C.E. On the other hand, we do not know how long the latter stayed in office. It may be assumed that the pro-Babylonian minister fell into disfavor not long after 594 B.C.E. when Zedekiah rebelled against his former Babylonian overlord. Gedalyahu the son of Ahiqam may subsequently have become the head of the opposition party against Zedekiah's anti-Babylonian politics and there is positive evidence from Lachish letter VI that such a party indeed had existed among the Jerusalem elite. It therefore seems unlikely to me that Gedalyahu the son of Ahiqam would have continued in office alongside Gedalyahu the son of Pashhur until the very end of

Nevertheless, if indeed all four bullae mention the same person, as I suggest, then it would mean that all four could have served different administrative purposes. While the City of David bulla, which only gives the personal name and patronymic of the seal bearer, may have been used predominantly for close colleagues and family members, the Lachish bulla gives his precise office held at the court in Jerusalem. As "Minister over the Royal House" he surely held one of the most prestigious positions within the Judahite bureaucracy.[28] A bulla bearing this title would have been used primarily for sealing documents related directly to the administration of the palace and royal properties, both in and outside Jerusalem. The unprovenanced Moussaieff and Sasson bullae endow him with the honorific epithet "servant/minister of the king" and these may have been used for a wider spectrum of bureaucratic correspondence, emphasizing his proximity and loyalty to the Judahite monarch.[29]

There is one more point that may be seen as a bonus to the work done so far. The discovery of the City of David bulla also supports the authenticity of the Moussaieff and Sasson bullae. Their letter forms could not have been copied from the provenanced City of David seal impression with which they show such strong affinities. Surely this evidence could not have been known to any forger back in the 1970s and 1980s as the City of David bulla was only discovered recently in 2007.

Bibliography

Avigad, Nachman, and Benjamin Sass. *Corpus of West Semitic Stamp Seals*. Jerusalem: The Israel Academy of Sciences and Humanities, 1997.

Becking, Bob. *From David to Gedaliah: The Book of Kings as Story and History*. OBO 228. Fribourg: Universitäts Verlag, 2007.

Deutsch, Robert. *Messages from the Past: Hebrew Bullae from the Time of Isaiah through the Destruction of the First Temple*. Tel Aviv: Archaeological Center Publications, 1999.

———. "Tracking Down Shebnayahu, Servant of the King: How an Antiquities Market Find Solved a 42-Year-Old Excavation Puzzle." *BAR* 35 (2009): 45–49, 67.

Finkelstein, Israel et al. "Has King David's Palace in Jerusalem Been Found?" *TA* 34 (2007): 142–64.

---

the reign of Zedekiah when the former had probably already moved to Mizpah in support of the besieging Chaldean army. On the political role played by the son Ahiqam see van der Veen, "Gedalyahu ben Ahiqam," 58–62, esp. pp. 60–61.

28. Nili Sacher Fox, *In the Service of the King: Officialdom in Acient Israel and Judah* (Cincinnati: Hebrew Union College Press, 2000), 95–96.

29. Fox, *In the Service of the King*, 62–63.

Fox, Nili Sacher. *In the Service of the King: Officialdom in Acient Israel and Judah.* Cincinnati: Hebrew Union College Press, 2000.
Freud, Liorah. "Pottery." in *Tel 'Ira: A Stronghold in the Biblical Negev.* Edited by Itzhaq Beit-Arieh. Tel Aviv: Emery ad Claire Sass Publications in Archaeology, 1999.
James, Peter J., and Peter G. van der Veen. "Geschichtsbild in Scherben?" *Spektrum der Wissenschaft* (December 2008): 88–93.
Mazar, Eilat. *The Palace of King David: Excavations at the Summit of the City of David: Preliminary Report of Seasons 2005–2007.* Jerusalem: Shoham Academic Research and Publication, 2009.
Shoham, Yair. "Hebrew Bullae." *Qedem* 41. Edited by Donald T. Ariel. Jerusalem: The Institute of Archaeology, The Hebrew University of Jerusalem, 2000.
Vaughn, Andrew G. "Palaeographic Dating of Judaean Seals and Its Significance for Biblical Research." *BASOR* 313 (1999): 43–64.
Veen, Peter G. van der. "Gedaliah ben Ahiqam in the Light of Epigraphic Evidence (A Response to Bob Becking)." Pages 55–70 in *New Seals and Inscriptions, Hebrew, Idumean and Cuneiform.* Edited by Meir Lubetski. Sheffield: Sheffield Phoenix, 2007.
———. "The Final Phase of Iron Age IIC and the Babylonian Conquest: A Reassessment with Special Emphasis on Names and Bureaucratic Titles on Provenanced Seals and Bullae from Israel and Jordan." Ph.D. diss., University of Bristol, 2005.
Zimhoni, Orna. "The Pottery of Levels III and II." Pages 1789–1906 in *The Renewed Archaeological Excavations at Lachish (1973–1994),* vol. 2. Edited by David Ussishkin. Tel Aviv: Emery and Claire Sass Publications in Archaeology, 2004.

Chapter Three
Sixteen Strong Identifications of Biblical Persons (Plus Nine Other Identifications) in Authentic Northwest Semitic Inscriptions from before 539 b.c.e.

Lawrence J. Mykytiuk

The goal of this paper is to report the strongest results of a complicated book, as now corrected and updated in a recent journal article, because almost half of these strongest results do not appear among the book's conclusions.[1] The book is titled *Identifying Biblical Persons in Northwest Semitic Inscriptions of 1200–539*

---

1. I dedicate this paper to collegial acquaintances among the scholars on the continent of Europe whom I have been privileged to meet or communicate with directly: Bob Becking, C. H. J. de Geus, Josette Elayi, Viktor Golinets, Martin Heide, Izaak J. de Hulster, Jens Bruun Kofoed, Reinhard G. Lehmann, André Lemaire, Gotthard G. G. Reinhold, Paul Sanders, Henry Stadhouders, and Peter van der Veen. I wish to thank our Section Chair, Meir Lubetski, for permission to have a substitute present this paper due to my unavoidable absence from the 2007 SBL International Meeting in Vienna. I am especially grateful to Peter van der Veen for very graciously agreeing to present this paper on my behalf. Since the meeting, besides revising and updating this paper, I have inserted "(Plus Nine Other Identifications)" into the title as a reference to the identifications (IDs) in sections 4, 5, and 6 below.

I hope for as fair and open a consideration of this paper in written form as it received at the Vienna meeting. In his insightful 2006 review of *IBP*, C. H. J. de Geus offers a plea for openness: "The book under review deserves to be received as a very serious ... piece of research.... [S]everal colleagues will push a work like this aside as an impossible project. However, the author deserves better than such a 'nihilistic' attitude.... Mykytiuk is well aware of the problems.... [He] has seen almost everything that is relevant for this subject.... [He] goes to great lengths to develop a workable and acceptable method of identifying names/persons. But his real opponents are not the 'nihilistic' academics, but enthusiastic authors who come with quick and premature unwarranted identifications" (C. H. J. de Geus, review of *IBP*, *BO* 63 [2006]: col. 356.)

B.C.E. (henceforth *IBP*), and the article, which appeared in *Maarav*, is designated below as Mykytiuk, "Corrections."[2] This presentation of results is needed in order to gather the strongest identifications (below, *identification* is abbreviated as ID) within the parameters of its title from three sources: *IBP*'s conclusions, *IBP*'s appendixes, and Mykytiuk, "Corrections." Because of circumstances that affected the arrangement of its contents,[3] *IBP* actually obscures five of its strongest IDs, found in its appendixes.[4] Below, these are briefly described along with some of the IDs treated in Mykytiuk, "Corrections."[5] All told, seven of the sixteen strongest IDs described below do not appear among *IBP*'s conclusions.

Readers who are interested only in "new" inscriptions should see below under the heading "Four Identifications that Currently Hover between Two Grades." Two bullae discovered in 2005 and 2008 are treated there.

Current Totals of Results and Scope of Coverage

From among inscriptions published as early as 1828 and gathered by Diringer,[6] through others published until July 2002, *IBP* attempts to glean all pre-Persian-era, Northwest Semitic inscriptions that seem to refer to figures in the Hebrew Bible. Within these same parameters, Mykytiuk, "Corrections," covers discoveries made through July 31, 2008. By subjecting all potential IDs in gleaned inscriptions to certain criteria, *IBP* and Mykytiuk, "Corrections," place them in various

---

2. Lawrence J. Mykytiuk, *Identifying Biblical Persons in Northwest Semitic Inscriptions of 1200–539 B.C.E.* (AcBib 12; Atlanta: SBL, 2004); idem, "Corrections and Updates to 'Identifying Biblical Persons in Northwest Semitic Inscriptions of 1200–539 B.C.E.'" *Maarav* 16 (2009): 49–132.

3. The SBL Academia Biblica series in which *IBP* was published had a rule stipulating that no substantial change from the content of the dissertation should be made in the content of the book. Therefore, updates and expansions beyond the original dissertation are confined to *IBP*'s footnotes, appendixes, and bibliography.

In *IBP*, 197–98, the conclusions chapter lists only nine biblical persons from before the Persian era having reliable IDs in inscriptions of known authenticity. These nine are discussed within the main body of text, specifically in *IBP*, 95–163. But besides these, *IBP*'s appendixes B and C include five other IDs, also in authentic inscriptions, which are reliable to certain but *not* mentioned in the conclusions chapter. These additional IDs do not receive any discussion in the main body of text and have frequently gone unnoticed.

4. Viz., Hazael, Ben-Hadad the son of Hazael, Sennacherib, Tiglath-pileser III, and Sargon II.

5. The strongest of these are IDs of Hadadezer and Ben-hadad, the son of Hadadezer.

6. David Diringer, *Le iscrizioni antico-ebraiche Palestinesi* (Florence: Felice Le Monnier, 1934).

grades, according to the degree of reliability or unreliability of the IDs and non-IDs they offer.

Now that the corrections article has improved on *IBP*'s results, more accurate numerical results are available. From among eighty-four persons[7] named in ninety-four gleaned inscriptions,[8] by judicious use of *IBP*'s evaluation protocols, one can discern strong IDs of sixteen biblical persons in Northwest Semitic inscriptions that are authentic. These sixteen strong IDs are graded from reliable to certain, as reflected in the title of this report. Four other IDs appear below that are reasonable and potentially strong, along with three other IDs that are classified as reasonable but not strong, plus two of literary and religious value, whose historical value is unclear.

There are four limits on coverage. First, this report covers no IDs from the Persian era onward, which in Palestine began in 539 B.C.E. Second, it treats IDs in inscriptions written only in Northwest Semitic languages (exceptions, in Egyptian and Akkadian, are mentioned in footnotes). Third, this report does not consider IDs in inscriptions of unknown authenticity, that is, those that are inscribed on unprovenanced (alias marketed) epigraphs, nor does it include those that show signs of having modern additions inscribed on genuinely ancient epigraphs to create fakes. Inscriptions of unknown authenticity must not serve as a basis for any conclusions. At best, they render conclusions unreliable and suspect, and at worst, they can lead to completely erroneous results. Because someday they might be authenticated, it is worth noting them, as in *IBP*, 153–96. But one must protect the pool of authentic inscriptional data from possible pollution by forged data by separating such inscriptions from those of known authenticity.[9] Therefore, this

---

7. Seventy-nine biblical persons appear in the list in *IBP*'s Appendix B (*IBP*, 211–43), as noted in *IBP*, 243 n. 111. A footnote names one more person mentioned in Scripture (ibid., 260 n. 54), two appear in Eilat Mazar, "Did I Find King David's Palace?" *BAR* 32 (2006): 26, and two more appear in idem, "The Wall that Nehemiah Built," *BAR* 35 (2009): 29, for a total of eighty-four persons.

8. Considering only published epigraphs, ninety-four gleaned, mostly unprovenanced Northwest Semitic inscriptions seem—before being evaluated—*potentially* to refer by name to eighty-four persons whom the HB places in the period before the Persian era. In some instances, two or more inscriptions refer to the same person. (Ninety-four is the total of ninety-one inscriptions in the list in appendix B [*IBP*, 211–43], one in a footnote [ibid., 260 n. 54], one in E. Mazar, "Did I Find King David's Palace," 26, 70 n. 11, and one more in idem, "The Wall that Nehemiah Built," 29.)

9. This approach to the proper basis for conclusions follows the example of Nili S. Fox, *In the Service of the King: Officialdom in Ancient Israel and Judah* (Monographs of the Hebrew Union College 23; Cincinnati: Hebrew Union College, 2000), 32. Later, Rollston's five principles for the handling of data from unprovenanced materials led to the major reorganization of *IBP* envisioned in Mykytiuk, "Corrections," 51–62 (Christopher A. Rollston, "Non-Provenanced

paper, which is intended to present the strongest conclusions in *IBP*, generally omits data from unprovenanced inscriptions.[10]

The only exceptions to the rule against using unprovenanced materials to reach conclusions are inscriptions that have socio-politically and chronologically appropriate paleographic details but were acquired before appropriate paleographic details became known to anyone, including both scholars and forgers. Normally, these inscriptions were acquired in the nineteenth century.[11] This logic

---

Epigraphs I: Pillaged Antiquities, Northwest Semitic Forgeries, and Protocols for Laboratory Tests," *Maarav* 10 [2003]: 135–93).

10. Possible forgery is the first reason for this paper's exclusion of an ID of Jezebel, queen of Israel (r. ca. 873–852; 1 Kgs 16:31, etc.), in the unprovenanced, iconic stone seal "*yzbl*" or "[ ]*yzbl*" (*WSS* no. 740), proposed by Marjo C. A. Korpel, "Seals of Jezebel and Other Women in Authority," *Tidskrif vir Semitistiek / Journal of Semitics* 15 (2006): 349–71; idem, "Queen Jezebel's Seal," *UF* 328 (2006): 379–98; idem, "Fit for a Queen: Jezebel's Royal Seal," *BAR* 34 (2008): 32–37. Besides the real possibility that this seal might be forged, Rollston, "Prosopography and the יזבל Seal," *IEJ* 59 (2009): 86–91, indicates several additional ways in which such an ID is very precarious. Cf. the grade 1 "Doubtful" classification of such an ID in this seal in *IBP*, 216 no. (8), *IBP*'s description of grade 1 IDs (*IBP*, 77–79), and its observations on the absence of particular kinds of identifying marks (*IBP*, 21–22). *IBP*'s structured approach implies a firm rejection of making IDs in an *ad hoc* manner, which can be a facile path to desired results. To avoid such practice, one should first establish sound principles and criteria for comprehensive application, as *IBP* attempts, and then vet potential IDs (see below, under the heading Identification Methodology, and *IBP*, 9–89).

11. There is at least one unprovenanced seal published in the twentieth century that has the potential to be demonstrably authentic. Chronologically appropriate paleographic details that were not known in 1940, it might be possible to demonstrate authenticity of the stone seal "Belonging to 'Ushna' [or 'Ashna'], minister of 'Ahaz" (king of Judah), purchased on the antiquities market during 1940 or earlier (Charles C. Torrey, "A Hebrew Seal from the Reign of Ahaz," *BASOR* 79 (1940): 27–29; *WSS*, no. 5; *IBP*, 163–69, 200, 220 seal [23], 249 seal [23]). Although Ahaz, son of Jotham, king of Judah (r. 742/1–726), can be identified in a summary inscription of Tiglath-pileser III (r. 745–727; *IBP*, 167), demonstrating this seal to be authentic would be the final step in establishing the first ID of him in a Northwest Semitic inscription of known authenticity. At least part of such an argument for authenticity of the seal of 'Ushna'/'Ashna' would be that Frank Moore Cross's series of three foundational articles on Hebrew paleography, published in the early 1960s, had not yet been written. These are: Frank Moore Cross, "Epigraphic Notes on Hebrew Documents of the Eighth–Sixth Centuries B.C.: I. A New Reading of a Place Name in the Samaria Ostraca," *BASOR* 163 (1961): 12–14; idem, "Epigraphic Notes on Hebrew Documents of the Eighth–Sixth Centuries B.C.: II. The Murabba'ât Papyrus and the Letter Found near Yabneh-yam," *BASOR* 165 (1962): 34–46; idem, "Epigraphic Notes on Hebrew Documents of the Eighth–Sixth Centuries B.C.: III. The Inscribed Jar Handles from Gibeon," *BASOR* 168 (1962): 18–23; all three reprinted (possibly with light revisions by Cross?) in *Leaves from an Epigrapher's Notebook: Collected Papers in Hebrew and West Semitic Palaeography and Epigraphy* (HSS 51; Winona Lake, Ind.: Eisenbrauns, 2003), 114–15, 116–24, 125–28, respectively.

To demonstrate that the chronologically appropriate or indicative paleographic details

is nothing new; it underlies Patrick D. Miller's observation over two decades ago in support of the authenticity of the Mesha Inscription, "The form of the letters is consistent with other inscriptions of the ninth century B.C.E. and could not have been known when the stone was discovered."[12] Below, under ID 10. Uzziah, two unprovenanced stone seals of King Uzziah's ministers are accepted as authentic on similar grounds.

The fourth limit concerns the strength of the IDs that appear here. This paper considers only published IDs in inscriptions of known authenticity in the following two groups:[13] 1) strong IDs, a term that embraces those that are reliable, virtually certain, or certain. All strong IDs are in *IBP*'s grades S or 3, which are explained below. 2) IDs that are reasonable but not known to be certain. These are in *IBP*'s grade 2, also explained below. Weaker IDs, as well as non-IDs, are not covered herein.

IDENTIFICATION METHODOLOGY

A summary of the identification protocols (*IBP*, 9–89) is as follows: As a precondition, avoid circular reasoning. Three decades ago, J. Maxwell Miller observed, "Obviously, when a written source has served as a determining factor in the interpretation of any given archaeological data, it is misleading to cite the interpreted archaeological data as 'proof' of the accuracy of the written source."[14] Therefore, *IBP*'s identification protocols first attempt to interpret a given inscription in light of authentic inscriptions and avoid as much as possible the use of biblical data to interpret them. Only *after* interpreting the inscriptional and the biblical data separately, using well-grounded data, should one compare them.[15]

---

contained in the seal of 'Ushna'/'Ashna' were not known in 1940 would require an exhaustive search of publications on Hebrew and West Semitic epigraphy and paleography before 1941. It would also be necessary to demonstrate fully that this seal's paleographic traits are suitable for the period of the reign of Ahaz, king of Judah, mid-to-late eighth century (see *IBP*, 164–66).

12. Patrick D. Miller Jr., "Moabite Stone," *ISBE* 3:396.
13. The overall schema for grading IDs appears in *IBP*, 212–13.
14. J. Maxwell Miller, *The Old Testament and the Historian* (GBS OT Series; Philadelphia: Fortress, 1976), 47.
15. *IBP* first uses authentic inscriptions as the basis for interpreting the thirteen inscriptions it treats in detail, before going on to compare inscriptional and biblical data. Because of space considerations, *IBP*'s appendixes and Mykytiuk, "Corrections," however, offer only preliminary evaluations of potential IDs and do not include this step. In many instances, these would be simple parallels to items already interpreted using data from inscriptions of known authenticity.

After this precondition, *IBP*'s identification protocols lead researchers to ask three questions, which serve as a matrix[16] for evaluating IDs:

- Are the initial data reliable, in the sense that epigraphic data are authentic, not forged, and that biblical data are well based in the ancient manuscripts, as determined by sound text criticism?[17]
- Do the settings (time and socio-political "place") of the inscriptional person and of the biblical person *permit* a match? They should normally be within about fifty years of each other and members of the same socio-political group, for example, late-eighth-century Israelite.
- How strongly do identifying marks that help to specify an individual, such as name, patronym, and title, count for or against an ID? For a reliable ID, they need to be sufficient to insure that the inscription and the biblical text are not referring to two different persons.

This third question is to distinguish between contemporaries in the same society who happened to have the same name, keeping them from being mistakenly identified as one and the same person. The number of matching identifying marks of an individual is built into the grade number of IDs in grades 3 (for three or more marks), 2, 1, and 0 (zero). Of course, IDs having more of these marks are better established than those having fewer marks. Another kind of ID, made on grounds of singularity, is defined in section 3.1 below. IDs of this last kind are strongest of all and are placed in grade S (for singularity).

Strong Identifications of Sixteen Biblical Persons

The sixteen strong IDs that result from using the above identification protocols appear in the lists below, each with brief mention of the answer to the third question: the identifying marks of the individual. Question 1 has already been answered in the affirmative for all of the IDs below, and question 2 above some-

---

16. I wish to thank Bob Becking for this descriptive term and especially for demonstrating that these three questions can be used as a quick and effective means to establish an ID (Bob Becking, "The Identity of Nabu-sharrussu-ukin, the Chamberlain: An Epigraphic Note on Jeremiah 39,3. With an Appendix on the Nebu⁽ˡ⁾sarsekim Tablet by Henry Stadhouders," *BN* NF 140 [2009]: 38–39).

17. This question has grown from its original form by adding biblical text criticism in response to de Geus, review of *IBP*, col. 357, with my thanks to the reviewer. Although text criticism has not affected any IDs that I have evaluated thus far, this requirement is of course necessary.

times requires long answers, which are available in *IBP* for most of the persons whose IDs are listed below. Therefore, as a space-saving expedient, the list below generally omits questions 1 and 2.

IDENTIFICATIONS MADE ON GROUNDS OF SINGULARITY

The following ten biblical figures, all kings, can be identified with certainty, because their IDs are made on grounds of singularity. Singularity involves the connection of the person to a singular circumstance, such as participation in a particular historical event. In order to have an ID based on singularity, the biblical and/or inscriptional data must refer to one and only one person, and the correspondence between the biblical and the inscriptional data must *require* that the ID be made.

For example, the Ashur ostracon (*KAI* 233) names Sennacherib, king of Assyria (r. 704–681). The singular feature evident in this inscription, according to both Assyrian and biblical records, is that he can only be the same Sennacherib who besieged King Hezekiah in Jerusalem (see ID 6 below).

These, the strongest IDs, result from the presence of at least one singular feature, sometimes called a point of singularity, in the following *loci*: 1) in both the inscriptional data and the biblical data; 2) in the inscriptional data alone; or, 3) in the biblical data alone. Accordingly, such IDs are listed below in three categories: singularity that is inscriptional and biblical, only inscriptional, and only biblical. Within each category, they are in approximate chronological order.

Identifications Based on Singularity in Inscriptional and Biblical Data

1. David, founder of the dynasty that ruled Judah (r. ca. 1010–970), 1 Sam 16:13, etc. (*IBP*, 110–32, 265–77; Mykytiuk, "Corrections," 119–21). Terms that incorporate his name in monumental Northwest Semitic inscriptions, leading to IDs, are as follows:

    a. David's name is an element in the phrase *bytdwd* in the Tel Dan stele, line 9.[18]

    b. David's name is also an element in the phrase *bt[d]wd* in the Mesha Inscription, line 31, though its presence is unclear at *prima vista*, due to the fragmentation in that line.[19]

---

18. Avraham Biran and Joseph Naveh, "An Aramaic Stele from Tel Dan." *IEJ* 43 (1993): 81–98; idem, "The Tel Dan Inscription: A New Fragment." *IEJ* 45 (1994): 1–18; *IBP*, 110–32.

19. André Lemaire, "La dynastie Davidique (*bytdwd*) dans deux inscriptions ouest-sémitiques du IXe s. av. J.-C.," *SEL* 11 (1994): 17–19; idem, "'House of David' Restored in Moabite Inscription," *BAR* 20 (1994): 30–37; with the agreement of, among others, Anson

Aramaic usage of $b(y)t$ + personal name in a variety of Aramaic sources, including the Tel Dan stele, is a way of indicating a dynasty by a phrase pattern that incorporates the name of its founder.[20] That this phrase pattern has this significance is especially clear in instances where the incorporated personal name is known to be a royal name or where the phrase is known to refer to a kingdom. Since a dynasty governs a territorial realm, $b(y)t$ + personal name is also a geographical name referring to that territorial realm.[21] Thus, this term in the Tel Dan stele incorporates a conventional phrase pattern that indicates that the David to whom it refers was the founder of a dynasty. This point of singularity is also found in the biblical text: both the Bible and the inscription refer to the one and only David who was the founder of the dynasty of Judah.

F. Rainey, "Mesha' and Syntax," in *The Land That I Will Show You: Essays on the History and Archaeology of the Ancient Near East in Honor of J. Maxwell Miller* (ed. J. Andrew Dearman and M. Patrick Graham; JSOTSup 343; Sheffield: Sheffield Academic, 2001), 293–94; *IBP*, 265–73. Moreover, there is no convincing alternative to Lemaire's reading of line 31. It was one full year after it was published that Baruch Margalit's reading actually appeared ("Studies in NWSemitic Inscriptions," *UF* 26 [1994]: 275–76). It attracted no significant support and seems quite forced (*IBP*, 272 n. 19, 273). Pierre Bordreuil, "A propos de l'inscription de Mesha' deux notes," in *Studies in Language and Literature in Honour of Paul-Eugène Dion*, vol. 3 of *The World of the Aramaeans* (ed. P. M. Michèle Daviau, John W. Wevers, and Michael Weigl; Sheffield: Sheffield Academic, 2001), 162–63, states no more than that some experts could not confirm Lemaire's reading. This statement is not a resounding refutation. More significantly, it offers no viable alternative reading.

20. Gary A. Rendsburg, "On the Writing ביתדוד in the Aramaic Inscription from Tel Dan," *IEJ* 45 (1995): 22–25; Kenneth A. Kitchen, "A Possible Mention of David in the Late Tenth Century B.C.E., and Deity *Dod as Dead as the Dodo?" *JSOT* 76 (1997): 38–39. George Athas rejects any indication of a dynastic founder in this term. He does find that in line A9 of the Tel Dan Inscription, "at least one other king was mentioned alongside the king of Israel. The most logical solution to this is to understand the second king as the ruler of a place called ביתדוד." But he contends that ביתדוד is a reference to Jerusalem and is strictly "a *toponym* and *not* a reference to a Davidic *dynasty*. Although this label may have had an etymology going back to a Davidic dynasty, this is not how the author of the Tel Dan Inscription used it" (George Athas, *The Tel Dan Inscription: A Reappraisal and a New Interpretation* [JSOTSup 360; Copenhagen International Seminar 12; Sheffield: Sheffield Academic, 2003], 225, 226, emphasis his). Still, in Athas' view, "The Tel Dan Inscription provides us with good evidence for the historicity of David which is in line with biblical testimony, and suggests the reliability of the biblical record" (idem, "Setting the Record Straight: What Are We Making of the Tel Dan Inscription?" *JSS* 51 [2006]: 241, Abstract). Athas, *The Tel Dan Inscription*, appeared too late for *IBP* to discuss it, as noted in *IBP*, 110 n. 34.

21. "Bit-Dawid (like Bit-Khumri [Omri]) is the name of a state, *and therefore is also a geographic entity*.... In my JSOT 1997 paper [Kitchen, "Possible Mention of David"], I listed a whole series of Bit-names all round the 1st-millennium Near East in various geographical locations" (K. A. Kitchen, review of *IBP*, third paragraph from the end, emphasis his).

Also, it can then be argued, from internationalization of this Aramaic usage and resulting—or simply parallel—Moabite usage, that *bt* + personal name in line 31 of the Mesha Inscription contains the same point of singularity. Besides such inscriptional-biblical singularity, the fact that there is only one David in the biblical king lists, which purport to be complete, gives his ID also what can be called biblical singularity.

c. An inscription written within about forty-five years of David's lifetime by Pharaoh Sheshonq I sheds additional light on "the house of David" mentioned in the Tel Dan stele as a possible geographical reference to the territory ruled by "[the kin]g of the house of David." Sheshonq's inscription contains the phrase *hadabiyat-dawit*, "the heights (or highland) of David." According to the geographically organized sequence in the inscription, this area should be in the southern part of Judah or the Negev, where the book of 1 Samuel places David when he was hiding from King Saul. An ID of King David as the person whose name is included in this phrase is entirely plausible, both in view of Kitchen's research into the rendering of the name and in view of other ancient Hebrew phrases, such as "the city of David" and "the house of David," which include a geographical dimension. It seems extremely doubtful that we shall suddenly discover some other, previously unknown David who was famous enough to have lent his name to the region mentioned in Sheshonq's timely inscription.[22]

2. Omri, king of Israel (r. 884–873), 1 Kgs 16:16, etc., in the Mesha Inscription from Dhiban, lines 4–5 (*IBP*, 108–10). The point of singularity in common between the inscription and the biblical text is that both refer to only one Omri as the founder of the Israelite dynasty against which Mesha rebelled. A second, biblical-only point of singularity is that in the Bible's lists of Hebrew kings, which purport to be complete, only one Omri appears.

3. Mesha, king of Moab (r. early to mid-ninth century), 2 Kgs 3:4, etc., in the Mesha Inscription from Dhiban, line 1 (*IBP*, 95–108). The singular feature in common between the inscription and the biblical text is that both refer to the only Mesha, king of Moab, who ever successfully rebelled against the Israelite dynasty of Omri.

---

22. Looking briefly beyond the scope of Northwest Semitic inscriptions, I find an eminently reasonable grade 2 ID of the biblical King David in this Egyptian inscription. See Kitchen, "Possible Mention of David," 39–41; idem, review of *IBP*, *SEE-J Hiphil* 2 (2005): fourth paragraph from the end, cited September 7, 2005, online: http://www.see-j.net/index.php/hiphil/article/viewFile/19/17; and the evaluation in Mykytiuk, "Corrections," 119–21. That same paragraph of Kitchen's review also mentions what I agree is a good case for a strong, grade S ID of the biblical Shishak in Egyptian inscriptions that name Pharaoh Sheshonq I.

4. Hazael, king of Aram at Damascus (r. 844/42–ca.800), 1 Kgs 19:15; 2 Kgs 8:8, etc.; 2 Kgs 13:3, etc., in the Aleppo-area Zakkur stele (*KAI* 202), line 4, which refers to "Bar-hadad, the son of Hazael, the king of Aram" (*IBP*, 238).[23]

The interpretation of the Zakkur stele, dated to ca. 780, is according to several inscriptions of Shalmaneser III, king of Assyria, which refer to Hazael, "son of nobody," as a successor (not necessarily the immediate successor) of Hadadezer to the throne of Damascus.[24] Singularity arises partly from the fact that there was only one king on the Damascus throne at a given time. The point of singularity in common between the Zakkur stele and the biblical text is that both refer to only one Hazael, king of Aram at Damascus and father of Bar-hadad (Hebrew: Ben-hadad), during approximately the last four decades of the ninth century as his regnal years.

5. Ben-hadad, son of Hazael, king of Aram at Damascus (r. early-eighth century), 2 Kgs 13:3, etc., in the Aleppo-area Zakkur stele (*KAI* 202), lines 4–5 (*IBP*, 240). On the interpretation of the Zakkur stele, see the entry on Hazael immediately above. The singular feature in common between the inscription and the biblical text is that there was only one Bar-hadad, son of Hazael, king of Aram at Damascus, during the early-eighth century.

6. Sennacherib, king of Assyria (r. 704–681), 2 Kgs 18:13, etc. in the Ashur ostracon (*KAI* 233), in a list of Assyrian kings and the locations from which they deported prisoners, line 16, restoring the first two consonants of his name (*IBP*, 241–42). The singular feature evident in this inscription, according to both Assyrian and biblical records, is that he can only be the Sennacherib who besieged King Hezekiah in Jerusalem.[25] Also, inscriptional singularity arises from

---

23. *IBP*, 238–39, lists other inscriptions in which are found IDs of Hazael that are generally not as strong as the ID in the Zakkur stele: 1) Hazael is named in three inscribed bronze pieces for a horse bridle (a frontlet and two blinders), war booty "from Umqi," which the deity "Hadad gave to Lord Hazael." 2) Two ivories inscribed with Hazael's name were found in Assyrian contexts at Arslan Tash (ancient Hadattah) and at Nimrud (biblical Calah), and are presumably war booty from Aram.

24. A. Kirk Grayson, *Assyrian Rulers of the Early First Millennium BC, II (858–745 BC)* (RIMA 3; Toronto: University of Toronto, 1996), 118, A.0. 102.40 (an inscribed, fragmentary statue of Shalmaneser III from Aššur), lines i 25–ii 6. Other references to Hazael in Shalmaneser III's inscriptions appear in ibid., 48, 49, 60, 62, 67, 77, 78, 151. On Hadadezer as "the king of Aram" in 1 Kgs 22:4–2 Kgs 6:23 and his son Ben-hadad in 2 Kgs 6:24–8:15, see IDs 11 and 12 below and Mykytiuk, "Corrections," 69–85, IDs no. 15 and 16.

25. Several Assyrian inscriptions record Sennacherib's account of the siege of Hezekiah's Jerusalem (see the ancient final edition of the Annals of Sennacherib, found in the Oriental Institute Prism of Sennacherib [and in the Taylor Prism], trans. Daniel D. Luckenbill, lines ii 37–iii 49 in *ANET*, 287–88; *COS* 2.119B:302–3; *TUAT* 1/4:388–90).

there being only one Sennacherib in the Assyrian king list, which purports to be complete.

Identifications Based on Singularity according to Inscriptional Data Only

7. Tiglath-pileser III, king of Assyria (r. 744–727), 2 Kgs 15:19, etc., (*IBP*, 240). A total of four Northwest Semitic inscriptions refer to him. In the Ashur ostracon (*KAI* 233), he is named in a brief list of Assyrian kings and the locations from which they deported prisoners, line 15. In addition, three Aramaic monumental inscriptions from near Zenjirli, north Syria, refer to him:

a. the monument in honor of Panamu II (*KAI* 215), lines 13, 15, 16

b. Bar Rekub inscription 1 (*KAI* 216), now in Istanbul, lines 3, 6

c. Bar Rekub inscription 8 (*KAI* 217), now in Berlin, with the first four consonants of his name restored in lines 1–2.

The singular feature that underlies the ID in the Ashur ostracon is that after the death of Tiglath-pileser II in 935, there is only one Tiglath-pileser in the Assyrian king list, which, as observed above, purports to be complete. Therefore, the singular feature that is evident in the Panamu II and both Bar Rekub inscriptions is that there is only one Tiglath-pileser during that period who could have invaded Syria-Palestine, as also explicitly corroborated in this Assyrian king's cuneiform inscriptions.[26]

8. Sargon II, king of Assyria (r. 721–705), Isa 20:1 (*IBP*, 240–41).[27] In the Ashur ostracon, a list of Assyrian kings and their deportations refers to Sargon

---

26. Hayim Tadmor, *The Inscriptions of Tiglath-pileser III, King of Assyria* (2nd printing with addenda et corrigenda; Fontes ad Res Judaicas Spectantes; Jerusalem: Israel Academy of Sciences and Humanities, 2008), 9 and 273–82 for discussions, inscriptions *passim*. Beyond the scope of Northwest Semitic inscriptions, in the realm of Assyrian Akkadian inscriptions, an ID of Tiglath-pileser III based on inscriptional and biblical singularity is found in his military campaigns in Galilee and conquest of "the entire region of Naphtali" (2 Kgs 15:29). These invasions are recorded in 2 Kgs 15:29 (cf. 1 Chr 5:6, 26 HB versification) and in Tiglath-pileser III's Calah Annal 18, lines 3'–7' with parallel Calah Annal 24, lines 3'–11' (ibid., 80–83, esp. 81, n. re. 3'–7' and Ann. 24:3'–11'. For a synopsis of biblical and Assyrian texts about Tiglath-pileser III's campaigns against Israel in 733–732, see Tadmor's "Supplementary Study G," ibid., 279–82.

27. Within the purview of this article, i.e., Northwest Semitic inscriptions, this ID is correctly classified as one based on inscriptional singularity. To look briefly beyond Northwest Semitic inscriptions, however, there is a point of singularity in common between Assyrian Akkadian inscriptions and a biblical text, in that there was only one Sargon (II), king of Assyria, who (in the year 712/711) presided over the conquest of Ashdod, as stated in Isa 20:1 and, along with other inscriptions, in lines 90–109 of his Khorsabad Summary Inscription, dated ca. 707 (Annals, lines 249–62, trans. Daniel D. Luckenbill, *ANET*, 286; *COS* 2.118A:294, 2.118E:296–7; *TUAT* 1/4:383–5; Mordechai Cogan, ed. and trans., *The Raging Torrent: Historical Inscriptions from Assyria and Babylonia Relating the Ancient Israel* [Jerusalem: Carta, 2008], 82–89). Norma Franklin describes

II.[28] Mention of him there also involves singularity, in that the Assyrian king list, purportedly complete, has only one Sargon in the period between 1000 and the year 609. Thus, this identification is made on grounds of inscriptional singularity.

Identifications based on Singularity according to Biblical Data Only

9. Jeroboam II, king of Israel (r. 790–750/49), 2 Kgs 13:13, etc., in the iconic stone seal *lšmʿ / ʿbd yrbʿm*, "belonging to *Šemaʿ*, / minister of *Yārobʿam*" discovered at Megiddo (*WSS*, no. 2; *IBP*, 133–39, 217). In seals and bullae, the title *ʿebed* signifies that the master of the *ʿebed* is a monarch or a deity. In this Hebrew seal from a royal administrative complex at Megiddo, *Yārobʿam* is a king of the northern kingdom of Israel. From the ninth century onward, there is only one Jeroboam in the biblical king list, which purports to be complete. An ID of his tenth-century namesake, Jeroboam I (r. 931/30–909), seems most unlikely in this seal, for two reasons. First, according to the discoveries currently known to epigraphers, during the ninth century and earlier, Israelite, Aramaic, and Phoenician epigraphic seals and bullae are either rare or possibly non-existent.[29] Second, it is an eighth-century seal. Ambiguities in stratigraphic dating are resolved by paleographic considerations, especially regarding the two *mem*s, which date it to the eighth century B.C.E. (*IBP*, 133–37).

10. Uzziah, king of Judah (r. 788/7–736/5), 2 Kgs 14:21, etc., in two iconic stone seals, the first of which is inscribed *lʾbyw ʿbd / ʿzyw*, "belonging to *ʾabiyaw*, minister of / *ʿUziyaw*" and the second of which is inscribed (obv.) *lšbnyw*, "belonging to *Shubnayaw*" (rev.) *lšbnyw ʿ / bd ʿzyw*, "belonging to *Shubnayaw*, minister of / *ʿUziyaw*"[30] (*WSS*, nos. 4 and 3 respectively; *IBP*, 153–59, 219). The fact that

---

the inscriptions that include references to Sargon II's presiding over the conquest of Ashdod on p. 260 of her illuminating essay, "A Room with a View: Images from Room V at Khorsabad, Samaria, Nubians, the Brook of Egypt and Ashdod," in *Studies in the Archaeology of the Iron Age in Israel and Jordan* (ed. Amihai Mazar; JSOTSup 331; Sheffield: Sheffield Academic, 2001), 257–77. On whether Sargon II conquered Ashdod specifically by sending his *turtānu/tartānu* (Hebrew: *tartān*) on that mission, as stated in Isa 20:1, see Tadmor's approach (1958) as briefly summarized in *COS* 2.118A:294 n. 14.

28. *KAI* 233, line 15, as "Sarkon;" *IBP*, 240–41.

29. Christopher A. Rollston, "Prosopography and the יזבל Seal," 88, point 4, contra David Ussishkin, "Gate 1567 at Megiddo and the Seal of Shema, Servant of Jeroboam," in *Scripture and Other Artifacts: Essays on the Bible and Archaeology in Honor of Philip J. King* (ed. Michael D. Coogan, J. Cheryl Exum, and Lawrence E. Stager; Louisville, Ky.: Westminster John Knox, 1994), 419–24; also contra Gösta W. Ahlström, "The Seal of Shema," *SJOT* 7 (1993): 208–15.

30. Pierre Bordreuil, *Catalogue des sceaux ouest-sémitiques inscrits de la Bibliothèque Nationale, du Musée du Louvre et du Musée biblique de Bible et Terre Sainte* (Paris: Bibliothèque Nationale, 1986), 45, 46.

there is only one Uzziah in the purportedly complete biblical king list (disregarding his common alias, Azariah), gives this ID singularity based on biblical data.

Note that these IDs are made in two unprovenanced but presumably authentic inscriptions published in 1858 and 1863, respectively. These dates are long before forgers or anyone else could have known the appropriate paleographic details of the formal cursive script used in the kingdom of Judah during the early to mid-eighth century.

IDENTIFICATIONS MADE ON THE BASIS OF THREE OR MORE IDENTIFYING MARKS OF AN INDIVIDUAL

The following six biblical persons, three father-and-son pairs, can each be identified by at least three marks pertaining to an individual (such as name, relationship, and title), therefore, they are called grade 3 IDs. These marks do not provide absolute certainty, but enough likelihood for the IDs to be considered either reliable or virtually certain.[31]

11. Hadadezer, king of Aram at Damascus (r. early-eighth century), nameless in the Hebrew Bible, which calls him only "the king of Aram";[32] 1 Kgs 22:4, 31; 2 Kgs 5; 6:8–23, and

12. Ben-hadad, son of Hadadezer, king of Aram at Damascus, whom Hazael assassinated; 2 Kgs 6:24; 8:7–15; in the Melqart stele, from Bureij, 7 km. north of Aleppo (Mykytiuk, "Corrections," 69–85[33]). In line 2, Hadadezer's name appears

---

31. To note a grade 3 ID outside of Northwest Semitic epigraphs, in July 2007, Michael Jursa discovered a Babylonian reference to the biblical "Nebo-Sarsekim, Rab-saris" (*rab ša-rēši*, chief official) of Nebuchadnezzar II (r. 604–562). The three identifying marks are name, title, and royal master. The biblical reference in Jer 39:3 is to the year 586. Jursa identified this official in an Akkadian cuneiform inscription on Babylonian clay tablet BM 114789 (1920-12-13, 81), dated to 595 B.C.E. See Michael Jursa, "Nabû-šarrūssu-ukīn, *rab ša-rēši*, und 'Nebusarsekim' (Jer. 39:3)," *NABU* 2008/1 (March): 9–10; Becking, "Identity of Nabu-sharrussu-ukin," 35–46; Mykytiuk, "Corrections," 121–24, re *IBP*, 242.

32. On the anonymity of some royal personages in scripture, see Robert L. Hubbard Jr., "'Old What's-His-Name': Why the King in 1 Kings 22 has No Name," in *Biblical Studies in Honor of Simon John De Vries* (vol. 1 of *God's Word for Our World*; ed. J. Harold Ellens; JSOTSup 388; London: T&T Clark, 2004), 294–314.

33. The detailed, extended discussion in Mykytiuk, "Corrections," 69–85, regarding IDs nos. 15 and 16, corrects *IBP*, 237, 237–38 n. 89, 261, by accepting Cross's paleographic dating of the Melqart stele to between 860 and 840 and by adopting Cross's and Reinhold's virtually identical readings of the Melqart stele. These are found in Cross, "Stele Dedicated to Melqart by Ben-Hadad of Damascus," in *Leaves from an Epigrapher's Notebook*, 173–77, repr. with rev. from *BASOR* 205 (1972): 36–42; Gotthard G. G. Reinhold, "Zu den Stelenbruchstücken der altaramäischen Inschrift von Tēl Dân, Israel," in *Bei Sonnenaufgang auf dem Tell, At Sunrise on*

as a hypocoristicon, the patronym *'Ezer*. The name of the son of Hadadezer and author of the Melqart stele, Bar-hadad, is in lines 1–2.

The three identifying marks for each of these two individuals are:

a. the name of the son, Bar-hadad,

b. the name of the father, (Hadad)ezer, and

c. the son's self-designation "the Damascene," which occurs in line 2 of the Melqart stele.

13. Shaphan the scribe, who served Josiah, king of Judah (r. 640/39–609), 2 Kgs 22:3, etc., and

14. Gemariah the official, son of Shaphan the scribe, Jer 36:10, etc., in the aniconic city of David bulla *lgmryhw* / [*b*]*n špn*, "belonging to *Gᵊmaryāhû*, / [so]n of *Šāfān*" (*WSS*, no. 470; *IBP*, 139–47, 228, 232).

The three identifying marks for each of these two individuals are:

a. the name of the son, the seal owner, Gemaryahu,

b. the name of the father, Shaphan, and

c. the striking provenance, namely, a public archive within 250 meters from where the Bible depicts the official activities of both men.[34] The infrequency of

---

the Tell: Essays about Decades Researches in the Field of Near Eastern Archaeology* (Remshalden, Germany: Bernhard Albert Greiner, 2003), 129; idem, "The Bir-Hadad Stele and the Biblical Kings of Aram," *AUSS* 24/2 [Summer 1986]: 115–126, esp. 117–21, 123; ibid., cited September 30, 2008, online: via the "Archives" link at http://www.auss.info/index.php. Their reading is contra that in Wayne T. Pitard, *Ancient Damascus: A Historical Study of the Syrian City-State from Earliest Times until Its Fall to the Assyrians in 732 B.C.E.* (Winona Lake, Ind.: Eisenbrauns, 1987), 141–43; idem, "The Identity of the Bir-Hadad of the Melqart Stela," *BASOR* 272 (1988): 3–21. It should be noted that Reinhold directly examined the stele itself, over a considerable period of time, as Pitard did. For a fuller list of Reinhold's many publications that treat this stele, see Mykytiuk, "Corrections," 71 n. 68.

34. "A recent examination of this bulla and the one mentioned immediately below [which is also mentioned immediately below in the present chapter] has demonstrated that these bullae were made of the particular kind of clay locally available in Jerusalem. Therefore, these bullae were not attached to documents from elsewhere. Rather, the officials who made them, namely, Gemariah ben Shaphan and Azariah ben Ḥilqiyahu, were physically present in the city of David. The petrographic analysis [of the fifty-one bullae discovered in Shiloh's 1982 excavations in the city of David, including the bullae of Gemaryahu ben Shaphan and Azaryahu ben Ḥilqiyahu,] revealed that the entire group of bullae from the City of David in Jerusalem ... was made of terra rosa soil, having the same mineralogical composition of silt and sand temper.... Moreover, this composition is identical to the fabric of the numerous local pillar figurines from the City of David.... Therefore, the entire set of bullae from the City of David may be regarded as the local production of this site." (Eran Arie, Yuval Goren, and Inbal Samet, "Indelible Impression: Petrographic Analysis of Judahite Bullae," in *The Fire Signals of Lachish: Studies in the Archaeology and History of Israel in the Late Bronze Age, Iron Age, and Persian Period in Honor of David Ussishkin* [ed. Israel Finkelstein and Nadav Na'aman; Winona Lake, Ind.: Eisenbrauns, 2011], 10.)

the name Shaphan both in the Bible and in Hebrew inscriptions strengthens this ID. Further, it is most likely that the group of fifty-one bullae, which included this one, formed a government archive,[35] which is consistent with the royal administrative positions of both father and son, as mentioned in Scripture.

Note that paleographically, the distinctive form of the Hebrew letter *nun* in [*b*]*n* clearly narrows down the date to the late-seventh to early-sixth century, precisely the period in which the book of Jeremiah places Gemariah.[36]

15. Hilkiah the high priest, 2 Kgs 22:4, etc., and

16. Azariah, son of Hilkiah the high priest, 1 Chr 5:39; 9:11; Ezra 7:1 in the aniconic city of David bulla *l'zryhw b / n ḥlqyhw*, "belonging to *ʿazaryāhû*, so/n of / Ḥilqîyāhû" (*WSS*, no. 596; *IBP*, 148–52, 229)

The three identifying marks for each of these two individuals are:

a. the name of the seal owner, Azaryahu,

b. the name of the father, Ḥilqiyahu, and

c. the striking provenance, namely, a public archive within 250 meters from the Jerusalem temple precincts, where the Bible depicts the official activities of the priesthood.[37]

Although both father and son have common names, the combination of these two specific names, in a father-and-son pair in which Ḥilqiyahu is the father and Azaryahu is the son, is not nearly as common. This combination of names, along with the additional limits of provenance and date, greatly reduces the possibility of confusion with other persons. Regarding date, in the lower register, the paleographically distinctive form of the Hebrew letter *he* in *-yhw* of the patronym narrows down the date to the late-seventh to early-sixth century.[38] According to 2 Kgs 22:3, 4 and 1 Chr 5:39–41 (6:13–15 in English and German translations),

---

I thank Peter van der Veen for pointing out this finding and publication.

35. As Shiloh observed, "The fact that the names do not overly repeat themselves, as would be expected in a private or family archive, ... would indicate that this find may represent a public archive, located in some bureau close to the administrative centre in the City of David" (Yigal Shiloh, *Excavations in the City of David I, 1978–1982: Interim Report of the First Five Seasons* [Qedem 19; Jerusalem: The Institute of Archaeology, The Hebrew University, 1984], 20, quoted in *IBP*, 146). Arie, Goren, and Samet further observe that "both in Jerusalem and Lachish the bullae were found in rooms together with standard weights." This fact that strengthens their assumption that "these rooms may have functioned as the place where legal affairs physically took place and where the documents were written, sealed, and stored (Arie, Goren, and Samet, "Indelible Impression," 13)

36. Vaughn, "Palaeographic Dating," 54–55.

37. See notes 34 and 35 above.

38. Vaughn, "Palaeographic Dating," 47, 52–53.

the biblical Hilkiah and his son Azariah lived and worked at that particular location during precisely this same, relatively narrow time period.

These six IDs that are virtually certain to reliable, based on three identifying marks of an individual, plus the ten IDs listed above that are certain, based on singularity, bring the number of strong IDs in inscriptions of known authenticity to sixteen. To mark the end of this group, the strongest IDs, the numbering of biblical persons below does not continue from 16.

Four Identifications that Currently Hover between Two Grades

The following four IDs are at least grade 2, reasonable, because they are based on two identifying marks of an individual, but they might turn out to be grade 3, reliable to virtually certain. It would be premature to settle on a specific grade at this time, because the grading of these IDs may potentially depend on new data or understanding from the ongoing excavation in the city of David that is being directed by Eilat Mazar. These four IDs receive as complete a treatment as currently available data allow in Mykytiuk, "Corrections," 85–100, regarding its IDs no. 17–20. As with the bulla of Azaryahu treated immediately above, the bullae of Yehukal and of Gedalyahu below both contain a distinctive letter *he* that dates them to the late-seventh or early-sixth century.[39]

1. J(eh)ucal, son of Shelemiah (Jer 37:3 and 38:1), and

2. Shelemiah, father of J(eh)ucal (Jer 37:3 and 38:1) in city of David bulla *lyhwkl b / [n] šlmyhw /bn šby*,[40] "belonging to *Y^əhûkal*, so / [n] of *Šelemyāhû*, / son of *Šōbî*" (Mykytiuk, "Corrections," 85–92)

For both IDs, the two identifying marks of an individual that are thus far available are:

    a. the seal owner's name, Yehukal, and

    b. the patronym, Shelemyahu.

3. Gedaliah, son of Pashhur (Jer 38:1) and

---

39. Ibid.

40. Eilat Mazar, "Did I Find," 26; idem, *Preliminary Report on the City of David Excavations 2005 at the Visitors Center Area* (Jerusalem: Shalem, 2007), 67–69; idem, *The Palace of King David: Excavations at the Summit of the City of David: Preliminary Report of Seasons 2005-2007* (Jerusalem: Shoham Academic Research and Publication, 2009), 66, 67, 69.

4. Pashhur, father of Gedaliah (Jer 38:1) in city of David bulla *lgdlyhw / bn [p]šḥwr*,[41] "belonging to *Gᵃdalyāhû, / son of [P]ašḥûr*" (Mykytiuk, "Corrections," 92–100).

For both IDs, the two identifying marks of an individual that are thus far available are:

a. the seal owner's name, Gedalyahu, and
b. the patronym, [P]ashḥur.

The last four bullae above, belonging to Gemaryahu ben Shaphan, Azaryahu ben Ḥilqiyahu, Yehukal ben Shelemyahu, and Gedalyahu ben [P]ashḥur, were discovered within a few dozen meters of each other along the eastern edge of the city of David, and all date between the late-seventh century and the destruction of Jerusalem in 586 B.C.E, the time of the last generation in the kingdom of Judah. It is appropriate to ask whether the fact that these IDs were discovered so close to each other might strengthen the IDs they offer. Although such mutual strengthening cannot be argued with airtight, inexorable logic, as pointed out in Mykytiuk, "Corrections," 96–100, nevertheless, the proximity of these four bullae to each other suggests that they may be scattered remnants from sealed records in a royal administrative center. Thus, without changing the objectively determined grades of the eight individual IDs they offer, their collocation plainly seems to imply a common origin that strengthens their plausibility (cf. Mykytiuk, "Corrections," 100, second-to-last paragraph).

THREE REASONABLE BUT UNCERTAIN IDENTIFICATIONS IN AUTHENTIC INSCRIPTIONS

The following IDs of three biblical persons are reasonable but not certain. They should be treated with varying degrees of tentativeness. These persons are identified by the same two marks of an individual in both the inscriptional and biblical data.

1. Shebna, overseer of the palace (Isa 22:15–19; probably the scribe of 2 Kgs 18:18, etc., before being promoted) in a Silwan epitaph, line 1, in which the name is effaced except for its very common theophoric ending on many Hebrew names, "[ ]*yhw*" (*IBP*, 225).

The two identifying marks of an individual are:

a. The inscriptional title, *ʾšr ʿl hbyt*, matches the title *ᵃšer ʿal habbāyit* in Isa 22:15.

---

41. Mazar, "Wall," 29; idem, *Palace of King David*, 68, 69, 71.

b. This epitaph is carved over the entrance to a rock-cut tomb in a hill near Jerusalem, which corresponds to Isaiah's description.

2. Jaazaniah or Jezaniah, son of the Maacathite (2 Kgs 25:23; Jer 40:8), in the iconic Tell en-Nasbeh seal *ly'znyhw / 'bd hmlk*, "belonging to Ya'^azanyāhû, the king's minister" (*WSS*, no. 8; *IBP*, 235).

The two identifying marks of an individual are:

a. The seal owner's name, Yaazanyahu, corresponds to the biblical name in 2 Kgs 25:23.

b. The biblical Jaazaniah died at Mizpah. This seal was discovered at that site, but, oddly, in a Roman-era tomb.

Note that, as with some inscriptions listed above, paleographically, the distinctive form of the Hebrew letter *he* in this seal, in the word *hmlk*, narrows the date to the late-seventh to early-sixth century,[42] the same time period as that of the biblical Jaazaniah.

3. Baalis, king of the Ammonites (Jer 40:14), in a Tell el-Umeiri ceramic cone (bottle-stopper?) with an Ammonite sealing on the larger end: *lmlkm'wr / 'b / d b'lyš'*.[43] (*WSS*, no. 860; *IBP*, 242 no. (77) in [89]).

The two identifying marks of an individual are:

a. seal owner *Milkom'ûr*'s title is *'ebed*, which here implies that he is the minister of a king (*IBP*, 207–10).

b. the royal master's name is *Ba'alyiša'* or *Ba'alîša'*, if the vocalization here is correct, but the precise Ammonite vocalization may be unavailable to us. The differences between the king's name in this seal impression and the biblical rendition, *Ba'^alîs*, have been debated and are not irreconcilable.[44] They can be understood as variant dialectical renderings of the same name.

This ID seems quite likely, but it is not entirely secure without an ancient Ammonite king list that purports to be complete and includes the monarchs of the early-sixth century. King lists being developed by modern scholars cannot currently be known to be complete.

---

42. Vaughn, "Palaeographic Dating," 47, 52–53.
43. Larry G. Herr, "The Servant of Baalis," *BA* 48 (1985): 169–72.
44. See the bibliography in M. O'Connor, "The Ammonite Onomasticon: Semantic Problems," *AUSS* 25 (1987): 62 paragraph (3), supplemented by Lawrence T. Geraty, "Back to Egypt: An Illustration of How an Archaeological Find May Illumine a Biblical Passage," *RefR* 47 (1994): 222; Emile Puech, "L'inscription de la statue d'Amman et la paleographie ammonite," *RB* 92 (1985): 5–24.

Two Identifications in an Inscription Lacking Clear Historical Value

1. Beor, father of Balaam (Num 22–24, etc.), and
2. Balaam, son of Beor (Num 22–24, etc.) in the Tell Deir 'Allā inscription on plaster, combination 1: *bʿr* in lines 2, 4 and *blʿm* in lines 3, 4[45] (*IBP*, 236, 252; Mykytiuk, "Corrections," 111–13).

The three identifying marks of an individual are
a. name of son, Bilʿam,
b. name of father, Buʿur, and
c. the son's abilities as a seer of divine visions.

The genre of this inscription, which recounts a vision, renders the IDs of the biblical Balaam and his father Beor in the inscription without clear historical value. No date appears in its content, and the epigraph itself is dated to ca. 700 B.C.E., whereas biblical reckoning dates Balaam and Beor to several centuries earlier. Therefore, it is not possible to date this pair of inscriptional persons within fifty years of the biblical persons. As a result, according to *IBP*'s identification protocols, no historical ID can be established. The match between the biblical geographical setting and the Transjordanian provenance of the wall inscription, hence of the folk tradition, suggests but does not establish historicity of this father and son.

The question of an ID or a non-ID *per se*, although useful in historical study, is not limited to the field of history. Many scholars, following Hackett's lead, readily assume the IDs of the Balaam and Beor of Numbers chapters 22–24 in the folk tradition found in the Tell Deir 'Alla inscription. All in all, because a date is lacking, it is best to transfer these two IDs to a newly created, nonhistorical, folk-tradition category.

Summary and Conclusion

In the texts of authentic Northwest Semitic inscriptions, using sound protocols (based on the three questions above and detailed in *IBP*, 9–89), one can identify with certainty at least ten biblical persons from before the Persian era who

---

45. Jo Ann Hackett, *The Balaam Text from Deir 'Allā* (HSM 31; Chico, Calif.: Scholars Press, 1984), 29, 33–34, 36; idem, "Some Observations on the Balaam Tradition at Deir 'Allā," *BA* 49 (1986): 216–22; P. Kyle McCarter Jr., "The Balaam Texts from Deir 'Allā: The First Combination," *BASOR* 239 (1980): 49–60.

are mentioned in the Hebrew Bible. Another six such persons can be identified reliably or with virtual certainty. The IDs of these sixteen persons deserve to be counted among the known, fixed points in the biblical presentation of history, not least because archaeological data verify their historical existence.

Two other authentic inscriptions, bullae discovered recently in an ongoing excavation, offer four more IDs, two in each bulla, which are at least to be included among reasonable grade 2 IDs and might potentially come to be recognized as stronger IDs. The future verdict on this possibility should become clear as more data and interpretive insights into their archaeological context become available from the excavation that has unearthed them. If they turn out to be stronger, that is, grade 3 IDs, they would be reliable enough to be added to the sixteen above-mentioned strong IDs, raising that number to twenty.

Three other authentic inscriptions offer an additional three IDs which, while not quite certain, are reasonable IDs and can be used as reasonable hypotheses.

The total of these IDs, from a minimum of sixteen to possibly as many as twenty-three, currently approximately doubles the nine biblical persons whom *IBP* presents as most clearly identified in inscriptions of known authenticity in its concluding chapter (*IBP*, 197–98).

The direct significance of the twenty-three IDs above relates only to the historical existence of the biblical persons identified, variously including such data as their name, title, ancestry, location, sociopolitical group, and approximate date. Their indirect significance, however, is suggestive of the *activities* of identified individuals. Except for narrative inscriptions, such as that of Mesha, usually the most that can be said is that persons named both in the Bible and in inscriptions were at one time *in a position* (usually indicated by setting and title or lineage) to do what the Bible says they did. From a purely inscriptional standpoint, compatibility between the person's position as observable in inscription(s) and his or her biblical actions can ... make the biblical narratives plausible.[46]

Of course, the IDs reported above, being within specified time and language boundaries, are only one part of a larger picture. Footnotes 22, 26, 27, and 31 above mention just five of a significant number of biblical persons who can be identified in Akkadian and Egyptian inscriptions of known authenticity from before the Persian era. Such additional IDs in inscriptions written in languages outside the Northwest Semitic group, as well as others from the Persian era, only increase the number of biblical persons who deserve to be recognized as known points in history. A conservative estimate is that the current, overall grand total of

---

46. *IBP*, 201–2.

strong and of reasonable IDs of persons whom the Bible places between 1000 and 400 B.C.E. in inscriptions of known authenticity reaches well beyond forty.

BIBLIOGRAPHY

Ahlström, Gösta W. "The Seal of Shema." *SJOT* 7 (1993): 208–15.
Arie, Eran, Yuval Goren, and Inbal Samet. "Indelible Impression: Petrographic Analysis of Judahite Bullae." Pages 1–16 of *The Fire Signals of Lachish: Studies in the Archaeology and History of Israel in the Late Bronze Age, Iron Age, and Persian Period in Honor of David Ussishkin*. Edited by Israel Finkelstein and Nadav Na'aman. Winona Lake, Ind.: Eisenbrauns, 2011.
Athas, George. "Setting the Record Straight: What Are We Making of the Tel Dan Inscription?" *JSS* 51 (2006): 241–55.
———. *The Tel Dan Inscription: A Reappraisal and a New Interpretation*. JSOTSup 360. Copenhagen International Seminar 12. Sheffield: Sheffield Academic, 2003.
Avigad, Nahman, and Benjamin Sass. *Corpus of West Semitic Stamp Seals*. Jerusalem: Israel Academy of Sciences & Humanities, Israel Exploration Society, and The Institute of Archaeology, The Hebrew University of Jerusalem, 1997.
Becking, Bob. "The Identity of Nabu-sharrussu-ukin, the Chamberlain: An Epigraphic Note on Jeremiah 39,3. With an Appendix on the Nebu$^{(l)}$sarsekim Tablet by Henry Stadhouders." *BN* NF 140 (2009): 35–46.
Biran, Avraham, and Joseph Naveh. "An Aramaic Stele from Tel Dan." *IEJ* 43 (1993): 81–98.
———. "The Tel Dan Inscription: A New Fragment." *IEJ* 45 (1994): 1–18.
Bordreuil, Pierre. "A propos de l'inscription de Mesha' deux notes." Pages 158–67 of *Studies in Language and Literature in Honour of Paul-Eugène Dion*. Vol. 3 of *The World of the Aramaeans*. Edited by P. M. Michèle Daviau, John W. Wevers, and Michael Weigl. 3 vols. Sheffield: Sheffield Academic, 2001.
———. *Catalogue des sceaux ouest-sémitiques inscrits de la Bibliothèque Nationale, du Musée du Louvre et du Musée biblique de Bible et Terre Sainte*. Paris: Bibliothèque Nationale, 1986.
Cogan, Mordechai, ed. and trans. *The Raging Torrent: Historical Inscriptions from Assyria and Babylonia Relating to Ancient Israel*. Jerusalem: Carta, 2008.
Cross, Frank Moore. "Epigraphic Notes on Hebrew Documents of the Eighth–Sixth Centuries B.C.: I. A New Reading of a Place Name in the Samaria Ostraca." Pages 114–15 in *Leaves from an Epigrapher's Notebook: Collected Papers in Hebrew and West Semitic Palaeography and Epigraphy*. HSS 51. Winona Lake, Ind.: Eisenbrauns, 2003. Repr. from *BASOR* 163 (1961): 12–14.
———. "Epigraphic Notes on Hebrew Documents of the Eighth–Sixth Centuries B.C.: II. The Murabba'ât Papyrus and the Letter Found near Yabneh-yam." Pages 116–24 in *Leaves from an Epigrapher's Notebook: Collected Papers in Hebrew and West Semitic Palaeography and Epigraphy*. HSS 51. Winona Lake, Ind.: Eisenbrauns, 2003. Repr. from *BASOR* 165 (1962): 34–46.
———. "Epigraphic Notes on Hebrew Documents of the Eighth–Sixth Centuries B.C.: III. The Inscribed Jar Handles from Gibeon." Pages 125–28 in *Leaves from an Epigrapher's*

Notebook: Collected Papers in Hebrew and West Semitic Palaeography and Epigraphy. HSS 51. Winona Lake, Ind.: Eisenbrauns, 2003. Repr. from *BASOR* 168 (1962): 18–23.

———. "The Stele Dedicated to Melqart by Ben-Hadad of Damascus." Pages 173–77 in *Leaves from an Epigrapher's Notebook: Collected Papers in Hebrew and West Semitic Palaeography and Epigraphy.* HSS 51. Winona Lake, Ind.: Eisenbrauns, 2003. Repr. with rev. from *BASOR* 205 (1972): 36–42.

Diringer, David. *Le iscrizioni antico-ebraiche Palestinesi.* Florence: Felice Le Monnier, 1934.

Donner, Herbert, and Wolfgang Röllig. *KAI.* 3 vols. 3d ed. Wiesbaden: Harrassowitz, 1971–1973.

Fox, Nili S. *In the Service of the King: Officialdom in Ancient Israel and Judah.* Monographs of the Hebrew Union College 23. Cincinnati: Hebrew Union College, 2000.

Franklin, Norma. "A Room with a View: Images from Room V at Khorsabad, Samaria, Nubians, the Brook of Egypt and Ashdod." Pages 257–77 in *Studies in the Archaeology of the Iron Age in Israel and Jordan.* Edited by Amihai Mazar. JSOTSup 331. Sheffield: Sheffield Academic, 2001.

Geraty, Lawrence T. "Back to Egypt: An Illustration of How an Archaeological Find May Illumine a Biblical Passage." *RefR* 47 (1994): 221–27.

Geus, C. H. J. de. Review of Lawrence J. Mykytiuk, *Identifying Biblical Persons in Northwest Semitic Inscriptions of 1200–539 B.C.E. BO* 63 (2006): cols. 356–58.

Grayson, A. Kirk. *Assyrian Rulers of the Early First Millennium BC, II (858–745 B.C.).* RIMA 3. Toronto: University of Toronto, 2006.

Hackett, Jo Ann. *The Balaam Text from Deir 'Allā.* HSM 31. Chico: Scholars Press, 1984.

———. "Some Observations on the Balaam Tradition at Deir 'Allā." *BA* 49 (1986): 216–22.

Hallo, William W., ed. *Monumental Inscriptions from the Biblical World.* Vol. 2 of *Context of Scripture.* Leiden: Brill, 2000.

Herr, Larry G. "The Servant of Baalis." *BA* 48 (1985): 169–72.

Hubbard, Robert L. Jr. "'Old What's-His-Name': Why the King in 1 Kings 22 has No Name." Pages 294–314 in *Biblical Studies in Honor of Simon John De Vries.* Vol. 1 of *God's Word for Our World.* Edited by J. Harold Ellens. JSOTSup 388. London: T&T Clark, 2004.

Jursa, Michael. "Nabû-šarrūssu-ukīn, *rab ša-rēši,* und 'Nebusarsekim' (Jer. 39:3)." *NABU* 2008/1 (2008): 9–10.

Kaiser, Otto, ed. *Rechts- und Wirtschaftsurkunden, historisch-chronologische Texte.* Vol. 1 of *TUAT.* Gütersloh: Mohn, 1984–.

Kitchen, Kenneth A. "A Possible Mention of David in the Late Tenth Century B.C.E., and Deity *Dod as Dead as the Dodo?" *JSOT* 76 (1997): 29–44.

———. Review of Lawrence J. Mykytiuk, *Identifying Biblical Persons in Northwest Semitic Inscriptions of 1200–539 B.C.E. SEE-J Hiphil* 2 (2005), cited September 7, 2005. Online: http://www.see-j.net/index.php/hiphil/article/viewFile/19/17.

Korpel, Marjo C. A. "Seals of Jezebel and Other Women in Authority." *Tidskrif vir Semitistiek / Journal of Semitics* 15 (2006): 349–71.

———. "Queen Jezebel's Seal." *UF* 328 (2006): 379–98.

———. "Fit for a Queen: Jezebel's Royal Seal." *BAR* 34 (2008): 32–37.

Lemaire, André. "La dynastie Davidique (*bytdwd*) dans deux inscriptions ouest-sémitiques du IXe s. av. J.-C." *SEL* 11 (1994): 17–19.

———. "'House of David' Restored in Moabite Inscription." *BAR* 20 (1994): 30–37.

Lipschits, Oded. *The Fall and Rise of Jerusalem.* Winona Lake, Ind.: Eisenbrauns, 2005.

Margalit, Baruch. "Studies in NWSemitic Inscriptions." *UF* 26 (1994): 271–315.
Mazar, Eilat. "Did I Find King David's Palace?" *BAR* 32 (2006): 16–27, 70.
———. *The Palace of King David: Excavations at the Summit of the City of David: Preliminary Report of Seasons 2005-2007*. Jerusalem: Shoham Academic Research and Publication, 2009.
———. *Preliminary Report on the City of David Excavations 2005 at the Visitors Center Area*. Jerusalem: Shalem, 2007.
———. "The Wall that Nehemiah Built." *BAR* 35 (2009): 24–33, 66.
McCarter, P. Kyle Jr. "The Balaam Texts from Deir ʿAllā: The First Combination." *BASOR* 239 (1980): 49–60.
Miller, J. Maxwell. *The Old Testament and the Historian*. GBS OT Series. Philadelphia: Fortress, 1976.
Miller, Patrick D. Jr. "Moabite Stone." Pages 396–98 in vol. 3 of *ISBE*. Edited by Geoffrey W. Bromiley. 4 vols. Rev. ed. Grand Rapids, Mich.: Eerdmans, 1986.
Mykytiuk, Lawrence J. "Corrections and Updates to 'Identifying Biblical Persons in Northwest Semitic Inscriptions of 1200–539 B.C.E.'" *Maarav* 16 (2009): 49–132.
———. *Identifying Biblical Persons in Northwest Semitic Inscriptions of 1200–539 B.C.E.* SBL AcBib 12. Atlanta: Society of Biblical Literature, 2004.
O'Connor, Michael. "The Ammonite Onomasticon: Semantic Problems." *AUSS* 25 (1987): 51–64.
Pitard, Wayne T. *Ancient Damascus: A Historical Study of the Syrian City-State from Earliest Times until its Fall to the Assyrians in 732 B.C.E.* Winona Lake, Ind.: Eisenbrauns, 1987.
———. "The Identity of the Bir-Hadad of the Melqart Stela." *BASOR* 272 (1988): 3–21.
Pritchard, James B., ed. *ANET*. 3d ed. Princeton: Princeton University Press, 1969.
Puech, Emile. "L'inscription de la statue d'Amman et la paleographie ammonite." *RB* 92 (1985): 5–24.
Rainey, Anson F. "Meshaʿ and Syntax." Pages 287–307 in *The Land That I Will Show You: Essays on the History and Archaeology of the Ancient Near East in Honor of J. Maxwell Miller*. Edited by J. Andrew Dearman and M. Patrick Graham. JSOTSup 343. Sheffield: Sheffield Academic, 2001.
Reinhold, Gotthard G. G. "The Bir-Hadad Stele and the Biblical Kings of Aram," *AUSS* 24 (1986): 115–26. Cited September 30, 2008. Online: http://www.auss.info/index.php.
———. "Zu den Stelenbruchstücken der altaramäischen Inschrift von Têl Dân, Israel." Pages 121–29 in *Bei Sonnenaufgang auf dem Tell, At Sunrise on the Tell: Essays about Decades Researches in the Field of Near Eastern Archaeology*. Remshalden, Germany: Bernhard Albert Greiner, 2003.
Rendsburg, Gary A. "On the Writing ביתדוד in the Aramaic Inscription from Tel Dan." *IEJ* 45 (1995): 22–25.
Rollston, Christopher A. "Non-Provenanced Epigraphs I: Pillaged Antiquities, Northwest Semitic Forgeries, and Protocols for Laboratory Tests." *Maarav* 10 (2003): 135–93.
———. "Prosopography and the יובל Seal." *IEJ* 59 (2009): 86–91.
Shiloh, Yigal. *Excavations in the City of David I, 1978–1982: Interim Report of the First Five Seasons*. Qedem 19. Jerusalem: The Institute of Archaeology, The Hebrew University, 1984.
Tadmor, Hayim. *The Inscriptions of Tiglath-pileser III, King of Assyria*. 2nd printing with

addenda et corrigenda. Fontes ad Res Judaicas Spectantes. Jerusalem: Israel Academy of Sciences and Humanities, 2008.

Torrey, Charles C. "A Hebrew Seal from the reign of Ahaz." *BASOR* 79 (1940): 27–29.

Ussishkin, David. "Gate 1567 at Megiddo and the Seal of Shema, Servant of Jeroboam." Pages 410–28 in *Scripture and Other Artifacts: Essays on the Bible and Archaeology in Honor of Philip J. King*. Edited by Michael D. Coogan, J. Cheryl Exum, and Lawrence E. Stager. Louisville, Ky.: Westminster John Knox, 1994.

Vaughn, Andrew G. "Palaeographic Dating of Judaean Seals and Its Significance for Biblical Research." *BASOR* 313 (1999): 43–64.

Chapter Four
Six Hebrew Fiscal Bullae from the Time of Hezekiah

Robert Deutsch

The ancient site of Keilah was a biblical fortified town (Josh 15:44), located 13.5 kilometers northwest of Hebron. Keilah has preserved its name in Arabic as Qila. The name of this town is mentioned in the Amarna letters during the conflict between Abdi-Heba of Jerusalem and Shuwardata of Hebron.[1] David established his headquarter at Keilah and used the town as a place of refuge from Saul (2 Sam 23:1–13). During the First Temple Period the town of Keilah was a part of the district of Mareshah and later, during the Persian period, Keilah was a district capital in the province of Judah.

At the turn of the millennium, over one thousand Hebrew bullae were recovered in nonprofessional excavations at the site and found their way to several private collections. The rich assemblage was discovered in a library from the time of Hezekiah, king of Judah. This epigraphic treasure contained many royal bullae, including bullae of high officials in the royal court. Over six hundred bullae have been published in the past,[2] and several hundred are still to be published this year by the author.[3] The discovery is of prime importance for the study of ancient Israel and its geographical history. The aim of this paper is to present a group of

---

1. *ANET* 489, 289–90.
2. Robert Deutsch, "Biblical Period Hebrew Bulla," *Messages from the Past, Hebrew Bullae from the Time of Isaiah through the Destruction of the First Temple* (Tel Aviv-Jaffa, Archaeological Center Publications, 1999); "A Hoard of Fifty Hebrew Clay Bullae from the Time of Hezekiah," in *Shlomo: Studies in Epigraphy, Iconography, History and Archaeology in Honor of Shlomo Moussaieff* (ed. R. Deutsch; Tel Aviv-Jaffa: Archaeological Center Publications, 2003), 45–98.
3. Robert Deutsch, *Biblical Period Epigraphy: The Josef Chaim Kaufman Collection; Seals, Bullae, Handles* (vol. 2; Tel Aviv-Jaffa: Archaeological Center Publications, 2011).

six "fiscal bullae,"[4] seal impressions used for taxation, revealing the names of biblical towns, some previously unknown from extra-biblical sources.[5]

All six bullae are inscribed in Hebrew script and in the Hebrew language. Four bullae are dated and described as belonging to the king who is unnamed, and two are undated. The bullae presented in this paper belong to Group I. The formula used on the fiscal bullae of this group is constant: 1) The date, marked in hieratic numerals; 2) the name of a town; and 3) the king's ownership.[6] The use of Egyptian hieratic numerals is due to the fact that an individual Hebrew numeric system had not yet developed in Judah in the First Temple period; they are also used on Hebrew ostraca and weights.[7] Two bullae feature Egyptian iconography, a four-winged serpent *uraeus* wearing the horned sun disk crown of Hathor. Egyptian iconography is often used in the glyptic art of the Iron Age and is also found on seals and seal impressions.[8]

The Bullae

A Dated Brown-Clay Bulla

The field is divided into three registers by two double lines and is surrounded by a double framing line (fig. 1). Two pointed circles are placed at the end of the second and third line serving as space fillers.

The Hebrew inscription reads:

ב 13 שנה / גבעה / למלך
b 13 šnh / gbʻh / lmlk
"In the 13th year, Gibeah, to/belonging to the king"

Gibeah, meaning "Hill," is the name of four biblical towns. Gibeah mentioned on this bulla is probably located in the hill country of Judah south of Hebron, yet its

---

4. The term "fiscal bullae" was first coined by Nahman Avigad in his 1990 article: "Two Hebrew Fiscal Bullae," *IEJ* 40 (1990): 262–66.

5. The bullae are kept in a private collection and the owner prefers to remain anonymous.

6. The bullae of Group II mention personal names instead of town names.

7. Stefan Wimmer, *Palästinisches Hieratisch, Die Zahl- und Sonderzeichen in der althebräischen Schrift* (Wiesbaden: Harrasowitz, 2008).

8. F. M. Cross, Jr., "King Hezekiah's Seal Bears Phoenician Imagery," *BAR* 25 (1999): 42–45, 60; Robert Deutsch, "Lasting Impressions; New Bullae Reveal Egyptian-Style Emblems on Judah's Royal Seals," *BAR* 28 (2002): 42–51, 60–61.

Fig. 1. A brown-clay bulla with the inscription: "In the 13th year, Gibeah, to/belonging to the king."

precise location is unknown (Josh 15:57). This is the first occurrence of this town name in extra biblical sources of the Iron Age.

A Dated Fragmentary and Damaged Black-Clay Bulla

The field is divided into three registers by two double lines (fig. 2). A section of the surrounding double frame line is preserved on the right edge. The letters *mem* and *lamed* are partly visible and the last letter *kaf* is missing, yet the reading is certain.

The Hebrew inscription reads:

ב 21 שנה / לכש / למל[ך]
b 21 šnh / lkš / lml[k]
"In the 21st year, Lachish, to/belonging to the king"

The ancient site of Lachish (Tell ed-Duweir), is situated about 40 kilometers north of Beer-Sheva and covers an area of about 30 acres. In Iron Age II (eighth–seventh century B.C.E.), Lachish was the most important city after Jerusalem, and its destruction level, called "Lachish III," is dated to the conquest of the city by the Assyrian king Sennacherib in 701 B.C.E. The conquest was commemorated by paneling the walls of a room in the palace in Nineveh with scenes of the siege of

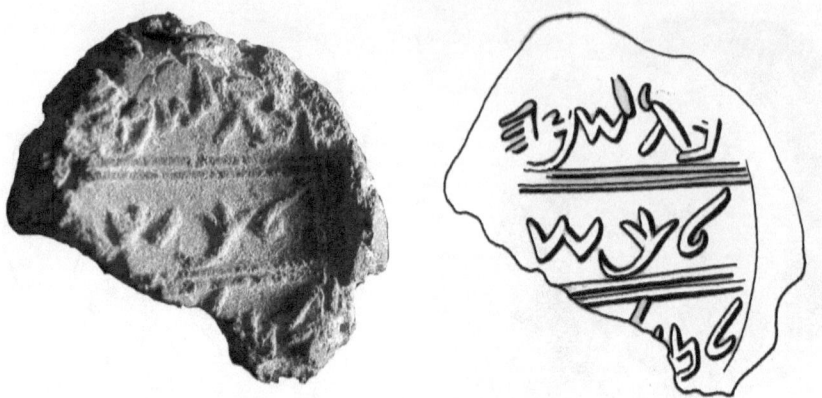

Fig. 2. A fragmentary and damaged black-clay bulla with the inscription: "In the 21st year, Lachish, to/belonging to the king."

the city. The city was conquered again in 586 B.C.E. by the Babylonian king Nabuchadnezzar II, and its destruction level is called "Lachish II."

In 1966, on the floor of a small room, Yohanan Aharoni found a rich group of ceramic vessels. One of the vessels, a typical Iron Age II cylindrical juglet, contained a group of seventeen Hebrew clay seal impressions. Evidently, an official at Lachish was collecting the seal impressions, which he removed from the incoming mail, and kept them in the juglet. The finds were dated to the "Lachish II destruction Level," ca. 586 B.C.E. Unfortunately, only seven bullae are fully or partly legible, while the reminder are poorly preserved and are illegible. Six of them bear personal names while one, which is damaged and its lower right corner is missing, belonged to the high official "Shebanyahu." In the light of the new epigraphic evidence from Keilah, we have to reconsider the attribution of the Lachish juglet and its content to the Lachish II level.[9]

A Dated, Complete, Brown-Clay Bulla

The field is divided into three registers by two double lines and is surrounded by a double framing line (fig. 3). The edges are covered by finger prints. The inscription is carelessly executed.

The Hebrew inscription reads:

---

9. Robert Deutsch, "Tracking Down Shebnayahu, Servant of the King," *BAR* 8 (2009): 45–49, 67.

Fig. 3. A complete brown-clay bulla with the inscription: "In the 20th year, 'Adullam, to/belonging to the king."

ב 20 שנ/ה עדלם / למלך
b 20 šn/h ʿdlm / lmlk
"In the 20th year, 'Adullam, to/belonging to the king"

Adullam (Adollam in Greek spelling), is a town in the Shephelah between Socoh and Keilah. It has been identified with modern Tell esh Sheikh Madhkur. The king of Adullam is mentioned as one of the local kings defeated by the Israelites (Josh 12:15), and the city was allotted to the tribe of Judah (Josh 15:35). David fled from Saul to a cave in the Adullam area, and there he surrounded himself with about four hundred men (1 Sam 22:1). Rehoboam fortified the city preparing it against the invasion of Judah by Shishak (2 Chr 11:7). Micah mourns over Adullam in the time of Hezekiah (Mic 1:15), and it is one of the towns in which the people of Judah settled after the exile (Neh 11:30). This is the first occurrence of this town name in extra biblical sources of the Iron Age.

An Undated Reddish-Brown Clay Bulla

The field is divided into three registers by two double lines and is surrounded by a triple framing line (fig. 4). Two pointed circles and a lotus flower are placed at the end of the second and third line serving as space fillers. In the upper register a four-winged serpent *uraeus* is depicted, wearing the horned sun disk crown of Hathor.

The Hebrew inscription reads:

64 NEW INSCRIPTIONS AND SEALS

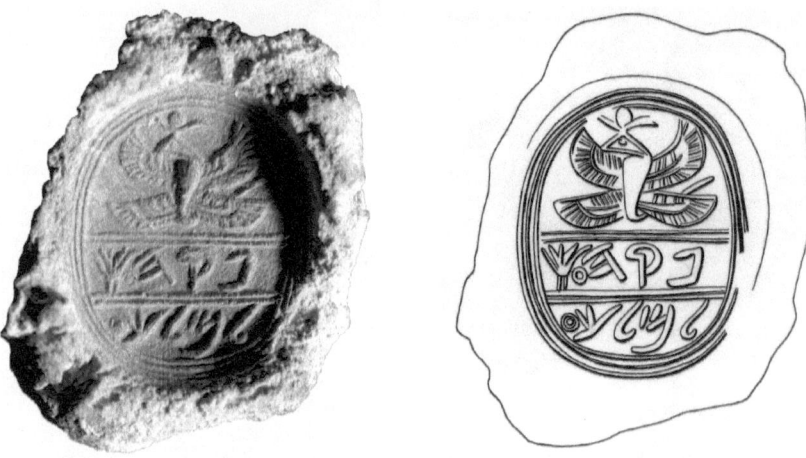

Fig. 4. A reddish-brown clay bulla with the inscription: "('A)pheqah, to/belonging to the king."

(א)פקה / למלך
(')pqh / lmlk
"('A)pheqah, to/belonging to the king"

The name of the town is written in *scriptio defectiva* with the dropped prefix *alef* (same as Hiram for Ahiram). The name probably means "enclosure" or "fortress." Aphek(ah) is one of the nine towns listed in the sixth district of Judah, the capital of which is presumed to have been Hebron (Josh 15:53). This is the first occurrence of this town name in extra biblical sources of the Iron Age.

An Undated Reddish-Brown Clay Bulla

The field is divided into three registers by two double lines (fig. 5). The surrounding triple framing line is preserved on the lower edge. A dot is placed at the end of the inscription serving as a space filler. In the upper register a four-winged serpent *uraeus* is depicted, wearing the horned sun disk crown of Hathor. The surface is slightly damaged but the reading is certain

The Hebrew inscription reads:

צאננם / למלך
s'nnm / lmlk
"Tza'ananim, to/belonging to the king"

Fig. 5. A reddish-brown clay bulla with the inscription: "Tza'ananim, to/belonging to the king."

The biblical town of Zeanan (Zeananim in plural), is mentioned in the district of Lachish (Josh 16:37). The name of the town is also mentioned in Mikha (1:11). This is the first occurrence of this town name in extra biblical sources of the Iron Age.

A Dated Complete Black-Clay Bulla

The field is divided into four registers by three single lines and is surrounded by a framing line (fig. 6).

The Hebrew inscription reads:

בשנה / השלשת / שוכה / למלך
bšnh /hšlšt / šwkh / lmlk
"In the third year, Socoh, to/belonging to the king"

Socoh on this bulla is possibly the biblical town located in the Hebron district (Josh 15:48), identified as the double tell called "The Upper and Lower Shuwaikah," about 6 kilometers southwest of Eshtamoa. Socoh served as an administrative or storage center, being one of the four cities mentioned on the *LMLK* stamps of the Judean monarchy.

Another candidate is the town named Socoh that is found in the lower hill country in the Ela Valley between Adullam and Azekah (Josh 15:35). The Philistines camped between the Ela Valley, Socoh, and Azekah before the encounter

Fig. 6. A complete black-clay bulla with the inscription: "In the third year, Socoh, to/belonging to the king."

of David and Goliath (1 Sam 17:1). Rehoboam fortified the place (2 Chr 11:7). It was also one of the cities occupied temporarily by the Philistines in the time of Ahaz, Hezekia's father (2 Chr 28:18).

Conclusions

The six fiscal bullae presented above, naming the towns of Gibeah, Lachish, Adullam, (A)pheqah, Tzaananim, and Socoh, are to be added to the eleven fiscal bullae previously deciphered, recording eight cities: Eltolad, Arab, Arubboth, Gebim, Lachish, Maon, Nasib, and Keilah.[10] The thirteen different towns mentioned on the fiscal bullae are situated in Judah, with the borders of Keilah in the north, Eltolad in the south, Maon in the east, and Lachish in the west. Within the same borders, on the eastern part of Judah, we find the towns of Hebron, Ziph, and Socoh, mentioned on the *LMLK* storage-jar handles. Therefore, we can safely determine that both artifacts, the fiscal bullae and the *LMLK* storage jars, which are chronologically coexistent, are to be attributed to Hezekiah's taxation system, and are probably connected with his efforts to confront and resist the Assyrian threat, realized in the invasion that took place in 701 B.C.E.

---

10. Deutsch, "Biblical Period Hebrew Bulla," 87.

Bibliography

Avigad, Nahman. "Two Hebrew Fiscal Bullae." *IEJ* 40 (1990): 262–66.
Cross, Frank M., Jr. "King Hezekiah's Seal Bears Phoenician Imagery." *BAR* 25 (1999): 42–45, 60.
Deutsch, Robert. "A Hoard of Fifty Hebrew Clay Bullae from the Time of Hezekiah." Pages 45–98 in *Shlomo: Studies in Epigraphy, Iconography, History and Archaeology in Honor of Shlomo Moussaieff.* Edited by R. Deutsch. Tel Aviv-Jaffa: Archaeological Center Publications, 2003.
———. *Biblical Period Epigraphy: The Josef Chaim Kaufman Collection; Seals, Bullae, Handles*, vol. 2. Tel Aviv-Jaffa: Archaeological Center Publications, 2011.
———. *Biblical Period Hebrew Bulla: The Josef Chaim Kaufman Collection.* Tel Aviv-Jaffa, Archaeological Center Publications 2003.
———. "Lasting Impressions; New Bullae Reveal Egyptian-Style Emblems on Judah's Royal Seals." *BAR* 28 (2002): 42–51, 60–61.
———. *Messages from the Past, Hebrew Bullae from the time of Isaiah through the Destruction of the First Temple.* Tel Aviv-Jaffa, Archaeological Center Publications, 1999.
———. "Tracking Down Shebnayahu, Servant of the King," *BAR* 8 (2009): 45–49, 67.
Wimmer, Stefan. *Palästinisches Hieratisch, Die Zahl- und Sonderzeichen in der althebräischen Schrift.* Wiesbaden: Harrasowitz, 2008.

Chapter Five
Dml': A Seal from the Moussaieff Collection

Meir Lubetski

There is a dome-shaped unperforated scaraboid seal in Shlomo Moussaieff's collection (fig. 1). Purchased in Jerusalem, it is made of blue-gray lapis lazuli and its dimensions are 16.0 long, 12.1 wide, and 6.1 mm high.[1] The seal cutter engraved an ornamented feline icon on the upper part, while the lower part contains a two-line inscription. Robert Deutsch and Michael Heltzer, in their book, *Windows to the Past*, read it:

לדמלא ב
ן פקחיו
[belonging to] *dml'* son of *pqḥyw*

The authors indicate that the father's name is included in biblical onomastics[2] while the seal owner's name is not. The latter, however, is found in collateral epigraphic sources of the late-Israelite monarchical preexilic period.[3] Deutsch and Heltzer are inclined to agree with Pritchard's and Avigad's supposition that *dml'* is a hypocoristic form of the full personal name *dmlyhw* or *dml'l*. Pritchard adapted Prof. Jonas Greenfield's assumption that "the element *dml* may be explained as

---

1. *Editio princeps* in Robert Deutsch and Michael Heltzer, *Windows to the Past* (Tel Aviv: Archaeological Center Publication, 1997), 45–46.

2. Ibid. For the current explanation of the patronymic name see the summary of Robert Deutsch, *Biblical Period Hebrew Bullae* (Tel Aviv: Archaeological Center Publication, 2003), 425; See also Jeaneane D. Fowler, *Theophoric Personal Names in Ancient Hebrew* (JSOTSup 49; Sheffield: JSOT, 1988), 94, 164, 357.

3. Deutsch and Heltzer, *Windows to the Past*, 45. Cf. F. W. Dobbs-Alsopp et al., eds., *Hebrew Inscriptions* (New Haven: Yale University Press, 2005), 595. The authors offer a short explanation of the name and a bibliography. For a detailed discussion of the name see Fowler, *Theophoric Personal Names*, 126, 165, 341.

Fig. 1. לדמלא בן פקחיו. From the Moussaieff Collection, courtesy of Robert Deutsch and Andre Lemaire.

the root *dmm* plus the preposition *l*. The meaning of the name would then be something like "Wait on the Lord" as in Ps 37:7."⁴ The verse referred to is דום לה׳ והתחולל לו, and is translated by JPS as "Be patient and wait for the Lord."⁵ As for the suffix *aleph*, Pritchard believed that the *aleph* changes into a *yod*, so that the *aleph* in this name is a shortened version of the theophoric *yhw*. The full name, according to Pritchard, would be *dmlyhw.⁶

Avigad, who also deciphered an inscribed iconic bulla, *ldml'*, belonging to *dml'*, assumed that the name is a hypocoristic form of the theophoric name *dml'l/dmlyhw* found on other seals. He suggested that we understand the name as composed of three elements, *dm*, an imperative of the verb *dmm*, the preposition *l* and the theophoric element *aleph*, standing for the whole name *'l*. Accordingly, it is a verbal sentence *dm l'l* or *dm lyh*, similar to Ps 37:7, as above, and the sense is: "Be silent before *'l* or *yhw*.⁷

---

4. James B. Pritchard, *Hebrew Inscriptions and Stamps from Gibeon* (Philadelphia: University Museum of Pennsylvania, 1959), 11.

5. *Tanakh* (Philadelphia: JPS, 1985). For an explanation of *dmm* see BDB, 198–99; *HALOT*, 226. A lesser known yet well-documented explanation is "whisper." Mosheh Zaidel, *Ḥikre Lashon* (Jerusalem: Mosad Harav Kook, 1986), 16–17. See also BDB, 199, under the entry דממה; *HALOT*, 226. It is astonishing that commentators neglected this approach in comprehending the verse.

6. *Dml'* > *dmlyhw* on the analogy of *nr'*> *nryhw*. Pritchard, *Hebrew Inscriptions and Stamps from Gibeon*, 11.

7. Nahman Avigad, "New Names on Hebrew Seals," *ErIsr* 18 (1975): 70–71 (Hebrew). See also Nahman Avigad and Benjamin Sass, *Corpus of West Semitic Stamp Seals* (Jerusalem: Israel

The scholars who advanced the above explanation took for granted that the *aleph* was the shortened form of the word *'l*, similar to the suffix *yh*, the shortened version of *yhw*.[8] However, it is possible that they built their theory on an incorrect assumption and that the *aleph* is not hypocoristic.[9] I have not found examples of this and nor did Lawrence Mykytiuk who has researched the subject.[10] To the contrary, the shortest word for the name of god is the letter *l*, and hence Ebla's *Ilum* the common name of god, is written *lum*.[11] Similarly, in Hebrew, the dominance of the *lamed* is clearly indicated through the diacritical marks in such a name as יחזקאל. In this name the sound of the *lamed* is heard but the aleph is silent. The Masoretes vocalized the word so that the suffix אל has an aleph in the *ktib*, but the *qre perpetuum* is without a consonantal aleph since the *tsere* vowel is dotting the ק.[12] Consequently, there may very well be three separate names, *dmlyhw, dml'l* and *dml'*. The first two have the same meanings, whereas the third, which appears on a number of artifacts, is not only constructed in another way but also means something else.

Diringer, in discussing the name *dmlyhw* engraved on a Samaria ostracon, divided the components of the name differently than Avigad or Pritchard. He proposed that the first element was composed of three letters, *dml*, and he connected it to the Arabic verb *damal* in the sense of "to cure," "to heal," or to "make peace,"

Academy of Sciences and Humanities, 1997), 193, 494; Avigad cited the article of Bezalel Porten, "'Domlaèl' and Related Names," *IEJ* 21 (1971): 47–49, as support to his approach. Cf. the cautious comments of Fowler on the same article. *Theophoric Personal Names*, 87, 125, 126, 165, 341.

8. Nahman Avigad, Michael Heltzer, and André Lemaire, *West Semitic Seals Eighth–Sixth Centuries BCE* (Haifa: University of Haifa, 2000), 30. The authors conjectured that the names *dmlyhw* and *dml'l*, prevalent on seals, are cognate to the hypocristicon, *dml'*. Deutsch lists many bullae that contain all three names and he feels that they are all connected. Robert Deutsch, *Biblical Period Hebrew Bullae* (Tel Aviv: Archaeological Center Publication, 2003), 37–40, 157–59, 390–91.

9. If *dml'* is originally a Hebrew name then the final *aleph* sign cannot represent the short form of the deity's name. It is used merely as an orthographical letter without designating a consonantal *aleph*. Hence, it marks a long vowel before it. For a thorough discussion of the role and the weakness of the letter *aleph* see GKC §23.

10. I would like to thank my colleague Lawrence J. Mykytiuk, author of *Identifying Biblical Persons in Northwest Semitic Inscriptions of 1200–539 B.C.E.* (Atlanta: Society of Biblical Literature, 2004) for researching this topic for me. In an email communication from September 9, 2009, he writes: "I find no clear, unambiguous example of final *aleph* bearing a theophoric meaning."

11. The personal name *i-ti-lum* is indeed *Itti-(I)lum* with mimation. Franco D'Agostino, *Testi Amministrativi di Ebla* (Rome: University of Rome, 1996), Text 3, verso XIV.15; Text 21, verso I.1.

12. For the same model see the names of Daniel (Dan 1:6) and Ishmael (Gen 16:11). In postbiblical Hebrew the prefix אל in a variety of names is shortened to *l*. Thus the Talmudic sage לעזר is really אלעזר.

and thus the personal name presented the imperative request: "Cure (O) god"; or "make peace (O) god."[13] Diringer's interpretation of a two syllable name where the prefix *dml* describes the nature or function of the deity whose name constitutes the second component is a viable explanation for the name, *dmlyhw* or *dml'l*.

There is an additional reason to suggest that the prefixes of the two names were based on *dml*. Ugaritic onomastics include the word *dml* among the list of deities,[14] so that *dmlyhw* or *dml'l* could have originated with the usual addition of *yhw* or *'l* to a deity's name and the meaning would be "*dml* is (my) god."[15] However, the prefixes of *dmlyhw* or *dml'l* do not match the prefix of *dml'* and there is no compelling reason to tie them together. Therefore, I would like to suggest a different explanation of *dml'*

A linguistic search indicates that *dml'* has antecedents in early vocabularies and onomastics of eastern Mediterranean communities. We find *dm* in Ugaritic literature as an emphatic particle: "lo, now"[16] or "behold."[17] It is possible that the word *dm* in Ps 37:7 has the same quality. And the emphatic word calls attention to the statement that follows it.[18] Thus the verse דום לה׳ והתחולל לו would mean "Lo, now unto God (or heed to God), and [place your] hope in Him." So, too, *dm* in the personal name *dml'* would reflect the same sense, "lo, now."[19]

The suffix *l'*, in the personal name, *dml'*, may be related to the Ugaritic elements *l'y/lan* [20] in the meaning "strong," or "being mighty."[21] In Ugaritic

---

13. David Diringer, *Le iscarizioni antico-ebraiche palestinesi* (Florence: le Monnier, 1934), 178–79, 217. Cf. Siegfried H. Horn, "An Uninscribed Seal from Jordan," *BASOR* 189 (1968): 41–43. See also J. C. L. Gibson, *Textbook of Syrian Semitic Inscriptions: Hebrew and Moabite* (Oxford: Clarendon, 1971), 1:56.

14. *UT* (1998), §19.673. See also Gregorio del Olmo Lete and Joaquín Sanmartín, *A Dictionary of the Ugaritic Language in the Alphabetic Tradition* (trans. Wilfred G. E. Watson; Leiden: Brill, 2003), 1:273; Josef Tropper, *Kleines Wörterbuch des ugaritischen* (Weisbaden: Harrassowitz, 2008), 30, dm_1.

15. For additional examples of a common type of a god's name plus *il*, see *UT* (1998), §8.62.

16. *UT* (1998), §19.670.

17. del Olmo Lete and Sanmartín, *A Dictionary of the Ugaritic Language*, 1:272#2.

18. GKC, §105b; §147b, d.

19. Another verse where Ugaritic *dm* might suit the contents is Ezek 24:17. When the prophet's wife dies he is ordered: "lo now" wail [yet] do not mourn for the dead. This translation is based on Radak's suggestion to reverse the order of the latter words in the verse. Further, the Sages perceive the first part of that verse as an order to cry out loud. y. *Mo'ed Qat.* 3:5.

20. The suffix *n* added to the same name often represents *ân* and the same personal name might add or delete the *ân*. For instance, *ily* or *ilyn*.

21. *UT* (1998), §19.1342; See also Svi Rin and Shifra Rin, *Acts of the Gods* (Philadelphia: Inbal, 1996), 790, 537, 539. [Hebrew]. See also *l-'-w* in Stanislav Segert, *A Basic Grammar of the Ugaritic Language* (Berkeley and Los Angeles: University of California Press, 1984), 190.

ononmastics, the elements are found as integral parts of the epithet *aliyn.b'l*,[22] the honorific title of Baal, the strong one, and in other personal names as well.[23] The combination *dm+ l'* is present in a narrative relating that *El* orders *Mt* to cease harmful activities against *Krt*, commanding *Š^{e}tqt* to cure the patient: Hence, the father of the gods says: *dm lan* = lo be strong...[24] [and cure *Krt*]. The two elements, *dm* and *lan* are juxtaposed in one phrase, transmitting a forceful imperative to carry out the deity's order. Thus, the command *dmla(n)* [25] is strikingly similar to the personal name *dml'*. Furthermore, the suffix *l'y*, known from the Ugaritic onomastics, is anticipated by the El Amarna cuneiform spelling of the personal name, ^{m}*li-e-ia* (*lêia*),[26] and its cognate, as Albright had already recognized occurs in Egyptian syllabical spelling *r3l3*.[27] The Egyptian prefix *r(3)* is prone to undergo the regular substitution of Egyptian *r* for Semitic *l* by an Egyptian scribe well-trained to write in cuneiform.[28]

---

22. *UT* (1998), §19.1342; See Svi Rin and Shifra Rin's comment on this name. *Acts of the Gods*, 67–68.

23. Frauke Gröndahl, *Die Personennamen der Texte aus Ugarit* (Rome: Pontifical Biblical Institute, 1967), 154. Also, Joseph Aisleitner, *Wörterbuch der ugaritischen Sprache* (Berlin: Akademie, 1974), 79 #759.

24. *UT* (1998), text 127, lines 13–14. For an example of a biblical personal name that originates as a result of a deity's action, see Gen 16:11.

25. See Mitchell J. Dahood's comments on the connection between Ugaritic *l'y* and its Hebrew cognate *l'y* in his commentary on Ps 22:30. *Psalms 1–50* (AB 16; New York: Doubleday, 1966). See also his review of Y. Yadin et al. (eds.), *Hazor II*, *Biblica* 42 (1961): 475. He says: "The root [*l'y*] occurs more frequently in Hebrew than we suspect, and P. Haupt may be correct in understanding the biblical name לאה as *domina*."

26. El Amarna tablet 162, line 70. See Samuel A. B. Mercer, *The Tell El-Amarna Tablets* (2 vols.; Toronto: Macmillan, 1939), 2:524–25; William L. Moran, *The Amarna Letters* (Baltimore: John Hopkins University, 1992), 248–51, esp. line 70.

27. William F. Albright, "Cuneiform Material for Egyptian Prosopography," *JNES* 5 (1946): 14, #20a, #20b, Albright cites the fact that Ramses II sends a royal officer with the same name to the Hittite king. For a very close parallel of personal names in the Egyptian Nineteenth Dynasty and the New Kingdom, see also Hermann Ranke, *Die ägyptischen Personennamen* (3 vols.; Glückstadt: Augustin, 1935), 1:216#28, #29, 1.217#1, 1.425#3,#4.

28. Kurt Sethe, *Das ägyptische Verbum im altägyptischen, neuägyptischen, und koptischen* (3 vols.; Leipzig: Hinrichs, 1899–1902), 1:134–35. See also James E. Hoch, *Semitic Words in Egyptian Texts of the New Kingdom and Third Intermediate Period* (Princeton: Princeton University Press, 1994), 202 #273, #274, 407; Yoshiyuki Muchiki indicates the change of Egyptian *r>l* at the initial of the personal Northwest Semitic name Leya* in his *Egyptian Proper Names and Loan words in North-West Semitic* (SBLDS 173; Atlanta: SBL, 1999), 306. The transposition of Egyptian *r* into *l* is prevalent in Coptic. For instance, Egyptian *rw-3bw*, lioness; demotic *lbj*; Hebrew לביא. See the Coptic and later Arabic forms in Wolfhart Westendorf, *Koptisches Handwörterbuch* (Heidelberg: Winter, 1965), 75.

Li-e-ia is the name of an Egyptian family head on the list of enemies of the King of Egypt. Aziru of Amurru is requested to extradite the head of the family li-e-ia and his sons to Egypt.[29] Late Egyptian texts record the name as rȝlȝ[30] and the element lȝ in Late Egyptian personal names connotes the theophoric name 'l.[31] The rȝ prefix conveys, literally, the idea of "mouth" or "utterance," but figuratively, "the mighty voice."[32] Accordingly, the Late Egyptian rȝlȝ provides the meaning of the personal name, "the utterance of 'l," a very appropriate blended designation for an Egyptian living in Amurru outside of Egypt.

Dml', the inscription, ends with two letters, lamed and aleph. The Egyptian cognate offers the meaning of the suffix as: the utterance of 'l while the cuneiform syllabary transliterates the Egyptian spelling into prevalent Amarna script. And for this reason, the aleph is not the short form of 'l or yhw, as was assumed. Rather, it is the disguised spelling of Late Egyptian onomastics transmitted by the royal scribe of the King of Egypt, to Aziru, the Prince of Amurru. Not only did the name of 'l remain in existence but the mighty deity 'l and his utterance had been introduced by the familiar Ugaritic emphatic prefix, dm, "lo, now."[33] And so, the extrabiblical personal name dml' is formed out of three elements; dm an emphatic call for attention that introduces the l; the mouth, that is, "the mighty word"; and the aleph, a specific god, 'l. Thus, dml' connotes: Lo, now, the (mighty) utterance of 'l. An understanding of the meaning of dml' provides more

---

29. King Amenophis IV (Ikhnaton) demanded from Aziru, governor of Amurru, to hand over to Egypt an Egyptian family whose name was on the king's foes' list.

30. Ranke, *Die ägyptischen Personennamen*, 1:216#23; Mercer, *The Tell El-Amarna Tablets*, 2.524; tablet 162, line 70. Cf. Richard S. Hess, *Amarna Personal Names* (Winona Lake, Ind.: Eisenbraun, 1993), 104 #105. Hess assumes that the name is Egyptian but might be of West Semitic origin as well. Muchiki lists lêia as the cognate name of r(ȝ)l(ȝ) in his analysis of phonological correspondences between Egyptian proper names and those appearing in the El Amarna tablets. Yoshiyuki Muchiki, *Egyptian Proper Names*, 292.

31. As of the Eighteenth Dynasty and on the lȝ sign in Egyptian onomastics is cognate to the term *'ēl(u), the Northwest Semitic term for the deity. Hoch, *Semitic Words*, 27–8#16, 506. It is important to note the approach of the Masoretes to consonantal l' with an aleph in Job 13:15. They suggest that we read the word as lô (spelled with the vocalic consonant waw) in the sense of Him. This, in a sense, was an answer to the Talmudic query in b. Sotah 27b regarding the meaning of the above verse. Note that the LXX, composed in Hellenistic Egypt, perceives consonantal l' in that verse as ὁ δυνάστης, the Omnipotent. The translators seem to continue the old Egyptian tradition.

32. Leonard H. Lesko, ed., *A Dictionary of Late Egyptian* (2 vols.; Fall River, Mass.: Fall River Modern Printing, 2002), 1:259. See also Alan H. Gardiner, *Egyptian Grammar* (3rd rev. ed.; London: Oxford University Press, 1973), 577.

33. Similarly, in the Bible, the words הנה or הן emphasize the phrase following it. To wit: "Behold, I give," Gen 1:29; "Lo, a people that rises like a lion," Num 23:24.

than just a linguistic analysis. It offers a window into the thinking of an Israelite family. The name conveys the awe approaching the deity: Pay attention to the mighty voice of God.

That *dml'* has an Egyptian-inspired tone is evident through the special iconography carved on the seal: A feline divinity[34] sits on top of a semicircular shield in the form of a broad collar.[35] A row of small squares at the outer edge of this collar frames the bottom with a floral motif. Perhaps it represents the zoned petals that frequently comprise the outermost row of beads on such collars. The choice of a collar adds another dimension to this seal, security. The collar, symbolically, would endow the seal bearer with divine protection and keep him away from peril.[36]

The identity of the feline is a bit of a puzzle. The two thick strands of hair falling over the shoulders are normally associated with feline figures; these lappets of the so-called tripartite wig often appear on the leonine goddess Sakhmet. This goddess represented, on the one hand, the might of Egypt, and on the other, disease and pestilence, since she was known as the ruler of the desert.[37] But, in order to diminish the negative effects, the seal cutter decorated the feline with what seems to be three pellets of medicaments.[38] In addition, he formed the

---

34. For examples of other felines on Hebrew scarab seals see Robert Deutsch and André Lemaire, *Biblical Period Personal Seals* (Tel Aviv: Archaeological Center Publications, 2000), 8; Avigad and Sass, *Corpus of WSS*, 137 #298.

35. For similar seal scarabs with beaded collars, see Alice Greenfell, "Amuletic Scarabs, etc., for the Deceased," *Recueil de travaux relatifs à la philology et á l'archéologie égyptiennes et assyriennes* 30 (1908): plate I, #9, #10. See also Steffen Wenig, *Africa in Antiquity: The Art of Nubia and Sudan* (Brooklyn: The Brooklyn Museum, 1978), 2:237, 239. To research the preexilic seal of the late Hebrew monarchy, we should give priority to corresponding items that are as close as possible in time and place to the particular article in question. For our period, the Nubian material may be expected to furnish the valid outside factors.

36. Ambrose Lansing, "A Faience Broad Collar of the Eighteenth Dynasty," *The Metropolitan Museum of Art Bulletin* 35 (1940): 65–68; cf. E. A.Wallis Budge, *The Book of the Dead* (trans. E. A. Wallis Budge; 2d ed.; London: Routledge & Kegan Paul, 1960), Chapter CLVIII, 525. One has to bear in mind the dominant role a collar plays in the journey of the deceased to his cherished afterlife.

37. See Alfred Wiedemann, *Religion of the Ancient Egyptians* (London: H. Greval, 1897), 137–38. Sakhmet brings forward the twofold feature of most Egyptian deities; a characteristic that permits the deity to substitute function and icon easily. For an illustration of the goddess as a leonine-headed woman see Stephen Quirke and Jeffrey Spenser, eds., *The British Museum Book of Ancient Egypt* (New York: Thames & Hudson, 1992), 63.

38. Gardiner, *Egyptian Grammar*, 490, Sign List N33.

pointed ears to give the impression that the likeness is the benevolent cat goddess, Bastet.[39]

That the image of the deity is not of one specific divinity, but rather is a composite of similar antithetical gods, Sakhmet and Bastet, [40] was intentional by the engraver. Sakhmet conveys the idea of "power"[41] while Bastet, the feline deity of the *bas* or unguent jar, functions like the ointment itself, a shield from harm and a cure for sickness.[42] Bastet, then, reflects the desire for divine kindliness and care.[43] Bubastis, her city in the Delta, attained national status[44] and her cult in a cat form gained prominence especially during the late-Hebrew monarchical period.[45]

Both aspects of the feline are of importance to the seal owner as they remind him of attributes of the divine. In the Bible, the Hebrew god is referred to by His attributes. Indeed, Rashi, in his explanation of Exod 20:2, vividly portrays two aspects that are particularly relevant to our discussion. He says that God has revealed himself at the Red Sea as a "mighty man of war" and at Mount Sinai as an "elderly man filled with compassion." Adherence to aniconism eliminated the option for Hebrew seal owners to represent God artistically so that the engraver

---

39. Quirke and Spenser, *The British Museum Book*, 46.
40. Siegfried Morenz, *Egyptian Religion* (trans. Ann E. Keep; Ithaca: Cornell University Press, 1990), 260, 268. A well-known Philae text portrays Isis-Hathor who personifies all the female deities as: "kindly is she as Bastet, terrible is she as Sakhmet." Hermann Junker, *Der Auszug der Hathor-Tefnut aus Nubien* (Berlin: Verlag der Königlichen Akademie der Wissenschaften, in Commission bei Georg Reimer, 1911), appendix, S.32=Philae, Photo 57–8. The duality of Sakhmet-Bastet, the lioness-cat is discussed by Hellmut Brunner in "Das Besänftigungslied im Sinuhe (B269–279)," *ZÄS* 80 (1955): 7, and also notes 3 and 5.
41. "*Sḫm*" = The powerful one, in Raymond O. Faulkner, *A Concise Dictionary of Middle Egyptian* (Oxford: Griffith Institute, 1986), 241.
42. Gardiner, *Egyptian Grammar*, 527, Sign List W1,2.
43. It is a prevalent supplication to God in Psalms requesting to "take refuge under your protecting wings," Ps 61:5, repeated in Pss 17:8; 36:8; 57:2, and in many other texts. For the Egyptian pictorial representation, see Grenfell, "Amuletic Scarabs for the Deceased," 107. Plate 1 #14 indicates the connection between Bastet and the ability to hover. The Egyptian scarab cutter engraved the pintail duck since the dead Egyptian requests the ability to flutter daily over his piece of land. It is expressed with words and pictorially with the pintail duck either flying or alighting (for pictographs see Gardiner, *Egyptian Grammar*, 472, Sign List G40 or G41).

The engraver who chose the pictography of the kind deity Bastet for the seal bearer might have had in mind the same idea.

44. Ezekiel, who describes the humiliation of Egypt, specifically discusses the calamity of the city Bubastis and its inhabitatnts (Ezek 30:17).
45. Kenneth A. Kitchen, *The Third Intermediate Period in Egypt 1000–650 BC* (Warminster: Aris & Phillips, 1973), 291. See also Douglas J. Brewer and Emily Teeter, *Egypt and the Egyptians* (Cambridge: Cambridge University Press, 1999), 53.

displayed Egyptianized pictorial designs as a substitute to express the Hebrew's outlook. Even though he used Egyptianized religious imagery for his iconography, that did not mean that he or his client ascribed to the Egyptian religious mythology. My revered professor, Cyrus H. Gordon, used to comment on striking literary parallels between Ugaritic literature and the Hebrew Bible: "Just as John Milton was a good Christian despite his profuse allusions to pagan mythology, the Hebrew poets were monotheists who worshiped God and God alone."[46] So the dual icon was able to reflect the idea of the strength of a powerful god on the one hand and compassionate protection by the deity on the other.

The engraver chose to adorn the feline figure with a crown. Headdresses are designed to signify authority. Conferring them on a person meant investing him with power.[47] However, this Egyptianized head covering signifies a person with a non-ruling position since it lacks the vital authority symbol of a skullcap or streamer.[48] Yet, *dml'* son of *pqḥyw*, the bearer, carried considerable weight because of the unusual engraved glyph. The iconography would have had a profound meaning to the owner and his close associates, and possibly also served as a charm. The artisan shaped an impressive product that was laden with meaning for his important client.

There is another clay bulla that reads לדמלא, [belonging] to *dml'* (fig. 2)[49] that also shows Egyptian inspiration. The seal cutter engraved on this seal one of the most popular Egyptian icons, a beetle holding the sun ball between its hind legs.[50] This glyph is one of the most characteristic designs on official royal pre-exilic *lmlk* stamps.[51] Underneath is an icon that Avigad deems to be a pedestal for the beetle. However, the design might also be perceived as the Egyptian ideogram *nb*, the wicker basket,[52] and therefore it represents the seal bearer's status as a wealthy property owner.[53] Not only does the Egyptian ideogram on the bulla

---

46. He made these comments in a post-doctoral seminar at New York University.
47. Gen 41:41–43; Esth 6:6–10.
48. László Török, *The Royal Crowns of Kush* (Oxford: B.A.R., 1987), 40.
49. See note 7. See fig. 2, p. 78.
50. This beetle has four wings, whereas the common Egyptian model has two wings.
51. For the explanation of *lmlk* stamps and the iconography on the jar handles, there are many sources. The following is a small selection that highlights the complexities of the subject matter: A. D. Tushingham, "A Royal Israelite Seal(?) and the Royal Jar Handle Stamps (part one)," *BASOR* 200 (1970): 71–78; idem, "A Royal Israelite Seal(?) and the Royal Jar Handle Stamps (part two)," *BASOR* 201 (1971): 23–35. Yossi Garfinkel, "A Hierarchic Pattern in the Private Seal-Impression on the '*lmlk*' Jar Handles," *ErIsr* 18 (1985): 108–15 (Hebrew); Gavriel Barkay, "A Group of Stamped Handles from Judah," *ErIsr* 23 (1992): 113–28.
52. Gardiner, *Egyptian Grammar*, 525, Sign List V30.
53. "*Nb*," in Leonard H. Lesko, ed., *A Dictionary of Late Egyptian*, 232. For example, *ink nb*

Fig. 2. לדמלא. With permission of the Israel Museum.

imply the sense of "possessor of property"⁵⁴ but it is also found in Egyptian onomastics as an independent name.⁵⁵ And if so, it could also fulfill the patronymic function in this bulla.

Dml', the extra-biblical name, seems to have been prevalent in the region south of Jerusalem. Avigad assumes that the bulla was unearthed in the vicinity of Hebron. It is interesting to note that not far away, north of Jerusalem in Gibeon, wine producers register the name *dml'* five times on jar handles over the course of a few centuries⁵⁶ and thus Pritchard suggests the possibility of a distinct

---

ʿ3w nb ḫbsw "I was a possessor of donkeys and a possessor of plough lands"; Alan Gardiner, *Egyptian Grammar*, 423, §115a. Also, in a literary piece dedicated to the god Amun as the ultimate helper, the narrative praises the one who … bw šbn nb wnw (and) "mingles not with a possessor of property"; Alan H. Gardiner, *Late Egyptian Miscellanies* (Brussells: Reine Elisabeth, 1937), Papyrus Anastasi II 18.9, 3. Lack of space on a seal is the cause for different kinds of omissions and especially abbreviations in spelling names, titles, and missing determinatives. This topic is treated at length by Alice Grenfell in her article, "Amuletic Scarabs for the Deceased," 105–20.

54. Alan Gardiner, *Egyptian Grammar*, 573.

55. Hermann Ranke, *Die ägytischen Personennamen*, 1:112, 17, 18. and the word might serve as a component in compound names. To wit, ibid., 1:184, 1, 12.

56. Pritchard, *Hebrew Inscriptions and Stamps from Gibeon*, 16.

family that utilizes the name *dml'* in succession.⁵⁷ Is it a coincidence for the name to be used in that particular region?

Cuneiform *lêia* is a familiar name in the Amurru and Hittite regions during the Amarna era.⁵⁸ Genesis 23:1-20 tells about an enclave of "the children of Heth" living in Hebron. The narrator lists Hittites ⁵⁹ among the pre-Hebrews that lived in the region between Jerusalem and Hebron prior to the arrival of the Israelites. Even in Ezek 16:3 and 45 there is mention of Amorites and Hittites living close to Jerusalem.⁶⁰ In addition, Pharaoh Shishak's renewed trade interests in the area left their footprints.⁶¹ The Egyptian army invaded this region at the beginning of the divided monarchy of Israel and captured many cities, Gibeon among them.⁶² As there was an evolution in the ethnic composition of the population, there was a gradual transformation in choosing names for newborns.⁶³ It is the diversity of the ethnic groups that inhabited the area prior to and during the period of

---

57. Ibid., 17.

58. Albright, "Cuneiform Material for Egyptian Prosopography," 14.

59. Although the descriptions of the Hittite Empire expansion never reached southeast Canaan, the Bible reports the presence of Hittites in different regions of the land and prominent biblical figures have contacts with individuals of Hittite origin. See Nahum M. Sarna, *Genesis* (Philadelphia: JPS, 1989), 395-96; excursus 19. What is of interest is that the episode of selling real estate in Hebron to Abraham had characteristics of Hittite law. See Manfred R. Lehmann, "Abraham's Purchase of Machpelah and Hittite Law," *BASOR* 129 (1953): 15-18. Recently, J. D. Hawkins pieced together the historical aftermath of the disintegration of the Hittite Empire. His research shows numerous Luwian hieroglyphic inscriptions belonging to small independent city states that continued to exist ca. 1000-700 B.C.E. The cities and their ruling circles were still characterized as Hittite by their neighbors, an identity that they themselves seem to have promoted. J. D. Hawkins, "Cilicia, the Amuq, and Aleppo: New Light in a Dark Age," *Near Eastern Archaeology* 72 (December 2009): 164-73. The emerging political landscape molded by forces of continuity and change left their impressions on the surrounding neighbors who refer to the Hittites as "Kings of the Hittites." Accordingly, in a war between the Aramaens and the Kingdom of Israel, the biblical narrator reports that the Aramaen army surrounding Israel retreated because they believed, "Lo the King of Israel hath hired against us the Kings of the Hittites" (2 Kgs 7:6).

60. The spies who return from their mission in the southern part of the Land of Canaan report that Hittites and Amorites are settled in the hills (Num 13:29). King Solomon mentions the existence of Hittites and Amorites (1 Kgs 9:20-22). Cf. Mercer, *The Tell El-Amarna Tablets*, 2:704-5, line 2; 711, line 25.

61. 1 Kgs 14:25-26; 2 Chr 12:2-9.

62. See John D. Currid, *Ancient Egypt and the Old Testament* (Grand Rapids: Baker Books, 1997), 172-202, esp. 192.

63. Eduard Yechezkel Kutscher provides examples of Northwest Semitic names that are adapted as part of biblical onomastics. Prefixes and suffixes of the prevalent names in the region that the Kingdom of Israel inherited are altered. *Hebrew and Aramaic Studies* (Jerusalem: Magnes, 1977), 9-10 (Hebrew).

Israelite settlement that provide the background for the name *dml'*. How much influence was actually transmitted from the previous traditions to the newcomers is impossible to say, but if the El Amarna *lêia* or Egyptian *rʒlʒ* appealed to the original wine producers of Gibeon, it did not pass from one generation to the next without modification. When the name surfaced as *dml'* it wore an Hebraic costume, which concealed the original alien source.

The Israelites inherited the Land of Canaan, a crossroads of the great civilizations of the era. They engaged in active interchange with their neighbors so that they had the richest possible sources from which to draw upon to create their own distinctive culture. The diverse origins of Hebraic onomastics never cease to amaze and challenge the investigator of treasures buried thousands of years ago.

Bibliography

Aisleitner, Joseph. *Wörterbuch der ugaritischen Sprache*. Berlin: Akademie, 1974.
Albright, William F. "Cuneiform Material for Egyptian Prosopography." *JNES* 5 (1946): 14.
Avigad, Nahman. "New Names on Hebrew Seals." *ErIsr* 18 (1975): 70–71 (Hebrew).
Avigad, Nahman, and Benjamin Sass. *Corpus of West Semitic Stamp Seals*. Jerusalem: Israel Academy of Sciences and Humanities, 1997.
Avigad, Nahman, Michael Heltzer and André Lemaire. *West Semitic Seals Eight-Sixth Centuries BCE*. Haifa: University of Haifa, 2000.
Barkay, Gavriel. "A Group of Stamped Handles from Judah." *ErIsr* 23 (1992): 113–28.
Brewer, Douglas J., and Emily Teeter, *Egypt and the Egyptians*. Cambridge: Cambridge University Press, 1999.
Brown, Francis, S. R. Driver, Charles A. Briggs, Edward Robinson, and Wilhelm Gesenius. *A Hebrew and English Lexicon of the Old Testament: With an Appendix Containing the Biblical Aramaic*. Oxford: Clarendon, 1952.
Brunner, Hellmut. "Das Besänftigungslied im Sinuhe B269–279." *ZÄS 80 (1955):* 7.
Budge, E. A. Wallis. *The Book of the Dead*. Translated by E. A. Wallis Budge. 2d ed. London: Routledge & Kegan Paul, 1960.
Currid, John D. *Ancient Egypt and the Old Testament*. Grand Rapids: Baker Books, 1997.
D'Agostino, Franco. *Testi Amministrativi di Ebla*. Rome: University of Rome, 1996.
Dahood, Mitchell J. *Psalms 1–50*. Anchor Bible 16. New York: Doubleday, 1966.
———. Review of Y. Yadin et al., eds., *Hazor II*. *Biblica* 42 (1961): 475.
Deutsch, Robert. *Biblical Period Hebrew Bullae*. Tel Aviv: Archaeological Center Publications, 2003.
Deutsch, Robert, and Michael Heltzer. *Windows to the Past*. Tel Aviv: Archaeological Center Publication, 1997.
Deutsch, Robert, and André Lemaire. *Biblical Period Personal Seals*. Tel Aviv: Archaeological Center Publications, 2000.
Diringer, David. *Le iscarizioni antico-ebraiche palestinesi*. Florence: le Monnier, 1934.
Dobbs-Alsopp, F. W. et al., eds. *Hebrew Inscriptions*. New Haven: Yale University Press, 2005.

Faulkner, Raymond O. *A Concise Dictionary of Middle Egyptian*. Oxford: Griffith Institute, 1986.
Fowler, Jeaneane D. *Theophoric Personal Names in Ancient Hebrew*. JSOTSup 49. Sheffield: JSOT, 1988.
Gardiner, Alan H. *Egyptian Grammar*. 3rd rev. ed. London: Oxford University Press, 1973.
———. *Late Egyptian Miscellanies*. Brussells: Reine Elisabeth, 1937.
Garfinkel, Yossi. "A Hierarchic Pattern in the Private Seal-Impression on the "*lmlk*" Jar Handles." *ErIsr* 18 (1985): 108–15 (Hebrew).
Gibson, J. C. I. *Textbook of Syrian Semitic Inscriptions: Hebrew and Moabite*. Oxford: Clarendon, 1971.
Gesenius' Hebrew Grammar. Edited by E. Kautzsch. Translated by A. E. Cowley. 2d. ed. Oxford, 1910.
Gordon, Cyrus H. *Ugaritic Textbook*. Rev. repr. AnOr 38. Rome: Pontifical Biblical Institute, 1998.
Grenfell, Alice. "Amuletic Scarabs for the Deceased." *Recueil de travaux relatifs à la philology et á l'archéologie égyptiennes et assyriennes* 30 (1908): 105–20.
Gröndahl, Frauke. *Die Personennamen der Texte aus Ugarit*. Rome: Pontifical Biblical Institute, 1967.
Hawkins, J. D. "Cilicia, the Amuq, and Aleppo: New Light in a Dark Age." *NEA* 72 (December 2009): 64–73.
Hess, Richard S. *Amarna Personal Names*. Winona Lake, Ind.: Eisenbraun, 1993.
Hoch, James E. *Semitic Words in Egyptian Texts of the new Kingdom and Third Intermediate Period*. Princeton: Princeton University Press, 1994.
Horn, Siegfried H. "An Uninscribed Seal from Jordan," *BASOR* 189 (1968): 41–43.
Junker, Hermann. *Der Auszug der Hathor-Tefnut aus Nubien*. Berlin: Verlag der Königlichen Akademie der Wissenschaften, in Commission bei Georg Reimer, 1911. Appendix.
Kitchen, Kenneth A. *The Third Intermediate Period in Egypt 1000–650 BC*. Warminster: Aris & Phillips, 1973.
Koehler, L., W. Baumgartner, and J. J. Stamm, *The Hebrew and Aramaic Lexicon of the Old Testament*. Translated and edited under the supervision of M. E. J. Richardson. 4 vols. Leiden, 1994–1999.
Kutscher, Eduard Yechezkel. *Hebrew and Aramaic Studies*. Jerusalem: Magnes, 1977 (Hebrew).
Lansing, Ambrose. "A Faience Broad Collar of the Eighteenth Dynasty." *The Metropolitan Museum of Art Bulletin* 35 (1940): 65–68.
Lehmann, Manfred R. "Abraham's Purchase of Machpelah and Hittite Law." *BASOR* 129 (1953): 15–18.
Lesko, Leonard H. ed. *A Dictionary of Late Egyptian*. 2 vols. Fall River, Mass.: Fall River Modern Printing, 2002.
Mercer, Samuel A. B. *The Tell El-Amarna Tablets*. 2 vols. Toronto: Macmillan, 1939.
Moran, William L. *The Amarna Letters*. Baltimore: John Hopkins University, 1992.
Morenz, Siegfried. *Egyptian Religion*. Translated by Ann E. Keep. Ithaca: Cornell University Press, 1990.
Muchiki, Yoshiyuki. *Egyptian Proper Names and Loanwords in North West Semitic*. SBLDS 173. Atlanta: SBL, 1999.

Mykytiuk, Lawrence J. *Identifying Biblical Persons in Northwest Semitic Inscriptions of 1200–539 B.C.E.* AcBib 12. Atlanta: SBL, 2004.

Olmo Lete, Gregorio del, and Joaquín Sanmartín. *A Dictionary of the Ugaritic Language in the Alphabetic Tradition.* Translated by Wilfred G. E. Watson. Leiden: Brill, 2003.

Porten, Bezalel. "'Domla'el' and Related Names." *IEJ* 21.4 (1971): 47–49

Pritchard, James B. *Hebrew Inscriptions and Stamps from Gibeon.* Philadelphia: University Museum of Pennsylvania, 1959.

Quirke, Stephen, and Jeffrey Spenser, eds. *The British Museum Book of Ancient Egypt.* New York: Thames & Hudson, 1992.

Ranke, Hermann. *Die ägyptischen Personennamen.* 3 vols. Glückstadt: Augustin, 1935.

Rin, Svi, and Shifra Rin. *Acts of the Gods.* Philadelphia: Inbal, 1996 (Hebrew).

Sarna, Nahum M. *Genesis.* Philadelphia: JPS, 1989.

Segert, Stanislav. *A Basic Grammar of the Ugaritic Language.* Berkeley and Los Angeles: University of California Press, 1984.

Sethe, Kurt. *Das ägyptische Verbum im altägyptischen, neuägyptischen, und koptischen.* 3 vols. Leipzig: Hinrichs, 1899–1902.

Török, László. *The Royal Crowns of Kush.* Oxford: B.A.R., 1987.

Tropper, Josef. *Kleines Wörterbuch des ugaritischen.* Weisbaden: Harrassowitz, 2008.

Tushingham, A. D. "A Royal Israelite Seal? and the Royal Jar Handle Stamps, part one," *BASOR* 200 (1970): 71–78; part two, *BASOR* 201 (1971): 23–35.

Wenig, Steffen. *Africa in Antiquity: The Art of Nubia and Sudan.* Brooklyn: The Brooklyn Museum, 1978.

Westendorf, Wolfhart. *Koptisches Handwörterbuch.* Heidelberg: Winter, 1965.

Wiedemann, Alfred. *Religion of the Ancient Egyptians.* London: H. Greval, 1897.

Zaidel, Mosheh. *Ḥikre Lashon.* Jerusalem: Mosad Harav Kook, 1986 (Hebrew).

Chapter Six
Who Was *Bat Pharaoh*,
the Daughter of Pharaoh?

*Claire Gottlieb**

When we study the inscriptions and iconography on ancient seals and related artifacts we are usually dealing with names of people with few or no clues as to their identity or place in history. It is only through careful and painstaking investigation and comparison with other objects that we can sometimes gain some insight as to who these people might have been and what their roles in their respective societies were. In the study of biblical literature we sometimes have the opposite problem. Some of the stories present us with a saga that can take place over many years but the names of some or all of the principal characters are never revealed.

Numbers 12:8 records that God speaks to Moses פה אל-פה, mouth to mouth, ולא בחידת, and not in riddles. The rest of us are not so fortunate. Therefore, we will have to heed the advice of Prov 1:6 and learn to understand דברי חכמים וחידתם, the words of the wise and their riddles. The problem is that often when we read the Bible we do not recognize a riddle and therefore produce a mistranslation and consequently a wrong interpretation of the verse in question. This is the dilemma in the Exodus story beginning with Exod 2 and in the Solomon story beginning with 1 Kgs 3. Biblical exegetes from Josephus to Philo, to modern-day scholars have wrestled with the question of who Bat Pharaoh (the daughter of Pharaoh) was.

One Bible scholar has decided that it makes no sense to raise questions about her identity or the location of the event because the writer is not interested in historical details.[1] Others are skeptical of any biblical reference to a connection

---

*A version of this paper was first presented at the SBL International Meeting, Cambridge, England, July 2003. I would like to thank Prof. Meir Lubetski for his invaluable support, insight and suggestions for references that enhanced the clarity of the paper.

between the United Monarchy and the Bible. They maintain that the stories are merely "plausible" history and themes for midrash.[2] This appears to be a somewhat defeatist position. If we look at the term from another perspective, the one in which the story takes place, and forget our modern preconceived notions, we can come up with a new solution to this old problem.

In the chapters of the books of the Bible where we find the term Bat Pharaoh, her Hebrew name appears in only one instance. Furthermore, in most cases none of the other characters in the story are identified, not even Pharaoh himself. In order to discover the identity of the Bat Pharaoh being referred to we must first analyze the Egyptian term Pharaoh.

Chapter 1 of Exodus does not reveal the name of the ruler of Egypt. He is called מלך מצרים, the king of Egypt (Exod 1:8, 15, 17, and 18). The term Pharaoh by itself is used three times in the chapter (Exod 1:11, 19, and 22). The Egyptian term *pr-ʿ3* means "great house" and refers to the palace or home of the king.[3] According to Gardiner it is not until the fourteenth century B.C.E. that the word actually refers to the king. This occurs at the beginning of the New Kingdom period (Eighteenth Dynasty), during the reign of Tuthmosis III (1504–1450) and any use of the term as meaning "king" before this period should be regarded as an anachronism.[4] Later, one of the Amarna letters sent to Amenophis IV (Akhenaten, 1372–1355), addresses the king as *pr-ʿ3 ʿnḫ wḏ3 snb nb*, Pharaoh, life, prosperity, health, the master.

The final development of the usage of the word occurs when a proper name is added to the title. The earliest Egyptian example of this is not found until the Twenty-Second (Libyan) Dynasty, referring to one of the Shoshenks (945–924?).[5] However the Shoshenk (Shishak) of the Bible is not given the title Pharaoh in the

---

1. See, e.g., in Cornelis Houtman, *Exodus: Vol. 1* (Kampen: KOK, 1993), 280.
2. John D. Currid, *Ancient Egypt and the Old Testament* (Grand Rapids: Baker Books, 1997), 161.
3. Yoshiyuki Muchiki, *Egyptian Proper Names and Loanwords in North West Semitic* (Atlanta: Society of Biblical Literature, 1999), 253.
4. Sir Alan Gardiner, *Egypt of the Pharaohs* (New York: Oxford University Press, 1966), 52. See also A. S. Yahuda, *The Language of the Pentateuch in Its Relation to Egyptian* (London: Oxford University Press, 1933), 44–50. For another dating see Thomas O. Lambdin, "Egyptian Loan Words in the Old Testament," *JAOS* 73 (1953): 153.
5. Sir Alan Gardiner, *Egyptian Grammar* (Oxford: Griffith Institute, 1976), 75. For a hieroglyphic text naming Sheshonq (Shishak) king and pharaoh see Robert K. Ritner, *The Libyan Dynasty* (WAW 21; Atlanta: Society of Biblical Literature, 2009), 174–75 See also p. 493 for Dakhleh Stela, line 2, naming Pharaoh Piye (*Pr-ʿ3 Py*). For kings of the Twenty-Second Dynasty see Gardiner, *Egypt of the Pharaohs*, 448.

Bible. He is שישק מלך-מצרים, Shishak, king of Egypt.⁶ Similarly the title of King So of 2 Kgs 17:4 is סוא מלך-מצרים, So, king of Egypt.⁷

Similarly, the Twenty-Fifth Dynasty king mentioned in the Bible is not given the prefix title Pharaoh. Tirhaka (Taharqa) (690–664) king of Ethiopia is תרהקה מלך-כוש, Tirhaka, king of Kush (Nubia).⁸ The Bible does not pick up on the usage of the complete title until the Egyptian Twenty-Sixth Dynasty. In 2 Kgs 23 we have the title Pharaoh prefaced to the name: פרעה נכה מלך-מצרים, Pharaoh Necho, king of Egypt (609–594).⁹ Jeremiah 44:30 speaks of פרעה חפרע מלך-מצרים, Pharaoh Hophra, (Apries) king of Egypt (also Twenty-Sixth Dynasty, 589–570).

We will now examine some portions of the Bible where the appellative Bat Pharaoh is found and see how the development of the term fits into the historical time frame and clarifies the narratives. We read in 1 Kgs 3:1: ויתחתן שלמה את-פרעה מלך מצרים ויקח את-בת-פרעה ויביאה אל-עיר דוד, "Solomon made a marriage alliance with Pharaoh, king of Egypt,¹⁰ and he took Bat Pharaoh and he brought her to the city of David." The only person named in this verse is Solomon. Again we have no clue as to the identity of Pharaoh or Bat Pharaoh. It also does not say that Solomon married Bat Pharaoh. The usual marriage terms are not used. He did not take her to himself as a wife (לאשה), and he did not know (ידע) her. He did not go to her (בא אל).¹¹ In fact if the verse had been omitted it would not change the context of the narrative in any way since it is not until chapter 7 verse 8 that we have another mention of Bat Pharaoh. This text reads: ובית יעשה לבת-פרעה אשר לקח שלמה "Solomon built a house for Bat Pharaoh who he had taken." Although it is possible to assume from the context that he did marry her, the Hebrew phrase again is ambiguous as it does not utilize the usual words for marriage and gives no clue as to who she was. The thread continues in chapter

---

6. 1 Kgs 11:40; 14:25; 2 Chr 12:2, 5, 9. See also P. J. Achtemeier, ed., *Harpers Bible Dictionary* (San Francisco: Harper & Row, 1985), 945.

7. Possibly Shabako, 716–701. Kitchen says he is an earlier king, Osorkon IV, Twenty-Second Dynasty. K. Kitchen, *On the Reliability of the Old Testament* (Grand Rapids: Eerdmans, 2003), 15–16, 24. For discussion see Currid, *Ancient Egypt and the Old Testament*, 238 n. 58. See also Achtemeier, *Harpers Bible Dictionary*, 961.

8. 2 Kgs 19:9; Isa 37:9. Egyptian and Assyrian documents testify that he was an historical king although it is not certain if he was involved in one or two campaigns against the Assyrians in Egypt at this time. See George Arthur Buttrick, ed., *The Interpreters Dictionary of the Bible*, vol. 4 (Nashville: Abingdon, 1962), 652. See also *ABD* 6:572.

9. 2 Kgs 23:29, 33–35; 2 Chr 35:20, 22; 36:4.

10. Translation "marriage alliance" attested in Simon J. DeVries, *1 Kings* (Waco, Tex.: Word, 1985), 45, 50. See also Jerome T. Walsh, *1 Kings* (Minnesota: Liturgical, 1996), 70.

11. See BDB, 394, col. A, note 3; 543, col. A, note 4e. Also *HALOT*, 532 n. 7. See 1 Kgs 16:31 for Hebrew for "take a wife." For "go to" as to marry see 2 Sam 17:25 and A. A. Anderson, *2 Samuel* (Dallas: Word, 1989), 217, 219 n. 25.c.

9 verse 24 as Bat Pharaoh comes up from the city of David to the house that Solomon built for her.

Verse 9:16 is more specific. It says that Pharaoh captured and destroyed the city of Gezer and gave it as שלחים, a portion or dowry, to his daughter, Solomon's wife. This verse appears to be a parenthetical note explaining how Gezer became part of Solomon's realm.[12] A dowry is not usually given so long after the supposed marriage and Solomon had to rebuild the burned city himself. The story does not inform us as to the identity of the Pharaoh or tell us if the woman is the same person spoken of in the aforementioned verses. In fact the verses are disconnected and add nothing to the understanding of the story. The narrator tells us that Solomon had many foreign wives and concubines and a Bat Pharaoh, who could be one of the many, is mentioned several times.[13] It is known that kings of Egypt cemented diplomatic alliances by taking foreign princesses as wives and also by having their sons marry the daughters of foreign rulers. However, there is no Egyptian evidence attesting to the fact that a king of Egypt sent any of his daughters to be the wife of a foreign ruler.[14] So we must ask ourselves if a king of Egypt would have given one of his daughters to be the wife of a non-Egyptian ruler.

Some biblical evidence can be adduced from 1 Kgs 11:14–20 where we read of Hadad the Edomite, who fled to Egypt after Edom was defeated by David's forces under Joab. The Egyptian king is unnamed and is referred to as Pharaoh, king of Egypt. As a token of his esteem for Hadad, the king of Egypt gives him his wife's sister in marriage. The names of the king's wife and her sister are not revealed. The title of the king's wife is תחפנים, Tahpanes, which in Egyptian is $t3$-nt-$ḥt$-$p3$-nsw, "she who belongs to the house of the king"[15] or $t3$-$ḥ(mt)$ $p3$-nsw, "the wife of the king."[16] The Bible clarifies this by saying that she is הגבירה, the *Gevirah*, signifying that she is the principal lady of the country. This would be equivalent to our First Lady. So although the Egyptian king holds Hadad in high esteem, giving him sustenance, a house, and land, he does not give him one of his daughters. Even though the woman would not be sent out of Egypt he gives Hadad his wife's sister as a wife.

---

12. Mordechai Cogan, *1 Kings* (New York: Doubleday, 2001), 301.

13. See 1 Kgs 11:1–3.

14. Donald B. Redford, *Egypt, Canaan and Israel in Ancient Times* (Princeton: Princeton University Press, 1992), 165–69. William L. Moran, *The Amarna Letters* (Baltimore: Johns Hopkins University Press, 1992), xxv; EA 3, 11, 13 and others. See also Gay Robins, *Women in Ancient Egypt* (Cambridge: Harvard University Press, 1993), 30–33. For other opinions see Currid, *Ancient Egypt and the Old Testament*, 162–65.

15. Muchiki, *Egyptian Proper Names*, 228.

16. Cogan, *1 Kings*, 332. Note that אשה denotes "wife" in reference to both women.

Evidence is also found in Amarna Letter 4, written in Babylonian, to Amenophis III quoting Amenophis as stating indignantly that "from time immemorial no daughter of the king of Egypt is given to anyone." If the marriage of the daughter of an Egyptian king to a foreign monarch is such an unheard of event why does the Bible gloss over it as though it were an ordinary occurrence?[17] Why are the woman and the Pharaoh both unnamed?

A later mention of a Bat Pharaoh appears in the genealogy lists in Chronicles. First Chronicles 4:18 mentions בתיה בת-פרעה אשר לקח מרד, Bithiah, *bat pharaoh* who Mered took.[18] There is no evidence that a marriage occurred. However it is interesting to note that the same terminology (לקח) as in 1 Kgs 3:1 is used. It does not say Mered took her in marriage or as a wife. As with Solomon we do not know if he took her into his household as a wife, a concubine or to fill some important domestic position.

Before we can discuss the heroine who is probably the most famous and intriguing of the Bat Pharaohs of the Bible we must look at the Egyptian terms for Daughter of the Pharaoh or Daughter of the King. In Hebrew Daughter of the King is בת(ה)מלך.[19] The Egyptian correlation to this is $s3t\ nsw$ (daughter of the king).[20] Daughter or son of the great house (pr-$'3$) is not attested in Egyptian.

This takes us back to Exod 2:1–9, another portion in which no one is named. It is the tale of the birth of the national hero *par excellence* of Israel, the one who is larger than life. This birth requires special recognition. Therefore, here we have a typical "Birth of a Hero" story. In the words of my late beloved teacher and dear friend, Cyrus Gordon, the details of the story make it "worthy of saga." We are informed in verse 5 that a תבה, an ark, carrying a baby is found by בת-פרעה, usually translated as the daughter of Pharaoh.[21] Who is this בת-פרעה? If she is the daughter of Pharaoh why isn't she named? Why would the daughter of Pharaoh defy her father, save the baby, give him to a Hebrew woman to be nursed, and then take him as her own son? If she were the daughter of Pharaoh it is probable that she could have brought him into $ḥrd\ n\ k3p$, the Royal Nursery, and raised

---

17. For a recent interpretation of the marriage see Jerome T. Walsh, *1 Kings*, 69–72. For an earlier twentieth century interpretation see James A. Montgomery, *A Critical and Exegetical Commentary on the Books of Kings* (Edinburgh: T&T Clark, 1951), 102–3.

18. For discussion of this verse see R. C. Steiner, "Bitte-Ya, daughter of Pharaoh (1 Chr. 4:18, and Bint(i)-'Anat, daughter of Ramesses II", *Biblica* 79 (1999): 394–408.

19. See 2 Kgs 9:34.

20. Kurt Sethe, *Urkunden der 18. Dynastie* (Leipzig: Hinrichs, 1907), 669; Raymond O. Faulkner, *A Concise Dictionary of Middle Egyptian* (Oxford: Griffith Institute, 1976), 207; L. H. Lesko, *A Dictionary of Late Egyptian*, Vol. 3 (Providence: Scribe, 1987), 4.

21. The Egyptian word for 'ark' is $ḏb(3.t)$, cognate to the Hebrew word *tevah*. The Hebrew word is first found in the flood story, Gen 6:14–19; 18. Muchiki, *Egyptian Proper Names*, 258.

him in the royal household. There is evidence that during the Eighteenth Dynasty many foreign princes were reared and schooled in the Egyptian court.[22] Surely an Egyptian princess, not wanting her father to know that she had rescued and adopted a Hebrew child, would have had him brought up to believe that he was either an Egyptian or a member of some foreign household other than that of the Hebrews. Therefore how did the child grow up knowing that he was a Hebrew? The clue to the answer can be found in Gen 13, which depicts the household of Abraham, the Hebrew who was very rich in cattle, silver and gold; and in Gen 14 where we learn that he is a warrior chieftain who is able to muster 318 trained men who were officially recognized as ילידי ביתו, born in his household, to rescue Lot.[23] These numbers indicate possession of a huge household. In antiquity it was not unusual for a noble person to take a well-born foreigner into his household, treat him well and even give him a position of the highest responsibility.[24] Eliezer has the title בן-בית, Ben Bayit, in Gen 15:3. Abraham informs God that "Eliezer, בן-ביתי, son of my house, will inherit my estate" (Gen 15:3). This indicates that בן-בית is the legal designation given to one who holds an official high position in a noble household and is also regarded as a family member. I propose that in a Hebrew household Bat Pharaoh, referring to a woman from Egypt, is the female equivalent of Ben Bayit. She is the woman in charge of the household or *pr ꜥ3*, great house. As such she would have many women serving under her. In the context of the Exodus story it is probable that she is a Hebrew woman serving in an important position of trust in the Egyptian king's household. This makes the story plausible and accounts for her ensuing actions, and for Moses knowing that he was a Hebrew.

It also explains who the Bat Pharaoh sent to King Solomon by the Egyptian king was. She was a highly regarded woman, either taken into or born into the Egyptian king's household. As a token of his regard for King Solomon, the Egyptian king sent her to him to assume a high position in his household, similar to the position of Eliezer in Abraham's household. Her Hebrew title is Bat Pharaoh since she came from the "great house" of the Egyptian king. This clarifies the

---

22. James K. Hoffmeier, *Israel in Egypt* (New York: Oxford University Press, 1996), 224. See also A. Bernard Knapp, *The History and Culture of Ancient Western Asia and Egypt* (Chicago: Dorsey, 1988), 172.

23. For ילידי ביתו see Gen 14:14; 17:23, 27. See also Lev 22:11 for the special privilege given to one born into the household of the priest.

24. See the Joseph saga, Gen 39–41. Also as in the Story of Sinuhe. See Miriam Lichtheim, *Ancient Egyptian Literature*. Vol. 1, *The Old and Middle Kingdom* (Berkeley and Los Angeles: University of California Press, 1975), 222–35.

usage of the Hebrew word לקח, "took," in place of the usual Hebrew marriage terms used when these women entered a Hebrew household.

Some of the Egyptian equivalents for these positions of trust are *šmsw pr-ʿ₃*, "servant of the palace,"[25] *ḥry - pr n pr-ʿ₃* "majordomo of the palace" or the feminine counterpart *ḥry.t -pr*, "mistress or woman in charge of the house."[26] We also have the office of *ḥnwt nt ḥmwt nsw*, "mistress of the king's women."[27] Another office is *ḥmt-nsw*, "king's maidservant."[28] Note that when he is being referred to, the king is called *nsw* and not pharaoh. The persons with these positions are reported to have had significant roles in the Egyptian community and some became quite affluent.[29] In the Middle Kingdom tomb scenes they appear to be regarded as members of the family as they are frequently represented with the tomb owner's sons and daughters.[30]

The references to *bat pharaoh* in the Bible are drawn together by the fact that except for the verse in 1 Chr 4:18, we do not know the name of *bat pharaoh* or of most of the protagonists. Furthermore, some of the verses merely furnish us with extraneous information. If they were omitted from the texts the outcome of the events would not really be changed. We might loose some of the action that makes stories interesting or "worthy of saga." However, a hero for the deliverance of the Israelites from Egypt would still arise and Solomon would still build his edifices and his empire. What is important is that we can now discern from these texts that there is an alternate interpretation for the term *bat pharaoh*. In both Israel and Egypt certain persons of trust who had either been born into or taken into the household of a royal or aristocratic family were considered to be members of that household. In Hebrew this would be the *ben bayit* or the corresponding equivalent in the case of an Egyptian woman, the *bat pharaoh*. The introductory term *ben* or *bat* indicates the position or title and gender of the person being referred to.

There is further evidence that *ben* can be a title in 1 Kgs 4:7–13. The first six prefects who were governors over Israel and responsible for providing the king

---

25. Stephen Quirke, *Titles and Bureaux of Egypt 1850–1700 BC* (London: Golden House, 2004), 47.

26. Ibid. William A. Ward, *Index of Egyptian Administrative and Religious Titles of the Middle Kingdom* (Beirut: American University, 1982), 117–18. See also Barbara Watterson, *Women in Ancient Egypt* (Phoenix Mill: Sutton, 1998), 37.

27. *Urk*. IV, 603, 9. William C. Hayes, *A Papyrus of the Late Middle Kingdom in the Brooklyn Museum* (New York: John B. Watkins Co., 1972), 103.

28. Hayes, *A Papyrus of the Late Middle Kingdom*, 91.

29. Ibid., 103–4.

30. Ibid., 83–84, 121, 132.

and his household with food for one month have *Ben* preceding their names. These men may have had a higher rank than the following six prefects.[31]

There are many instances in the Bible where the term *bat* is used to personify a city or other location such as in Jer 46:11 and 24 where we have *bat mitsrayim* and Isa 1:8 where we have *bat tsiyyon*. In these cases *bat* does not mean daughter but may be a title referring to inhabitants in general or women belonging to a particular group.[32]

The above illustrations indicate that in ancient languages just as in modern languages many words can have more than one meaning. The words son and daughter can have several interpretations that are not necessarily indications of a familial relationship. Before we give what may appear to be a literal translation to any passage of the Bible the evidence from the era the portion in question is portraying must be taken into consideration. In addition to explaining the meaning of the term *bat pharaoh* the evidence presented illustrates that we can discern from the dating of the development of the use of the word *pr-'ȝ*, pharaoh, that whether or not the Exodus or the Solomon stories are historically accurate, the literary style and the use of terminology place them in a known historical time frame.

Bibliography

Achtemeier, P. J. ed. *Harpers Bible Dictionary*. San Francisco: Harper & Row, 1985.
Anderson, Arnold. A. *2 Samuel*. Dallas: Word, 1989.
Buttrick, George Arthur, ed. *The Interpreters Dictionary of the Bible*, vol. 4. Nashville: Abingdon, 1962.
Cogan, Mordechai. *1 Kings*. New York: Doubleday, 2001.
Currid, John D. *Ancient Egypt and the Old Testament*. Grand Rapids: Baker Books, 1997.
DeVries, Simon J. *1 Kings*. Waco, Tex.: Word, 1985.
Faulkner, Raymond O. *A Concise Dictionary of Middle Egyptian*. Oxford: Griffith Institute, 1976.
Gardiner, Sir Alan. *Egyptian Grammar*. Oxford: Griffith Institute, 1976.
———. *Egypt of the Pharaohs*. New York: Oxford University Press, 1966.
Hayes, William C. *A Papyrus of the Late Middle Kingdom in the Brooklyn Museum*. New York: John B. Watkins Co., 1972.
Hoffmeier, James K. *Israel in Egypt*. New York, Oxford University Press, 1996.
Houtman, Cornelis. *Exodus*. Vol. 1. Kampen: KOK, 1993.
Kitchen, Kenneth. *On the Reliability of the Old Testament*. Grand Rapids: Eerdmans, 2003.

---

31. *TDOT* 2:152–53; *HALOT*, 138.
32. *TDOT* 2:334–36; *HALOT*, 166.

Knapp, A. Bernard. *The History and Culture of Ancient Western Asia and Egypt*. Chicago: Dorsey, 1988.
Lambdin, Thomas O. "Egyptian Loan Words in the Old Testament." *JAOS* 73 (1953): 145–55.
Lesko, Leonard H. *A Dictionary of Late Egyptian*, vol. 3. Providence: Scribe, 1987.
Lichtheim, Miriam. *Ancient Egyptian Literature*. Vol. 1, *The Old and Middle Kingdom*. Berkeley and California: University of California Press, 1975.
Montgomery, James A. *A Critical and Exegetical Commentary on the Books of Kings*. Edinburgh: T&T Clark, 1951.
Moran, William L. *The Amarna Letters*. Baltimore: Johns Hopkins University Press, 1992.
Muchiki, Yoshiyuki. *Egyptian Proper Names and Loanwords in North-West Semitic*. Atlanta: Society of Biblical Literature, 1999.
Quirke, Stephen. *Titles and Bureaux of Egypt 1850–1700 BC*. London: Golden House, 2004.
Redford, Donald B. *Egypt, Canaan and Israel in Ancient Times*. Princeton: Princeton University Press, 1992.
Ritner, Robert K. *The Libyan Dynasty*. WAW 21. Atlanta: Society of Biblical Literature, 2009.
Robins, Gay. *Women in Ancient Egypt*. Cambridge: Harvard University Press, 1993.
Sethe, Kurt. *Urkunden der 18. Dynastie*. Leipzig: Hinrichs, 1907.
Steiner, R. C. "Bitte-Ya, daughter of Pharaoh (1 Chr. 4:18, and Bint(i)-'Anat, daughter of Ramesses II." *Biblica* 79 (1999): 394–408.
Walsh, Jerome T. *1 Kings*. Minnesota: Liturgical, 1996.
Ward, William A. *Index of Egyptian Administrative and Religious Titles of the Middle Kingdom*. Beirut: American University, 1982.
Watterson, Barbara. *Women in Ancient Egypt*. Phoenix Mill: Sutton, 1998.
Yahuda, A. S. *The Language of the Pentateuch in Its Relation to Egyptian*. London: Oxford University Press, 1933.

Chapter Seven
New Perspectives on the Trade between Judah and South Arabia

André Lemaire

Ancient Near Eastern maps show that South Arabia is approximately 2000 kilometers from the kingdom of Judah. The history of the ancient South Arabian civilization during the first millennium B.C.E. is obscure and its chronology uncertain. However the Hebrew Bible mentions Sheba twenty-four times,[1] Hadramawt two times (Gen 10:26; 1 Chr 1:20) and the Minaeans approximately four times (Esd 2:40; Neh 7:52; 1 Chr 4:41; 2 Chr 26:7). The Table of Nations in Gen 10, illustrates that South Arabia was part of the cultural horizon of the Judaeans around 600 B.C.E.[2]

According to the first book of Kings, chapter 10, the international trade between Judah and Sheba probably started near the end of Solomon's reign. The historical interpretation of the tale of the visit of the Queen of Sheba (1 Kgs 1-10) has been and is still a topic for much discussion. However, following Mario Liverani,[3] I have tried to show that the beginning of the international trade with Sheba in the second half of the tenth century B.C.E. is not unlikely and that the earliest level of this story could well go back to the end of the tenth century B.C.E.[4] I do not intend to discuss this historical problem again or the conditions of the

---

1. Gen 10:7, 28; 25:3; 1 Kgs 10:1, 4, 10, 13; Isa 60:6; Jer 6:20; Joel 4:8; Ezek 27:22, 23; 38:13; Ps 72:10, 15; Job 1:15; 6:19; 1 Chr 1:9, 22, 32; 2 Chr 9:1, 3, 9, 12.

2. Edward Lipiński, "Les Japhétites selon Gen 10,2-4 et 1 Chr 1,5-7," *ZAH* 3 (1990): 40-53, esp. 53 : "premier quart du VIe siècle av. J.-C."

3. Mario Liverani, "Early Caravan Trade between South-Arabia and Mesopotamia," *Yemen* 1 (1992): 111-15.

4. See André Lemaire, "La reine de Saba à Jérusalem: la tradition ancienne reconsidérée," in *Kein Land für sich allein. Studien zum Kulturkontakt in Kanaan, Israel/Palästina und Ebirnâri für Manfred Weippert* (ed. Ulrich Hübner and Ernst Axel Knauf; OBO 186; Fribourg:

emergence of the incense road at the end of the second millennium B.C.E.,[5] but will try to explain further the trade between Judah and Sheba taking into account an important new Sabaean inscription.

"The Towns of Judah" in a New Sabaean Inscription

This new inscription, recently published by François Bron and I,[6] appeared on the market of antiquities early in 2008. It is unprovenanced but its content indicates that it was probably found in the ancient city of Nashq, today Al-Bayḍâʾ. It is broken and incomplete having only the remains of 25 lines. It was dedicated by "Ṣabaḥḥumû, son of ʿAmmshafaq, (from the clan) of Rashwân, (inhabiting) Nashq" (lines 1–2). This man was a messenger of "Yadaʿil Bayin, son of Ythaʿʾamar, king of Sheba" (lines 17–18). He fought with the army of Sheba against the army of Maʿin as far as Ḥaḍramawt (lines 5–9) and was also the leader of an important trade expedition mentioned in lines 13–16 (fig. 1):

13 … when he carried on international trade and led a caravan to Dedan, [Gaz]a
14. and the towns of Judah ('HGR YHD), and when he was safe and sound
15. as sent from Gaza to Kition (KTY) during the war (ḌR)
16. of Chaldea (KŠDM) and Ionia (YWN)…

This is the first mention of "the towns of Judah" in a Sabaean and more generally South Arabian inscription, as well as the first mention of Kition in this type of inscription. To understand the significance of this new discovery, it is necessary to try to date this inscription as precisely as possible and then to put it in its proper Judean context.

Univesitätsverlag; Göttingen: Vandenhoeck & Ruprecht, 2002), 43–55 (*pace* Ernst Axel Knauf, ibid., 2–3).

5. See Israel Finkelstein, "Arabian Trade and Socio-Political Conditions in the Negev in the Twelfth-Eleventh Centuries B.C.E.," *JNES* 47 (1988): 241–52; idem, *Living on the Fringe: The Archaeology and History of the Negev, Sinai and Neighbouring Regions in the Bronze and Iron Age* (Monographs in Mediterranean Archaeology 6; Sheffield: Sheffield Academic, 1995), 120–26; Michael Jasmin, "Les conditions d'émergence de la route de l'encens à la fin du IIe millénaire avant notre ère," *Syria* 82 (2005): 49–62.

6. "Nouvelle inscription sabéenne et le commerce en Transeuphratène," *Transeuphratène* 38 (2009): 11–29.

Fig. 1. "The Towns of Judah" in a New Sabaean Inscription.

Dating

As noted above, the chronology of South Arabia in the first millennium B.C.E. is still very uncertain. The Sabean king mentioned in this inscription, "Yada'il Bayin, son of Yitha''amar," is mentioned in several inscriptions commemorating his building of the city wall in Nashq (*CIH* 634). However Jacqueline Pirenne dated him to about 350 B.C.E.[7] and Hermann von Wissmann himself proposed

---

7. Jacqueline Pirenne, *Paléographie des inscriptions sud-arabes. Contribution à la chronologie et à l'histoire de l'Arabie du Sud antique I. Des origines jusqu'à l'époque himyarite* (Brussel: Paleis der Academiën, 1956), 164.

two different dates: the first, in about 590,[8] and the second, two centuries later, in about 394.[9]

In such a context, we may try to date the inscription from the mention of "the war of Chaldea and Ionia." This war took place during the epoch of the Chaldean Empire (ca. 610–539), but it is difficult to determine its exact date during this period since our documentation does not seem to mention explicitly a war between Chaldea and Ionia. However since the time of the Neo-Assyrian Empire, especially since Sargon II, a confrontation between a Near Eastern empire and Ionia is well attested in Cilicia.[10] In 1939, Ernst F. Weidner suggested that the Ionians mentioned in Babylonian tablets were probably inhabitants of Cilicia: "Die Leute von Jam(w)an werden schon damals, wie später unter Dareios I., die Bewohner von Kilikien, Teilen von Zypern und einzelnen Distrikten des syrischen Festland gewesen sein."[11] This Cilician interpretation seems to be confirmed by the fact that the personal names of these "Ionians" are not Greek and at least one of them, "Kunzumpiya," is clearly Luwian.[12] One may also note that this Cilician

---

8. Hermann von Wissmann, "Die Geschichte des Sabäerreichs und der Feldzug des Aelius Gallus," in *ANRW* II,9.1 (ed. Hildegard Temporini; Berlin: de Gruyter, 1976), 308–544, esp. 351–54.

9. Hermann von Wissmann, *Die Geschichte von Saba' II. Das Grossreich der Sabäer bis zu seinem Ende im frühen 4. Jh. v. Chr.* (SAWW 402. Band; Wien; Verlag der österreichischen Akademie der Wissenschaften; 1982), 329–39.

10. See Josette Elayi, "Sargon II et les Ioniens," *Oriens Antiquus* 18 (1979): 59–75; Anna Margherita Jasink, "I Greci in Cilicia nel periodo neo-assiro," *Mesopotamia* 24 (1989): 117–28; Andreas Fuchs, *Die Inschriften Sargons II. aus Khorsabad* (Göttingen: Cuvillier, 1994), 109, 290, 304, 440; W. Mayer, "Zypern und Ägäis aus der Sicht der Staaten Vorderasiens in der 1. Hälfte des 1. Jahrtausends," *UF* 28 (1996): 463–84, esp. 470–73; Stephanie Dalley, "Sennacherib and Tarsus," *Anatolian Studies* 49 (1999): 73–80; Giovanni B. Lanfranchi, "The Ideological and Political Impact of the Assyrian Imperial Expansion on the Greek World in the 8th and 7th Centuries BC," in *The Heirs of Assyria* (ed. Sanna Aro and R. M. Whiting; Melammu Symposia I; Helsinki: The Neo-Assyrian Text Corpus Project, 2000), 7–34, esp. 13–31. This does not mean that Ionia = Cilicia and Robert Rollinger, "Überlegungen zur Frage der Lokalisation von Jawan in neuassyrische Zeit," *State Archives of Assyria Bulletin* 16 (2007): 64–90, is right to emphasize this point even though he is probably wrong in locating Assyrian Tarsis in Spain (see *infra*, n. 13).

11. Ernst F. Weidner, "Jojachin, König von Juda, in babylonischen Keilschrifttexten," in *Mélanges syriens offerts à René Dussaud II* (BAH 30; Paris: Geuthner, 1939), 923–35, esp. 932.

12. Ibid., 933; Albrecht Goetze, "Cilicians," *JCS* 16 (1962): 48–58; J. A. Brinkman, "The Akkadian Words for 'Ionia' and 'Ionian,'" in *Daidalikon: Studies in Memory of Raymond V. Shoder* (ed. R. F. Sutton; Wauconda Ill., 1989), 53–71, esp. 59; Francis Joannès, "L'Asie mineure méridonale d'après la documentation cunéiforme d'époque néo-babylonienne," in *De Anatolia Antiqua I* (Bibliothèque de l'Institut Français d'Études Anatoliennes d'Istanbul 32; Paris: Maisonneuve, 1990), 261–66, esp. 266. For the two Luwian elements, see P. H. J. Houwink ten Cate, *The Luwian Population Groups of Lycia and Cilicia Aspera during the Hellenistic Period*

interpretation fits into the "table of nations" in Gen 10:4: "Elisha (Cyprus), Tarshish (the country around Tarsus[13]), Kittim and Rodanim" were all considered as "sons of Iawan."

In this context, a war between Chaldea and Iawan—as mentioned in the Sabaean inscription—is very probably connected with a Neo-Babylonian campaign in Cilicia. Such a Neo-Babylonian campaign was not waged before the battle of Karkemish in 605 and not after the campaign and stay of Nabonidus in Arabia in 553/2–543.[14] A look at the fragmentary Neo-Babylonian chronicles seems to reveal two Neo-Babylonian campaigns in Cilicia while administrative texts[15] could reveal a third one.[16]

- The first Neo-Babylonian campaign in Cilicia, clearly mentioned in the fragments of the Neo-Babylonian Chronicles is that of Neriglissar, in his third year (557/6). It is presented as a reaction to an invasion of Ḫume (Cilician plain) by Appuashu, king of Pirindu (Cilicia Trachea).[17] Neriglissar defeated Appuashu, took his capital Ura (near Silifkeh), and

---

(Documenta et Monumenta Orientis Antiqui 10; Leiden: Brill, 1965), 138–39, 177, 191; Walter Kornfeld, *Onomastica Aramaica aus Ägypten* (SAWW 333; Wien: Verlag der österreichischen Akademie der Wissenschaften, 1978), 114–15; Ran Zadok, "On Anatolians, Greeks and Egyptians in 'Chaldean' and Achaemenid Babylonia," *TA* 32 (2005): 76–106, esp. 100.

13. See André Lemaire, "Tarhish-*Tarsisi*: Problème de topographie historique biblique et assyrienne," in *Studies in Historical Geography and Biblical Historiography Presented to Zecharia Kallai* (ed. Gershon Galil and Moshe Weinfeld; VTSup 81; Leiden: Brill, 2000), 44–62; Aurelio Padilla Monge, "*Taršiš y Tartessos* de nuevo a examen," *Aula Orientalis* 24 (2006): 233–42; Françoise Briquel-Chatonnet, "Taršiš," in *Supplément au Dictionnaire de la Bible* XIV/fasc. 77–78 (Paris: Letouzey et Ané, 2008), col. 1–8.

14. See, for example, André Lemaire, "Nabonidus in Arabia and Judah in the Neo-Babylonian Period," in *Judah and the Judeans in the Neo-Babylonian Period* (ed. Oded Lipschits and Joseph Blenkinsopp; Winona Lake, Ind.: Eisenbrauns, 2003), 285–98 (with bibliography); Alasdair Livingstone, "Taimā' and Nabonidus: It's a Small World," in *Writing and Ancient Near Eastern Society: Papers in Honour of Alan R. Millard* (ed. Piotr Bienkowski et al.; New York: T&T. Clark, 2005), 29–39.

15. See Brinkman, "The Akkadian Words for 'Ionia' and 'Ionian,'" in *Daidalikon*, 53–71; Rollinger, "Zur Bezeichnung von 'Griechen' in Keilschrifttexten," *RA* 91 (1997), 167–72.

16. See Francis Joannès, "L'Asie mineure méridionale…," in *De Anatolia Antiqua I*, 261–66, esp. 262–63.

17. On this kingdom, see André Lemaire, "Hiwwites, Perizzites et Girgashites: Essai d'identification ethnique," in *Stimulation from Leiden: Collected Communications to the XVIIIth Congress of the International Organization for the Study of the Old Testament, Leiden 2004* (ed. Hermann Michael Niemann and Matthias Augustin; Beiträge zur Erforschung des Alten Testaments und des Antiken Judentums 54; Frankfurt: Lang, 2006), 219–24, esp. 220–22.

then Kirshu in the mountains (=Meydancikkale).[18] He took possession of the island of Pitusu/Pityoussa (Dana Adasi) with its garrison of 6,000 soldiers (probably Ionians) and followed the coast as far as the Lydian border.

- The second campaign "against Ḫume" could have taken place in the first year of Nabonidus (555/4) but his accession year is also possible (556/5). Actually the text of the Chronicles is very fragmentary and one could wonder whether this second campaign is not the prolongation of the first one since Neriglissar could have returned to Babylon "in the month of Adar" 556 while Nabonidus could have arrived, with most of the army, a few months later.[19]

- The existence of another Neo-Babylonian campaign against Cilicia can be deduced from the mention of probable prisoners coming from Ionia, Ḫume, Pirindu, and Lydia in tablets from Nebuchadnezzar's palace. Some of these tablets have been published by Ernst F. Weidner and they generally date from the tenth to the thirty-fifth year of Nebuchadnezzar II (595/4 to 570/569). Prisoners from Pirindu are more precisely mentioned in a tablet from the thirteenth year (592/1).[20] Since Nebuchadnezzar claimed to control the countries "from Egypt to Ḫume, Piriddu/Pirindu and Lydia,"[21] as proposed by D. J. Wiseman, "this could have occurred early in his reign"[22] and is probably connected with Nebuchadnezzar's campaign similar to the one of Neriglissar in 557/6.

The date of this campaign is not easy to date precisely. One could think, first, of a campaign after the eleventh year of Nebuchadnezzar (594/3), the last year of Nebuchadnezzar mentioned in the fragments of his Chronicle that we are

---

18. See Alain Davesne, André Lemaire, and Hélène Lozachmeur, "Le site archéologique de Meydancikkale (Turquie): du royaume de Pirindu à la garnison ptolémaïque," *Comptes rendus de l'Académie des Inscriptions et Belles-Lettres* (1987): 359–82; Lemaire and Lozachmeur, "Les inscriptions araméennes," in *Gülnar I. Le site de Meydancikkale* (ed. Alain Davesne and Françoise Laroche-Traunecker; Paris: Éditions Recherche sur les Civilisations, 1998), 307–44.

19. For this possible historical interpretation, see André Lemaire, "Remarques sur la datation des campagnes néo-babyloniennes en Cilicie," to be published in *La famille dans le Proche-Orient ancien: réalités, symbolismes et images, 55ᵉ Rencontre Assyriologique Internationale, Paris, 6–9/07/2009* (ed. Jean-Marie Durand; Paris).

20. D. J. Wiseman, *Chronicles of Chaldaean Kings (626–556 B.C.) in the British Museum* (London: British Museum, 1956), 87.

21. W. G. Lambert, "Nebuchadnezzar King of Justice," *Iraq* 27 (1965): 1–11.

22. D. J. Wiseman, *Nebuchadrezzar and Babylon* (The Schweich Lectures of the British Academy 1983; Oxford: Oxford University Press, 1985), 9.

aware of. In this case, it should probably be dated to the twelfth year[23] since Pirindu is mentioned in a tablet of the thirteen year of Nebuchadnezzar.[24] However, since the tablets of Nebuchadnezzar's palace are generally dated from his tenth to thirty-fifth years,[25] although not impossible, a date after 595/4 does not seem very likely. Furthermore, as we will see below, the mention of "the towns of Judah" in our inscription does not fit very well into such a dating.

One could also think about "the sec[ond year]" of Nebuchadnezzar II (603/2), since the description of the contemporary campaign in Nabuchadnezzar's Chronicle is very fragmentary but it suggests that it was an important one: he "strengthened his large army" ... and used "large siege towers."[26] D. J. Wiseman, A. K. Grayson, and J.-J. Glassner thought of a new "Hatti" campaign but other commentators have proposed Ekron/Tel Miqneh, Kimuhu, or Cilicia.[27] This last interpretation would fit well all the Neo-Babylonian texts, including the mention of Iawan, Pirindu and Ḫume in the cuneiform tablets from Nebuchadnezzar's palace.

Finally, for this Cilician campaign early in his reign, although a date in 593/2 cannot be excluded, a date in his second year (603/2) seems preferable due to the mention of "the towns of Judah (*Yahud/Yahudu*)" in the Sabaean inscription, line

---

23. See Paolo Desideri and Anna Margherita Jasink, *Cilicia. Dall'età di Kizzuwatna alla conquista macedone* (Torino: Casa Editrice Le Lettere, 1990), 167: "Gli stati de Pirindu e Ḫume furono presumibilmente attaccati e conquistati da Nabucodonosor fra il 593 e il 591."

24. Wiseman, *Chronicles of Chaldaean Kings*, 87.

25. Weidner, "Jojachin, König von Juda," 924 ; see also Zadok, "On Anatolians," 79: "Greeks with Lycian names are recorded in Babylon between 595/4 and 570/69, when some of them were employed as carpenters (presumably shipwrights) in the (royal) boathouse."

26. Wiseman, *Chronicles of Chaldaean Kings*, 29, 70; A. K. Grayson, *Assyrian and Babylonian Chronicles* (Texts from Cuneiform Sources 5; Locust Valley, N.Y.: Augustin, 1975), 100; Jean-Jacques Glassner, *Chroniques mésopotamiennes* (Paris: Les Belles Lettres, 1993), 199.

27. Tel Miqneh: Trude Dothan and Seymour Gitin, "Ekron," *ABD* 2:415–22, esp. 420; idem, "Miqne, Tel," in *The Oxford Encyclopedia of Archaeology in the Near East* (ed. Eric M. Meyers; New York: Oxford University Press, 1997), 4:30–35, esp. 33; Martin Alonso Corral, *Ezechiel's Oracles Against Tyre: Historical Reality and Motivations* (Biblica et orientalia 46; Rome: Pontificio Istituto Biblico, 2002), 35, 91, but Ekron was probably destroyed with Ascalon in 604 (see Nadav Na'aman, "Ekron under the Assyrian and Egyptian Empires," *BASOR* 332 [2003]: 81–91, esp. 85, 88; Seymour Gitin, "Neo-Assyrian and Egyptian Hegemony over Ekron in the Seventh Century BCE: A Response to Lawrence E. Stager," in *Hayim and Myriam Tadmor Volume* (ed. Israel Eph'al et al.; Eretz-Israel 27; Jerusalem: Israel Exploration Society, 2003), 55*–61*, esp. 58*.

Kimuhu: Nadav Na'aman, "Nebuchadrezzar 's Campaign in Year 603 BCE," *BN* 62 (1992): 41–44.

Cilicia: David Stephen Vanderhooft, *The Neo-Babylonian Empire and Babylon in the Latter Prophets* (HSM 59; Atlanta: Scholars Press, 1999), 82 n. 83.

14. HGR, the South Arabian word used to designate towns, implies that they are somehow fortified towns with walls.[28] Such "towns of Judah" had to face three Neo-Babylonian campaigns around 600 B.C.E.:

- In his seventh year, "in the month Kislev," Nebuchadnezzar "mustered his army and marched to Hattu. He encamped against the city of Judah and, on the second day of the month Adar (= March 16, 597), he captured the city and seized (its) king."[29] In this quick campaign Nebuchadnezzar does not seem to have destroyed many Judean towns but the Edomites, sent in the beginning of the revolt, apparently did destroy the towns of the Negev (see 2 Kgs 24:2, correcting "Aram" into "Edom") and occupied the southern part of Judah.[30]
- The destructions seem to have been much more important during the second campaign, in 587. Jerusalem, and all the towns of the Shephelah (see Lachish and Azekah: Jer 34:7), as well as probably in the mountains of Judah (Hebron) were taken and burnt down. Only the land of Benjamin to the north of Jerusalem, with the new capital at Mizpah (Tell en-Nasbeh) was somehow spared.[31]
- The Neo-Babylonian campaign of 582 was apparently directed against Ammon and Moab[32] and Judah suffered a new deportation (Jer 52:30).

Although it is difficult to determine whether the Edomite control of the Shephelah (Lachish, Maresha) and the south of the Judean mountain (Hebron) started in 587 or in 582, it is clear enough that this part of the country was heav-

---

28. See A. F. L. Beeston, "Functional Significance of the Old South Arabian 'Town,'" *Proceedings of the Seminar for Arabian Studies* 1 (1971): 26–28 = *A. F. L. Beeston at the Arabian Seminar and Other Papers* (ed. M. C. A. Macdonald and C. S. Phillips; Oxford: Archaeopress, 2005), 87–88.

29. Grayson, *Assyrian and Babylonian Chronicles*, 102.

30. See, for example, André Lemaire, "D'Édom à l'Idumée et à Rome," in *Des Sumériens aux Romains d'Orient: la perception géographique du monde. Espaces et territoires au Proche-Orient ancien* (ed. Arnaud Sérandour; Antiquités sémitiques 2; Paris: Maisonneuve, 1997), 81–103, esp. 80 (with bibliography).

31. See Oded Lipschits, "Nebuchadrezzar's Policy in 'Ḫattu-Land' and the Fate of the Kingdom of Judah," *UF* 30 (1998): 467–87; idem, "The History of the Benjamin Region under Babylonian Rule," *TA* 26 (1999): 155–90; idem, *The Fall and Rise of Jerusalem: Judah under Babylonian Rule* (Winona Lake, Ind.: Eisenbrauns, 2005), 237–45, 267–71; idem, "Demographic Changes in Judah between the Seventh and the Fifth Centuries B.C.E.," in *Judah and the Judeans*, 323–76.

32. *Jewish Antiquities* X, 181–182.

ily destroyed in 587. After 587, Mizpah was probably the only fortified town of the Neo-Babylonian province of *Yehud*, therefore South Arabian trade with "the towns of Judah" very probably took place before this date. Actually, because of its connection with Gaza, the mention of "the towns of Judah" was probably referring to the Judean towns and forts of the south of the kingdom of Judah, namely, the Beersheba region. Since these towns were destroyed in 597 and this part of the country fell under Edomite control, the mention of "the towns of Judah" (and not of "Edom"!) in this inscription probably dates to before 597. Finally among the possible dates of Neo-Babylonian campaigns against Cilicia—603, 593, 557, or 556/5—the earliest date (603) seems preferable but not certain.

Incidentally, since the author of this inscription is the contemporary of the king of Sheba "Yada'il Bayin son of Yitha'amar" (lines 17–22), the dating of this inscription seems to confirm a date very close to 600 for this Sabaean king and the first approximate date of his reign (590) proposed by Hermann von Wissmann.[33]

The Sabaean Trade with Judah in Context

This first mention of Judah in a Sabaean inscription dating to approximately 600 B.C.E. is not completely unexpected in the historical context of contemporary Judah.

The phrase "the towns of Judah" is not an innovation of the Sabaean inscription. Although probably also attested at the end of the eighth century (2 Kgs 18:13; Isa 36:1) and in the fifth century B.C.E. (Neh 11:3), this phrase is well known in the book of Jeremiah (1:15; 4:16; 7:17, 34; 11:6, 12…), and is contemporary with the new inscription. Actually, several oracles of the prophet Jeremiah announce their destruction/abandonment (9:10; 10:22; 34:22; cf. 4:26; 25:18; 33:10; 44:6) as realized in 597 and mainly 587. Archaeology and palaeo-Hebrew epigraphy seem to document the prosperity of the towns of Judah at the end of the seventh century B.C.E.[34]

---

33. Von Wissmann, "Die Geschichte des Sabäerreichs," 351–54.
34. See Nadav Na'aman, "The Kingdom of Judah under Josiah," *TA* 18 (1991): 3–71; Israel Finkelstein, "*Ḥorvat Qiṭmit* and the Southern Trade in the Late Iron Age II," *ZDPV* 108 (1992): 156–70, esp. 160–62 (however the Edomite character of Horvat Qitmit is clear enough, especially from its inscriptions); Yifat Thareani-Sussely, "The 'Archaeology of the Days of Manasseh' Reconsidered in the Light of Evidence from the Beersheba Valley," *PEQ* 139 (2007): 69–77.

As clearly shown by the Elegy on Tyre in Ezek 27, international trade seems to have been blooming in the Levant around 600 B.C.E.[35] and various commentators have emphasized the prosperity of the region before the Neo-Babylonian destructions.[36] The reference to the incense road from South Arabia is clear:

> Dedan dealt with you in coarse woolens for saddle-cloths.
> Arabia and all the chiefs of Kedar were the source of your commerce
> in lambs, rams and he-goats;
> this was your trade with them.
> Dealers from Sheba and Raamah[37] dealt with you,
> Offering the choicest spices, every kind of precious stone and gold, as your staple wares. (Ezek 27:21–22)

The archaeological excavations of Beersheba have revealed a few traces of the South Arabian trade, apparently from the end of the eighth century B.C.E.[38] but probably going on later. One should also mention the discovery of a probable South-Arabic graffito in Beersheba,[39] as well as a Sabaean chiselled letter in Aroer.[40]

The excavations of Jerusalem have brought to light three fragmentary incised inscriptions on vases that are probably South Arabian. Two of them are connected with the destruction level of the city in 587.[41] The interpretation of these

---

35. See Mario Liverani, "The Trade Network of Tyre according to Ezek. 27," in *Ah Assyria !... Studies in Assyrian History and Ancient Near East Historiography Presented to H. Tadmor* (ed. Michael Cogan and Israel Eph'al; Jerusalem, 1991), 65–79, esp. 79: "between the fall of Niniveh in 612 B.C.E. and the beginning of the siege of Tyre by Nebuchadnezzar in 585 B.C.E."

36. See Edward Lipiński, "Products and Brokers of Tyre according to Ezekiel 27," in *Studia Phoenicia III: Phoenicia and Its Neighbours* (ed. Éric Gubel and Edward Lipiński; Leuven: Peeters, 1985), 213–20; Liverani, "Trade Network of Tyre," 65–79; I. M. Diakonoff, "The Naval Power and Trade of Tyre," *IEJ* 42 (1992): 168–98; Corral, *Ezechiel's Oracles Against Tyre*; Markus Saur, *Der Tyroszyklus des Ezechielbuches* (BZAW 386; Berlin: de Gruyter, 2008).

37. Probably Ragmatum in the oasis of Nagrân, see Walter W. Müller, "Raamah," *ABD* 5:597.

38. See Lily Singer-Avitz, "A Gateway Community in Southern Arabian Long-Distance Trade in the Eighth Century B.C.E.," *TA* 26 (1999): 3–74, esp. 40–61.

39. François Bron, "Vestiges de l'écriture sud-sémitique dans le Croissant fertile," in *Présence arabe dans le Croissant fertile avant l'Hégire* (ed. Hélène Lozachmeur; Paris: Éditions Recherche sur les Civilisations, 1995), 81–91, esp. 51.

40. Yifat Thareani-Sussely, "Desert Outsiders: Extramural Neighborhoods in the Iron Age Negev," in *Bene Israel: Studies in the Archaeology of Israel and the Levant during the Bronze and Iron Ages in Honour of Israel Finkelstein* (ed. Alexander Fantalkin and Assaf Yasur-Landau; Leiden: Brill, 2008), 198–212 and 288–303, esp. 208 and 302.

41. Yigal Shiloh, "South Arabian Inscriptions from the City of David, Jerusalem," *PEQ* 119 (1987): 9–18; Albert Jamme, "A World-Class Expert Reads A South Arabian Inscription," *BAR*

small fragmentary inscriptions has been somewhat discussed,[42] the South Arabian character of one of them seems certain. The two other ones are not so clear, and might also have a connection to Greek epigraphy.[43]

Our inscription apparently reveals a direct connection between Gaza and Kition, probably by a sea route. This apparent maritime trade connection reveals the extent of the South Arabian trade in the eastern Mediterranean and may also help us to understand the presence of "Kittiyim" in the Beersheba Valley around 600 B.C.E. as revealed by the palaeo-Hebrew Arad ostraca.[44] Although the text of the ostraca does not explain the reason for the presence of these "Kittiyim" in the Judean Negev, the context suggests a group of mercenaries rather than a group of merchants.[45] This presence in the Negev is more easily understood if there were direct naval relations between Gaza and Kition.

The dating of this inscription seems to confirm the "long chronology" of the South Arabian inscriptions and is the last blow to the "short chronology" proposed by Jacqueline Pirenne.[46] This "short chronology" suffered from a severe fault in methodology, being clearly "Helleno-centered." It did not take into account the history and epigraphy of the ancient Near East,[47] and the geographical proximity to South Arabia. Actually the "Assyrian synchronism,"[48] which

---

14 (1988): 66; Yonatan Nadelman, "'Chiselled' Inscriptions and Markings on Pottery Vessels from the Iron Age II (Discussion and Catalogue)," *IEJ* 40 (1990): 31–41, esp. 34, 39–41; Maria Höfner, "Remarks on Potsherds with Incised South Arabian Letters," in *Excavations at the City of David 1978–1985, Directed by Yigal Shiloh*. Vol 6, *Inscriptions* (ed. Donald T. Ariel; Qedem 41; Jerusalem: The Institute of Archaeology, The Hebrew University of Jerusalem, 2000), 26–28.

42. Benjamin Sass, "Arabs and Greeks in Late First Temple Jerusalem," *PEQ* 122 (1990): 59–61.

43. Bron, "Vestiges de l'écriture," esp. 84.

44. Yohanan Aharoni, *Arad Inscriptions* (Judean Desert Studies; Jerusalem: Israel Exploration Society, 1981), 12–13.

45. André Lemaire, *Inscriptions hébraïques I. Les ostraca* (LAPO 9; Paris: Cerf, 1977), 159–61; Johannes Renz, *Die althebräischen Inschriften* (Handbuch der althebräischen Epigraphik I; Darmstadt: Wissenschaftliche Buchgesellschaft, 1995), 353–54 ; Shmuel Ahituv, *Echoes from the Past, Hebrew and Cognate Inscriptions from the Biblical Period* (Jerusalem: Carta, 2008), 94.

46. Jacqueline Pirenne, *La Grèce et Saba. Une nouvelle base pour la chronologie sud-arabe* (Extrait des Mémoires présentés par divers savants à l'Académie des Inscriptions et Belles-Lettres XV; Paris: Imprimerie nationale, 1955); eadem, *Paléographie des inscriptions sud-arabes*.

47. With strange mistakes in dealing with West Semitic epigraphy, apparently knowing only three Phoenician inscriptions from the eighth century B.C.E. but considering as one of them the Hadad inscription (ead., *La Grèce et Saba*, 26/[114]) that is well known to be in Samalian, a dialect of Aramaic (see Mark Lidzbarski, *Handbuch der nordsemitischen Epigraphik nebst ausgewählten Inschriften I* [Weimar, 1898], 440–42).

48. Recognized by François Lenormant, *Manuel d'histoire ancienne de l'Orient* (3rd ed.; Paris, 1968), 2, 90; see lately Annie Caubet and Iwona Gajda, "Deux autels en bronze provenant de

is one of the bases of the "long chronology," is now generally accepted, even by scholars who originally defended the "short chronology."[49]

The dating of this inscription also throws some light on the problem of the transition between a Sabaean and a Minaean control of the incense trade road. Although several scholars still propose a date in 343,[50] the "revolt" mentioned in Minaean inscription RES 3022 must be dated to the fifth century B.C.E.[51] because the events of 343 B.C.E. cannot be interpreted as a revolt of Egypt against the Persian Empire, but were exactly the opposite. Thus Minaean control of the incense road started at least during the Achaemenid period while the new inscription reveals that this road was still under Sabaean control early in the Neo-Babylonian period, at least to 603 B.C.E.

One may note that a great part of this incense road was directly under the control of Nabonidus during his ten year stay in Teima (552–543),[52] which is well

---

l'Arabie méridionale, suivi d'un appendice de F. Demange," *Comptes rendus de l'Académie des Inscriptions et Belles-Lettres* (2003): 1219–42; Dan T. Potts, "The Mukarrib and His Beads: Karib'il Watar's Assyrian Diplomacy in the Early 7th Century B.C.," *Isimu* 6 (2003): 197–206; Norbert Nebes, "Ita'amar der Sabäer: Zur Datierung der Monumentalinschrift des Yita'ʾamar Watar aus Ṣirwāḥ," *Arabian Archaeology and Epigraphy* 18 (2007): 25–33.

49. See, for example, Giovanni Garbini, "La piu antica storia sabea e il sincronismo assiro," *Rendiconti dell'Academia Nazionale dei Lincei* ser. IX,9 (1998): 387–94; idem, *Introduzione all'epigrafia semitica* (Studi sul Vicino Oriente antico; Brescia: Paideia, 2006), 281, 295.

50. Christian J. Robin, "Les premiers états du Jawf et la civilisation sudarabique," in *Arabia Antiqua: Early Origins of South Arabian States* (ed. C. J. Robin; Serie Orientale Roma 70/1; Rome: Istituto italiano per il Medio ed Estremo Oriente, 1996), 49–65, esp. 64; idem, "Les fondements de la chronologie sudarabique," in Yves Calvet and Christian Robin, *Arabie heureuse, Arabie déserte. Les antiquités arabiques du Musée du Louvre* (Notes et documents des musées de France 31; Paris: Musée du Louvre, 1997), 39; Gherardo Gnoli, "Ancora sui 'Medi' in RES 3022," in *Sabaean Studies: Archaeological, Epigraphical and Historical Studies in Honour of Yūsūf M. ʿAbdallah, Alessandro de Maigret, Christian J. Robin* (ed. Amida M. Sholan, Sabina Antonini, and Mounir Arbach; Naples/Sanʿāʾ: Universita degli Studi di Napoli "L'Orientale," 2005), 295–300; Garbini, *Introduzione all'epigrafia semitica*, 291.

51. See André Lemaire, "Histoire du Proche-Orient et chronologie sudarabique avant Alexandre," in *Arabia Antiqua*, 35–48, esp. 47.

52. See idem, "Nabonidus in Arabia and Judah in the Neo-Babylonian Period," in *Judah and the Judeans*, 285–98 (with bibliography).

illustrated by North Arabian Teimanite inscriptions.[53] Actually Nabonidus went as far as Dedan/al-'Ula, Fadak, Khaybar, Yadi', and Yatrib/Medine.[54]

These conditions may lead one to think that Nabonidus's campaign led to the end of Sabaean control of the incense road[55] and was probably the origin of the decline of the Sabaean kingdom. At the beginning of the Persian period, Minaeans probably sought an alliance with the kingdom of Kedar and could take control of the incense road from the end of the sixth century B.C.E. on. At least in the present state of the documentation, this appears to be a good working hypothesis that would fit the Bible accounts where Minaeans appear in the books of Chronicles (1 Chr 4:41; 2 Chr 16:7) as well as in Ezra (2:50) and Nehemiah (7:52), probably dating from the fourth century B.C.E.

Thus this new Sabaean inscription throws new light on the trade between South Arabia and Judah and one can only hope that it is only a beginning.

Bibliography

Aharoni, Yohanan. *Arad Inscriptions*. Judean Desert Studies. Jerusalem: Israel Exploration Society, 1981.
Ahituv, Shmuel. *Echoes from the Past, Hebrew and Cognate Inscriptions from the Biblical Period*. Jerusalem: Carta, 2008.
Alonso Corral, Martin. *Ezechiel's Oracles Against Tyre: Historical Reality and Motivations*. Biblica et orientalia 46. Rome: Pontificio Istituto Biblico, 2002.
Beeston, A. F. L. "Functional Significance of the Old South Arabian 'Town.'" *Proceedings of the Seminar for Arabian Studies* 1 (1971): 16–18 = Pages 87–88 in *A. F. L. Beeston at the Arabian Seminar and Other Papers*. Edited by M. C. A. Macdonald and C. S. Phillips. Oxford: Archaeopress, 2005.
Brinkman, J. A. "The Akkadian Words for 'Ionia' and 'Ionian.'" Pages 53–71 in *Daidalikon. Studies in Memory of Raymond V. Shoder*. Edited by R. F. Sutton. Wauconda, Ill., 1989.

---

53. See Hani Hayajneh, "First Evidence of Nabonidus in the Ancient North Arabian Inscriptions from the Region of Tayma,'" *Proceedings of the Seminar for Arabian Studies* 31 (2001): 81–95; idem, "Der babylonische König Nabonid und der RBSRS in einigen neu publizierten früh-nordarabischen Inschriften aus Taymâ," *Acta Orientalia* 62 (2001): 22–64; Walter W. Müller and Said F. Al-Said, "Der babylonische König Nabonid in taymanischen Inschriften," *BN* 107/108 (2001): 109–19; Yaakov Grundfest and Michael Heltzer, "Nabonid, King of Babylon (556–539) B.C.E. in Arabia in Light of New Evidence," *BN* 110 (2001): 25–30.

54. See C. J. Gadd, "The Harran Inscriptions of Nabonidus," *Anatolian Studies* 8 (1958): 35–92, esp. 58–59; W. Röllig, "Erwägungen zu neuen Stelen Königs Nabonids," *ZA* 56 (1964): 218–60, esp. 220–26; A. Leo Oppenheim, "Nabonidus and His God," in *The Ancient Near East: Supplementary Texts and Pictures Relating to the Old Testament* (ed. James B. Pritchard; Princeton: Princeton University Press, 1969), 562–63.

55. See von Wissmann, "Die Geschichte der Sabäerreichs," 354.

Briquel-Chatonnet, Françoise. "Taršiš." Col. 1–8 in *Supplément au Dictionnaire de la Bible* XIV/fasc. 77–78. Paris: Letouzey et Ané, 2008.
Bron, François. "Vestiges de l'écriture sud-sémitique dans le croissant fertile." Pages 81–91 in *Présence arabe dans le Croissant fertile avant l'Hégire*. Edited by Hélène Lozachmeur. Paris: Éditions Recherche sur les Civilisations, 1995.
Bron, François, and André Lemaire. "Nouvelle inscription sabéenne et le commerce en Transeuphratène." *Transeuphratène* 38 (2009): 11–29.
Caubet, Annie, and Iwona Gajda. "Deux autels en bronze provenant de l'Arabie méridionale, suivi d'un appendice de F. Demange." *Comptes rendus de l'Académie des Inscriptions et Belles-Lettres* (2003): 1219–42.
Dalley, Stephanie. "Sennacherib and Tarsus." *Anatolian Studies* 49 (1999): 73–80.
Davesne, Alain, André Lemaire, and Hélène Lozachmeur. "Le site archéologique de Meydancikkale (Turquie): du royaume de Pirindu à la garnison ptolémaïque." *Comptes rendus de l'Académie des Inscriptions et Belles-Lettres* (1987): 359–82.
Desideri, Paolo, and Anna Margherita Jasink. *Cilicia. Dall'età di Kizzuwatna alla conquista macedone*. Torino: Casa Editrice le Lettere, 1990.
Diakonoff, I. M. "The Naval Power and Trade of Tyre." *IEJ* 42 (1992): 168–98.
Dothan, Trude, and Seymour Gitin. "Ekron." *ABD* 2:415–22.
———. "Miqne, Tel." Pages 30–35 in *The Oxford Encyclopedia of Archaeology in the Near East IV*. Edited by Eric M. Meyers. New York: Oxford University Press, 1997.
Elayi, Josette. "Sargon II et les Ioniens." *Oriens Antiquus* 18 (1979): 59–75.
Finkelstein, Israel. "Arabian Trade and Socio-Political Conditions in the Negev in the Twelfth-Eleventh Centuries B.C.E." *JNES* 47 (1988): 241–52.
———. "Ḥorvat Qiṭmît and the Southern Trade in the Late Iron Age III." *ZDPV* 108 (1992): 156–70.
———. *Living on the Fringe: The Archaeology and History of the Negev, Sinai and Neighbouring Regions in the Bronze and Iron Age*. Monographs in Mediterranean Archaeology 6. Sheffield: Sheffield Academic, 1995.
Fuchs, Andreas. *Die Inschriften Sargons II. Aus Khorsabad*. Göttingen: Cuvillier, 1994.
Gadd, C. J. "The Harran Inscriptions of Nabonidus." *Anatolian Studies* 8 (1958): 35–92.
Garbini, Giovanni. "La piu antica storia sabea e il sincronismo assiro." *Rendiconti dell'Academia Nazionale dei Lincei* ser. IX,9 (1998): 387–94.
———. *Introduzione all'epigrafia semitica*. Studi sul Vicino Oriente antico; Brescia: Paideia, 2006.
Gitin, Seymour. "Neo-Assyrian and Egyptian Hegemony over Ekron in the Seventh Century BCE: A Response to Lawrence E. Stager." Pages 55*–61* in *Hayim and Myriam Tadmor Volume*. Edited by Israel Eph'al et al. Eretz-Israel 27. Jerusalem: Israel Exploration Society, 2003.
Glassner, Jean-Jacques. *Chroniques mésopotamiennes*. Paris: Les Belles Lettres, 1993.
Gnoli, Gherardo. "Ancora sui 'Medi' in RES 3022." Pages 295–300 in *Sabaean Studies: Archaeological, Epigraphical and Historical Studies in Honour of Yūsūf M. 'Abdallah, Alessandro de Maigret, Christian J. Robin*. Edited by Amida M. Sholan, Sabina Antonini, Mounir Arbach. Naples/San'ā', Universita degli Studi di Napoli "L'Orientale." 2005.
Goetze, Albrecht. "Cilicians." *JCS* 16 (1962): 48–58.
Grayson, A. K. *Assyrian and Babylonian Chronicles*. TCS 5. Locust Valley, N.Y.: Augustin, 1975.

Grundfest, Yaakov, and Michael Heltzer. "Nabonid, King of Babylon (556–539 B.C.E.) in Arabia in Light of New Evidence." *BN* 110 (2001): 25–30.
Hayajneh, Hani. "First Evidence of Nabonidus in the Ancient North Arabian Inscriptions from the Region of Tayma." *Proceedings of the Seminar for Arabian Studies* 31 (2001): 81–95.
Hayajneh, Hani. "Der babylonische König Nabonid in taymanischen Inschriften." *BN* 107/108 (2001): 109–19.
Höfner, Maria. "Remarks on Potsherds with Incised South Arabian Letters." Pages 26–28 in *Excavations at the City of David 1978–1985, Directed by Yigal Shiloh*. Vol. 1, *Inscriptions*. Edited by Donald T. Ariel. Qedem 41. Jerusalem: The Institute of Archaeology, The Hebrew University of Jerusalem, 2000.
Houwink ten Cate, P. H. J. *The Luwian Population Groups of Lycia and Cilicia Aspera During the Hellenistic Period*. Documenta et Monumenta Orientis Antiqui 10. Leiden: Brill, 1965.
Jamme, Albert. "A World-Class Expert Reads A South Arabian Inscription." *BAR* 14 (1988): 66.
Jasmin, Michael. "Les conditions d'émergence de la route de l'encens à la fin du IIe millénaire avant notre ère." *Syria* 82 (2005): 49–62.
Jasink, Anna Margherita. "I Greci in Cilicia nel periodo neo-assiro." *Mesopotamia* 24 (1989): 117–28.
Joannès, Francis. "L'Asie mineure méridionale d'après la documentation cunéiforme d'époque néo-babylonienne." Pages 261–66 in *De Anatolia Antiqua I*. Bibliothèque de l'Institut Français d'Études Anatoliennes d'Istanbul 32. Paris: Maisonneuve, 1990.
Kornfeld, Walter. *Onomastica Aramaica aus Ägypten*. SAWW 333. Wien: Verlag der österreichischen Akademie der Wissenschaften, 1978.
Lambert, W. G. "Nebuchadnezzar King of Justice." *Iraq* 27 (1965): 1–11.
Lanfranchi, Giovanni B. "The Ideological and Political Impact of the Assyrian Imperial Expansion on the Greek World in the 8th and 7th Centuries BC." Pages 7–34 in *The Heirs of Assyria*. Edited by Sanna Aro and R. M. Whiting. Melammu Symposia I. Helsinki: The Neo-Assyrian Text Corpus Project, 2000.
Lemaire, André. "D'Édom à l'Idumée et à Rome." Pages 81–103 in *Des Sumériens aux Romains d'Orient: la perception géographique du monde. Espaces et territoires au Proche-Orient ancien*. Edited by Arnaud Sérandour. Antiquités sémitiques 2. Paris: Maisonneuve, 1997.
———. "Histoire du Proche-Orient et chronologie sudarabique avant Alexandre." Pages 35–48 in *Arabia Antiqua: Early Origins of South Arabian States*. Edited by Christian Robin. Serie orientale Roma 70/1. Rome: Istituto italiano per il Medio ed Estremo Oriente, 1996.
———. "Hiwwites, Perizzites et Girgashites: Essai d'identification ethnique." Pages 219–24 in *Stimulation from Leiden: Collected Communications to the XVIIIth Congress of the International Organization for the Study of the Old Testament, Leiden 2004*. Edited by Hermann Michael Niemannn and Matthias Augustin. Beiträge zur Erforschung des Alten Testaments und des Antiken Judentums 54. Frankfurt am Main: Lang, 2006.
———. *Inscriptions hébraïques I. Les ostraca*. Littératures anciennes du Proche-Orient 9. Paris: Cerf, 1977.
———. "Nabonidus in Arabia and Judah in the Neo-Babylonian Period." Pages 285–98 in *Judah and the Judeans in the Neo-Babylonian Period*. Edited by Oded Lipschits and

Joseph Blenkinsopp. Winona Lake, Ind.: Eisenbrauns, 2003.

———. "La reine de Saba à Jérusalem: la tradition ancienne reconsidérée." Pages 43–55 in *Kein Land für sich allein. Studien zum Kulturkontakt in Kanaan, Israel/Palästina und Ebirnâri für Manfred Weippert*. Edited by Ulrich Hübner and Ernst Axel Knauf. OBO 186. Fribourg; Universitätsverlag. Göttingen: Vandenhoeck & Ruprecht, 2002.

———. "Remarques sur la datation des campagnes néo-babyloniennes en Cilicie." *La famille dans le Proche-Orient ancien: réalités, symbolismes et images, 55e Rencontre Assyriologique Internationale, Paris, 6–9/07/2009*. Edited by Jean-Marie Durand. Paris, forthcoming.

———. "Tarshish-*Tarsisi*: Problème de topographie historique biblique et assyrienne." Pages 44–62 in *Studies in Historical Geography and Biblical Historiography Presented to Zecharia Kallai*. Edited by Gershon Galil and Moshe Weinfeld. VTSup 81. Leiden: Brill, 2000.

Lemaire, André, and Hélène Lozachmeur. "Les inscriptions araméennes," Pages 307–44 in *Gülnar I. Le site de Meydancikkale*. Edited by Alain Davesne and Françoise Laroche-Traunecker. Paris: Éditions Recherche sur les Civilisations, 1998.

Lenormant, François. *Manuel d'histoire ancienne de l'Orient*. 3d ed. Paris, 1968.

Lidzbarski, Mark. *Handbuch der nordsemitischen Epigraphik nebst ausgewählten Inschriften*. Weimar, 1898.

Lipiński, Edward. "Products and Brokers of Tyre according to Ezekiel 27." Pages 213–30 in *Studia Phoenicia III: Phoenicia and Its Neighbours*. Edited by Éric Gubel and Edward Lipiński. Leuven: Peeters, 1985.

———. "Les Japhétites selon Gen 10,2–4 et 1 Chr 1,5–7." *ZAH* 3 (1990): 40–53.

Lipschits, Oded. "Demographic Changes in Judah between the Seventh and the Fifth Centuries B.C.E." Pages 323–76 in *Judah and the Judeans in the Neo-Babylonian Period*. Edited by Lipschits and Joseph Blenkinsopp. Winona Lake, Ind.: Eisenbrauns, 2003.

———. *The Fall and Rise of Jerusalem. Judah under Babylonian Rule*. Winona Lake, Ind.: Eisenbrauns, 2005.

———. "Nebuchadrezzar's Policy in 'Ḫattu-Land' and the Fate of the Kingdom of Judah." *UF* 30 (1998): 467–87.

Liverani, Mario. "The Trade Network of Tyre according to Ezek. 27." Pages 65–79 in *Ah Assyria!... Studies in Assyrian History and Ancient Near Eastern Historiography Presented to H. Tadmor*. Edited by Michael Cogan and Israel Eph'al. Scripta Hierosolymitana 33. Jerusalem: Magnes / The Hebrew University, 1991.

———. "Early Caravan Trade Between South Arabia and Mesopotamia." *Yemen* 1 (1992): 111–15.

Livingstone, Alasdair. "Taimā' and Nabonidus: It's a Small World." Pages 29–39 in *Writing and Ancient Near Eastern Society: Papers in Honour of Alan R. Millard*. Edited by Piotr Bienkowski et al. New York: T&T Clark, 2005.

Mayer, W. "Zypern und Ägäis aus der Sicht der Staaten Vorderasiens in der 1. Hälfte des 1. Jahrtausends." *UF* 28 (1996): 463–84.

Müller, Walter W. "Raamah." *ABD* 5:597.

Na'aman, Nadav. "Ekron under the Assyrian and Egyptian Empires." *BASOR* 332 (2003): 81–91.

———. "The Kingdom of Judah under Josiah." *TA* 18 (1991): 3–71.

———. "Nebuchadrezzar's Campaign in Year 603 BCE." *BN* 62 (1992): 41–44.

Nadelman, Yonatan. "'Chiselled' Inscriptions and Markings on Pottery Vessels from the

Iron Age II (Discussion and Catalogue)." *IEJ* 40 (1990): 31–41.

Nebes, Norbert. "Ita'amar der Sabäer: Zur Datierung der Monumentalinschrift des Yita"amar Watar aus Ṣirwāḥ." *Arabian Archaeology and Epigraphy* 18 (2007): 25–33.

Oppenheim, A. Leo. "Nabonidus and His God." Pages 562–63 in *The Ancient Near East: Supplementary Texts and Pictures Relating to the Old Testament*. Edited by James B. Pritchard. Princeton: Princeton University Press, 1969.

Padilla Monge, Aurelio. *"Taršiš* y *Tartessos* de nuevo a examen." *AuOr* 24 (2006): 233–42.

Pirenne, Jacqueline. *La Grèce et Saba. Une nouvelle base pour la chronologie sud-arabe*. Extrait des Mémoires présentés par divers savants à l'Académie des Inscriptions et Belles-Lettres XV. Paris: Imprimerie nationale, 1955.

Pirenne, Jacqueline. *Paléographie des inscriptions sud-arabes. Contribution à la chronologie et à l'histoire de l'Arabie du Sud antique I. Des origines jusqu'à l'époque himyarite*. Brussel: Paleis der Academiën, 1956.

Potts, Dan T. "The Mukarrib and His Beads: Karib'il Watar's Assyrian Diplomacy in the Early 7th Century B.C." *Isimu* 6 (2003): 197–206.

Renz, Johannes. *Die althebräischen Inschriften*. Handbuch der althebräischen Epigraphik I. Darmstadt: Wissenschaftliche Buchgesellschaft, 1995.

Robin, Christian J. "Les fondements de la chronologie sudarabique." Pages 37–41 in Yves Calvet and Christian Robin, *Arabie heureuse, Arabie déserte. Les antiquités arabiques du Musée du Louvre*. Notes et documents des musées de France 3. Paris: Musée du Louvre, 1997.

———. "Les premiers états du Jawf et la civilisation sudarabique." Pages 49–65 in *Arabia Antiqua: Early Origins of South Arabian States*. Edited by Robin. Serie orientale Roma 70/1. Rome. Istituto italiano per il Medio ed Estremo Oriente, 1996.

Röllig, W. "Erwägungen zu neuen Stelen Königs Nabonids." *ZA* 56 (1964): 218–60.

Rollinger, Robert. "Überlegungen zur Frage der Lokalisation von Jawan in neuassyrischer Zeit." *State Archives of Assyria Bulletin* 16 (2007): 64–90.

Sass, Benjamin. "Arabs and Greeks in Late First Temple Jerusalem." *PEQ* 122 (1990): 59–61.

Saur, Markus. *Der Tyroszyklus des Ezechielbuches*. BZAW 386. Berlin: de Gruyter, 2008.

Shiloh, Yigal. "South Arabian Inscriptions from the City of David, Jerusalem." *PEQ* 119 (1987): 9–18.

Singer-Avitz, Lily. "A Gateway Community in Southern Arabian Long-Distance Trade in the Eighth Century B.C.E." *TA* 26 (1999): 3–74.

Thareani-Sussely, Yifat. "The 'Archaeology of the Days of Manasseh' Reconsidered in the Light of Evidence from the Beersheba Valley." *PEQ* 139 (2007): 69–77.

———. "Desert Outsiders: Extramural Neighborhoods in the Iron Age Negev." Pages 198–212, 288–303 in *Bene Israel: Studies in the Archaeology of Israel and the Levant during the Bronze and Iron Ages in Honour of Israel Finkelstein*. Edited by Alexander Fantalkin and Assaf Yasur-Landau. Leiden: Brill, 2008.

Vanderhooft, David Stephen. *The Neo-Babylonian Empire and Babylon in the Latter Prophets*. HSM 59. Atlanta: Scholars Press, 1999.

Weidner, Ernst F. "Jojachin, König von Juda, in babylonischen Keilschriften." Pages 923–35 in *Mélanges syriens offerts à René Dussaud II*. BAH 30. Paris: Geuthner, 1939.

Wiseman, D. J. *Chronicles of Chaldaean Kings (626–556 B.C.) in the British Museum*. London: British Museum, 1956.

———. *Nebuchadrezzar and Babylon*. The Schweich Lectures of the Britsh Academy 1983.

Oxford: Oxford University Press, 1985.

Von Wissmann, Hermann. "Die Geschichte des Sabäerreichs und der Feldzug des Aelius Gallus." Pages 308–544 in *ANRW* II,9.1. Edited by Hildegard Temporini. Berlin: de Gruyter, 1976.

———. *Die Geschichte von Saba' II. Das Grossreich der Sabäer bis zu seinem Ende im frühen 4. Jh. v. Chr.* SAWW 402. Band. Wien: Verlag der österreichischen Akademie der Wissenschaften, 1982.

Zadok, Ran. "On Anatolians, Greeks and Egyptians in 'Chaldean' and Achaemenid Babylonia." *TA* 32 (2005): 76–106.

Chapter Eight
A Unique Bilingual and Biliteral Artifact from the Time of Nebuchadnezzar II in the Moussaieff Private Collection

Kathleen Abraham*

Babylonia in the first millennium B.C.E., under the reigns of the Chaldean, Achaemenid, and Seleucid dynasties, was a multilingual society, with Aramaic and Akkadian as its major languages. It was also a society in which more than one script was in use, with cuneiform signs used to write Akkadian,[1] and alphabetic characters for writing Aramaic or other West Semitic languages.[2] The relation-

---

* This research was made possible through the generous support of Dr. Shlomo Moussaieff under the aegis of "The Shlomo Moussaieff Program for the Study of Cuneiform Tablets" at Bar-Ilan University.

1. For a rare example of cuneiform signs being used to write Aramaic, see M. Geller, "The Aramaic Incantation in Cuneiform Script (AO 6489 = TCL 6,58)," *JEOL* 35–36 (1997–2000): 127–46 and Ch. Müller-Kessler, "Die aramäische Beschwörung und ihre Rezeption in den Mandäisch-magischen Texten. Am Beispiel ausgewählter aramäischer Beschwörungsformulare," in *Charmes et sortilèges. Magie et magiciens* (ed. R. Gyselen; Res Orientales 14; Bures-sur-Yvette: Groupe pour l'étude de la civilisation du Moyen-Orient, 2002), 193–208.

2. For examples of this biliteralism in Babylonia, see, for instance, the Aramaic epigraphs on cuneiform legal documents, the ever-increasing number of Aramaic dockets (but mostly from Assyria and northern Mesopotamia), the Aramaic labels on bricks of Nebuchadnezzar and several scribal exercises pertaining to learning the West Semitic (presumably Aramaic) alphabet. Ch. Müller-Kessler, "Eine aramäische 'Visitenkarte': Eine spätbabylonische Tontafel aus Babylon," *MDOG* 130 (1998): 189–95; F. M. Fales, "The Use and Function of Aramaic Tablets," *Ancient Near Eastern Studies Supplement* 7 (2000): 89–124; F. M. Cross and J. Huehnergard, "The Alphabet on a Late Babylonian Cuneiform School Tablet," *JCS* 72 (2003): 223–28; A. Lemaire, *Nouvelles tablettes araméennes* (Hautes Études Orientales 34; Moyen et Proche Orient 1; Geneva: Droz, 2001; E. Lipiński, *Studies in Aramaic Inscriptions and Onomastics*, vol. 3 (OLA 200; Leuven: Peeters, 2010).

ship between these languages and scripts is still not fully understood, mainly because the Aramaic alphabetic evidence that has come to us from Babylonia is rather limited. It is also becoming more and more clear today that these languages and scripts were each used in specific spheres of activity,[3] and that the process of replacing Akkadian by Aramaic was more complex and probably not so intrusive as had been originally thought.[4]

I hope to add some new evidence that will prove important for this still ongoing discussion on the linguistic landscape of Babylonia in the first millennium B.C.E. with the publication of a rather unique artifact from the Shlomo Moussaieff collection. It is bilingual and biliteral, and it allows us a certain understanding of the workings of the royal administration at the time of Nebuchadnezzar II, and of how Akkadian and Aramaic were used by the administration, so it seems, simultaneously. It also bears, directly or indirectly, on many other intriguing issues of various nature, such as the development of the Aramaic lapidary script in the late-seventh century B.C.E. and the circumstances surrounding Nebuchadnezzar's succession.

A Description of the Object

Let us start with a description of the physical characteristics of the object in question. The object is circular with a diameter of 12 cm; it is made of clay (see figs below). It is a perfectly preserved piece with no chipped off or broken edges and no cracks on either of its surfaces. Its obverse side is flat and bears an imprint in the middle and a cuneiform inscription around the outer edge. The imprint consists of three vertical strokes, two of which have a wedge-shaped head resembling that of a cuneiform sign. The small vertical stroke in the middle is of different shape, lacking the triangular head present in the other verticals. An alphabetic inscription encircles the three vertical strokes. The cuneiform inscription was written by hand (not stamped like the Aramaic one) exceeding the contour of the

---

3. See most recently, P.-A. Beaulieu, "Official and Vernacular Languages: The Shifting Sands of Imperial and Cultural Identities in First-Millennium B.C. Mesopotamia," in *Margins of Writing, Origins of Cultures* (ed. S. L. Sanders; Chicago: University of Chicago Press, 2006), 187–216, in particular on the (diglossic) relationship between Aramaic and Akkadian and the related question of cultural identity.

4. For a reassessment of the question of Aramaic influence on Akkadian and the role the former may have played in the eventual demise of the latter, see K. Abraham and M. Sokoloff, "Aramaic Loanwords in Akkadian: A Reassessment of the Proposals," *AfO* 52 (2007–2009) forthcoming.

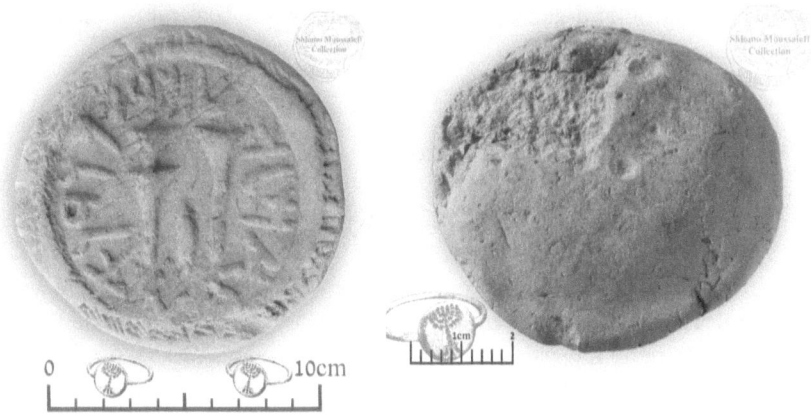

Fig. 1. Bilingual and Biliteral Artifact from the Time of Nebuchadnezzar II, obverse and reverse.

stamped imprint. The reverse side is basically flat and uninscribed. The object has a thickness of a bit more than one centimeter.

The Inscriptions

The reading of the inscriptions does not pose any specific problems. The cuneiform inscription reads:

qaq-qar šá ᵐŠEŠ-ZALAG₂ ˡúENGAR šá ᵐᵈAMAR.UTU-na-din-ŠEŠ A-šú šá ᵐᵈAG-NÍG.DU-URU₃ LUGAL TIN.TIRᵏⁱ is-ba-tu MU.3ᵏᵃᵐ ᵈAG-NÍG.DU-UR[U₃ LU]GAL ⌜E⌝ᵏⁱ

The plot of land which Aḫu-nūrī, the farm-laborer of Marduk-nādin-aḫi, son of Nabû-kudurri-uṣur, King of Babylon, took possession of. Third year of Nabû-kudurri-uṣu[r, Ki]ng of ⌜Babylon⌝.[5]

The text engraved on the stamp in the alphabetic script reads:
למרדכנדנאח בר מלך.

---

5. The third year of Nebuchadnezzar's equals the year 602–601 B.C.E., according to R. A. Parker and W. H. Dubberstein, *Babylonian Chronology 626 B.C.–A.D. 75.* (Providence, R.I.: Brown University Press, 1956), 27.

Belonging to (and guaranteed by) Marduk-nādin-aḫi, son of the (ruling) King.

Philological Notes

The language of the alphabetic inscription is probably Aramaic in view of the use of בר for "son."

The ל, being a polysemic preposition,[6] can be interpreted in three ways:[7] as an indication of ownership or origin (ל = "of"),[8] an indication of destination (ל = "to, for"), or an indication of a standard of measurement (ל = "by").[9] In the case under consideration it first and foremost identifies the owner of the artifact ("Belonging to Marduk-nādin-aḫi"). Whether or not the other meanings apply as well, much depends on how one defines the function of the artifact on which the phrase למרדכנדנאח was stamped. This is a complicated matter that will need a separate discussion (see briefly below pp. 119–22).

Assuming the language is Aramaic, the lack of the emphatic *aleph* in מלך is noteworthy. The idiom "Son of the king" should have been בר מלכא, with an emphatic *aleph*, in proper Aramaic of the seventh century. In Aramaic epigraphs on Assyrian tablets from the seventh century B.C.E., for instance, we find בר מלכא in the phrase שערן (סנה) זי בר מלכא על "barley, (deputy of) the 'son of the king,' owed by (so-and-so)."[10]

---

6. *DNWSI*, 549–58.

7. Cf. the difficulties in interpreting the למלך inscriptions that were stamped on thousands of storage jars from various sites in Judea (eighth–seventh centuries B.C.E.). The reason for stamping the jars with למלך is still under debate.

8. Cf. *WSS*, 470 (ל indicating ownership on West Semitic seals, only rarely replaced by חתם "Seal of" or זי "Of").

9. Cf. the use of זי on the lion weights from Nineveh (F. M. Fales, "Assyro-Aramaica: The Assyrian Lion-Weights," in *Immigration and Emigration within the Ancient Near East: Festschrift E. Lipinski* [ed. K. Van Lerberghe and A. Schoors; OLA 65; Leuven: Peeters, 1995], 33–55) where minas were measured by the standard "of the king" (מלך or זי מלך), or by the standard "of the land" (זי ארקא).

10. Delaporte, EA nos 21–24 = F. M. Fales, *Aramaic Epigraphs on Clay Tablets of the Neo-Assyrian Period* (Rome: La Sapienza, 1986), nos. 2, 6, 7 and 9. Cf. the expression ארדכל זי מלכא "builder of the king" in a legal document from fifth century B.C.E. Elephantine (C 15: 2); and the phrase אדנלרם סכן בית מלכה "Adūnu-larām, governor of the house of the king" on two Hamath graffiti from ca. 720 B.C.E. (B. Otzen et al., *Hama II.2. Les Objets de la Période dite Syro-Hittite [Âge du fer]. Fouilles et recherches de la Fondation Carlsberg 1931–1938* [Nationalmuseets Skrifter, Større Beretninger 12; Copenhagen: Nationalmuseet, 1990], 275). Note that by the "house of the king" in this specific case is probably meant a building, namely, the king's palace (277), whereas

One may explain בר מלך without the expected emphatic *aleph* in our text as poor Aramaic and the result of Akkadian influence. It is indeed possible that the scribe who wrote it was not thinking freely in Aramaic, but rather translated the Akkadian *mār šarri* automatically into Aramaic. As Akkadian does not distinguish between definite and indefinite forms of the noun, the idiom *mār šarri* means "a (or the) son of a (or the) king."

The idiom בר מלך in our text means "prince" and it refers to a member of the royal family.[11] It expresses a kinship relationship. Its first element, בר, is the important and contrastive component; its second element, מלך, conveys incidental information. It could be left indefinite because it was self-evident which king was meant, namely, the ruling king.[12]

The indefinite מלך meaning "of the (ruling) king" in our passage finds its closest parallel in the Nineveh lion weights of the late-eighth century B.C.E. They bear Aramaic inscriptions pertaining to the weight standard that was being used. Minas were measured by the standard "of the king" (מלך or זי מלך),[13] or by the standard "of the land" (זי ארקא).[14] Fales argued that the later formula was original, and that the one regarding the "royal mina" was later added to it by scribes in the court of Shalmaneser V.[15] They added on the body of each lion not only an Akkadian text mentioning the king's name, but also a further Aramaic inscription "denoting that while the weight-standard remained unchanged, the guarantee of the Assyrian Crown was henceforth on the piece."[16] The mina or minas "of the king" were weights guaranteed by the ruling king, *in casu* Shalmaneser V.

בית מלכא in sources from Achaemenid Egypt means "royal domain" (M. L. Folmer, *The Aramaic Language in the Achaemenid Period: A Study in Linguistic Variation* [OLA 68; Leuven: Peeters, 1985], 290–301, esp. 300–301).

11. The meaning of בר מלכא in the epigraphs may refer to a member of the royal family or to a kind of functionary in the royal administration. Cf. the ambiguity regarding the Hebrew title בן המלך on seals of the eighth to seventh centuries B.C.E. More at *DNSWI*, 637–38.

12. Cf. בת מלך "palace" in the Mesha inscription, with the emphasis on the building being built rather than on its builder, who was self-evidently Mesha (*KAI* 181:23 ואנך בנתי בת מלך); בית מלך in the Sfire inscription (*KAI* 222A:6 ועם כל עלל בית מלך); and מערב שמש "west" versus מערב שמשא "sunset" in Egyptian Aramaic, T. Muraoka and B. Porten, *A Grammar of Egyptian Aramaic* (Leiden: Brill, 1998), 179.

13. מנה מלך, and in the plural מני מלך and מנ(י)ן זי מלך.

14. E.g., CIS II/1, no. 1 (re-edited by Fales, "Assyro-Aramaica," 35).

15. Fales, "Assyro-Aramaica," 52–55.

16. Ibid., 54. The Aramaic epigraphs on the lion weights could then belong to two different strands in the Aramaic language, one originating in the Aramaic homelands in the west (זי ארקא) and one in Assyria at the time of Shalmaneser V (מלך and זי מלך).

Qaqqaru is a generic term for "plot of land."[17] It is apparently used indiscriminately from similar words such as zēru, eqlu, or kirû in contemporary archival texts, but statistically it appears less frequently than the latter ones. It does not say much about the use of the land or its quality, and it is, therefore, different from terms such as bīt gišimmarē "date palm grove," taptû "land newly prepared for cultivation," tamirtu "irrigated land," or mērešu "cultivated land" and others that frequently turn up in the description of land in Neo-Babylonian sale and lease contracts.[18]

The verb ṣabātu means "to take possession of real estate," in general, and "to hold in feudal tenure, to lease,"[19] in particular. In the present case it is difficult to determine whether it is to be understood in its general or in its specific meaning. In other words, it is hard to know if Aḫu-nūrī who "took" Marduk-nādin-aḫi's land had specifically "leased" it from him. Note in this respect that terms such as sūtu "rent," errēšūtu "crop-sharing," zittu "share (in the yield)," ana zāqipūti "for planting trees," e.a., which belong to the stock formulary of Neo-Babylonian land leases are suspiciously lacking from our inscription.[20] Therefore, it is also possible that Aḫu-nūrī who cultivated Marduk-nādin-aḫi's land was after all not a lessee or tenant-farmer but rather someone who worked for Marduk-nādin-aḫi on a different basis. What this could have been may be clarified with the help of the term ikkaru.

The ikkaru was a type of farm laborer who cultivated cereal-crop land belonging to the temple or the palace, and who delivered almost the entire crop

---

17. CAD Q, 119–121 s.v. qaqqaru meaning 4.
18. M. Jursa, "Pacht. C. Neubabylonische Bodenpacht," in RlA 10 (2004): 173.
19. CAD Ṣ, 14–15. On ṣabātu as a technical term for "to lease," see further G. Ries, Die neubabylonischen Bodenpachtformulare (Berlin: Schweitzer, 55 and 61–62 (Pachtklausel B$_1$) and M. Jursa, Neo-Babylonian Legal and Administrative Documents: Typology, Contents and Archives (Guides to the Mesopotamian Textual Record 1; Münster: Ugarit Verlag, 2005), 22–25. Normally, Neo-Babylonian lease contracts were formulated from the point of view of the lessor, meaning that the object was normally given (nadānu) by A to B. M. Jursa, Die Landwirtschaft in Sippar (Archiv für Orientforschung Beiheft 25; Institut für Orientalistik der Universität Wien, 1995), 117 n. 225, points out that ṣabātu seem to have been preferred over nadānu in those cases in which the lessor's identity was self-evident, as for instance in the case of temple land leases. In those cases, indeed, it was obvious that the land was being leased out by agents of the temple only, so that naming the lessor was unnecessary. This explanation for the use of ṣabātu instead of nadānu may also apply to leases of land owned by the king or members of his family, and it may therefore apply to the case currently under consideration.
20. These terms are essential for establishing the economic and legal nature of the lease agreement. Without them it cannot be determined to which part of the yield Aḫu-nūrī was entitled, if any, what kind of agricultural work he had to perform, which other dues he may have had to pay to the king's son, etc.

directly to the landowner in the form of rent (*sūtu*). He belonged for the most part to the category of temple or state dependants and was paid in the form of subsistence rations during the work period.[21] As part of a team he was allocated a plough and draught animals and placed under the administrative responsibility of a *rab ikkari*. The institutions' date-palm groves were cultivated in a similar way, namely, by *nukarribū*, or dependent gardeners, who received a salary (*sissinnu*) in return for their work. In addition, the institutions called on independent farmers, the *errēšū*, who were employed on a contractual basis in a tenant-like position, and are, therefore, a different category of farmers.

The expression *qaqqara ṣabātu* occurs a few times in Babylonian texts from the Neo-Assyrian and early Neo-Babylonian periods in the context of land allocations by the palace to its clients or by the temple to its prebendaries. These allocations seem to have been part of a larger policy aimed at reclaiming land. The administrative document Pohl 1934: no. 1 from Uruk, for instance, lists the names of ninety-one individuals, foremen of units of fifty in the service of the king (*rab ḫanšê ša ina pāni Marduk-apla-iddin šar Bābili*, ll. 1–2).[22] These men had each seized a plot of land of 150 cubits (*qaqqara ṣabtū*, ll. 4 and 97) that had been allocated to them (*ša ušaṣbitu*, l. 100) by a royal official. The document is to be dated around Merodach-Baladan's fourth year (ca. 718 B.C.E.). In VS 6 255+,[23] dated in Nebuchadnezzar's accession year (604 B.C.E.), six gardeners receive a share in temple-owned land in return for their services ([*zēr gišimmarē ša rab banê itti*] *aḫameš i*[*ṣbatū*], "[gardens which the prebendary temple-gardener]s s[eized] together," obv. l. 1, cf. rev. ll. 4'–5'). These examples show that *qaqqara ṣabātu* can have the specific connotation of taking land under the plough.

Another interesting parallel usage of the expression *qaqqara ṣabātu* with respect to royal land from the time of Nebuchadnezzar II occurs in one of the

---

21. See F. Joannès, *The Age of Empires: Mesopotamia in the First Millennium BC* (Edinburgh: Edinburgh University Press, 2004), 270 and G. Van Driel, *Elusive Silver: In Search of a Role for a Market in an Agrarian Environment: Aspects of Mesopotamia's Society* (Leiden: Brill, 2002), 224 on the ongoing discussion about the social and legal position of the *ikkaru* and his economic function.

22. D. Cocquerillat, *Palmeraies et cultures de l'Eanna d'Uruk (559–520)* (Berlin: Mann, 1968), 25 n. 45 and 107. See further the letter published by S. Cole, *Nippur IV: The Early Neo-Babylonian Governor's Archive from Nippur* (OIP 114; Chicago: Oriental Institute of the University of Chicago, 1996), 189–90; and see also CT 56, 44+ (Jursa *Die Landwirtschaft in Sippar*, 12–13).

23. Jursa, *Die Landwirtschaft in Sippar*, 59–60 and R. Da Riva, *Der Ebabbar-Tempel von Sippar in frühbabylonischer Zeit (640–580 v. Chr.)* (AOAT 291; Münster: Ugarit Verlag, 2002), 159–66.

Larsa private archives.[24] A certain Itti-Šamaš-balāṭu declares in the course of a fragmentarily preserved legal dispute that he seized Nebuchadnezzar's land in Larsa and built a house on it. The text is as yet unpublished but the relevant passage has been cited by Beaulieu and reads as follows: *qaqqar* ⌜x x⌝ *ti*[25] *ša Nabû-kudurri-uṣur šar Bābili*^(ki) *ina Larsa*^(ki) *aṣṣabat u bīti ina libbi ētepuš* (ll. 3–5), "the plot of land x x *ti* of Nebuchadnezzar, king of Babylon, in Larsa, I took, and I built a house on it." The text does not say exactly how or why Itti-Šamaš-balāṭu had obtained (lit. "taken") the land from the king. However, it was probably done in order to cultivate it. In fact, we know that Itti-Šamaš-balāṭu was actively involved in the cultivation of royal land from another text in the archive.[26] According to this text, he and a man named Nusku-ušabši had to pay rent to the king,[27] meaning that they had, apparently, obtained land from the king in tenure. They subsequently assigned their own farmer (*ikkaru*) and gardener (*nukarribu*) to cultivate it.[28] The farmer and the gardener were entitled to a share in the yield,[29] hence the recorded transaction is tantamount to sublease. These texts from Larsa show that private persons could be allocated royal land, build a house on it and partake in its cultivation, which they did with the help of *ikkaru*-farmers and *nukarribu*-gardeners and through a hierarchical system of lease and sublease. The same picture emerges from texts in the archive of Zababa-šarra-uṣur who was the manager of the crown prince's estate (*rab bīti ša bīt redûti*) in Bīt-abi-rāmi under the reign of Darius I.[30]

The date "third year of Nebuchadnezzar, King of Babylon" (i.e., 602–601 B.C.E.) comes at the end of the cuneiform inscription as revealed by the handwriting. With only little space left after having written the main text, viz. *qaqqar ... iṣbatu*, the scribe had to squeeze the signs of the date formula tightly together to have them fit in. For the same reason, he wrote "(king of) Babylon" with the signs

---

24. YBC 3526 unpublished, see P.-A. Beaulieu, "A Finger in Every Pie: The Institutional Connections of a Family of Entrepreneurs in Neo-Babylonian Larsa," in *Interdependency of Institutions and Private Entrepreneurs* (ed. A. C. V. M. Bongenaar; PIHANS 87; Leiden: Brill, 2000), no. 22 and n. 14.

25. Perhaps read ⌜*ab-tu*⌝-*ti* "unclaimed."

26. NCBT 1021, published as no. 8 by P.-A. Beaulieu, "A Finger in Every Pie," 43–72.

27. They had to pay *zitti šarri* "a share (in the yield) of the King" (Beaulieu, "A Finger in Every Pie," no. 8, lines 9–10).

28. Ibid., no. 8, lines 1–5: ^(lú)*ikkaru ša Itti-Šamaš-balāṭu itti* PN₁ ^(lú)*nukarribu ša Nusku-ušabši u Itti-Šamaš-balāṭu ušēziz*, "He has employed the farm laborer of IŠB as well as PN₁, the gardener of Nusku-ušabši and of IŠB."

29. Beaulieu, "A Finger in Every Pie," no. 8, lines 5–10: *aḫi ina uḫinnī ikkalū*.

30. F. Joannès and A. Lemaire, "Contrats babyloniens d'époque achéménide du Bīt-Abī râm avec une épigraphe araméenne," *RA* 90 (1996): 41–60.

E^ki, which take up relatively little space, rather than with the longer TIN.TIR^ki (which he had used in the main text).

The Three Vertical Strokes

The three vertical strokes that were stamped in the middle of the round clay artifact are enigmatic. They may be interpreted in various ways. In my opinion they are best explained as a mark of capacity written with cuneiform numerals. In other words, I read them, or at least the two wedge-shaped ones, as cuneiform signs.[31] When read as cuneiform writing, they stand in for the amount of 3 PI (=108 liters), and accordingly, they relate to a certain amount of commodities. In all likelihood, what is meant here are commodities from the land Aḫu-nūrī farmed on behalf of the king's son.

The Function and Practical Meaning of the Object

The correct interpretation of this artifact is severely hampered by the lack of an archaeological context, and the scarcity of comparative material. The major problem is how to understand its function: what purpose was it used for and by whom, why was it labeled with a stamp, and why was it inscribed with two different messages, in two different languages and with two different scripts?

The questions raised by this artifact need a thorough investigation the scope of which by far exceeds the frame of the present article. What follows below is, therefore, only a summary of what I think was the function of this artifact and a brief outline of the importance of the artifact for the socio-economic, linguistic and political history of the Neo-Babylonian empire. A more detailed discussion in which all the above issues will be examined in full and which will also provide hand copies of the inscriptions is currently in preparation.

The relatively large size of this piece of clay, the fact that it lacks any string holes, and the smooth surface of its reverse side (with no marks or imprints of any kind), exclude the possibility that the object in question was a tag or a bulla,[32]

---

31. Other interpretations for the verticals in the middle of the stamp are possible: a decorative filler, a royal emblem of unknown origin, and a symbolic representation of Marduk (viz. a spade) and Nabû (viz. a stylus).

32. A tag, or *Tonverschluss* is a round or oval piece of clay pressed directly against jars, bags, baskets, boxes, trunks, and doors as a means to seal them off. The best-known examples are those from the Neo-Assyrian period, see S. Herbordt, *Neuassyrische Glyptik 8.-7. Jh.v.Chr.*

and strongly suggest it was the lid of a jar. The clue to identifying the nature of this object lies in the characteristic features of its reverse side. Indeed, a closer look at it shows that its central part, namely, that facing the stamped imprint on the obverse, is slightly spherical, and that the outer circular edge, which corresponds to the circular cuneiform inscription on the other side, recedes inwards. Thus, it has the characteristic shape of a lid. Jar lids were typically flat disc-shaped pieces of clay,[33] or the bottom of broken bowls put on top of the jar's opening directly or on its cloth or leather cover.[34] The use of lids was one of the three ways that were current in Mesopotamia to close and seal off jars.[35]

As we saw above, the lid is marked in three ways: in Aramaic, in Akkadian, and by means of vertical strokes. The Aramaic inscription states that the lid, and by implication the jar to which it belonged and its contents, were the property of Marduk-nādin-aḫi, the ruling king's son; the Akkadian tells us who cultivated his land and in which year. The three vertical strokes indicate the jar's capacity.

In my opinion, the markings had the double function of indicating ownership and guaranteeing capacity. The royal name was stamped on the jar lid by

---

Unter besonderer Berücksichtigung der Siegelungen auf Tafeln und Tonverschlüsse (SAAS 1; Helsinki: Neo-Assyrian Text Corpus Project, 1992), 56–62, figs. 7–11. For similar illustrations from Babylonia, see R. Zettler, "Sealings as Artifacts of Institutional Administration in Ancient Mesopotamia," *JCS* 39 (1987): 297–340, figs. 4–8 and 10–13 (Ur III Nippur); C. D. Reichel, "Seals and Sealings at Tell Asmar a New Look," in *Historiography in the Cuneiform World* (Proceedings of the 45th Rencontre Assyriologique Internationale; ed. Tzvi Abusch et al. Bethesda, Md.: CDL, 2001), 110–12, figs. 7–10 (OB Asmar); and for Anatolia, see S. Herbordt, *Die Prinzen- und Beamtensiegel der hethitischen Grossreichszeit auf Tonbullen aus dem Nisantepe-Archiv in Hattusa. Mit Kommentaren zu den Siegelinschriften und Hieroglyphen von J. D. Hawkins* (Boğazköy-Hattuša: Ergebnisse der Ausgrabungen 19; Mainz: von Zabern, 2005), 33–39 (Neo-Hittite Nisantepe). Further note that some of the inscribed Neo-Assyrian tags were bilingual, e.g. Herbordt, *Neuassyrische Glyptik*, 202 (table 10 no. 29).

On the distinction between bullae and tags, see Herbordt, *Die Prinzen- und Beamtensiegel*, 25 and 32 (with illustrative drawings); and F. M. Fales and J. N. Postgate, *Imperial Administrative Records. Part II* (SAA 11; Helsinki: Helsinki University Press, 1995), xxi–xii.

33. See for instance the lids from Neo-Babylonian Uruk: E. Strommenger, *Gefässe aus Uruk von der neubabylonischen Zeit bis zu den Sasaniden* (Der deutschen Forschungsgemeinschaft in Uruk-Warka 7; Berlin, Mann, 1967), 16–17; Tables 11/3–10 and 35/1–6.

34. For the use of broken bowls as lids, see K. Radner, *Das Mittelassyrische Tontafelarchiv von Giricano/Dunnu-ša-uzibi* (Subartu 14; Turnhout: Brepols, 2004), 12–13 (for the English summary see p. 135).

35. U. Moortgat-Correns, "Glyptik," in *RlA* 3 (1957–1971): 451–52; A. Von Wickede, *Prähistorische Stempelglyptik in Vorderasien* (Münchener vorderasiatischen Studien 6; Munich: Profil, 1990), 30; and P. Ferioli and E. Fiandra, "Clay Sealings from Arslantepe VI A: Administration and Bureaucracy," *Origini. Preistoria e protostoria delle civilta antiche* 12, no. 2 (1983): 479.

the king's son himself, or rather by certain of his staff, in order to mark the jar as palace property. The vertical strokes in the middle were stamped on the jar lid in order to give royal endorsement to its content. They are a mark of capacity and put next to the king's name they guaranteed that what was inside the jar had been measured by the royal standard and found equal to 108 liters, or at least, that the jar when it would be filled up would contain the exact amount of 108 liters.

There remains some uncertainty as to what exactly the jar to which this lid belonged may have contained. It could have contained (part of) the yield of Marduk-nādin-aḫi's land that had been harvested by Aḫu-nūrī in Nebuchadnezzar's third year,[36] or (part of) the seeds for the land in question. It could have served as a container for tablets concerned with the cultivation of the land by Aḫu-nūrī up till Nebuchadnezzar's third year.[37] However, it is also possible that the supposed jar with its "royal capacity" lid was not meant for storing but rather was used to measure out the large amounts of crop from Marduk-nādin-aḫi's land. If that is the case, we can consider the supposed jar a measuring unit under royal warrant.

Containers with a standard capacity used as measures are well attested in Neo-Babylonian textual sources. One of the better-attested Neo-Babylonian measuring vessels was the *mašīḫu*, which could contain between 30 and 54 liters.[38] The standard *mašīḫu*-container had a capacity of 36 liters,[39] which is exactly one *pān* (PI), and it was the standard measure used for barley and dates. Our jar would have been three times the standard one in size.

---

36. However, note that 108 liters is a very small amount for a royal domain. The tenants on the Crown Prince's domain in Bīt-Abī-rām, for instance, delivered each 18 kor (3240 liters), 30 kor (5400 liters) and 100 kor (18000 liters) of dates as their rent for the same year (Joannès and Lemaire, "Contrats babyloniens").

37. We may speculate that Aḫu-nūrī had stopped working for Marduk-nādin-aḫi after he had been drafted together with other farmers in the wake of the military events of Nebuchadnezzar's third year. W. Tyborowski, "The Third Year of Nebuchadnezzar II (602 B.C.) According to the Babylonian Chronicle BM 21946—An Attempt at an Interpretation," ZA 86 (1996): 211–16 argues that when Nebuchadnezzar claimed he "strengthened his powerful army" in his second year, thousands of peasants from the villages of Babylonia were gathered in anticipation of a hard campaign, one of which was most probably (but not certainly) against Judah. Aḫu-nūrī may have been among the conscripted men.

38. A. Salonen, *Die Hausgeräte der alten Mesopotamier nach sumerisch-akkadischen Quellen. Teil II: Gefässe* (Annales academiae scientiarum fennicae 144; Helsinki, 1966), 288–89; and CAD M_1, 366.

39. This can be inferred from the phrase found in several Neo-Babylonian texts that five *mašīḫu* equal 1 *kurru* (=180 liters), as for instance in TCL 12 56, 7: 5 *ma-ši-ḫu akî* 1 GUR "at the rate of five *mašīḫu*-s per *kor*."

Furthermore, we know that the Neo-Babylonian king and crown prince had a policy of guaranteeing container capacity. When a *mašīḫu* container, for instance, was guaranteed by the king, it was called *mašīḫu ša šarri*, "the *m*-measure of the king," or more specifically *mašīḫu ša šarri ša 1 pānu*, "the 36 liter *m*-measure of the king."[40] There is also evidence for "a *m*-measure of the crown prince (*mašīḫu ša mār šarri*)," attested to in a debt note for dates, the assessed rent (*imittu*) from Darius's twenty-first year.[41]

It was not unusual to indicate the capacity of a container or specify its content in Mesopotamia. Admittedly, it was never done the way we have it here, namely, on the lid. Usually inscribed and eventually also sealed clay tags or bullae, of the type we mentioned earlier, were used for identifying and quantifying the content of a container. Another practice was to inscribe the relevant details on the container's shoulder or neck,[42] and there are several examples known from the time of Nebuchadnezzar II, Amēl-Marduk, his son, and Neriglissar.[43] The inscriptions on these vases or on sherds from these vases, written close to the neck in cuneiform script, specify not only the vases' target capacity or the amount actually contained in them, but also their provenance or owner. Thus, it says, for instance, "[1 liter] 3 *akalu*[44] / Palace of Amēl-Marduk." Considering the fact that these were made out of stone and not out of clay, they were no doubt objects of value. They may have been used to store cosmetics, because they are comparable in size and material to the inscribed cosmetic bottle from the Persepolis Treasury.[45] If so, they were used in a different context from the marked clay jar to which our lid must have belonged. Nevertheless, they share the same practice according to which a container was marked, first, as belonging to the palace and secondly, as having a certain guaranteed capacity, regardless of whether it was a clay jar for daily commodities, or a stone vase for special occasions.

---

40. For examples, see CAD M₁, 366, 2'. For Nebuchadnezzar's *mašīḫu*-measure of 45 liters used in the palace administration in Babylon, see O. Pedersén, *Archive und Bibliotheken in Babylon* (Berlin: Mann, 2005), 114.

41. Joannès and Lemaire, "Contrats babyloniens," 45–46 (text no. 4).

42. M. A. Powell, "Masse und Gewichte," in *RlA* 7 (1990): 503–4; Salonen, *Die Hausgeräte*, 270–71.

43. P.-R. Berger, *Die neubabylonischen Königsinschriften. Königsinschriften des ausgehenden babylonischen Reiches (626–539 a. Chr.)* (AOAT 4/1; Neukirchen–Vluyn: Neukirchener Verlag, 1973), 148, 325, and 333.

44. The *akalu* (NINDA) was probably one-tenth liter (Powell, "Masse und Gewichte," 498–99 and 503–4).

45. OIP 69 pp. 108–9 and plate 83. For the bottle's capacity, indicated in one line at the level of the handles ("8 1/3 *akalu*"), see Powell, "Masse und Gewichte," 504a.

Importance of the Object and the Information Contained in Its Markings

Several other issues are raised by this unique artifact in addition to the question of its function and practical meaning. They pertain to the socio-economic, linguistic, and political history of Babylonia in the first millennium B.C.E., and to the history of the Aramaic script. They may be summarized as follows.

Socio-Economic History: The Royal Administration at the Time of Nebuchadnezzar II

The first area in which the artifact under consideration contributes to our knowledge is that of the agricultural and administrative organization of royal domains during the Neo-Babylonian Empire. Its inscriptions and the capacity mark in the middle each throw light on a different aspect. The cuneiform inscription, for instance, provides information on the kind of farmers that were employed on Crown land at the time of Nebuchadnezzar II and the conditions under which they farmed this land. Indeed, the land of one of Nebuchadnezzar's sons was farmed, as we saw above, by an *ikkaru*, i.e., a state-dependent farm laborer. This information, laconic as it may be, is a welcome addition, as the textual evidence on the exploitation of royal land for this period is extremely sparse.

We further learn that the royal administration at the time of Nebuchadnezzar II issued official stamps in Aramaic. Indeed, the artifact under consideration is, as we saw, stamped with an Aramaic inscription in alphabetic script. The stamp contains the name of its owner, who was a son of the ruling king, and a capacity mark. However, as the present artifact is hitherto the only known example of its kind, we do not know how widespread issuing royal stamps in Aramaic may have been at the time. Moreover, we cannot know whether it was practiced in the heartland of Babylonia or rather in those parts of the Neo-Babylonian Empire with a dense Aramaic-speaking population. This latter uncertainty is due to the fact that we have no information whatsoever on the artifact's provenance.

Finally, the capacity mark in the middle of the royal stamp shows the administration's concern for officially guaranteed measuring units. It finds its collateral in phrases such as *mašīḫu ša šarri* and others that are frequently found in economic and legal texts from the period, as we explained above.

The information on the Neo-Babylonian royal administration that may be gleaned from the artifact under consideration and its markings is extremely precious, because such information is very rare due to the fact that the main source, namely, the archives from the central administration in Babylon, is as yet not available.[46]

Linguistic History: Languages and Scripts

This artifact with its bilingual and biliteral inscriptions will no doubt play a central role in the still-ongoing discussion on the linguistic character of Babylonian society in the first millennium B.C.E. That Akkadian and Aramaic were used alongside each other in this society is an established fact, but when, where and for which purposes each language was used still largely escape us. It is also still not fully understood if and to what extent the spread of Aramaic, and with it the use of the alphabetic script, contributed to the eventual disappearance of Akkadian and the cuneiform script. The use of Aramaic on a stamp that officially belonged to a son of Nebuchadnezzar II attests to the spread of Aramaic in the administration of the Neo-Babylonian Empire and raises several intriguing questions on the status of Aramaic in the Neo-Babylonian period.

Political History: Nebuchadnezzar's Succession

A final matter that needs to be carefully looked into is the historical implications of this early attestation of Marduk-nādin-aḫi. He was hitherto known from only one legal document, dated to Ulūlu of his father's 42nd year (563 B.C.E.).[47] According to the artifact's cuneiform he is now attested in his father's third year (602–601 B.C.E.), and probably, not as a child, but as an adult in charge of his land. As a matter of fact, this is the earliest attestation of any of Nebuchadnezzar's children. His three other sons are attested only from 566 B.C.E. onwards.[48] His three daughters are attested relatively early, namely, between their father's thirteenth and eighteenth years (592–586 B.C.E.), with one of them perhaps attested as early as Nisannu of the fifth year (600 B.C.E.).[49] This is two (if not ten) years later than the earliest attestation of Marduk-nādin-aḫi. Hence, Marduk-nādin-aḫi may well have been Nebuchadnezzar's first-born child, or at least his eldest son.

---

46. O. Pedersén, *Archives and Libraries in the Ancient Near East 1500–300 B.C.* (Bethesda, Md.: CDL, 1998), 183–91 and *Archive und Bibliotheken in Babylon.*

47. For the text, viz. Nbk 382 (a quitclaim drafted in Babylon), see M. A. Dandamaev, *Slavery in Babylonia: From Nabopolassar to Alexander the Great (626–331 BC)* (DeKalb: Northern Illinois University Press, 1984), 335 and 435.

48. Viz., between Ulūlu of Nebuchadnezzar's 39th and Ayaru of his 42nd year (P.-A. Beaulieu, "Ba'u-asītu and Kaššaya, Daughters of Nebuchadnezzar II," *OrNS* 67 [1998]: 200 n. 45).

49. Beaulieu, "Ba'u-asītu and Kaššaya" (YBC 3449).

Considering the possibility that Marduk-nādin-aḫi was Nebuchadnezzar's eldest son, it follows that he was also the legitimate heir to the throne. If this was indeed the case, it has far-reaching historical implications regarding Nebuchadnezzar's succession. When Nebuchadnezzar II died in 562 B.C.E., Amēl-Marduk succeeded him on the throne of Babylon. How are we to account for Amēl-Marduk's ascension if he had an older brother, namely, Marduk-nādin-apli? Is there a link between this and the fact that Amēl-Marduk's reign was not of long duration? He was assassinated by Neriglissar, his sister's husband and a man of great political and military power, after barely two years in power. Whether his difficulties resulted from his earlier attempts at conspiracy for which he had been jailed by his father,[50] from tension between different fractions within the royal family after Nebuchadnezzar's death,[51] or from his mismanagement as king,[52] is a matter beyond the scope of the present paper. In any case, the evidence from the Moussaieff clay lid adds a new factor that needs to be taken into account in any renewed discussion on this subject, and that is that Amēl-Marduk almost certainly had an older brother.

History of the Aramaic Script

A final area on which our artifact sheds new light is palaeography. The alphabetic script of our stamped imprint is basically of the monumental type with an occasional display of cursive influence.[53] As we saw, it can be dated precisely to 602–601 B.C.E., thanks to the cuneiform inscription that accompanies it. Thus, it

---

50. Irving L. Finkel, "The Lament of Nabû-šuma-ukîn," in *Babylon: Focus mesopotamischer Geschichte, Wiege früher Gelehrsamkeit, Mythos in der Moderne* (ed. J. Renger; CDOG Band 2; Saarbrücken: SDV, 1999), 323–42.

51. Beaulieu, "Ba'u-asītu and Kaššaya"; M. Jursa, "Die Söhne Kudurrus und die Herkunft der neubabylonischen Dynastie," *RA* 101 (2007): 125–36.

52. This mismanagement was the reason for murdering Amēl-Marduk according to Berossus ("because he managed affairs in a lawless and outrageous fashion," see S. M. Burstein *The Babyloniaca of Berossus* (Sources from the Ancient Near East 1/5; Malibu: Undena, 1978), 28–32; G. P. Verbrugghe and J. M. Wickersham, *Berossos and Manetho, Introduced and Translated: Native Traditions in Ancient Mesopotamia and Egypt* [Ann Arbor: University of Michigan Press, 1996], 60) and is also reflected in the Bible where Amēl-Marduk is deliberately called Evil-Merodach.

53. J. Naveh, *The Development of the Aramaic Script* (The Israel Academy of Sciences and Humanities Proceedings 5/1; Jerusalem: Israel Academy of Sciences and Humanities, 1972), 10–15 and 51–64. Peculiar in our inscription are: the inversed *resh* in בר as against an upright, correct *resh* in מרדך (cf. the reversed *nun* in WSS no. 772), and the direction of the *heth*'s bar (it ascends from the bottom of the right vertical towards the top of the left vertical; cf. the *heth* in WSS 762 (Ahu-nuri's seal).

comes to fill in the gap that exists in dated Aramaic material from the late-seventh and sixth centuries B.C.E. This period is crucial for tracing the development of the Aramaic monumental ductus. The earlier monumental script that had been used indiscriminately to write Aramaic, Phoenician, and Hebrew, was still in use, but it was undergoing significant changes as it slowly absorbed cursive characteristics. As a result, a new and distinctively Aramaic monumental ductus started to develop, crystallizing not before the fifth century B.C.E. In view of this, it is clear that the monumental shape of the signs on our artifact of 602–601 B.C.E. are of prime paleographical importance.

Between the present paper's submission (2009) and its publication, considerable time elapsed, and some of the matters discussed above may have to be reviewed in light of the Aramaic, figural, and auxiliary cuneiform impressions on bricks from the time of Nebuchadnezzar, published by B. Sass and J. Marzahn (*Aramaic and Figural Stamp Impressions on Bricks of the Sixth Century B.C. from Babylon* [Ausgrabungen der Deutschen Orient-Gesellschaft in Babylon 10, WVDOG 127; Wiesbaden: Harrassowitz, 2010], esp. 141–48), and the function these impressions fulfilled in marking the bricks' destination. Further note Sass and Marzahn's detailed discussion of sixth-century B.C.E. Aramaic palaeography (ch. 6) and more examples of reversed alphabetic letters on stamps (pp. 158–61). Another point that may need to be looked into more carefully in the future regards the handleability of a 108-liter vessel, especially if it were to function as measuring vessel.

Bibliography

Abraham, K., and M. Sokoloff. "Aramaic Loanwords in Akkadian. A Reassessment of the Proposals." *AfO* 52 (2007–2009), forthcoming.

Beaulieu, P.-A. "Ba'u-asītu and Kaššaya, Daughters of Nebuchadnezzar II." *Or* NS 67 (1998) 173–201.

———. "A Finger in Every Pie: The Institutional Connections of a Family of Entrepreneurs in Neo-Babylonian Larsa." Pages 43–72 in *Interdependency of Institutions and Private Entrepreneurs*. Edited by A. C. V. M. Bongenaar. PIHANS 87. Leiden: Brill, 2000.

———. "Official and Vernacular Languages: The Shifting Sands of Imperial and Cultural Identities in First-Millennium B.C. Mesopotamia." Pages 187–216 in *Margins of Writing, Origins of Cultures*. Edited by S. L. Sanders. Chicago: University of Chicago Press, 2006.

Berger, P.-R. *Die neubabylonischen Königsinschriften. Königsinschriften des ausgehenden babylonischen Reiches (626–539 a. Chr.)*. AOAT 4/1. Neukirchen-Vluyn: Neukirchener Verlag, 1973.

Burstein, S. M. *The Babyloniaca of Berossus*. Sources from the Ancient Near East 1/5. Malibu: Undena, 1978.

Cocquerillat, D. *Palmeraies et cultures de l'Eanna d'Uruk (559–520)*. Berlin: Mann, 1968.
Cole, S. *Nippur IV: The Early Neo-Babylonian Governor's Archive from Nippur*. OIP 114. Chicago: Oriental Institute of the University of Chicago, 1996.
Cross, F. M., and J. Huehnergard. "The Alphabet on a Late Babylonian Cuneiform School Tablet." *JCS* 72 (2003): 223–28.
Da Riva, R. *Der Ebabbar-Tempel von Sippar in frühbabylonischer Zeit (640–580 v. Chr.)*. AOAT 291. Münster: Ugarit Verlag, 2002.
Dandamaev, M. A. *Slavery in Babylonia: From Nabopolassar to Alexander the Great (626–331 BC)*. DeKalb: Northern Illinois University Press, 1984.
Fales, F. M. *Aramaic Epigraphs on Clay Tablets of the Neo-Assyrian Period*. Rome: La Sapienza, 1986.
———. "Assyro-Aramaica: The Assyrian Lion-Weights." Pages 33–55 in *Immigration and Emigration within the Ancient Near East. Festschrift E. Lipinski*. Edited by K. Van Lerberghe and A. Schoors. OLA 65. Leuven: Peeters, 1995.
———. "The Use and Function of Aramaic Tablets." *Ancient Near Eastern Studies Supplement* 7 (2000): 89–124.
Fales, F. M., and J. N. Postgate. *Imperial Administrative Records. Part II*. SAA 11: Helsinki University Press, 1995.
Ferioli, P., and E. Fiandra. "Clay Sealings from Arslantepe VI A: Administration and Bureaucracy." *Origini. Preistoria e protostoria delle civilta antiche* 12, no. 2 (1983): 455–510.
Finkel, Irving L. "The Lament of Nabû-šuma-ukîn." Pages 323–42 in *Babylon: Focus mesopotamischer Geschichte, Wiege früher Gelehrsamkeit, Mythos in der Moderne*. Edited by J. Renger. CDOG Band 2. Saarbrücken: SDV, 1999.
Folmer, M. L. *The Aramaic Language in the Achaemenid Period: A Study in Linguistic Variation*. OLA 68. Leuven: Peeters, 1995.
Geller, M. "The Aramaic Incantation in Cuneiform Script (AO 6489 = TCL 6,58)." *JEOL* 35–36 (1997–2000): 127–46.
Herbordt, S. *Neuassyrische Glyptik 8.–7.Jh.v.Chr. Unter besonderer Berücksichtigung der Siegelungen auf Tafeln und Tonverschlüsse*. SAAS 1. Helsinki: Neo-Assyrian Text Corpus Project, 1992.
———. *Die Prinzen- und Beamtensiegel der hethitischen Grossreichszeit auf Tonbullen aus dem Nisantepe-Archiv in Hattusa. Mit Kommentaren zu den Siegelschriften und Hieroglyphen von J. D. Hawkins*. Boğazköy-Hattuša: Ergebnisse der Ausgrabungen 19. Mainz: von Zabern, 2005.
Joannès, F. *The Age of Empires. Mesopotamia in the First Millennium BC*. Edinburgh: Edinburgh University Press, 2004.
Joannès, F., and A. Lemaire. "Contrats babyloniens d'époque achéménide du Bīt-Abī râm avec une épigraphe araméenne." *RA* 90 (1996): 41–60.
Jursa, M. *Die Landwirtschaft in Sippar in neubabylonischer Zeit*. Archiv Für Orientforschung. 25. Vienna: Institut für Orientalistik der Universität Wien, 1995.
———. "Pacht. C. Neubabylonische Bodenpacht." *RlA* 10/3–4 (2004): 172–83.
———. *Neo-Babylonian Legal and Administrative Documents. Typology, Contents and Archives*. Guides to the Mesopotamian Textual Record 1. Münster: Ugarit Verlag, 2005.
———. "Die Söhne Kudurrus und die Herkunft der neubabylonischen Dynastie." *RA* 101 (2007): 125–36.

Moortgat-Correns, U. "Glyptik." *RlA* 3 (1957–1971): 440–62.
Muraoka, T., and B. Porten. *A Grammar of Egyptian Aramaic*. Leiden: Brill, 1998.
Müller-Kessler, Ch. "Eine aramäische 'Visitenkarte'. Eine spätbabylonische Tontafel aus Babylon." *MDOG* 130 (1998): 189–95.
———. "Die aramäische Beschwörung und ihre Rezeption in den Mandäisch-magischen Texten. Am Beispiel ausgewählter aramäischer Beschwörungsformulare." Pages 193–208 in *Charmes et sortilèges. Magie et magiciens*. Edited by R. Gyselen. Res Orientales 14. Bures-sur-Yvette: Groupe pour l'étude de la civilisation du Moyen-Orient, 2002.
Naveh, J. *The Development of the Aramaic Script*. The Israel Academy of Sciences and Humanities Proceedings 5/1. Jerusalem: Israel Academy of Sciences and Humanities, 1972.
Otzen, B., et al. *Hama II.2. Les Objets de la Période dite Syro-Hittite (Âge du fer). Fouilles et recherches de la Fondation Carlsberg 1931–1938*. Nationalmuseets Skrifter, Større Beretninger 12. Copenhagen: Nationalmuseet, 1990.
Parker, R. A., and W. H. Dubberstein. *Babylonian Chronology 626 B.C.–A.D. 75*. Providence, R.I.: Brown University Press, 1956.
Pedersén, O. *Archives and Libraries in the Ancient Near East 1500–300 B.C.* Bethesda, Md.: CDL, 1998.
———. *Archive und Bibliotheken in Babylon*. Berlin: Mann, 2005.
Powell, M.A. "Masse und Gewichte." *RlA* 7 (1990): 457–517.
Radner, K. *Das Mittelassyrische Tontafelarchiv von Giricano/Dunnu-ša-uzibi*. Subartu 14. Turnhout: Brepols, 2004.
Ries, G. *Die neubabylonischen Bodenpachtformulare*. Berlin: Schweitzer, 1976.
Reichel, C. D. "Seals and Sealings at Tell Asmar a New Look." Pages 101–32 in *Historiography in the Cuneiform World*. Proceedings of the 45th Rencontre Assyriologique Internationale. Edited by Tzvi Abusch et al. Bethesda, Md.: CDL, 2001.
Salonen, A. *Die Hausgeräte der alten Mesopotamier nach sumerisch-akkadischen Quellen. Teil II: Gefässe*. Annales academiae scientiarum fennicae 144. Helsinki: Academiae Scientiarum Fennicae, 1966.
Strommenger, E. *Gefässe aus Uruk von der neubabylonischen Zeit bis zu den Sasaniden*. Der deutschen Forschungsgemeinschaft in Uruk-Warka 7. Berlin: Mann, 1967.
Tyborowski, W. "The Third Year of Nebuchadnezzar II (602 B.C.) According to the Babylonian Chronicle BM 21946—An Attempt at an Interpretation." *ZA* 86 (1996): 211–16.
Van Driel, G. *Elusive Silver: In Search of a Role for a Market in an Agrarian Environment: Aspects of Mesopotamia's Society*. Leiden: Brill, 2002.
Verbrugghe, G. P., and J. M. Wickersham. *Berossos and Manetho, Introduced and Translated. Native Traditions in Ancient Mesopotamia and Egypt*. Ann Arbor: University of Michigan Press, 1996.
Von Wickede, A. *Prähistorische Stempelglyptik in Vorderasien*. Münchener vorderasiatischen Studien 6. Munich: Profil, 1990.
Zettler, R. "Sealings as Artifacts of Institutional Administration in Ancient Mesopotamia." *JCS* 39 (1987): 297–340.

CHAPTER NINE
BRICKS AND BRICK STAMPS IN THE
MOUSSAIEFF PRIVATE COLLECTION

*Kathleen Abraham**

Babylonian and Assyrian kings would often label bricks destined for public buildings with their name, title, and additional epithets (e.g., "provider of [*zānin*] / builder of [*bāni*] the temple of DN"). Some bricks bear long inscriptions detailing the historic and religious circumstances that led the king to (re)construct the building. These royal inscriptions were either stamped on the bricks or written by hand. Hundreds of such inscribed bricks are known from almost all periods of Mesopotamian history. Perhaps the best known are those from the time of Nebuchadnezzar, Neriglissar, and Nabunaid, which were discovered in German excavations at Babylon.[1] There are comparatively few specimens of the blocks that were used to print these bricks. They were probably made out of perishable material such as wood. Moreover, they were not needed in large quantities as one printing block probably sufficed to make a thousand bricks.

The private collection of Shlomo Moussaieff contains such a printing block, which was used in the construction of the Inanna/Ištar temple in Adab at the time of Narām-Sîn. It also contains an inscribed brick of Nebuchadnezzar II that commemorates his restoration of Ebabbar, the temple of the sun god Šamaš in Larsa. They are both published below with the kind permission of the owner.

---

* This research was made possible through the generous support of Dr. Shlomo Moussaieff under the aegis of "The Shlomo Moussaieff Program for the Study of Cuneiform Tablets" at Bar-Ilan University.

1. P.-R. Berger, *Die neubabylonischen Königsinschriften. Königsinschriften des ausgehenden babylonischen Reiches (629–539)* (AOAT 4/1; Neukirchen–Vluyn, Neukirchener Verlag, 1973); and R. Da Riva, *The Neo-Babylonian Royal Inscriptions: An Introduction* (Guides to the Mesopotamian Textual Record 4. Münster: Ugarit Verlag, 2008), 35–37 (with bibliography).

A Brick Stamp of Narām-Sîn

Narām-Sîn, king of Akkad (r. 2254–2218 B.C.E.),[2] was among the first kings to use a stamp with his name and titles for printing bricks. Prior to him the inscriptions on the bricks were written by hand. Two rare earlier exemplars are known from the time of his grandfather Sargon I.[3] The stamps are typically flat rectangular-shaped clay blocks, measuring 10–15 cm in length, with slightly rounded ends and equipped with a handle. The inscription runs over a few horizontal lines and is engraved in cuneiform lapidary script.[4]

The object published below is a nice example of such a brick stamp from the time of Narām-Sîn. It measures 9 × 9 cm and bears a three-line inscription in reversed writing on the obverse. Remnants of the handle are still visible on the reverse. The language of the inscription is Akkadian and reads as follows:

1. ^{d}na-ra-am-^{d}EN.ZU
2. ^{ba}DÍM[5]
3. É ^{d}INANNA

"Narām-Sîn, builder of the temple of the goddess Ištar."

The inscription makes it clear that the stamp was to be used to label bricks destined for the Ištar temple in Adab (modern Bismaya). The same inscription is found on three other brick stamps from the reign of Narām-Sîn. Two were discovered by Banks in Adab[6] and are housed in Chicago and Kalamazoo. They were

---

2. The dates given here follow the middle chronology, cf. M. Van de Mieroop, *A History of the Ancient Near East ca. 3000–323 BC* (Blackwell History of the Ancient World; Oxford: Blackwell, 2004), 302–17.

3. BE 1/1 plate 3 and plate II (= CBS 8754 and CBS 8755). These inscribed brick stamps are not included among the royal inscriptions of Sargon assembled in RIME 2. For another possible brick stamp from the time of Sargon I, viz. with the name of his son Šū-Enlil, see RIME 2, 36 (no. 17). The latter exemplar is exceptionally small in size, and may have been used to label objects other than bricks.

4. Similar artifacts, inscribed in alphabetic script, are known from the Levant, e.g. F. R. Cross, "Judean Stamps," *Eretz-Israel* 9 (1969): 26–27 and plate V 3–4; G.W. Van Beek and A. Jamme, "An Inscribed South Arabian Clay Stamp from Bethel," *BASOR* 151 (1958): 9–16.

5. On the use of the Akkadian verb ^{ba}DÍM = *bāni* in the Sargonic building inscriptions, see J. Klein, "Observations on the Literary Structure of Early Mesopotamian Building and Votive Inscriptions," in *Your Praise Is Sweet: A Memorial Volume for Jeremy A. Black from Students, Colleagues and Friends* (ed. H. D. Baker, E. Robson, and G. G. Zolyomi; Oxford, forthcoming), n. 20.

6. E. J. Banks, *Bismya or the Lost City of Adab* (New York: Putnam, 1912), 317 and 321; for a photo of one of them, see p. 342 (note its cylindrical handle). Note that Banks actually found

reedited by Frayne in RIME 2.[7] The third one belongs to the Schoyen collection and remains unpublished.[8]

Narām-Sîn also made stamps to label bricks destined for the Enlil-temple in Nippur (twelve exemplars)[9] and the Sîn-temple in Ur (two exemplars).[10] These eighteen brick stamps of Narām-Sîn are, therefore, among the earliest examples we have of blind printing.[11]

An Inscribed Brick of Nebuchadnezzar II

Larsa (modern Tell as-Senkereh) had been a largely deserted site after the Kassite period,[12] with its temple lying in ruins, until Nebuchadnezzar II took steps to revive it in the early part of his reign.[13] The inscription in Neo-Babylonian script on the brick published below commemorates this.

Transliteration (lines are ruled)
Obv.
1. ᵈAG-*ku-dúr-ri-ú-ṣu-úr*
2. LUGAL KÁ.DINGIR.RA^{ki}
3. *áš-ri ka-an-šu mu-ut-né-en-nu-ú*
4. *pa-li-iḫ* EN EN.EN
5. *za-ni-in é-sag-ila u é-zi-da*

---

three brick stamps in Adab: two pertaining to the temple of Ištar, and a third about which we know next to nothing. The content of its inscription and its whereabouts are unknown.

7. RIME 2, 120–21 (no. 16).

8. For its publication, see recently A. R. George et al., *Cuneiform Royal Inscriptions and Related Texts in the Schoyen Collection* (Cornell University Studies in Assyriology and Sumerology 17; Bethesda, Md.: CDL, 2011), no. 24.

9. For these twelve exemplars, see RIME 2, 119–20 (no. 15); for a photo of one of them, see BE 1/1, plate II/3 = Text no. 4, with a loop handle.

10. For these two exemplars, see RIME 2, 121–22 (no. 17).

11. Schoyen's website refers to two additional exemplars, namely, "one intact with a cylindrical handle in Istanbul, and a tiny fragment in the British Museum." I do not know if these have been published.

12. J. Margueron, "Larsa. B. Archäologisch," *RlA* 6 (1980–1983): 500–506.

13. D. Arnaud, "Larsa A. Philologisch," *RlA* 6 (1980–1983): 499–500; D. Wiseman, *Nebuchadnezzar and Babylon* (Oxford, 1985); R. H. Sack, *Images of Nebuchadnezzar: The Emergence of a Legend* (Selinsgrove, Pa.: Susquehanna University Press, 1991); P.-A. Beaulieu, "Neo-Babylonian Larsa: A Preliminary Study," *Or* ns 60 (1991): 58–81; P. H. Wright, "The City of Larsa in the Neo-Babylonian and Achaemenid Periods: A Study of Urban and Intercity Relations in Antiquity" (Ph.D. diss., Hebrew Union College, 1994).

6. IBILA ki-i-ni šá ᵈAG-IBILA-ú-ṣur
7. LUGAL KÁ.DINGIR.RAki a-na-ku
8. i-nu-um ᵈAMAR.UTU EN ra-bu-ú
9. IGI.GÁL DINGIRmeš mu-uš-ta-ar-ḫu
10. ma-a-ti ù ni-ši ana re-'-ú-ti id-di-na
11. i-na u₄-mi-šu é-bar₆-ra
12. É ᵈUTU šá qé-re-eb UD.UNUGki
13. šá iš-tu u₄-um ru-qu-ú-ti
14. i-mu-ú ti-la-ni-iš
15. qé-re-bu-uš-šu ba-aî-îa iš-ša-ap-ku-ma
16. la ud-da-a ú-ṣu-ra-a-ti
17. i-na pa-le-e-a ⌈EN⌉ ra-bu-ú ᵈAMAR.UTU
18. a-na É šu-a-ti i-ir-ta-šu sa-li-mu
19. ⌈IM⌉-LIMMU₂-BA ú-ša-at-ba-am-ma
Rev. (Empty)
Edges (Empty)

Translation[14]

[1]Nebuchadnezzar, [2]King of Babylon, [3]humble, submissive, pious. [4]Worshiper of the lord of lords. [5]Caretaker of Esagil and Ezida. [6]The legitimate heir of Nabopolassar, [7]king of Babylon. I, [8]when Marduk, the great lord, [9]the wisest among the gods, the proud one, [10]gave me the country and the people for shepherdship,—[11]at that time, Ebabbar, [12]the temple of Šamaš within Larsa, [13]which a long time ago [14]had become a mound of ruins, [15]in whose midst sand had accumulated so that [16]the buildings plans were no longer recognisable,—[17]during my reign Marduk, the great Lord [18]had mercy on that temple. [19]He aroused the four winds and.sic!

COMMENT

When compared to other bricks with the same portion of text,[15] the following variants are to be noted: BM 90275, BM 90695, BM 115036, and Brique A: 10:

---

14. This translation for the most part follows P.-A. Beaulieu, "Neo-Babylonian Inscriptions," COS 2:308–9.
15. BM 90275, BM 90695 and BM 115036 (see C. B. F. Walker, *Cuneiform Brick Inscriptions* [London: Published for the Trustees of the British Museum by British Museum Publications, 1981], 72–73), and Brique A (published by D. Arnaud, "Textes et objets inscrits trouvés au cours de la 9ᵉ campagne à Larsa [1981]," in *Larsa et Oueili, travaux de 1978–1981* [ed. J.-L. Huot et al.;

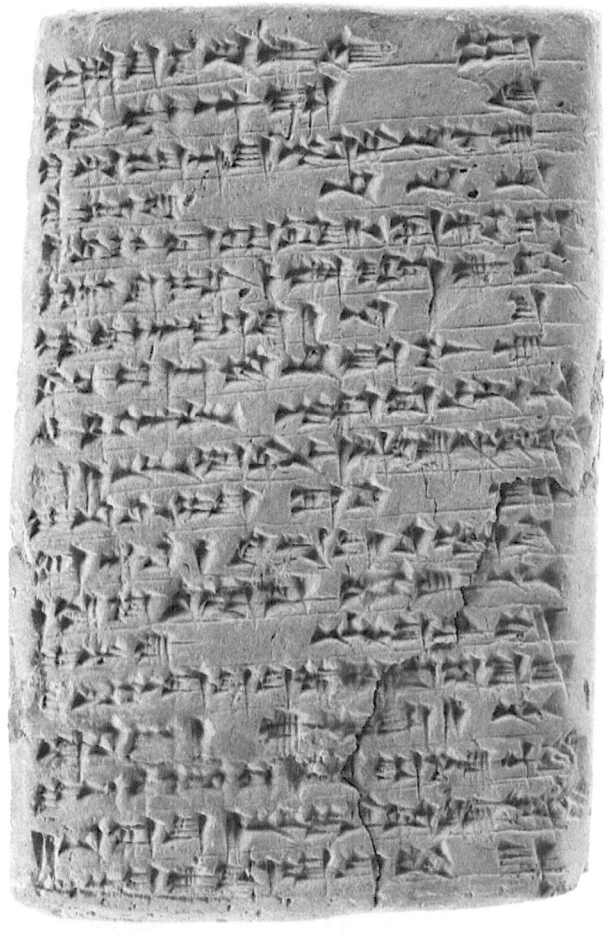

Fig. 1: Nebuchadnezzar's brick (obverse). Photo by Gabi Laron.

a-na; 16: la ú-ud-da-a. BM 115036: 10: un^{meš}; 13: u₄-mu; 15: qer-bu-uš-šu ... iš-šap-ku-ma; 18: ir-ta-šu. Brique A: 4 (// 5 above): ù; 9 (// 10 above): ni-ši-im; 15:

Paris: Éditions recherche sur les civilisations, 1983], 354–57). The text is the first part of a longer commemorative inscription, whose second part is found on the above mentioned bricks from the British Museum and Brique A, as well as on several other bricks that were found in Larsa by the French, but it is lacking from the Moussaieff brick (see more on this matter below).

qé-er-bu-uš-šu ... iš-ša-ap-ku (without -ma); 17: ra-bú-u; 20 (// 19 above): im^{meš}-limmu$_2$-ba.

The brick on which this inscription is written measures 10.7 (preserved length) × 7 (width) × 2.7 (thickness) cm. It is significantly different in size from the other inscribed bricks of Nebuchadnezzar, which are normally squares of 33 × 33 cm or 16 × 16 cm, or half squares of 33 × 16 cm.[16] Bricks from the time of Nebuchadnezzar that are similar in size to the Moussaieff brick are L. 70.86, L. 70.87 and the two bricks published by Arnaud in 1983 (Briques A and B).[17] These bricks are all from Larsa and are, moreover, engraved either with the same commemorative inscription as our text (Arnaud's Brique A) or with parts of it (Arnaud's Brique B, L. 70.86 and L. 70.87).

The text of the inscription on the Moussaieff brick is part of a commemorative inscription that is known, either in full or in part, from ten other bricks,[18] and it runs parallel to the text that is found on some of Nebuchadnezzar's clay

---

16. See Berger, *Die neubabylonischen Königsinschriften*, 21; Walker, *Cuneiform Brick Inscriptions*, 72–91; J.-L. Huot et al., "La structure urbaine de Larsa. Une approche provisoire," in *Larsa. Travaux de 1985* (ed. J.-L. Huot; Paris: Éditions recherche sur les civilisations, 1989), 28 and 32. The sizes as given above relate to fully preserved bricks, not to fragments. The statement made by Da Riva, *The Neo-Babylonian Royal Inscriptions*, 36 that "The sizes of Nebuchadnezzar's bricks, ..., vary enormously: 12×6.5×3 cm (...) versus 33×33×7 cm (...), ..." is based on bricks and brick fragments.

17. L. 70.86 measures 13.5 (preserved length) × 7 (width) cm. L. 70.87 measures 7.5 (preserved length) × 6.5 (width) cm. Brique A measures 32 (length) × 7 (width) cm. For Brique B only its width is known, viz., 7.4 cm. For the publication of these bricks, see n. 19. Note that Arnaud's Briques A and B are the only Nebuchadnezzar bricks found in a precise archaeological context—see J.-L. Huot et al., "Rapport préliminaire sur la dixième campagne à Larsa (1983)," in *Larsa (10e campagne, 1983), Oueili (4e campagne, 1983). Rapport préliminaire* (ed. J.-L. Huot et al.; Paris: Éditions recherche sur les civilisations, 1987), 173 (Mur M2). For a photo of one of them taken *in situ*, see Arnaud, "Textes et objets inscrits," 357.

18. All ten bricks are from Larsa. Three of them are currently in the British Museum (BM 90275, BM 90695, and BM 115036, see Walker, *Cuneiform Brick Inscriptions*, 72–73), and seven were found by the French during excavations in Larsa in 1967, 1970, 1971, 1974 and 1981: see M. Birot, "Découvertes épigraphiques à Larsa (Campagnes 1967)," *Syria* 45 (1968): 242–43 (two bricks, unpublished and without catalogue numbers); D. Arnaud, "Catalogue des textes trouvés au cours des fouilles et des explorations régulières de la mission française à Tell Senkereh-Larsa en 1969 et 1970," *Syria* 48 (1971): 293 (L. 70.86); "Larsa. Catalogue des textes et des objets inscrits trouvés au cours de la sixième campagne," *Syria* 53 (1976): 80 (L. 70.86 and L. 70.87); ibid., 48 and 81 (L. 74.9); and Arnaud, "Textes et objets inscrits," 354–57 (two bricks, A and B, published but without catalogue numbers). Cf. Da Riva, *The Neo-Babylonian Royal Inscriptions*, s.v. B26 (for the bricks in the British Museum) and s.v. C24/7–8 (for the three catalogued bricks from the French excavations, viz., L. 74.9, L. 70.86 and L. 70.87, but note that Da Riva mistakenly catalogued them as cylinders).

cylinders.[19] It opens with the standard royal titulary (ll. 1–7), followed by a description of the building works (ll. 8–19). However, it breaks off in the middle of this description and it lacks the prayer that is usually found at the end of this type of building inscription. In other words, the inscription on the Moussaieff brick is incomplete.

As can be seen, the brick published above ends in the middle of a sentence. Its last line (l. 19) relates how Marduk set the winds in motion (*ušatbâm-ma*), and the copulative *-ma* "and," which is affixed to the verb *ušatbâm*, suggests that a second verb followed: "he set the winds in motion and." From other exemplars of the same inscription, we know that it continued with a description of how the winds, after having been set in motion by Marduk, removed the sand and revealed to Nebuchadnezzar the original foundations(?) of the dilapidated temple of Šamaš in Larsa, which Nebuchadnezzar subsequently rebuilt. The inscription normally concluded with a prayer to Šamaš.

One of the bricks that was found during French excavations in Larsa in 1970 (L. 70.86) deserves our special attention.[20] It bears the second part of the text commemorating Nebuchadnezzar's restoration of the Ebabbar temple in Larsa, namely the part that runs parallel to Langdon 1911 no. 10 col. I 24–col. II 26. This is exactly the part that is missing on our brick, which has only the beginning of the text, namely the part that runs parallel to col. I 1–20. This fact, coupled with the fact that both L 70.86 and the Moussaieff brick have the same width, leads us to suggest that they once may have formed one piece that was sawed in two when it was removed from its original setting.[21] The two pieces, put together, would yield the entire text except for the lines paralleling col. I 21–23, which are lost.

We can, therefore, propose that the unprovenanced brick from the Moussaieff collection comes from Larsa and should be joined with L 70.86.

Bibliography

Arnaud, D. "Catalogue des textes trouvés au cours des fouilles et des explorations régulières de la mission française à Tell Senkereh-Larsa en 1969 et 1970." *Syria* 48 (1971): 291–93.

---

19. S. Langdon, *Die neubabylonischen Königsinschriften* (VAB 4; Leipzig: Hinrichs, 1911), 96–97 no. 10 col. I, lines 1–20. Cf. Da Riva, *The Neo-Babylonian Royal Inscriptions*, s.v. C24/1–6.

20. Arnaud, "Catalogue des textes," 293 (L. 70.86; for a copy see idem, "Larsa: Catalogue des textes," 80)

21. The smooth surface of the brick's lower edge could be the result of sawing. For another example in which the text of Langdon, *Die neubabylonischen Königsinschriften*, no. 10 is divided over two bricks, see Birot, "Découvertes épigraphiques à Larsa," 243 n. 1.

———. "Larsa. Catalogue des textes et des objets inscrits trouvés au cours de la sixième campagne." *Syria* 53 (1976): 47–82.

———. "Larsa A. Philologisch." *RlA* 6 (1980–1983): 496–500.

———. "Textes et objets inscrits trouvés au cours de la 9e campagne à Larsa (1981)." Pages 353–57 in *Larsa et Oueili, travaux de 1978–1981*. Edited by J.-L. Huot et al. Paris: Éditions recherche sur les civilisations, 1983.

Banks, E. J. *Bismya or the Lost City of Adab*. New York: Putnam, 1912.

Beaulieu, P.-A. "Neo-Babylonian Inscriptions." *COS* 2:306–14.

———. "Neo-Babylonian Larsa: A Preliminary Study." *Or* NS 60 (1991), 58–81.

Berger, P.-R. *Die neubabylonischen Königsinschriften. Königsinschriften des ausgehenden babylonischen Reiches (629–539)*. AOAT 4/1. Neukirchen–Vluyn: Neukirchener Verlag, 1973.

Birot, M. "Découvertes épigraphiques à Larsa (Campagnes 1967)." *Syria* 45 (1968): 241–47.

Cross, F. R. "Judean Stamps." *Eretz-Israel* 9 (1969): 20–27.

Da Riva, R. *The Neo-Babylonian Royal Inscriptions. An Introduction*. Guides to the Mesopotamian Textual Record 4; Münster: Ugarit Verlag, 2008.

George, A. R. et al. *Cuneiform Royal Inscriptions and Related Texts in the Schoyen Collection*. CUSAS 17. Bethesda: CDL, 2011.

Huot, J.-L. et al. "Rapport préliminaire sur la dixième campagne à Larsa (1983)." Pages 170–211 in *Larsa (10e campagne, 1983), Oueili (4e campagne, 1983). Rapport préliminaire*. Edited by J.-L. Huot, et al. Paris: Éditions recherche sur les civilisations, 1987.

Huot, J.-L. et al. "La structure urbaine de Larsa. Une approche provisoire." Pages 19–52 in *Larsa. Travaux de 1985*. Edited by J.-L. Huot. Paris: Éditions recherche sur les civilisations, 1989.

Klein, J. "Observations on the Literary Structure of Early Mesopotamian Building and Votive Inscriptions. In *Your Praise is Sweet: A Memorial Volume for Jeremy A. Black from Students, Colleagues and Friends*. Edited by H. D. Baker, E. Robson, and G. G. Zolyomi. Oxford (forthcoming).

Langdon, S. *Die neubabylonischen Königsinschriften*. VAB 4. Leipzig: Hinrichs, 1911.

Margueron, J. "Larsa. B. Archäologisch." *RlA* 6 (1980–1983): 500–506.

Sack, R. H. *Images of Nebuchadnezzar: The Emergence of a Legend*. Selinsgrove, Pa.: Susquehanna University Press, 1991.

Van Beek, G.W., and A. Jamme. "An Inscribed South Arabian Clay Stamp from Bethel." *BASOR* 151 (1958): 9–16.

Van de Mieroop, M. *A History of the Ancient Near East ca. 3000–323 BC*. Blackwell History of the Ancient World. Oxford: Blackwell, 2004.

Walker, C. B. F. *Cuneiform Brick Inscriptions*. London: Published for the Trustees of the British Museum by British Museum Publications, 1981.

Wiseman, D. *Nebuchadnezzar and Babylon*. Oxford, 1985.

Wright, P. H. "The City of Larsa in the Neo-Babylonian and Achaemenid Periods: A Study of Urban and Intercity Relations in Antiquity." Ph.D. diss., Hebrew Union College, 1994.

Chapter Ten
A Babylonian Boundary Stone in the Moussaieff Collection

W. G. Lambert†

Boundary stones, as they are conventionally called, are a well-known category of legal documents surviving mostly from the Kassite Dynasty and the following Second Isin Dynasty. Although a few appear later they thus cover the period ca. 1400–700 B.C.E.

They are called stones since a majority are carved on natural boulders with some trimming. A few offer similar texts but are written on clay tablets. The Moussaieff example is rare in that the stone has been cut to resemble a clay tablet: flat obverse and convex reverse, with sharp edges. Both text and relief sculpture commonly occur on a single stone. The text describes the borders and location of a plot of arable land, then states that it was given by the ruling king to a named man. Witnesses to the transaction are normally listed, then a series of curses by named gods, with their attributes specified. The curses were meant to stop anyone from overriding the terms of the deed. These commonly end the document, although the date by year of the reigning king may be given.

The relief sculpture normally depicts symbols of the gods invoked in the curses, but curiously, while most symbols are well known as belonging to well-known gods, there is never perfect agreement on one stone between the pictorial symbols and the gods named in the text. The symbols are most commonly arrayed around the top of the stone, but there are cases of one side being reserved for the symbols. Apart from symbols, the donating king is rarely portrayed. In addition the recipient may be shown facing the king, as happens on the stone under study. The king is of course the taller, the official the shorter. The king wears richly decorated robes, the official plain robes.

What actually took place is not exactly what is stated. It sounds like a king, in his generosity, giving a piece of land to a named person and his descendants in

Fig. 1. Obverse of the Boundary Stone. Dark Stone, 17 × 8.5 cm. Courtesy of Shlomo Moussaieff.

Fig. 2. Reverse of the Boundary Stone. Courtesy of Shlomo Moussaieff.

Fig. 3. Upper Edge of the Boundary Stone. Courtesy of Shlomo Moussaieff.

perpetuity. In fact the land was remuneration for unspecified duties to the king and as long as these duties were performed the recipient could indeed presume to keep hold of the land. Since professions were commonly passed down in families, the allusion to "in perpetuity" would easily be understood.

In this case the recipient of the land was an exorcist and "king's benediction (priest)." Exactly what the latter involved is unknown, but it was clearly a duty to the king. He is depicted as holding a small object in one hand, probably a cuneiform tablet. The right hand is raised, but it is not clear whether it is holding something; but if so it must have been very small. Probably it is raised in a gesture of benediction.

The king involved is Adad-apla-iddina, eighth king of the Second Isin Dynasty, and his accession year (the date of this stone) was about 1069 B.C.E. The witnesses were not just any suitable person around at the time, but a fixed group of high officers of state, a custom common under this dynasty, attesting to the importance of assignment of irrigated land.

The decision to create a tablet-like boundary stone resulted in some problems. The upper edge and top bands of area of each side are occupied with the symbols, although this resulted in overriding the normal rule that tablets were turned top-to-bottom, not side-to-side. The remainder of the side edges and bottom edge were notched. On the obverse, under the symbols, the portrait of king and courtier appears. The reverse has two quite separate parts: a 19-line section under the symbols describing the plot of land, its donation, listing the witnesses and the place and date of the action. These nineteen lines, though on the reverse, are not inverted. Below them is a short gap, then five lines that are inverted! To understand these we have to go back to the obverse. There, under the portraits is a sketch map of the land, with boundaries marked and specified, and areas given. Below this are two further lines stretching over the width of the tablet, and a little damaged. It is these two lines that are continued on the reverse with five more lines, but the section is damaged and its purpose not fully clear. What is lacking are curses. This is unusual but not without parallel.

The top edge of the stone (fig. 3) bears three symbols: (i) a crescent for the moon-god Sîn; (ii) an elaborate star for the sun god Šamaš; and (iii) a simpler star for Venus, Ištar. This is a very common collocation. However, the symbols on the tops of the two sides are not correctly placed by traditional standards. Normally they are set out in order of seniority of the gods in the Babylonian pantheon, though this involved much variation after the top half-dozen gods were represented. The correct hierarchical order here must begin on the reverse, half way along the area, and the result is: (iv) and (v) "seats" with tiaras resting on them (fig. 2): for Anu and Enlil, two old Sumerian gods once heads of the pantheon. The obverse now continues with three further "seats," distinguished by what appears on top, and by the front parts of recumbent horned animals projecting from their sides (fig. 1). The first of these (vi) offers the head of an ibex on top, on a very long neck, and the front parts of the mythological "fish-goat." This belongs to Ea, god of the subterranean waters. The next (vii) has part of a stylus on top and the front parts of the also mythological *mušḫuš*: a mixture of snake and lion, but in this case with animal horns. This represents Nabû, god of writing, who was powerful in the Babylonian pantheon at this time. The next (viii) has the same animal, but with a spade with pointed blade on top, a symbol of the god Marduk, who had recently been proclaimed "king of the gods." At this time Marduk was father of Nabû, which explains how the same animal serves for both. Three symbols on the reverse remain (fig. 2); the coiled snake (ix), the cosmic river Irḫan, which surrounded the earth conceived as a flat disc. The scorpion (x) represents Išḫara, goddess of love, and in this aspect paralleling Ištar, but lacking the astral presence. The omega-like symbol (xi)—the uterus?—stands for the Mother Goddess, Bēlet-ilī.

The disregard of tradition in this placing of the symbols was meant to enhance the position of the recently promoted Marduk. Ea was father of Marduk, and Marduk father of Nabû, so these three were represented by their symbols together on one side of the stone above the relief of king and courtier.

Text, Reverse

1. 10 *kurru*(gur) *zēru*(še.numun) 1 *ikû ṣimdu*(baneš) 1 *ammatu*(kùš) *rabītu*^{tu}
2. *ugār* (a.gàr) ^{uru}*ki-ri-ib-ti-* ^{d}*en-líl*
3. *kišād*(gú) ^{id}*sa-ḫi-ir-ti pīḫat*(nam) ^{uru}*ru-uq-ti*

4. ᵈadad-apla-i-din-nam šarru
5. ᵐᵈsin-na-ṣi-ir mār ᵐta-ri-bi āšipu(maš.maš)
6. ka-ri-ib-šu i-ri-im
7. ù a-na pa-aq-ra la ra-še-⌈e⌉
8. ik-nu-uk-ma a-na u₄-um ṣa-a-ti i[d-din]
9. i-na ka-na-ak tup-pi šu-[a-tu]
10. ᵐú-zib-šu-qab šakin (gar-kur) ᵘʳᵘi-š[i-in]
11. ᵐ[m]u-na-bit-tu mār ᵐpa-ḫa-ri š[a-rēši] (l[ú.sag])
12. [ᵐ]šu-ra-nu mār ᵐ nap-ši-ri sak-r[u-maš]
13. ᵐᵈnabû (nà)-šuma(mu)-iddina (sum)ⁿᵃ mār ᵐna-zi-ᵈmarūtuk ˡúsu[kkallu]
14. ᵐᵈen-líl-mudammiq(sig₅)ⁱᵠ mār ᵐpal-lu-la šākin(gar) ṭè-me
15. ᵐᵈen-líl-za-kir-šumi (mu) mār ᵐarad-ᵈé-a bēl pāḫiti (nam)
16. ⌈ù⌉ ᵐmu.nag.tu šà-tam bīt ú-na-a-ti izzazzu(gub)ᶻᵘ
17. [bāb]ilu ([ká]-dingir-ra)ᵏⁱ ⁱᵗⁱaraḫsamnu (apin.du₈.a) rēš šarrūti (mu.sag)
18. [ᵈ]adad-apla-i-din-nam šàr bābili (e)
19. [gaba]-ri ⁿᵃ⁴kunukki(kišib) šarri ša šip-re-e-ti

Translation

1. (A field requiring) 10 kurru of seed corn (at the rate of) one ṣimdu (measure) per ikû (of land, measured by) the big cubit,
2. the estate of Kiribti-Enlil,
3. on the bank of the Saḫirtu canal, province of (the town) Rūqtu:
4. Adad-apla-iddinam, the king,
5. granted to Sîn-nāṣir, son of Tāribu, the exorcist,
6. his (the king's) benediction priest.
7. So that there would be no claim
8. he (the king) sealed it and gave it for future days.
9. At the sealing of this tablet were present:
10. Uzib-šuqab, mayor of Isin,
11. Munnabittu, son of Paḫḫāru, the [officer],
12. Šurānu son of Napširu, the general,
13. Nabû-šuma-iddina, son of Nazi-Marduk, the vizier,
14. Enlil-mudammiq, son of Pallula, the administrator,
15. Enlil-zākir-šumi, son of Arad-Ea, provincial governor.
16. and MU.NAG.TU, supervisor of the stores.
17. Babylon, month Araḫsamnu, accession year of

18. Adad-apla-iddina, king of Babylon.
19. Copy of administrative royal document.
(20. ^{id}sa-ḫi-ir-tu: Saḫirtu [canal]).

Lower Obverse and Lowest Reverse

Below the relief is the sketch map of the land with captions, and beneath that are two lines of cuneiform written normally across the width of the tablet. These are followed by five such lines on the reverse, inverted as on a normal cuneiform tablet. The map begins with a single line of script within rulings marking the irrigation canal from which the plot was watered. The script (as shown on line 20 of the translation) reads: "Saḫirtu (canal)." Below, up to the two normal lines of script, all the writing is turned on its side in a top-to-bottom direction. The far right paragraph reads:

> šiddu elû iltānu (uš an-ta ^{im}si-sá)
> itû bīt ša-rēši (ús-sa-du é lú-sag)
> ša a-na pīḫati tu-ur-ru
> Translation: Upper side, north, adjacent to the estate of the officer, which turns toward the province.

The paragraph adjacent to the left edge of the stone reads:

> šiddu šaplû   (uš ki-ta)
> šūtu   (^{im}u$_{18}$-lu)
> itû   (ús-sa-du)
> pīḫat ^{uru}ru-uq-ti
> Translation: Lower side, south, adjacent to the province of Ruqtu.

The left-hand paragraph under canal reads:

> pūtu elītu   (sag an-ta)
> amurru   (^{im}mar-dú)
> kišād ^{id}sa-ḫi-ir-ti   (gú ^{id}sa-ḫi-ir-ti)
> Translation: Upper front, west, bank of the Saḫirtu canal.

The Horizontal line of signs immediately above the two normal lines reads:

> pūtu šaplītu šadû   (sag ki-ta ^{im}kur-ra)
> maḫar appāri   (igi ambar)
> itū pīḫat rūqti   (ús-sa-du nam ^{uru}ru-uq-ti)

Translation: Lower front, east, facing the marsh, adjacent to the province of Ruqtu.

These four boundaries enclose what turn out to be two adjacent plots of irrigated land, which make up what was being given by the king. Each is provided with measurements of the sides, and statements of the amount of seed corn needed according to their areas.

> Plot next to Saḫirtu canal:
> vertical right-hand side: 5 ninda (=60)
> side next to canal: 30
> the remaining: 45 seed-corn (še-numun) *ištēn*^{en} *eqlu*
> ("first field")
> Bigger plot under the first:
> vertical right hand side: 100
> vertical left hand side: 110
> upper and lower sides, both: 70
> the remaining: 44 seed-corn (še-numun) *šanû* (min^{ú}) *eqlu*
> ("second field")

The remaining seven lines of script covering the whole width of the tablet are:

> 1. [^{d}*adad*]-*apla-i-din-nam* š[*arru*]
> 2. [x x]-*im-bu-uš mār* ^{m}*tu-un-na* lú sag x [(x)]
> 3. ....] x *mār* ^{m} *arad-*^{d}*é-*[*a*]
> 4. ....] x ⌜*a-na*⌝ ^{md}*sin-nāṣir*(ùru) *āšipi* (maš-maš) *i*[*d-din*]
> 5. [x x x x x] ^{d}*adad-apla-i-din-nam šarru*
> 6. [*šá mi-šiḫ-t*]*i eqli li-lat-tík a-re-e*
> 7. [x x (x)] *bīt* ^{m}*arad-*^{d}*é-a*

> Translation
> 1. [Adad]-apla-iddina, the k[ing]
> 2. [. .]imbuš, son of Tunna, the . . . ,
> 3. . . .] . son of Arad-Ea,
> 4. . . .] g[ave] to Sîn-nāṣir the exorcist.
> 5. [. . . . .] Adad-apla-iddina, the king,
> 6. let him check the multiplication of the [measurements] of the field.
> 7. . . .] the house of Arad-Ea.

The point of these lines is largely lost due to damage. On the one hand they seem to repeat needlessly the substance of the main text. On the other hand persons not named in the text appear here for no clear reason. Line 6 is the most transparent, and appears to be unique in such a document, implying that some of the figures given are wrong. Therefore we must return to the captions on the plan. The ninda is commonly 12 cubits, so we assume that all the measurements are in cubits, although this is not stated. Therefore the two fields are 60 × 30 and 100/110 × 70 cubits. Since these figures were gotten by using a measuring tape we hope that they are correct. However, there is a blatant error in the seed-corn figures. The smaller field is "45" and the much larger field is "44." The very first line of the text gives "10 *kurru*" as the seed-corn for the two fields together. The *kurru* was a large unit in the system, so the figures on the plan must be in unstated smaller units of the system. There is no need to delve into the system further. The figures on the plan contain a serious error. This creates an apparent problem: a legal document declares itself to contain an error. The solution lies in the final line of the main text, line 19. The eighteen preceding lines were inscribed on a document in the royal archives and were the binding contract. The stones with their decoration and further inscriptions were made as records for the locality concerned and therefore, in order to save the labor of making a new stone, a note of needed correction was added.

The naming of Arad-Ea as father of several men involved in this document needs explanation. A Middle Babylonian custom is involved. Men in a particular profession professed descent from a famous man in that profession. The actual Arad-Ea lived much earlier, under or just before one of the kings Kurigalzu.[1] Furthermore, at least some of his offspring are known to have been "expert accountants" (um-mi-a níg-kas$_7$), which would have been relevant to matters on this stone.

The last phrase of the final line of these extra seven lines also occurs in a Middle Babylonian legal document from Ur,[2] where it occurs in a list of three witnesses. The first two had their fathers' names given. The third and last instead followed the personal name with "of the house of Arad-Ea (*ša bīt* ^{m}arad-^{d}é-a)." RG V 54 took Bīt-Arad-Ea as a place name, which is possible. However, identifying a witness by mention of his home town is surely unprecedented and unlikely. More likely, since it replaces the fathers' names of the other two witnesses, it is meant to indicate that he was a descendent of the famous scribe, not his immedi-

---

[1]. See W. G. Lambert, "Introduction," *Cuneiform Texts in the Metropolitan Museum of Art*, vol. 2 (I. Spar and W. G. Lambert; New York Metropolitan Museum of Art, 2005), xiii–xv.
[2]. *UET* VII 29, rev. 4.

ate son, as O. R. Gurney seems to have understood the phrase according to his translation: "of the house of Arad-Ea." ³

Note on the name Uzib-šuqab (rev. 10). While the variant readings GA/QA have long been noted in the divine name Šuqamuna, the same thing occurs with Šuqab. Hitherto only a writing with GA has been noted.⁴ However writing with QA occurs in a seal inscription:

x-x-^{d}U+DAR
dumu *ri-ib-^{d}šu-qa-ab*
ír *ilum-mu-ut-nin*

The style of the inscription is typical Old Babylonian, and the art is a crude variant of the Late Old Babylonian cut and/or drilled style. The man named in the last line need not have been a ruler. The name may have been that of a high official or wealthy individual. The seal is published in O. E. Ravn, *A Catalogue of the Oriental Cylinder Seals and Seal Impressions in the Danish National Museum* (København, 1960), no. 88.⁵

Bibliography

Balkan, Kemal. *Kassitenstudien*, vol. 1. New Haven: American Oriental Society, 1954.
Gurney, O. R. *Ur Excavation Texts:* 7. London: British Museum Publications Ltd for the British Museum, and the University Museum, University of Pennsylvania, 1974.
———. *The Middle Babylonian Legal and Economic Texts from Ur*. S. l. British School of Archaeology in Iraq, 1983.
Lambert, W. G. "Introduction." Pages xiii–xv in Ira Spar and W. G. Lambert, *Cuneiform Texts in the Metropolitan Museum of Art*, vol. 2. New York: Metropolitan Museum of Art, 2005.
Ravn, O. E. *A Catalogue of the Oriental Cylinder Seals and Seal Impressions in the Danish National Museum*. Copenhagen: National Museum, 1960.

---

3. O. R. Gurney, *The Middle Babylonian Legal and Economic Texts from Ur* (S. l.: British School of Archaeology in Iraq, 1983), 95.

4. Kemal Balkan, *Kassitenstudien*, vol. 1 (New Haven: American Oriental society, 1954), 115.

5. O. E. Ravn, *A Catalogue of the Oriental Cylinder Seals and Seal Impressions in the Danish National Museum* (Copenhagen: National Museum, 1960), no. 88.

Chapter Eleven
A New Inscribed Palmyrene Stone Bowl from the Moussaieff Collection

André Lemaire

The inscribed stone bowl (fig. 1) discussed here belongs to the collection of Mr. Shlomo Moussaieff.[1] It is 38.5 cm high with a diameter of 47 cm, or 58 cm if you take into account the 'handles'. The upper rim is 4.3 cm thick (fig. 1) and is decorated by two human heads with chubby faces (figs. 2 and 3). These faces have been identified as Dionysos' faces.[2] The two heads protruding 5.5 cm were placed in diametrical opposition and were probably used as a kind of handles to seize the bowl. The bowl is approximately half spherical with a base in the shape of a flat disk.

The rim of the stone bowl presents, on its upper part, an incised Palmyrene inscription ending with an ivy leaf, an ornament also well attested in Palmyrene funerary inscriptions. The inscription begins on the left of one of the heads/handles (fig. 4) and is inscribed around the upper rim (fig. 5), ending with the ivy leaf (fig. 6) on the right of and below the first head/handle.

The Palmyrene script is regular and well incised, showing many curves typical of semi-cursive writing. In this type of script, some of the letters may be easily confused: W with Y, Q with S, T with Ṣ, and D with R. Furthermore there are no word separators and the inscription is incised *scriptio continua*. However one can easily read it:

---

1. A similar bowl from the Moussaieff collection was published by Françoise Briquel-Chatonnet, "Un cratère palmyrénien inscrit: nouveau document sur la vie religieuse des Palmyréniens," *Aram* 7 (1995): 153–63, For another similar bowl, see, for example, Khaled Al-As'ad and Michał Gawlikowski, *The Inscriptions in the Museum of Palmyre: A Catalogue* (Palmyra/Warsaw: Archeo, 1997), 71: no. 109.

2. Briquel-Chatonnet, "Un cratère palmyrénien inscrit," 158–61 where the iconography is clearer and more detailed.

Fig. 1. Inscribed Palmyrene Stone Bowl.

QRB WHBY BR BLḤ' LGN'Y' ṬBY' WSKRY' 'L ḤYWHY WḤYY BN-
WHY ŠNT 465

(Which) offered Wahabay son of Bôlḥâ to the good and profitable *jinns* for his life and the life of his sons. Year 465

1. Paleographic Notes

- In the name WHBY, the W and the Y can be distinguished by the length of the vertical stroke but it is not always clear in this inscription.
- The R of BR is not completely clear.
- The third letter of the patronym is difficult to identify: one could choose between Ḥ and perhaps T. However it seems that, because of Palmyrene

Fig. 2. First handle in the shape of a head.

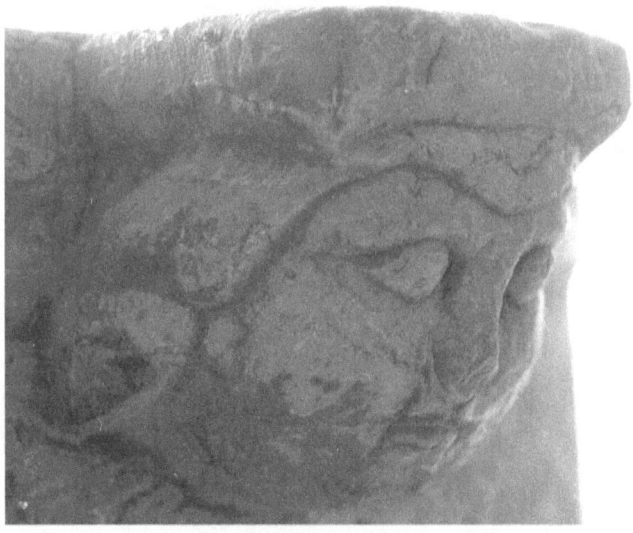

Fig. 3. Second handle in the shape of a head.

Fig. 4. Beginning of the inscription: QRB WHBY BR BLḤ LGN'Y' ṬBY' W.

Fig. 5. Middle of the inscription: SKRY' 'L ḤYWHY WḤYY BNWHY.

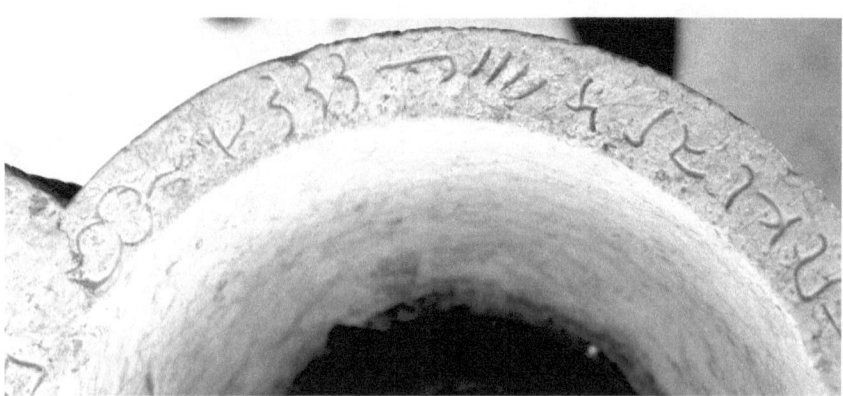

Fig. 6. End of the inscription: ŠNT 465.

onomastics, Ḥ is preferable. Actually BLḤ' is a personal name that has been mentioned at least four times in Palmyrene inscriptions,[3] and can be compared to BWLḤ', with *mater lectionis* W, and BWLḤZY/BLḤZY/BLḤY. It is probably an abbreviation with ending –' of BWLḤ'ZY, "Bôl has seen."[4]

- The Ṭ of ṬBY' is a little damaged on its upper part.
- The S of SKRY' might be easily confused with a Q or a M. Actually the angular shape would better fit a M than an S but, probably, toward the end of the third century C.E., there was some confusion in the shapes of both letters. Furthermore the Y of SKRY' is long and may be confused with a W.
- Both letters of the preposition 'L are clearly cursive.
- In the word ḤYWHY, one may note the tying of the first two letters. The same phenomenon appears at the beginning of ḤYY and between letters 2 and 3 in BNWHY. Most of the Y of these words are clearly long Y.
- In ŠNT, the first and the last letters could be classified as "baroque."

2. Commentary

The verb QRB, "to offer," is well known in Palmyrene inscriptions. One notes the absence of the indication of the object, which is the bowl itself.

The name WHBY is an abbreviated Arabic name with the ending –Y, meaning that the deity "gave." It is well known in Palmyrene inscriptions and already attested in the first Moussaieff bowl.[5] It is also already attested in fourth-century B.C.E. Idumean ostraca.[6] Here it is probably an abbreviation for WHBLT.[7]

GN'Y' is probably a common name. The phrase GN'Y' ṬBY' WSKRY' is to be compared to 'LHY' ṬBY' WSKRY'. The name GN'Y' instead of 'LHY' is especially well known in "the area northwest of Palmyra"[8] and the same phrase

---

3. See Jürgen Kurt Stark, *Personal Names in Palmyrene Inscriptions* (Oxford: Clarendon, 1971), 9.
4. See ibid., 74.
5. Briquel-Chatonnet, "Un cratère palmyrénien inscrit," 155–56.
6. See André Lemaire, *Nouvelles inscriptions araméennes d'Idumée II. Collections Moussaïeff, Jeselsohn, Welch et divers* (Supplément no. 9 à *Transeuphratène*; Paris: Gabalda, 2002), 173.
7. Stark, *Personal Names in Palmyrene Inscriptions*, 15, 85.
8. See Javier Teixidor, *The Pagan God: Popular Religion in the Greco-Roman Near East* (Princeton: Princeton University Press, 1977), 75; about *ginnayê*, see also idem, *The Pantheon of Palmyra* (Leiden: Brill, 1979), 77–80.

already appears on the first Moussaieff bowl.⁹ Both craters may come from the same place, northwest of Palmyra.¹⁰ From the point of view of orthography, one notes the presence of an ' *mater lectionis* in GN'Y' and the variant S for ŠKRY'. The alternation S/Š is well known at this time. Later on in the sentence, the alternation ḤYY BNWHY / ḤY' BNWHY is also well attested in Palmyrene inscriptions.

At the end of this inscription, the Palmyrene ciphers are clear. The dating refers to the Seleucid era and the date corresponds to 154/5 C.E. This dating is close to the dating of the first Moussaieff bowl, which is a few years later (474), another indication that both bowls could come from the same place and be made in the same workshop. However the paleographical comparison reveals important differences because the writing of this crater is more cursive than the one of the first crater where the writing is more formal. This comparison is all the more interesting that both inscriptions were incised in the same kind of stone, for the same kind of object. This comparison clearly reveals two aspects:

- the writing of the earlier bowl seems more developed than the writing of the later crater;
- in the same inscription, actually in the inscription of our bowl, you may find both formal and cursive shapes of the same letter. This is especially obvious in our inscription with the letter L.

Both aspects reveal the limits of any paleographical dating which is always approximate and, often, very approximate.

3. General Interpretation

As already indicated, several aspects of this stone bowl probably reveal that it was found northwest of Palmyra:

- This kind of stone bowl is frequent in this part of the country.¹¹

---

9. Briquel-Chatonnet, "Un cratère palmyrénien inscrit," 156.

10. About this area, see Daniel Schlumberger, *La Palmyrène du Nord-Ouest* (Paris: Geuthner, 1951), esp. 60–61, 112–13.

11. Ibid.; J. T. Milik, *Recherches d'épigraphie orientale I. Dédicaces faites par des dieux (Palmyre, Hatra, Tyr) et des thiases sémitiques à l'époque romaine* (Bibliothèque archéologique et historique 92; Paris: Geuthner, 1972), 108.

- The mention of the good and profitable *jinn*s is also frequent in this area.
- The writing of this bowl is not the usual formal Palmyrene script but the cursive Palmyrene writing (see especially the L) and this cursive Palmyrene writing is well known in the same area.

Furthermore, in this area, the stone bowls are generally found in sanctuaries, in the context of a kind of a banquet room. This probably means that they were used in the context of meetings of Hellenistic *thiases*. These bowls were probably used to mix water with wine. Actually the stone bowls were sometimes represented on Palmyrene *tesserae* that were used to take part in sacred banquets.[12] The possible identification of the heads/handles as faces of Dionysos would very well fit such an interpretation.

Now, as is well known, and has been noted by Françoise Briquel-Chatonnet,[13] these Hellenistic oriental *thiases* correspond to the institution of West Semitic *marzeah*. This West-Semitic *marzeah* is well attested not only in Palmyra but also in Nabatea, Phoenicia, and Ugarit.[14] Its characteristics are clear: "extensive upper-class drinking within a religious connection are the only features that are consistently present throughout the history of the *marzēaḥ*."[15]

The mention of a *marzeah* on a fifth-century B.C.E. Elephantine ostracon[16] shows clearly that this institution was not unknown in the Jewish tradition. Actually it is mentioned explicitly twice in the Bible:

Amos 6:7: "the sprawler's *marzeah* will cease";
Jeremiah 16:5: "do not enter the *marzeah* house."

---

12. See, for example, Khaled Al-Asʿad, Françoise Briquel-Chatonnet, and Jean-Baptiste Yon, "The Sacred Banquets at Palmyra and the Function of the *tesserae*: Reflections on the Tokens Found in the Arṣu Temple," in *A Journey to Palmyra: Collected Essays to Remember Delbert R. Hillers* (ed. Eleonora Cussini; Culture and History of the Ancient Near East 22; Leiden: Brill, 2005), 1–10.

13. Briquel-Chatonnet, "Un cratère palmyrénien inscrit," 162.

14. See, for example, John L. McLaughlin, *The* marzēaḥ *in the Prophetic Literature. References and Allusions in Light of the Extra-Biblical Evidence* (VTSup 86; Leiden: Brill, 2001), 9–79. Cf. also L. Miralles Maciá, *Marzeah y thiasos: Una institucion convival en el Oriente Proximo Antiguo y el Mediterraneo* (Anejos 20; Madrid, 2007).

15. Ibid., 79.

16. Ibid., 35–36; B. Becking, "Temple, *marzēaḥ*, and Power at Elephantine," *Transeuphratène* 29 (2005): 37–47.

These two examples show that prophets were aware of this contemporary institution against which they were generally critical. The verses of Amos 6:4–7[17] conclude with the explicit mention of the *marzeah*:

> You, lying on beds of ivory,
> sprawling on your couches
> eating lambs from the flock,
> and calves from the fattening stall;
> a singing to the sound of the lute,
> they compose on instruments of music;
> a drinking from bowls of wine,
> they anoint with finest oils,
> but are not grieved over the ruin of Joseph!
> Therefore, now they will be exiled, the first of the exiles,
> And the sprawler's *marzeah* shall cease.

From this text and other allusions (esp. Amos 2:7b–8; 4:1; Hos 4:16–19; Isa 28:7–8; Ezek 39:17–20), the *marzeah* "probably refers to an association of upper-class individuals who celebrated religious feasts characterized by excessive drinking."[18] "On the other hand, there is also evidence of some innovation in the prophetic period"[19] with some funerary connection. Actually, "in Jer. 16:5, the *marzeah* house is simply listed as a place where one might enact mourning rituals, but it is not denounced for that reason or even in itself."[20]

If excessive drinking is criticized by prophets and wise men (Prov 21:17; 23:20–21; 31:4), wine itself is not condemned in the biblical tradition. It is appreciated as a nice aspect of life created by God, as explicitly stated in Ps 104:14–15: "bringing bread out of the earth and wine to gladden men's hearts ($w^e yayin\ y^e sammah\ l^e bab$-$\check{}en\hat{o}\check{s}$)."

Bibliography

Al-As'ad, Khaled and Michał Gawlikowski. *The Inscriptions in the Museum of Palmyre: A Catalogue*. Palmyra/Warsaw: Archeo, 1997.

———, Françoise Briquel-Chatonnet, and Jean-Baptiste Yon. "The Sacred Banquets at Palmyra and the Function of the *tesserae*: Reflections on the Tokens Found in the Arṣu

---

17. See also Jonathan S. Greer, "A *Marzeaḥ* and a *Mizraq*: A Prophet's Mêlée with Religious Diversity in Amos 6.4–7," *JSOT* 32 (2007): 243–61.
18. McLaughlin, *The* marzēaḥ, 215.
19. Ibid.
20. Ibid., 216.

Temple." Pages 1–10 in *A Journey to Palmyra: Collected Essays to Remember Delbert R. Hillers*. Edited by Eleonora Cussini. Culture and History of the Ancient Near East 22. Leiden: Brill, 2005.

Becking, B. "Temple, *marzēaḥ*, and Power at Elephantine." *Transeuphratène* 29 (2005): 37–47.

Briquel-Chatonnet, Françoise. "Un cratère palmyrénien inscrit: nouveau document sur la vie religieuse des Palmyréniens." *Aram* 7 (1995): 153–63.

Greer, Jonathan S. "A *Marzeaḥ* and a *Mizraq*: A Prophet's Mêlée with Religious Diversity in Amos 6.4–7." *JSOT* 32 (2007): 243–61.

Lemaire, André. *Nouvelles inscriptions araméennes d'Idumée II. Collections Moussaïeff, Jeselsohn, Welch et divers*. Supplément n° 9 à *Transeuphratène*. Paris: Gabalda, 2002.

McLaughlin, John L. *The* marzēaḥ *in the Prophetic Literature. References and Allusions in Light of the Extra-Biblical Evidence*. VTSup 86. Leiden: Brill, 2001.

Milik, J. T. *Recherches d'épigraphie orientale. Dédicaces faites par des dieux (Palmyre, Hatra, Tyr) et des thiases sémitiques à l'époque romaine*. Bibliothèque archéologique et historique 92. Paris: Geuthner, 1972.

Miralles Maciá, L. *Marzeah y thiasos: Una institucion convival en el Oriente Proximo Antiguo y en el Mediterraneo*. Anejos 20. Madrid, 2007.

Schlumberger, Daniel. *La Palmyrène du Nord-Ouest*. Paris: Geuthner, 1951.

Stark, Jürgen Kurt. *Personal Names in Palmyrene Inscriptions*. Oxford: Clarendon, 1971.

Teixidor, Javier. *The Pagan God: Popular Religion in the Greco-Roman Near East*. Princeton: Princeton University Press, 1977.

———. *The Pantheon of Palmyra*. Leiden: Brill, 1979.

Chapter Twelve
Mandaic Magic Bowls in the Moussaieff Collection: A Preliminary Survey

*Matthew Morgenstern**

Amongst its many items, the Shlomo Moussaieff collection contains a sizeable number of magic texts inscribed on clay bowls or lead scrolls. To date, only a selection of these has been published, all of which have been texts written in the Jewish script.[1] However, the Moussaieff Collection also includes several items written in the Mandaic and so-called Manichaean Syriac scripts.[2] The "Manichaean" materials are being prepared for publication by the present author in collaboration with Dr. James Nathan Ford. The purpose of the present article is to present a preliminary survey of the magic texts written in the Mandaic script.

The corpus of published Mandaic magic texts has grown significantly in recent years. Since Yamauchi's survey in 1967,[3] several new collections have been

---

* The following conventions are employed: written Mandaean sources are cited in Mandaic script, followed by a letter-for-letter transliteration into Roman script. We have followed Macuch's system of transliteration and employed Roman "a" for the Mandaic halqa sign ₀ and ʿ for Mandaic ṣ. In contrast to Macuch, we have not distinguished between u and w in our transcription of Mandaic ⸺. Mandaic ⸺ is represented by ḍ. Dr. James Nathan Ford read a draft of this article and made several helpful suggestions which have been cited in his name. This research was supported by the Israel Science Foundation grant No. 38/10.

1. See in particular D. Levene, *A Corpus of Magic Bowls: Incantation Texts in Jewish Aramaic from Late Antiquity* (London: Kegan Paul, 2003), with M. Morgenstern, "Notes on Aramaic Magic Bowls in the Moussaieff Collection," *BSOAS* 68 (2005): 349–67 and J. N. Ford, *JSS* 51 (2006): 207–14 (review).

2. The entire collection of magic bowls in the Moussaieff Collection has been photographed by the present author in the form of some 2,500 high-resolution digital images.

3. E. Yamauchi, *Mandaic Incantation Texts* (New Haven: American Oriental Society, 1967). Yamauchi's linguistic description must be read along with M. Sokoloff, "Some Notes on Mandaic Magical Texts," *Or* 40 (1971): 448–58.

published, of which the most significant are the collections of bowls in the British Museum and in the Frau Hilprecht collection.[4] Other important collections are awaiting publication.[5] Both the publication of new and unknown formulae on the one hand, and the presentation of unpublished parallels that facilitate the collation and correction of the already published materials on the other, make a worthy contribution to the advancement of this field. Both improve our understanding of this aspect of Mandaean culture in late antiquity. Some of the contributions of the Moussaieff texts are discussed below.

A Note on the Numbering System

Some of the bowls have been examined previously by Professor Shaul Shaked and Dr. Dan Levene, and these have been ascribed numbers which are generally employed consistently in studies. However, the numbering of other bowls is uncertain, and as yet no comprehensive numbering system exists for these texts. Accordingly, in this article, I have referred to the Shaked and Levene numbers where they exist, but have refrained from ascribing new numbers to the unnumbered text until the complete inventory of the collection is prepared.

---

4. British Museum: J. B. Segal, *Catalogue of the Aramaic and Mandaic Incantation Bowls in the British Museum* (London: British Museum Press, 2000). The editions of the Mandaic texts in this volume are particularly inaccurate and must be read critically with the following reviews and articles in hand: J. N. Ford, review of J. B. Segal, *Catalogue of the Aramaic and Mandaic Incantation Bowls in the British Museum*, *Jerusalem Studies in Arabic and Islam* 26 (2002): 237–72; J. N. Ford, "Another Look at the Mandaic Incantation Bowl BM 91715," *JANES* 29 (2002): 31–47; C. Müller-Kessler, "Die Zauberschalensammlung des British Museum," *AfO* 48/49 (2001–2002): 115–45; M. Morgenstern, "The Mandaic Magic Bowl Dehays 63: An Unpublished Parallel to BM117872 (Segal 079A)," *JANES* 32 (forthcoming).

Frau Hilprecht Collection: C. Müller-Kesser, *Die Zauberschalentexte in der Hilprecht-Sammlung, Jena und weitere Nippur-Texte anderer Sammlungen* (Texte und Materialien der Hilprecht Collection 7; Wiesbaden: Harrassowitz, 2005); see M. Morgenstern, *JSS* 55 (2010), 280–89 (review).

5. The most substantial of these are the 150 Mandaic bowls in the Schøyen Collection, to be published by Shaul Shaked, James Nathan Ford and Siam Bhayro. Another 10–15 bowls in various collections are to be published by James Nathan Ford. At the time of writing, the long-awaited edition of 35 lead scrolls from the British Museum has yet to appear. On this, see C. Müller-Kessler, "Interrelations between Mandaic Lead Scrolls and Incantation Bowls," in *Mesopotamian Magic: Textual Historical, and Interpretative Perspectives* (ed. T. Abusch and K. van der Toorn; Groningen: Styx, 1999), 197–209, and C. Müller-Kessler, "The Mandaeans and the Question of Their Origin," *Aram* 16 (2004): 47–60, especially 54 n. 29.

Overview

To date, nine Mandaic magic bowls have been identified in the Moussaieff Collection. All these have been transcribed and will be published in a full scientific edition shortly. In addition, the Moussaieff collection contains several fragmentary lead scrolls, also written in Mandaic. These have yet to be photographed and studied in detail, and are not included in the present survey. The following is a brief description of the bowls:

M23

Eleven lines of well-preserved text written in a clear scribal hand for Asmandad son of Marta. This is perhaps the same client who is mentioned in a magic bowl published from a photograph by Müller-Kessler.[6] The formula itself comprises a series of bonds for various celestial realms, many of which are otherwise unknown to me.

M24

Fifteen lines of a well-preserved continuous text, despite some salting. The text is written in a clear scribal hand for Dād-Manda son of Iboi. The formula is partially paralleled by BM 91775 (086M in Segal's catalogue) and still more closely by MS 2054/34, but in contrast to the British Museum text it does not contain a repetition of the formula at the end. Its closest parallel comes from within the Moussaieff Collection, M45. Comparison of the versions of the formula that survive in multiple copies allows for several corrections to be made to the readings of the British Museum bowl, which is sometimes chipped or rubbed, particularly in its outer text. The previously unpublished formula contains some important grammatical forms. See below, §6.

M25

Seventeen lines of continuous text written for Yayai son of Emmoi and his wife Šerin daughter of Mama. The text is mostly readable in spite of some serious salting and abrasion, partially with the aid of the parallels. The bowl formula was apparently known to the scribes as ﾠﾠﾠ ('l klil nhur aiar), and this title is inscribed in whole or in part on the rear of several of the parallels,

---

6. Müller-Kessler, *Die Zauberschalentexte*, 116, but the bowl itself is different.

Fig. 1. A bound demon on M139.

including BM 117880 (081M in Segal's catalogue), MS 1928/25, and an unnumbered bowl in the Moussaieff collection (Unnumbered a, below). Again, our text provides several variants and enables us to improve some of the readings previously proposed in the research literature.

M26

The formula comprises nine lines of a well preserved continuous text, written for the client ͏ܒܘܗܟܣܪܐ ܒܪܚ ܒܗܪܬܘܝܐ (buhksra brḥ bhrtuia). The text presents several difficulties in interpretation, most significantly owing to the vulgar script and orthography. These are discussed in further detail below §4.

M45

A well-preserved continuous text, 16 lines in length. The bowl text was written for the children of Eboi: Tašmag, Mār-Sapin, Dād-Manda, Abbai and (if the reading is correct) Bar-Izi and their families. (The latter two clients are omitted from the second list of clients.) The formula closely parallels M24, and we may assume that the Dād-Manda mentioned here is the same client as that mentioned in M24.

M139

A large bowl of enormous proportions (355x175mm), bearing a large and impressive drawing of a demon (see fig. 1). The demon is characterized by long unruly hair and is bound at both the arms and legs. The first formula on the bowl is paralleled by several texts in the British Museum (BM 91775, 91779), the Hilprecht Collection (HS 3021, 3025), in the Collection of the Babylonian Section Philadelphia (CBS 16034) and in the Yale Babylonian Collection (YBC 15334),[7] while the second part is paralleled by BM 91715, 91780 and MS 2054/122.[8] A preliminary transcription of this text, prepared from the original some years ago, was put at my disposal by Prof. Shaul Shaked, and it has now been possible to improve on some of the readings in light of these recently published parallels.

M154

Thirteen continuous lines of a well-preserved formula, written for Azyazdan Khwast-Bindad son of Madukh. The formula comprises of a series of bindings for demons that are associated with certain Babylonian toponyms. Some of these are also mentioned on a Mandaic lead roll partially transcribed by C. Müller-

---

7. Published in ibid., 115–22.
8. The previously known witnesses to this formula have been collated in Ford, "Another Look."

Kessler. See below, §5. The text also contains some interesting expressions. See below, §6. On the reverse side of the bowl are a series of ten *halqa* (aleph) signs. The magical use of the halqa is known from the later period, but this is the clearest evidence that I have found for its use in the epigraphic texts. [9]

UNNUMBERED A

Nineteen lines of continuous text inscribed on the inner and outer portions of the bowl for Abanda Gušnaṣ son of Pidardost. A client by the same name is mentioned in several bowls in the Schøyen Collection which are mostly written in Mandaic. With the exception of a few words on the outer side, most of the text is well preserved, and the reading further facilitated by the fact that it is another parallel of the ࡀࡉࡀࡓ ࡍࡄࡅࡓ ࡊࡋࡉࡋ ࡋ ('l klil nhur aiar) formula (see notes on M25 above).

UNNUMBERED B

In contrast to all the other bowl-texts in this collection, this formula is written in a cursive as a series of short lines from the centre to the edge of the bowl. The bowl has been subject to considerable abrasion and much of the text is lost. These factors, along with the fact that so far I have not been able to identify any parallel formulae, have delayed progress on this difficult text and at the time of writing I am not able to comment upon its contents.

VULGAR SCRIPT AND ORTHOGRAPHY

The growing corpus of magic texts is revealing to us new forms of the Mandaic script and some unusual orthographic practices. The scribe of M26 employs an unusual practice of adding a circlet (the Mandaic halqa or possibly the -$ḥ$[10]) to the end of numerous words, as the example shown in fig. 2 illustrates:

In Classical Mandaic, the *halqa* is always employed to mark word-final –*a* and the digraph -ࡏࡉ (-ia) to mark word-final i/e. It is perhaps the latter usage,

---

9. On the magical use of the *halqa* see E. S. Drower, *The Mandaeans of Iraq and Iran* (Leiden: Brill, 1962), 240–41; B. Burtea, "Ein mandäischer magischer Text aus der Drower Collection," in *Festschrift Rainer Voigt zum sechzigsten Geburtstag* (ed. B. Burtea, J. Tropper, and H. Younansardaroud; Alter Orient und Altes Testament; Münster: Ugarit Verlag, 2004), 94.

10. The scribe makes a slight distinction between the two signs, in that the –$ḥ$ is slightly elongated and compressed.

Fig. 2. The vulgar script with the addition of *halqa*. The text reads ܩܕܟܠ ܚܠܝܢܢ (unitbr hiliuna) "May their power be broken" (M26:7).

along with a belief in the magical power of the letter mentioned above, that has led our scribe to employ this sign in what appears to be an arbitrary distribution in word-final position. Dr. James Ford informs me that same usage occurs in MS 2054/59: ܩܠܐܪܐܚܐ ܠܢ[ܘ]ܕܕܠ ܩܠܐܚܡܐܠ ܩܠܠܚܠ ܩܠܚ[ܘ]ܚܠܚܠ (bhumr[a]iuna udiuiuna ushraiuna ulili[a]tun … bbataiuna) "with their amulet spirits and their devs and their sahras and their liliths … in their houses." It is not known to me from other sources.

Relations to Other Texts

As mentioned in our summary above, several of these bowls contain formulae that parallel previously published texts. An important new parallel is provided by M154, which partially corresponds to a demon list found on a lead scroll from the British Museum mentioned in a recent publication (see below). The Moussaieff parallel is especially important given the difficulties involved in reading the lead scrolls, and it demonstrates once again the interrelationship of the texts written on the two media.[11] The Moussaieff text reads:

ܚܠܚܠ ܩܐܪܚܘܩܦܠܚܠ ܘ ܕܠܛ ܠܨ ܚܚܘܠ ܘ ܩܐܪܚܚܘ ܐܚܠ ܩܐܪܚܘ ܚܚܠܚܠ
ܐܚܠܠܘ ܐܠܚܠܐ ܚܚܠܐ ܚܠܚܠ ܐܪܐܠܚܩܠ ܪܠܚܚ ܕܠܛ ܠܨ ܚܚܘܠ ܘ ܠܚܕܝ
ܐܠܚܠܘܕܚ ܪܠܚ ܘ ܐܠܛ ܠܨ ܚܚܘܠ ܘ ܐܪܐܠܝܪܛ ܚܠܚܚܘܩܦ ܘ

'sirr (!) abugdana rba qrbtana ḏiatib 'l tila ḏbrišartai uʿsir nirig ḏiatib 'l tila ḏbit knariata uʿsir grud guria shra ḏšarim ptulata ḏiatib 'l tila ḏbit blahmia

Bound is the great Abugdana, the warrior, who dwells on the mound of Barišartai, and bound is Nirig who dwells on the mound of Bit Kanariata

---

11. On such parallels, see Müller-Kessler, "Interrelations."

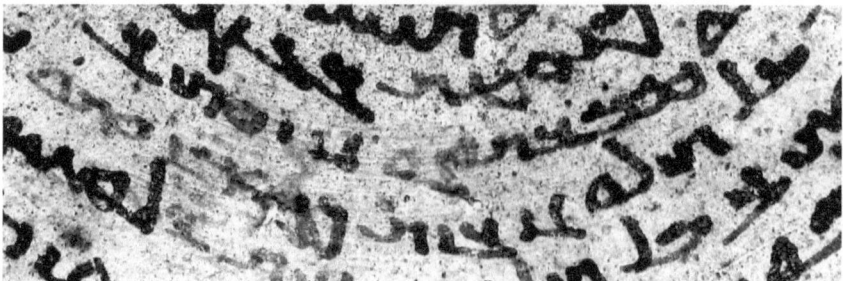

Fig. 3. The text of M154.

Fig. 4. The parallel passage in BM 132947.

(? – see below), bound is Garud the cub, the *sahir* who defiles (lit: rips) virgins[12] who dwells on the mound of Bit Balahmi. (M154:4–6)

This text is a direct parallel to that found on a lead roll in the British Museum (BM 132947). The reference to Nirig has already been noted by C. Müller-Kessler and K. Kessler, who have read in the British Museum text ܐܘܣܝܪ ܢܝܪܝܓ ܕܝܬܒ ܥܠ ܬܝܠܐ ܕܒܝܬ ܟܢܕܬܐ (uʿsir nirig ḏiatib ʿl tila ḏbit kndata).[13] In my opinion, this reading of the toponym is not correct, but the exact reading of both the BM text and of the Moussaieff bowl is difficult to determine, since both texts suffer from damage at this point (see figs. 3 and 4). A final reading may only be possible with the discovery of another clearer parallel.[14]

---

12. The expression ܕܫܪܝܡ ܦܬܘܠܬܐ (dšarim ptulata) "who defiles virgins" is discussed below, §6.

13. C. Müller-Kessler and K. Kessler, "Spätbabylonische Gottheiten in spätantiken mandäischen Texten," *ZfA* 89 (1999): 65–87; our text is cited on p. 79.

14. I wish to thank Professor Ran Zadok who took the time to examine the toponyms found in this formula and informed me that they were unknown to him from other sources.

6. Lexicographical and Linguistic Contributions.

Several new words and expressions appear in the Mandaic texts in this collection. Above, we saw the expression ࡀࡍࡀࡋࡉࡓࡕ ࡐࡕࡅࡋࡀࡕࡀ (dšarim ptulata) "who defiles the virgins" of M154:5. The root ࡔࡓࡌ (šrm) is not previously recorded in the scholarly literature for classical Mandaic, and to the best of my knowledge is not attested in the manuscript corpus. The root is not recorded in the literature from Jewish Babylonian Aramaic, and for Syriac Brockelmann cites the verbal usage only from a secondary source, i.e. the lexicon of Syriac poetry of Cardahi, and glosses 'fregit' (i.e., broke to pieces, shattered), which he identified with the Akkadian cognate šarāmu.[15] Specifically, the Akkadian root has the meaning of 'to break a seal, unseal', and is used in the context of breaking open the seal of a clay tablet, or to cut something to size.[16] In the context of our text, it seems best to interpret ࡔࡀࡓࡉࡌ (šarim) as 'copulate with (a virgin)'.

Remarkable confirmation for this interpretation arises from Neo-Mandaic. Dr. Hezy Mutzafi has drawn my attention to the fact that Neo-Mandaic contains a lexeme šᵊram, already recorded by Macuch, which is apparently a vulgar verb with the same meaning.[17] It therefore seems that the classical and modern idioms here complement one another. The classical idiom demonstrates the antiquity of the lexeme in the Mandaic language, while the modern idiom shows that the sexual connotations of the verb have remained well-understood until the present day.

n'mhia bmhita dkahia ukbira ubguaza dʿmra ušʿma bqurnasa drugza dhibula bšur šira ubzarzanit ʿzqta dainia lagṭa uhinkia dabqa

---

15. C. Brockelmann, *Lexicon Syriacum* (2d ed.; Halle: Max Niemeyer, 1928), 809 s.v. ܫܪܡ, citing P. Cardahi, *Al-Lolab* (Beirut: ex typogr. Catholica S. J., 1887–91), 591 s.v. ܫܪܡ.

16. *CAD* Vol. 17 (Š part 2), 1992, 48–49.

17. R. Macuch, *Handbook of Classical and Modern Mandaic* (Berlin: de Gruyter, 1965), 542b, as addendum to *Mandaic Dictionary* 476a: "ŠRM (cf P. šarm, shame) mod. To have a (sic!) sexual intercourse, cohabitate, copulate." Dr. Mutzafi tells me that his informants were hesitant to give him the exact meaning, simply stating in Arabic that the word is ʿār (obscene). The early attestation of this verbal use and the existence of a Semitic root ŠRM makes the Persian etymology suggested by Macuch less likely.

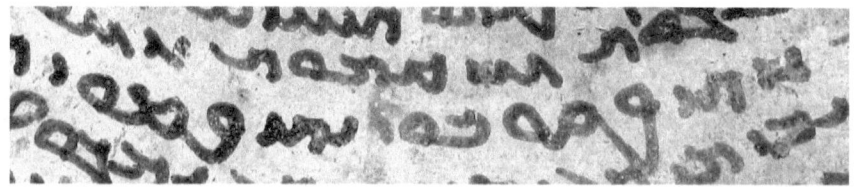

Fig. 5. Detail from M24:12, showing the t-ay morpheme of 2f.s. imperfect.

May he be struck by a blow that is strong and powerful, and by a staff of speech and hearing, and a hammer of wrath (and) of destruction, by the bond (šur šira) and by Zarzanit,[18] the seal that 'grabs' the eyes and **binds palates**. (M23:10–11)

The idiom ⟨lagiṭ ainia⟩ (lagiṭ ainia) is found in the Ginza Rba, where it is employed with the meaning of "blind" or, perhaps more accurately, "delude."[19] In our text the literal meaning is more appropriate. The expression ⟨uhinkia dabqa⟩ (uhinkia dabqa) has not been previously recorded, and here seems to similarly have a literal meaning of "bind the palate," i.e. render speechless. The entire context is one of inflictions to the senses: speech, hearing and sight. The use of the root DBQ with the palate recalls the language of Ps 137:6.

In several cases, the texts in this collection provide us with new linguistic information on the Mandaic language. For example, from the expression ⟨diša rbtia⟩ (diša rbtia) 'the great door' (M23:4) we may learn that this noun is feminine, a fact that is not recorded in the currently available Mandaic Dictionary. The noun is similarly feminine in Jewish Babylonian Aramaic.[20] Many such minor clarifications are now arising from the ever-increasing corpus of magic texts, and highlight the need to improve both the lexicographical and linguistic aspects of Mandaic lexicography.[21]

---

18. Dr. James Ford has suggested to me that Zarzanit is an alternative form of Zarzi'el, a personified seal, a name that often appears alongside šur-šira. See J. N. Ford, "Notes on the Mandaic Incantation Bowls in the British Museum (review of J. B. Segal, *Catalogue of the Aramaic and Mandaic Incantation Bowls in the British Museum*)," *Jerusalem Studies in Arabic and Islam* 26 (2002): 245–46.

19. Compare E. S. Drower and R. Macuch, *A Mandaic Dictionary* (Oxford: Clarendon, 1963), 230 s.v. LGṬ. A detailed semantic discussion of this expression will appear in the full text publication.

20. Contra Sokoloff, *DJBA*, p. 355. The examples cited therein demonstrate that the noun is feminine, e.g. חדא דשא "one door" (*b. Sanh* 96b).

21. The need for a new Mandaic dictionary is discussed in detail in M. Morgenstern, "The Present State of Mandaic Lexicography I: The Mandaic Dictionary," *AS* 7 (2009): 113–30.

Perhaps the most significant grammatical contribution of these texts comes in a formula that appears on both M24:13 and M45:12. We shall cite here from M24:12, wherein the text is better preserved and the reading entirely certain (see fig. 5):

uašbitilik aina bišta umuminalik bbil unbu unʿrig ḏtipšrai utipqai min hazin nišimta ubita

I have besworn you, Oh evil eye, and I adjure you by Bel, Nabu and Nerig, that you be exorcised and leave this soul and house... (M24:13).

The two verbs ⟨ⲥⲁⲣⲱⲁⲩ ⲥⲁⲣⲉⲁⲩⲁ⟩ (ḏtipšrai utipqai) show a 2 f.s. imperfect morpheme t-ay that is not found in sound verbs in other dialects. The morpheme is apparently further supported by evidence from a bowl in the Schøyen Collection: ⟨ⲧⲓⲥⲧⲁⲙⲣⲁⲓ⟩ (tisṭamrai kd hʿuia) "may you (f.s.) be crushed (?) like a snake" (MS 2054/20: 53–54). Another possible example is ⟨ⲧⲓⲡⲕⲁⲓ ⲧⲓⲧⲣⲓⲁⲓ⟩ (ḏtipqai titrhqai) "that you should exit and distance yourself" (MS 2054/2:10), but the text of the bowl is faded at this point and the reading remains somewhat uncertain.

The appearance of the 2 f.s. imperfect morpheme t-ay on several Mandaic magic bowls represents a significant discovery for Mandaic grammatical studies. Th. Nöldeke, whose grammar of Classical Mandaic still provides us with the most important reference tool for that idiom, wrote of this morpheme:

> Eine sehr seltsame Form für die 2. Sg. f. ist לאתימיתאי „stirb nicht" I, 161, 6; II, 132, 13.[22] (die Varr לאמיתאי, לאתימאיתא sind gar nichts werth). Vielleicht is תימיתיא zu schrieben mit der Endung î wie in Talm. und Hebr.[23]

Tarelko drew attention to similar forms in DC 40 (Šapta ḏmihla) but was apparently unacquainted with Nöldeke's example.[24] Furthermore, he assumed that the -ai morpheme was derived from the sound verb forms such as تقطلين teqṭlīn in

---

22. These references are to the first and second part of the Ginza Rba in the edition of H. Petermann: *Thesaurus sive Liber magnus vulgo Liber Adami* (Leipzig: P. O. Weigel, 1867).

23. T. Nöldeke, *Mandäische Grammatik* (Halle an der Salle: Waisenhaus, 1875), 250.

24. M. Tarelko, "Preliminary Remarks on the Unpublished Manuscript DC 40 from the Drower Collection of Mandaic Manuscripts," in *Und das Leben ist siegreich, And Life is Victorious* (ed. R. Voigt; Wiesbaden: Harrassowitz, 2008), 185–88, esp. 186, where he states explicity "Such ending is mentioned neither in the *Handbook of Classical and Modern Mandaic* by R. Macuch

Syriac and Jewish Babylonian Aramaic תדחלין/תדחלי.[25] However, Tarelko's proposed derivation does not account for the form; if the morpheme is derived from the affix *-ī(n), how is one to explain the diphthong –ay? I believe that we must look to the imperfect and imperative forms of the III-yod class of verbs for an answer. Whereas the apocopation of unstressed word-final vowels in other verb classes may have led to the neutralization in some dialects of the m.s. and f.s. forms of the imperfect,[26] the III-yod class distinguished historically between the morphemes –ē/ī for masculine and *-ay(n) > -ay for the feminine. Such forms are widely attested in classical Mandaic in the imperative, e.g. ࡒࡓࡀࡉ (qrai) 'Call!," ࡇࡆࡀࡉ (hzai) "See!,"[27] while one example of the imperfect is attested in the bowl corpus: ࡃࡕࡉࡕࡌࡄࡀࡉ (dtitmhai) "That you be struck" (Yamauchi, MIT, 21:6).[28] Furthermore, the form -ay was employed for the imperfect in the sister-dialect of Jewish Babylonian Aramaic, as demonstrated by examples such as לא תסתפאי "Do not fear" (b. Sanh 94b according to the manuscript of Yad Harav Herzog), and from

---

nor in the *Mandäische Grammatik* of Th. Nöldeke because usually the verb in Mandaic does not have a special ending in this form."

25. Incidentally, we may note that though the evidence for 2 f.s. imperfect forms in Rabbinic Babylonian Aramaic is extremely paltry, evidence for an –*īn* morpheme is even less forthcoming. The example תדחלין "(do not) fear!" (*b. B.M.* 84a) adduced by Tarelko, apparently drawn from J. N. Epstein, *A Grammar of Babylonian Aramaic* (Jerusalem: Magnes; Tel Aviv: Devir, 1960 [Hebrew]), 36, is not supported by the evidence of the best textual witnesses, which read תידיחלי (MS G1) and תידחלי (MS Hamburg 165).

26. See Nöldeke, *Mandäische Grammatik*, 217. The evidence of spoken Neo-Mandaic suggests that the distinction between the m.s. and f.s. imperative of the sound verb was maintained in at least those forms of Mandaic that were the forerunners of the surviving Neo-Mandaic dialects. In the G-stem of the sound verb, the m.s. and f.s. forms are distinguished by the vowel *o* for m.s. and *u* for f.s., e.g., $g^ətol$ 'kill!' (m.s.), vs. $g^ətul$ 'kill!' (f.s.). See R. Macuch (with G. Dankwarth), *Neumandäische Texte im Dialekt von Ahwāz* (Wiesbaden: Harrassowitz, 1993), 70; and C. G. Häberl, *The Neo-Mandaic Dialect of Khorramshahr* (Wiesbaden: Harrassowitz, 2009), 178. However, it is not certain that this distinction was maintained in all forms of Classical Mandaic. As I have tried to show elsewhere, Classical Mandaic already shows evidence for dialectal variation, while Neo-Mandaic contains many forms that cannot be explained as a direct linear development from classical language. See M. Morgenstern, "Diachronic Studies in Mandaic," *Or* 79 (2010): 505–25.

27. See Nöldeke, *Mandäische Grammatik*, 259. The reflex of this distinct feminine form may still be found in Neo-Mandaic in the contrast between the m.s. and f.s. imperative forms. See most recently $h^əzi$ "see" (m.s.) and $h^əze$ "see" (f.s. < * $h^əzay$), as presented in Häberl, *Khorramshahr*, 190. Compare Macuch, *Ahwāz*, 87.

28. In the same bowl text, we also find the bound form of the verb ࡅࡋࡀࡕࡉࡄࡆࡀࡉࡋࡅࡍ (ulatihzailun) "and do not appear to them" (Yamauchi, *MIT*, 21:14) with the –*ai* morpheme before the *l*-preposition. The examples cited here from *MIT* 21 for Mandaic confirm the doubts cast there (n. 76) on the existence of a 2 f.s. form identical to that of 2 m.s. and 3 f.s.

the magic corpus, אם לא תשנאי "if you (f.s.) will not change" (MS 1927/11:5).[29] We may assume that by analogy to such imperfect forms and imperative forms the -ay morpheme extended into the non-III-yod verb class, as witnessed in our examples. The evidence from the magic bowls is decisive in proving that the examples with the word-final –ay morpheme found in non-III-yod verbs in the mediaeval manuscripts of the Ginza are not the result of later scribal miscopying but rather reflect genuine Mandaic dialectal forms.

Conclusion

The unpublished Mandaic material in the Moussaieff Collection makes a welcome contribution to the growing corpus of Mandaic epigraphic materials. Within the scope of this brief survey, only some of the more significant examples have been presented. It is hoped that the full publication of these texts, which is currently in an advanced state of preparation, will both provide new material for scholarly study and further our understanding of the parallel texts that have already been published.

Bibliography

Brockelmann, C. *Lexicon Syriacum*. 2nd ed. Halle: Max Niemeyer, 1928.
Burtea, B. "Ein mandäischer magischer Text aus der Drower Collection." Page 94 in *Festschrift Rainer Voigt zum sechzigsten Geburtstag*. Edited by B. Burtea, J. Tropper, and H. Younansardaroud. Alter Orient und Altes Testament. Münster: Ugarit Verlag, 2004.
Cardahi, P. *Al-Lolab*. Beirut: ex typogr. Catholica S. J., 1887–91.
Drower, E. S. *The Mandaeans of Iraq and Iran*. Leiden: Brill, 1962.
Drower, E. S., and R. Macuch. *A Mandaic Dictionary*. Oxford: Clarendon, 1963.
Epstein, J. N. *A Grammar of Babylonian Aramaic*. Jerusalem: Magnes. Tel Aviv: Devir, 1960 (Hebrew).
Ford, J. N. "Another Look at the Mandaic Incantation Bowl BM 91715." *JANES* 29 (2002): 31–47.
———. "Notes on the Mandaic Incantation Bowls in the British Museum (review of J. B. Segal, *Catalogue of the Aramaic and Mandaic Incantation Bowls in the British Museum*)." *Jerusalem Studies in Arabic and Islam* 26 (2002): 245–46.

---

[29]. The evidence for Jewish Babylonian Aramaic is discussed in greater detail in M. Morgenstern, *Studies in Jewish Babylonian Aramaic Based Upon Early Eastern Manuscripts* (Harvard Semitic Studies 62; Winona Lake, Ind.: Eisenbrauns, 2011), 27–29. The typologically earlier form that both preserves the diphthong and bears the final *nun* is preserved in the example תימחיין "May you be struck" (JNF 1:8).

Häberl, C. G. *The Neo-Mandaic Dialect of Khorramshahr*. Wiesbaden: Harrassowitz, 2009.

Levene, D. *A Corpus of Magic Bowls: Incantation Texts in Jewish Aramaic from Late Antiquity*. London: Kegan Paul, 2003.

Macuch, R. *Handbook of Classical and Modern Mandaic*. Berlin: de Gruyter, 1965.

Macuch, R., with G. Dankwarth. *Neumandäische Texte in Dialekt von Ahwāz*. Wiesbaden: Harrassowitz, 1993.

Morgenstern, M. "Notes on Aramaic Magic Bowls in the Moussaieff Collection." *BSOAS* 68 (2005): 349–67.

———. "The Present State of Mandaic Lexicography I: The Mandaic Dictionary." *AS* 7 (2009): 113–30.

———. "Diachronic Studies in Mandaic." *Or* 79 (2010): 505–25.

———. *Studies in Jewish Babylonian Aramaic Based Upon Early Eastern Manuscripts*. Harvard Semitic Studies. Winona Lake: Eisenbrauns, 2011.

———. "The Mandaic Magic Bowl Dehays 63: An Unpublished Parallel to BM117872 (Segal 079A)." *JANES* 32 (forthcoming).

Müller-Kessler, C. "Interrelations between Mandaic Lead Scrolls and Incantation Bowls." Pages 197–209 in *Mesopotamian Magic: Textual Historical, and Interpretative Perspectives*. Edited by T. Abusch and K. van der Toorn. Groningen: Styx, 1999.

———. "Die Zauberschalensammlung des British Museum." *AfO* 48/49 (2001–2002): 115–45.

———."The Mandaeans and the Question of Their Origin." *Aram* 16 (2004): 47–60.

———. *Die Zauberschalentexte in der Hilprecht-Sammlung, Jena und weitere Nippur-Texte anderer Sammlungen*. Texte und Materialien der Hilprecht Collection 7. Wiesbaden: Harrassowitz, 2005.

Müller-Kessler, C., and K. Kessler."Spätbabylonische Gottheiten in spätantiken mandäischen Texten." *ZfA* 89 (1999): 65–87.

Nöldeke, T. *Mandäische Grammatik*. Halle an der Salle: Waisenhaus, 1875.

Segal, J. B. *Catalogue of the Aramaic and Mandaic Incantation Bowls in the British Museum*. London: British Museum Press, 2000.

Sokoloff, M. "Some Notes on Mandaic Magical Texts." *Or* 40 (1971): 448–58.

Tarelko, M. "Preliminary Remarks on the Unpublished Manuscript DC 40 from the Drower Collection of Mandaic Manuscripts." Pages 185–88 in *Und das Leben ist siegreich / And Life is Victorious*. Edited by R. Voigt. Wiesbaden: Harrassowitz, 2008.

Yamauchi, E. *Mandaic Incantation Texts*. New Haven: American Oriental Society, 1967.

Chapter Thirteen
Katuwas and the Masoretic Text of Kings: Cultural Connections between Carchemish and Israel

Richard S. Hess

The Luwian text of King Katuwas was excavated by Woolley at Carchemish in 1911–1914. Sometime after its discovery, it was largely destroyed. Fragments remain at the Anatolian Civilizations Museum in Ankara and at the British Museum. This study follows the text edition of John David Hawkins who was able to see the fragments and earlier photographs of the entire inscription.[1]

The first section of the text consists of the identification of the author:[2]

(§1) EGO-*wa/i-mi* ¹*ka-tú-wa/i-ss*|(IUDEX)*tara/i-wa/i-ni-sa*|*kar-ka-mi-si-za-sa*(URBS) RE|GIO DOMINUS… ¹*su-hi-si* REGIO DOMINUS]-[*ia-i-sa*] [|(INF]ANS)*ni-mu-wa/i-za-sa* ¹*á-sa-tú-wa/i-ta₄-ma-za-si-i* |REGIO-*ní* DO-MINUS-*ia-i-sa*|INFANS.NEPOS-*sa*

I (am) Katuwas the Ruler, Karkamišean Coun[try-Lord, the Country-Lord Suhis's] son, the Country-Lord Astuwatamanzas's grandson.

---

1. For transliteration and commentary, see John David Hawkins, *Inscriptions of the Iron Age. Part 1: Text. Introduction, Karatepe, Karkamiş, Tell Ahmar, Maraş, Malatya, Commagene* (Vol. 1 of *Corpus of Hieroglyphic Luwian Inscriptions*; Studies in Indo-European Language and Culture 8/1; Berlin: de Gruyter, 2000), 94–100. For photographs and hand copies, see idem, *Corpus of Hieroglyphic Luwian Inscriptions*. Vol. 1. *Inscriptions of the Iron Age. Part 3: Plates* (Studies in Indo-European Language and Culture 8/1; Berlin: de Gruyter, 2000), plates 10–12.

2. This and subsequent transliterations and translations follow Hawkins, *Inscriptions of the Iron Age. Part 1: Text*, 95.

This text provides the ruler's name Katuwas, his land Carchemish, and the names of his father and grandfather.

At first glance the text of Katuwas seems far removed from anything in the Bible. For one thing it is a monumental text positioned at a major gate that opened into the Iron Age city of Carchemish. Nothing similar, as far as is known, ever found its way into the biblical record. Further, as is appropriate for a monumental text, it is written in the first person by the king. In the Bible, first-person royal texts tend to occur only in the wisdom literature and the psalms, with rare and brief exceptions of letters embedded in narratives (for example, Josh 10:4). Psalms and prayers are directed toward God whereas the wisdom literature tends to consist of aphorisms. None of this is true of the Katuwas inscription. It is a first- person description of the king's exploits followed by a building description and concluding with a curse on any who deface the inscription or destroy the orthostats on which it is written.

However, the inscription contains several interesting connections with biblical details, especially those that are found in the books of Kings. This paper will consider several specific examples before turning to a consideration of the rebellion story. The purpose of this study is not to demonstrate comparisons for their own sake. Rather, the desire is to identify a cultural continuity between the Luwian peoples and kingdoms such as that at Carchemish, on the one hand, and those biblical traditions that may reach back into the Iron Age, on the other. In so doing, it is hoped that the understanding of the contexts of both texts may be broadened and hitherto overlooked implications may be suggested. Although written in a language and a script not at all resembling West Semitic, the reality of a common cultural inheritance remains a possibility. And it is this possibility that the paper will endeavor to examine with the one example of this text from the late-tenth or early-ninth century b.c.e.[3]

Prosperity

In his discussion of how the country prospered under his reign, King Katuwas mentions that,

(§10) *[a]-wa/i mi-ia-za-´DEUS.AVIS-ta-ní-ia-za* OV[IS...]*-wa/I* [ARGENTUM].DARE [x] ASINUS(ANIMAL) "HORDENTUM" || |CRUS+*RA/I*

---

[3]. Richard S. Hess, "Syria and the Bible: The Luwian Connection," in *Israel: Ancient Kingdom or Late Invention* (ed. D. I. Block; Nashville: Broadman & Holman, 2008), 169–84.

in my *days(?)* for a sheep the cost(?) (as) [so many] homers (of) *barley* stood.

Related costs of food commodities are referenced in a number of West Semitic documents in terms of curses. Best known are the Sefire treaty documents. However, the emphasis is not upon the cost in terms of monetary quantities but upon the lack of produce and its satisfaction; for example, "and (even if) seven [nurs]es anoin[t their breasts and] nurse a child, then may it not be sati[sfied ...]."[4] This compares to the curses in the Aramaic text of the Hadad-Yith'i inscription from Tell Fekheriye, which also dates to the eighth century B.C.E.: "And let him sow but not harvest. And let him sow one thousand barley (measures) and let him recover a *parīs* from it."[5] These bring to mind the curses of Deut 28:15–68. There, however, barley and grains do not appear. However, sheep and flocks are mentioned in verses 18, 31, and 51.

Because King Katuwas describes prosperity rather than destitution, a closer comparison may be found in the eighth century B.C.E. Panamuwa inscription. King Panamuwa's great achievements for the people of the land are described in lines 6b to 11a. There his son mentions how the land "abounded with wheat and barley and ewe and cow in his days."[6] Closest of all, however, are texts from the Bible where actual purchases are described. There is, for example, Hosea's purchase of Gomer, in Hos 3:2:

wāʾekkrehā lī baḥ^{a}miššāh ʾāśār kāsep w^{e}ḥōmer ś^{e}ōrîm w^{e}lētek ś^{e}ōrîm

I purchased her for myself for fifteen silver pieces and a homer and lethek of barley.

---

4. From Brent Strawn's translation of Sefire text I.A: 14b–42; see Sarah C. Melville, Brent A. Strawn, Brian B. Schmidt, and Scott Noegel, "10. Neo-Assyrian and Syro-Palestinian Texts I," in *The Ancient Near East: Historical Sources in Translation* (ed. Mark W. Chavalas; Oxford: Blackwell, 2006), 302. The text is found on lines 21b–22a: *wšbʿ [mhy]nqn ymšḥ[n šdyhn w]yhynqn ʿlym wʾl yšbʿ*. See Herbert Donner and Wolfgang Röllig, *Kanaanäische und Aramäische Inschriften. Band 1. Texte* (4th ed.; Wiesbaden: Harrassowitz, 1979), 41, number 222.

5. Stephen A. Kaufman, "Reflections on the Assyrian-Aramaic Bilingual from Tell Fakhariyeh," *Maarav* 3 (1982): 163. The text begins with the last word of line 18 and continues through line 19: *wlzrʿ. wʾl. wḥṣd. wʾlp. śʿryn. lzrʿ wprys. lʾḥz. mnh*. Kaufman (169) observes that this and other curses are dependent on Western Aramaic and biblical examples; not on Assyrian ones.

6. The text is sometimes referred to as Panamuwa II. See K. Lawson Younger, Jr., *COS* 2:159. The text is found as line 9 of the inscription: *wkbrt. ḥṭh. wśʿrh. wśʾh*. wśwrh*. bywmyh**. See Josef Tropper, *Die Inschriften von Zincirli* (ALASP 6; Münster: Ugarit-Verlag 1993), 116.

Perhaps the most important parallel is found in the story of 2 Kgs 7 where a siege of Samaria leads to a serious famine that the prophet Elisha predicts will end suddenly. He describes the reversal of fortune in terms of the cost of wheat and barley (2 Kgs 7:1):

> s^e'āh sōlet b^{e}šeqel w^{e}sā'tayim ś^e'ōrîm b^{e}šeqel b^{e}ša'ar šōm^{e}rôn
>
> a seah of flour will sell for a shekel and two seahs of barley will sell for a shekel at the gate of Samaria.

This is fulfilled in the story (cf. vv. 16 and 18). The low purchase price for food commodities becomes evidence of the prosperity that replaces the famine in the city. Although in the Katuwas inscription, barley buys sheep, while in 2 Kings silver buys barley, both texts describe the purchase of food commodities and use the staple of barley in order to demonstrate prosperity.

Temple Building

Well into the inscription, at paragraph 11, there begins the account of the actual building of a temple. A study of ancient temple Near Eastern building inscriptions can find only one West Semitic extra-biblical text that describes the building of a temple.[7] It is the Ugaritic Baal cycle, a mythical account in which Baal builds his "house" after military victory. However, there is nothing similar to the description of a historical person who oversees the construction of an actual temple. This occurs only in the Luwian inscription and in the biblical account among Iron Age West Semitic texts, despite the presence of many such inscriptions in ancient Mesopotamia.

The inscription of Katuwas introduces the construction account as follows:[8]

> (§11) *mu-pa-wa/i-'pi-na-*'LINGERE-*sa-ti kar-ka-mi-si-za*(URBS) (DEUS) TONITRUS-*ti* DEUS.DOMUS-*tà* [*261.]PUGNUS-*ru-ba* (§12) *wa/i-tù-ta-*'PANIS(-)*ara/i-si-na* PONERE-*wa/i-ha* (§13) |*za-ia-ha-wa/I* "PORTA"-*la/i/u-na á-ma* |AVUS-*ti-ia mu-*' |PRAE-*na* CRUS.CRUS-*ta* (§14) *a-wa/I* PURUS-*MI-ia* DEUS.DOMUS-*sa*(?) *ku-ma-na* AEDIFICARE + *MI-ha*

---

7. Victor Hurowitz, *I Have Built You an Exalted House: Temple Building in the Bible in Light of Mesopotamian and Northwest Semitic Writings* (JSOTSup 115; American Schools of Oriental Research Monograph Series 5; Sheffield: Sheffield Academic), 1992.

8. Hawkins, *Corpus of Hieroglyphic Luwian Inscriptions.* Vol. 1. *Inscriptions of the Iron Age. Part 1: Text*, 95.

But I myself then *constructed*(?) the temple(s) with luxury for Karkamišean Tarhunzas, for him I established ARASI-bread. And these gates (of) my grandfathers passed down to me. While I built the holies of the temple, (or: the Holy [One]'s temple) ...

There are several points of interest about this description. Like the other quotes from the Katuwas inscription, these have parallels in other Luwian compositions, from Carchemish and elsewhere.[9] Of special interest, however, is the connection of this description with the account of Solomon's construction of the Temple in 1 Kgs 5–9. Although the 1 Kings' account is in the third person in keeping with the narrative of the larger text, Solomon does speak in the first person beginning in 1 Kgs 8:12–13. Here he begins by stating in verse 13: *bānōh bānîtî bêt z^{e}bul lāk mākôn l^{e}šibt^{e}kā 'ôlāmîm* "I have indeed built a grand house for you, a place for your dwelling forever." Thus this claim occurs at the beginning of the description of what the king did in both cases. Both also describe the "house" or temple (DOMUS-*tà* in Luwian; *bêt* in Hebrew) with an adjective or descriptor that sets it apart. In Hebrew, this is the old West Semitic *z^{e}bul* with the sense of "lofty" or "grand." In the Luwian this term is LINGERE-*sa-ti*, which on the Karatepe bilingual corresponds to the Phoenician *mn'm* "luxury." Both terms thus describe a distinctively positive quality that sets the building apart.

Both texts also describe the presentation before the deity of a regular bread, whether the Luwian PANIS(-)*ara/i-si-na* or the Hebrew *leḥem happānîm*. These terms both describe an offering presented before the deity. If the Luwian is related to *ari-*, "season, time," then this describes a periodic presentation of bread before the storm god. In the case of the Israelite religion, the "bread of the Presence" includes twelve loaves of fine flour that are set in the Tabernacle and then the Temple weekly, with the old bread then consumed by the priests. This is described in Lev 24:5–9 but it appears in the description of the First Temple in 1 Kgs 7:48 as the sole food item amidst all the gold objects placed within the holy place of the Temple. It seems to have been practiced by the priests at Nob during David's time (1 Sam 21:6 [Heb. 7]). Although the Luwian text does not define how frequently the bread was served, the neighboring Hittites, with whom Carchemish seems to have had connections extending back into the Late Bronze Age, served fresh bread daily in temples. That may well have been in the case at Carchemish insofar as bread forms the primary food item designated for the consumption of the storm god. Jacob Milgrom suggests that the Israelite bread of the Presence was not primarily for divine consumption, and thus not presented daily,

---

9. Ibid.

but to symbolize a prayer to God for the nation and its fruitfulness.[10] Be that as it may, for both the summary of the construction of the Temple in 1 Kgs 6–7 and that in the Katuwas text, the only food mentioned is bread and it is described in the context of its regular presentation before the deity.

In addition to the special description of the temple and the presentation of bread in it, a third area of comparison has to do with the sequence of the building account. Note that the account of Katuwas begins with the temple (§11–12), then turns to the gates to which the inscription is attached (§13), and then turns back to the construction of the temple that is described as going on (§14) while Katuwas further enhanced the gates with the inscribed orthostats and other structures (§15–16). This parallel sequence, in which the construction of the temple is placed in tandem with other structures, occurs in the Masoretic Text of 1 Kgs 6–7. Chapter 6 describes the construction of the temple. First Kings 7:1–12 then turns to the building of the palaces, the courtyards, and the great foundations in Jerusalem. First Kings 7:13–51 then returns to the temple and provides details of its furnishings and the artistic embellishments of its architecture. This would appear to form the expected style for West Semitic temple building descriptions of the Iron Age. If so, this style did not continue. Both the Septuagint and Josephus alter the sequence of 1 Kgs 6–7 in their accounts. This is especially clear in the Septuagint where the description of the palaces, courtyards, and foundations in 1 Kgs 7:1–12 is placed subsequent to the details of the furnishings of the temple in 1 Kgs 7:13–51. As Percy S. F. van Keulen has argued, the effect of this secondary movement by the Septuagint tradition emphasizes the piety of King Solomon who does not begin work on his own palace and other "secular" buildings until all the details of the temple are completed.[11] Such repositioning serves to highlight the original style as found in the Masoretic Text and in the earlier description of Katuwas of Carchemish.

Thus there occur several parallels between these two unique descriptions of temple building: the prominent position of the king's own claim to build the temple, the description of the temple as a luxurious or magnificent house, the emphasis on the presentation of bread before the deity, and the sequence of

---

10. For the Hittite and Israelite practices, see Jacob Milgrom, *Leviticus 23–27: A New Translation and Commentary* (AB 3b; New York: Doubleday, 2000), 2092, 2094, 2098–99.

11. See Percy S. F. van Keulen, *Two Versions of the Solomon Narrative: An Inquiry Into the Relationship Between MT 1 Kgs. 2–11 and LXX 3 Reg. 2–11* (VTSup 104; Leiden: Brill, 2005), 130–41. For Josephus, see L. H. Feldman, "Josephus' View of Solomon," in *The Age of Solomon: Scholarship at the Turn of the Millennium* (ed. Lowell K. Handy; SHANE 11; Leiden: Brill, 1997), 348–74 (365).

temple building alongside the construction of other structures. While some of these comparisons occur elsewhere, their cumulative force remains unique.

Upper Floors

After this text of King Katuwas related his description of the construction of the temple, it began to consider the gate where the inscription was found. The Luwian hieroglyphs then describe a structure associated with the gate in §§18–19:[12]

(§18) wa/i-tà '"LIGNUM"-wa/i-ia-ti AEDIFICARE-MI-ha
(§19) |za-zi-pa=wa/i (DOMUS) ha + ra/i-sà-tá-ni-zi ¹á-na-ia BONUS-sa-mi-i FEMINA-ti-i DOMUS + SCALA(-)tá-wa/i-ni-zi i-zi-i-ha

I built them (also) with *wood,*
and these *upper floors* for Ana my beloved wife as TAWANI-apartments I made

Katuwas identifies an upper storey built of wood, also described elsewhere in a Luwian text from Carchemish.[13] In his edition, Hawkins compares women's quarters at the upper storey with references from Homeric Greek, Hittite wisdom literature from Ugarit, and Ottoman domestic architecture.[14] He relates the Luwian, *ha + ra/i-sà-tá-ni-zi,* to the Hittite *harištani-* that also occurs in the Hittite–Akkadian bilingual wisdom text from Ugarit.[15] There it has been identified as a place for holding grain, as established by the context.[16] However, a broader meaning of a structure that can contain grain or be used as apartments for living corresponds semantically to the Akkadian *ganūnu.*[17]

The connection of an upper storey with the queen's apartments may be made with texts from Kings. In particular, Jezebel looks from her palace window

---

12. Hawkins, *Corpus of Hieroglyphic Luwian Inscriptions.* Vol. 1. *Inscriptions of the Iron Age. Part 1: Text,* 95–96.
13. Ibid, 103–4 (II.11 + 12 §15, 33). This text also associates the upper storey with the queen.
14. Ibid, 99.
15. Emmanuel Laroche, "Textes de Ras Shamra en langue Hittite," in *Ugaritica V. Nouveaux texts accadiens, hourrites et ugaritiques des archives et bibliothèques privées d'Ugarit. Commentaires des texts historiques (première partie)* (ed. Jean Nougayrol et al.; Mission de Ras Shamra Tome XVI; Paris: Geuthner, 1968), 779–84, RS 22.439 line 38.
16. Ibid, 783.
17. *CAD* 5:42–43.

when Jehu approaches in 2 Kgs 9:30–33. A term for "upper room" or "upper storey" does not occur in the text. However, we read that Jehu *wayyiśā' pānāyw 'el haḥallôn* "looked up to the window." He called upon his supporters to *šimṭûhā* "throw her out" of the window. This resulted in Jezebel's death. Additional accounts from the Bible mention upper rooms. For example, there is the story of Eglon, the king of Moab. Ehud trapped Eglon in an upper room of his palace and there assassinated him (Judg 3:20–24). Returning to the books of Kings, the prophet Elijah also lived in the upper room of a house (1 Kgs 17:19). Also in the book of Kings, Ahaziah, king of Samaria, fell through the lattice of the upper room in his palace (2 Kgs 1:2). In Jerusalem, Jeremiah condemned King Shallum, for building a magnificent palace, including *'ăliyôtāyw* "his upper rooms," with injustice. The royal connection with the upper storeys, as well as their use as apartments for women, served as an architectural phenomenon throughout the Levant.

Katuwas and Rebellion Stories

After the first section where Katuwas introduces himself, there follow two somewhat broken sections that describe how the god or gods elevated the king to his position:[18]

(§2) *wa/i-m[u-x]* DE[US... ..."MA]NUS"-*tara/i-ti*|PUGN[US...||...]
(§3) [*wa/i-mu...á-ma-za t*]*á-ti-ia-za* "LIGNUM"[...]-*za* [||]*pi-[ia]-tá*

Me the god[...   ...]rai[sed] by the hand, [and to me my] paternal power he/she/they gave

The next section identifies Katuwas as strengthened by the gods due to his "justice."[19]

(§4) *wa/i-mu-*'DEUS-*ní-zi mi*|?-*ia-ti-*'<">IUSTITIA"-*wa/i-ní-ti* PUGNUS-*mi-la/i/u*|PUGNUS-*ri+i-ta*

me the gods *raised in strength* because of my justice.

---

18. Hawkins, *Corpus of Hieroglyphic Luwian Inscriptions*. Vol. 1. *Inscriptions of the Iron Age. Part 1: Text*, 95.
19. Ibid.

This is most important because it anticipates the revolt that follows and implies that the successful outcome of that revolt was already determined by the favor of the gods. Such favor was not indiscriminate but depended on the virtue of the king, specifically on the justice that he possessed. Following Hawkins' interpretation of section §5, Katuwas sees twenty of his TATI or kinsmen revolt and the lands governed by Carchemish would seem to follow suit:[20]

(§5) *mi-zi-pa-wa/i-mu-ta-'|20-tá-ti-zi ARHA CRUS+RA/I*
(§6) *[wa/i-m]a-tá [|]REGIO=ní-ia|*314(-)sá-pa-za |REL-a-ti SUB-na-na ARHA (PES₂)tara/i-za-nu-wa/i-tá*

But my 20-TATI's *revolted* against me,
wherefore they caused the lands to TARZA- from under me ...

The gods of Katuwas come to his aid and restore the lands that he and his forefathers governed:[21]

(§7) *wa/i-mu-' mi-i-sa-'*DOMINUS-*na-ni*||(DEUS)TONITRUS-*sa* (DEUS)*kar-hu-ha-sa-'*(DEUS)*ku*+AVIS-*pa-sa-ha mi-ia-ti-'*|*"*IUSTITIA*"-na-ti* (LITUUS) *á-za-ta*
(§8) *wa/i-mu-tá-' á-ma |tá-ti-ia* AVUS-*ha-ti-ia* |REGIO-*ní-ia* (*33(1))*mi-tà-sa₅+r/i-i-na* REL-*a-ti a-tá i-zi-ia-ta*

My lord Tarhunzas, Karhuhas and Kubaba loved me because of my justice, *wherefore* they made my father's and grandfather's lands MITASARI- for me, (or: *wherefore* my father's (and) grandfather's lands made (for) me(?) MITASARI-)

Note how important the emphasis is upon the king's justice. This alone receives a second mention. Katuwas possesses it, and the gods recognize it and reward him for it. The king portrays a picture that describes no grounds for the revolt. He simply relates that the TATIs carried out this rebellion. However, he emphasizes his own justice before, during, and after the revolt. It is that quality that restores his rulership and continues the dynasty that Katuwas inherited.

When we come to the stories of First Kings, we find examples of attempts to usurp authority from the first chapter. There Adonijah attempts a coup against the dying David. Like the revolt against Katuwas, it does not succeed. However, the solution is not so much the restoration of David as it is the succession of

---

20. Ibid.
21. Ibid.

Solomon as the chosen heir instead of Adonijah. Nevertheless, in a manner similar to the Luwian account we have the appearance of the "kinsmen," here $b^e n\hat{e}$ *hammelek,* as those who join in the revolt. These "sons of the king" appear three times, always in descriptions of those who have joined Adonijah, also a *ben hammelek* (1 Kgs 1:9, 19, 25). We also note the important role played by the deity. Although the narrative contains no miraculous acts or divine revelations, the report of the coronation of Solomon, as told by Jonathan, ends with David worshiping and praising Yahweh (1 Kgs 1:47–48). Both Katuwas and David ascribe their success to their deity.

A closer story in terms of plot occurs after King Solomon's death in 1 Kgs 12. There, Rehoboam, Solomon's son and successor, loses the northern part of his kingdom early in his reign. It happens when he refuses to lighten the corvée labor that Solomon had placed on the Israelites. However, in this case the rebellion is successful. Unlike the Katuwas inscription or the story of Adonijah, there is no mention of God except in the form of a prophetic warning to Rehoboam not to attempt to bring back the rebels by military force (1 Kgs 12:22–24). Nor do a group of "kinsmen" lead in the revolt. There is no suggestion of a common family, clan, or tribal identity between Rehoboam and the northerners.

Rather the issue here concerns the extent to which "justice" plays a role. It clearly does in the Katuwas inscription where the king credits his possession of this quality to his success over the rebels. Now concern for justice occurs in the early chapters of 1 Kings. Solomon asks God for the ability to rule Israel with justice. Yahweh is so pleased that he grants the king treasures, peace, and a long life, as well as the ability to rule with justice. In 1 Kgs 3:11 and 28, both God and all Israel recognize Solomon's justice, Hebrew *mišpaṭ.* However, this concern for justice gradually is lost. The last reference to *mišpaṭ* in the story of Solomon appears in 1 Kgs 11:33 where Solomon is condemned for no longer rendering justice, in the sense that the king no longer observes the statutes of Yahweh. This verse actually forms part of the prophet Ahijah's proclamation to Jeroboam that Yahweh will tear the kingdom from Solomon's son and give it to Jeroboam. Thus the text gives the deity the ultimate responsibility for all that happens with respect to the rebellion against the kingdom. As with Katuwas, the chief deity is given the credit for the events. In this case, however, the successor does not retain the kingdom; but loses it.

Of special significance is the role of justice in the Katuwas inscription. By repeating this quality in his brief account, the king of Carchemish explains the true basis for his continuation on the throne over his entire kingdom. On the other hand, the absence of the customary term for justice is here coupled with the obvious narrative slant that pictures King Rehoboam as acting without mercy and apart from concerns for what is just toward the people of Israel. The narrative pictures the king as without justice. Both the will of Yahweh and the actions and words of Rehoboam demonstrate that the lack of justice leads to the loss of the kingdom. In a mirror-image account, King Katuwas has victory over the rebels and retains his kingdom due to his justice, functioning along with the will of his gods.

Conclusion

This relatively brief inscription from the West Semitic cultural world of the eighth century B.C.E. demonstrates many wide-ranging cultural connections with the Hebrew biblical text, especially as reflected in the books of Kings. The result is evidence for a cultural continuum across the Levant in the first millennium B.C.E.

Bibliography

Donner, Herbert, and Wolfgang Röllig. *Kanaanäische und Aramäische Inschriften. Band 1. Texte.* 4th ed. Wiesbaden: Harrassowitz, 1979.

Feldman, L. H. "Josephus' View of Solomon." Pages 348–74 in *The Age of Solomon. Scholarship at the Turn of the Millennium.* Edited by Lowell K. Handy. SHANE 11. Leiden: Brill, 1997.

Hawkins, John David. *Corpus of Hieroglyphic Luwian Inscriptions.* Vol. 1. *Inscriptions of the Iron Age. Part 1: Text. Introduction, Karatepe, Karkamiş, Tell Ahmar, Maraş, Malatya, Commagene.* Studies in Indo-European Language and Culture 8.1. Berlin: de Gruyter, 2000.

———. *Corpus of Hieroglyphic Luwian Inscriptions.* Vol. 1. *Inscriptions of the Iron Age. Part 3: Plates.* Studies in Indo-European Language and Culture 8.1. Berlin: de Gruyter, 2000.

Hess, Richard S. "Syria and the Bible: The Luwian Connection." Pages 169–84 in *Israel: Ancient Kingdom or Late Invention.* Edited by D. I. Block. Nashville: Broadman & Holman, 2008.

Hurowitz, Victor. *I Have Built You an Exalted House: Temple Building in the Bible in Light of Mesopotamian and Northwest Semitic Writings.* JSOTSup 115. American Schools of Oriental Research Monograph Series 5. Sheffield: Sheffield Academic, 1992.

Kaufman, Stephen A. "Reflections on the Assyrian-Aramaic Bilingual from Tell Fakhariyeh." *Maarav* 3 (1982): 137–75

Keulen, Percy S. F. van. *Two Versions of the Solomon Narrative: An Inquiry Into the Relationship Between MT 1 Kgs. 2–11 and LXX 3 Reg. 2–11.* VTSup 104. Leiden: Brill, 2005.

Laroche, Emmanuel. "Textes de Ras Shamra en langue Hittite." Pages 769–84 in *Ugaritica V. Nouveaux texts acccadiens, hourrites et ugaritiques des archives et bibliothèques privées d'Ugarit. Commentaires des texts historiques (première partie).* Edited by Jean Nougayrol et al. Mission de Ras Shamra Tome XVI. Paris: Geuthner, 1968.

Melville, Sarah C., Brent A. Strawn, Brian B. Schmidt, and Scott Noegel. "10. Neo-Assyrian and Syro-Palestinian Texts I." Pages 280–330 in *The Ancient Near East: Historical Sources in Translation*. Edited by Mark W. Chavalas. Oxford: Blackwell, 2006.

Milgrom, Jacob. *Leviticus 23–27: A New Translation and Commentary*. AB 3b. New York: Doubleday, 2000.

Tropper, Josef. *Die Inschriften von Zincirli*. ALASP 6. Münster: Ugarit-Verlag, 1993.

Chapter Fourteen
Hebrew Seals, Stamps, and Statistics:
How Can Fakes Be Found?

Alan Millard

Hebrew seals have attracted collectors since the mid-nineteenth century, consequently, there have been forgers at work to try to profit from them. The energetic French scholar Charles Clermont-Ganneau was one who published a stone inscribed "Servant of Yahwe, David, king" (*'bd yhw dwd mlk*) in poorly executed imitation Old Hebrew letters, with other forgeries.[1] The problem of distinguishing true artifacts from fakes was not difficult in those cases. Today the problem is acute, exacerbated by the appearance of scores of seals and hundreds of bullae, some with the names of kings of Judah, which arouse great interest and command high prices. When Joseph Naveh wrote the Preface to Nahman Avigad's *Corpus of West Semitic Stamp Seals,* completed and edited by Benjamin Sass, he expressed his doubts about 46 out of the 399 seals, while noting that no one had proved them to be modern creations.[2] The *Corpus* itself concludes with "A Selection" of twenty "Questionable or Forged Seals" (nos. 1195–1215). Others have raised suspicions about one seal or another from time to time, but no one has offered systematic criteria for reaching a verdict. Recently Andrew Vaughn has set out a method that he believes may come close to doing that.[3] Through a statistical analysis of seals and bullae made in association with C. P. Dobler, he has argued that

---

1. David Diringer, *Le iscrizioni antico-ebraiche palestinesi* (Florence: Le Monnier, 1934), 320–21, no. 3, etc.

2. *WSS*, 12.

3. Andrew G. Vaughn and Carolyn P. Dobler, "A Provenance Study of Hebrew Seals and Seal Impressions: A Statistical Analysis," in *'I Will Speak the Riddle of Ancient Times': Archeological and Historical Studies in Honor of Amihai Mazar on the Occasion of his Sixtieth Birthday* (ed. Aren M. Maeir and Pierre de Miroschedji; Winona Lake, Ind.: Eisenbrauns, 2006), 757–71, cited hereafter by page number.

certain differences are significant, suggesting that some of the unprovenanced items "which have features quite different from those with known provenances may not be authentic." The study dealt with 495 seals of unknown provenance and 28 of known, 205 bullae of unknown provenance and 57 of known. For their comparisons, Vaughn and Dobler used the Avigad-Sass *Corpus* and the catalogue of the Moussaieff collection by Deutsch and Lemaire.[4] The present study is based only upon the Avigad-Sass *Corpus* because the Moussaieff collection comprises seals with unknown provenances alone.

The enormous increase in the harvest of Hebrew seals since the middle of the twentieth century suggests that, if there are forgeries, most are more likely to have been made since about 1950. An analysis of features on seals known before that date should show a pattern very close to that Vaughn and Dobler found for seals with known provenances. Comparing the same features on 73 seals known before 1950 with the 28 of known provenance yields percentages which (Table 1) are reasonably close, but the 12 percent difference between those with *bn* or *bt* and those without is notable.

Table 1. Comparison of features on seals known before 1950 with those of known provenance.

Features present	Old Seals 73	Known Seals 28
bn or *bt*	(30) 41%	(8) 29%
lamedh	(70) 96%	(25) 89%
Title	(8) 11%	(2) 7%
Icon	(31) 42%	(10) 36%
Dividing lines	(49) 67%	(19) 68%
1 line	(2) 3%	(2) 7%
2 lines	(43) 57%	(15) 54%
Other dividers	(4) 5%	(2) 7%
No divider	(33) 33%	(8) 30%
Height = Width	(34) 47%	(9) 32%
Register div.	(50) 67%	(20) 74%

If the differences between these two groups of seals are not great, then the probability of forgeries existing among the "Old Seals" is small on statistical grounds, although suspicions may be raised for other reasons. For example, Joseph Naveh raised a doubt about *Corpus* no. 180, which is very similar to no. 279. The former

---

4. Robert Deutsch and André Lemaire, *Biblical Period Personal Seals in the Shlomo Moussaieff Collection* (Tel Aviv: Archaeological Center Publications, 1997).

was acquired before 1898 and might copy the latter, which became known in 1849. However, both owners had the same patronym, *'bdyhw*, so the possibility that both seals were made by the same engraver for two brothers cannot be dismissed.

Now there should be no marked difference between the features on the seals and the features on the bullae, which, of course, were imprinted by seals. Yet Vaughn and Dobler's tables reveal some striking contrasts. For example, 32 percent of both known and unknown seals have *bn* or *bt*, while 72 percent of known bullae and 55 percent of unknown bullae have one or the other; 32 percent of known seals, 37 percent of unknown seals have an icon, whereas only 5 percent of known bullae and 14 percent of unknown bullae have one. On the other hand, the preposition *lamedh* is present on 93 percent of known seals, 81 percent of unknown, 95 percent of known bullae, and 55 percent of unknown.

Table 2. Comparison of features on seals and bullae of known and unknown provenance.

Features present	Known Seals	Unknown Seals	Known Bullae	Unknown Bullae
bn or *bt*	32%	32%	72%	55%
lamedh	93%	81%	95%	87%
Icon	7%	9%	5%	14%

According to the statistical analysis, the P(robability) value suggests that the two groups of bullae "do not both come from a larger group of authentic bullas" (p. 761).

On considering Vaughn and Dobler's study, the comparison of provenance bullae with unprovenanced seems likely to be skewed, since, as they admit, "we do not have truly random samples" (p. 761). The majority of those from known provenances (known bullae) come from two sites and from strata dated to the last days of the kingdom of Judah, namely the City of David hoard of 43 bullae impressed by different seals and the juglet from Lachish, yielding 6 bullae impressed by different seals (in both cases counting only those "readable and nearly complete" [p. 759]). That is, 49 out of 57. Assuming the unprovenanced bullae (unknown bullae) came from earlier periods and a wider range of sites, then a greater disparity might be expected, the sort of disparity seen between the known seals and the known bullae in regard to the presence of *bn* or *bt*. (The bullae bearing the names of kings Ahaz and Hezekiah or their servants published more recently show that.[5])

---

5. Robert Deutsch, *Biblical Period Hebrew Bullae: The Josef Chaim Kaufman Collection* (Tel Aviv: Archaeological Center Publications, 2003).

Vaughn and Dobler excluded "seal impressions found on jar handles because there were too few impressions of unknown provenance that did not have identical impressions of known provenance to make them worth including" (pp. 758–59). Yet introducing the jar stamps is worthwhile because they are really the same as bullae; they are imprints of seals on clay. Furthermore, few, if any, are likely to be the productions of modern craftsmen. On the one hand, the fact that there are too few examples of unknown provenance prevents a comparison between those of known provenance and those of unknown provenance among the stamps alone, as done for seals and for bullae: on the other hand, it does not preclude comparison of their features with the features on bullae of both classes. That is the comparison this paper presents. (I am not a statistician and have not sought the aid of one; the percentages are sufficient for the present purpose.) There are 399 seals in the *Corpus*, 29 with known provenances, and 262 bullae, 57 of them with known provenances. There are 50 jar stamps in the *Corpus* that have features Vaughn and Dobler used. Not all of the stamps are legible in every respect; 46 of them have known provenances.

Presence of *bn* or *bt*

Of 48 legible stamps, 3 have *bn*, 1 has *bt*, 8 percent, so 37 of 48 (77 percent) lack either term, but we should note that of the 48, 7 (15 percent) have only one personal name, so 37 of the 41 that could have *bn* or *bt* do not, that is, 90 percent. Vaughn and Dobler reckon 72 percent of known bullae (41 of 57) have *bn* or *bt*, whereas only 55 percent of unknown bullae (113 of 205) have such a term. They evidently used the total of all the bullae as their base, whether or not they had a patronym as well as the owner's name. The statistical difference is said to be "very important … and suggests that the sample of bullas of known provenance and the sample of unknown provenance do not both come from a larger group of authentic bullas" (p. 761). That is to say, the number of bullae of unknown provenance having *bn* or *bt*, being lower than the number from known provenances, 55 percent against 72 percent, indicates inauthenticity. As only 8 percent of the jar stamps bear either term, this criterion by itself could imply those jar stamps are inauthentic! It might also be argued that the stamps belonged to a particular class of official that did not need to state its patronym.

Presence of the Preposition *lamedh*

Of known bullae 95 percent have the possessive *lamedh*, of unknown bullae 87 percent. Among the jar handles, 45 are legible in this respect and of those 33 have *lamedh*, 12 do not, 73 percent against 27 percent. Here the percentage on the stamps is smaller than on the unknown bullae.

Titles

Only 2 of 50 stamps bear a title, that is 4 percent, whereas there are titles on 7 percent of known bullae and 9 percent of unknown bullae, so the stamps again underplay the known bullae and even more the unknown bullae.

Iconography

Here the reverse is true: 6 of 49 stamps have designs (12 percent), against only 5 percent of known bullae, but 14 percent of unknown bullae.

Dividing Lines

Dividing lines are present on 77 percent of known bullae and 92 percent of unknown bullae. The jar stamps fall between the two, 42 of 50 or 84 percent having them. Different numbers of dividing lines might be significant. The jar stamps show 7 of 50 (14 percent) with one line, 34 (68 percent) with two lines, compared with 7 percent of known bullae having one line, 2 percent of unknown bullae, 89 percent of known bullae with two lines and 93 percent of unknown bullae. In this case the jar stamps are distinct from each category of bullae.

Other Dividers

Vaughn and Dobler observed, "bullas of known provenance exhibited a much higher frequency of other types of dividers between the registers" (p. 763), the percentages being 18 percent to 4 percent. However, the jar stamps have no other types of divider. Of the jar stamps, 8 or 16 percent had no divider, a higher proportion than either the known bullae (5 percent) or unknown bullae (4 percent). They noted 3 percent of unknown bullae had a lotus bud or other lotus feature as a divider, but 16 percent of known bullae had a lotus divider and concluded, "We again see strong evidence that the two groups differ with respect to the presence of a lotus-bud divider.... It thus seems that the much smaller percentage of this feature represents a quite significant difference between the two groups" (p. 763). No Stamp in the *Corpus* has a lotus-bud divider!

Sizes

Measuring bullae, Vaughn and Dobler computed mean height and width for known bullae as 10.71 and 13 mm, and for unknown bullae as 10.69 and 11.64 mm. Assuming their calculation includes bullae of every shape, the 47 measurable stamps are closer to the known bullae at 12.6 and 13, although the measurements of the stamps may not always be exact. Another measurement, comparing the percentage of bullae with height at least as great as width, gives 14 percent of known bullae and 32 percent of unknown bullae. The stamps are closer to the unknown bullae at 26 percent, 12 of 47 measurable examples. (Measurement of depth, in which Vaughn and Dobler found "a large difference," is, of course, not possible for bullae and stamps.)

Table 3. Comparison of features occurring on known bullae, unknown bullae and stamps.

Features present	KnownB	Unk.B	Stamps
bn or *bt*	72%	55%	8%
lamedh	95%	87%	73%
Title	7%	9%	4%
Icon	5%	14%	12%
Dividing lines	95%	96%	84%
Other dividers	18%	4%	0%
No divider	5%	4%	16%
Height = Width	14%	32%	26%

Table 4. Comparison of features occurring on all seals and imprints.

Features present	KnownB	Unk.B	Stamps	Old Seals 73	Known Seals
bn or *bt*	72%	55%	8%	(30) 41%	(8) 29%
lamedh	95%	87%	73%	(70) 96%	(25) 89%
Title	7%	9%	4%	(8) 11%	(2) 7%
Icon	5%	14%	12%	(31) 42%	(10) 36%
Dividing lines	77%	92%	84%	(49) 67%	(19) 68%
1 line	7%	2%	14%	(2) 3%	(2) 7%
2 lines	89%	93%	68%	(43) 57%	(15) 54%
Other dividers	18%	4%	0%	(4) 5%	(2) 7%
No divider	5%	4%	16%	(33) 33%	(8) 30%
Height = Width	14%	32%	26%	(34) 47%	(9) 32%
Register divider	95%	96%	84%	(50) 67%	(20) 74%

The tabulation of these figures reveals no consistent agreement between the jar stamps and either the known bullae or the unknown bullae. The presence of *bn* or *bt* is extremely low on the stamps, much lower than on the bullae or the seals, and the presence of *lamedh* is also much lower than on both. The percentage of stamps bearing icons is closer to that of the unknown bullae, as is the absence of other dividers. In dividing lines the stamps fall between the known and the unknown bullae, all having more than the seals. In contrast, a higher percentage of stamps than bullae has no divider.

Keeping in mind the relatively small numbers of stamps available, 49 against 57 known bullae and 205 unknown bullae, these results suggest that Vaughn and Dobler's statistical analysis is not a satisfactory means for distinguishing authentic from inauthentic bullae. In particular, as already noted, they termed statistically very important the difference between bullae with *bn* or *bt* and bullae without, 72 percent against 55 percent, and found it "moderate-to-strong" following randomization tests. Yet that becomes very questionable in the light of the small percentage—6 percent—of stamps with *bn* or *bt*. With regard to the presence or absence of an icon, at 10 percent the stamps fall between the known bullae, 5 percent, and the unknown bullae, 14 percent, again raising a doubt about the validity of the comparison. The dividers also provided Vaughn and Dobler with "a statistically significant difference" between the known and unknown bullae, the probability of these differences occurring by chance was less than 3 in 1,000 for the difference in the frequency of "lines" (p. 763). They observed "the use of a lotus bud (or any lotus feature) as a register divider was much more common in bullas of known provenance than in bullas of unknown provenance," 16 percent against 3 percent, indicating two different groups. As observed above, none of the stamps has a lotus-bud divider, which, on those statistics, might lead to the unlikely conclusion that they are not genuine!

The figures now offered suggest that Vaughn and Dobler's analysis does not give sound reason for doubting the authenticity of unprovenanced Hebrew seals or bullae. They claim their statistics show "differences ... that are widespread," with the "least amount of variation ... seen in features that are the most common in the groups of known provenance" (p. 769). A forger, they say, would "craft a seal or seal impression that was similar to known seals and seal impressions. If there were indeed forgeries, one would expect the differences to be most apparent in features that are less well known or popular. One would also expect more variation in lesser-known features in the authentic seals and seal impressions because the forgers would tend to imitate features that are well known." (pp. 769–70). As an illustration, one might say the creator of *Corpus* no. 1210 was imitating a fairly common type of two-line Hebrew seal with a double line divider with fan-shaped ends in a manner that is inconsistent with ancient styles. Again, the doubt

Naveh expressed about the seal of Yeho'ahaz, son of the king (*Corpus* no. 13) with a fighting cock engraved below the legend, would find support in its similarity to the well-known seal of Ya'azanyahu, servant of the king (*Corpus* no. 8), excavated at Tell en-Nasbeh, which also bears the figure of a fighting cock. However, suspicions voiced repeatedly about the seal of the king's daughter Ma'adana (*Corpus* no. 30) do not arise from similarities to "features that are well known," but particularly from the unique form of the lyre it displays.

On the basis of the figures presented here, the stamps appear to form a distinct third group. In fact, their evidence points to a greater variety than Vaughn and Dobler's study allows. They presumably belonged to officials having responsibility in some way in the manufacture of the jars. Those officials would not have ranked among the highest in the land, so their seals would be utilitarian, they would not be the most ornate in design or skillfully engraved, nor, as noted already, would they necessarily need to include their father's names. Would the very roughly engraved seal of Koniyahu son of Hodiyahu (*Corpus* no. 220) be thought genuine if it had not been found in excavations at Gibeon, as recently remarked by A. Lemaire,[6] or one inscribed for Derashyahu, son of X, found at Arad (*Corpus* no. 132)?

The seals of those officials would not, therefore, display the features seen on many others. As pointed out earlier, 86 percent of the legible known bullae (49 of 57) come from two hoards of similar date (the City of David and Lachish), so the seals that impressed them may be expected to be comparable in style. The stamps encourage the idea that seals of earlier date might vary considerably, for they are almost all dated archaeologically to the end of the eighth century B.C.E., some occurring on the same handles as LMLK stamps, a century or more before the two hoards of bullae were deposited. Usually, ancient archives survive from the last phase of occupation at any site, according to evidence from other countries,[7] so the discovery of hoards of bullae from the last days of Samaria and of Judah was predictable, as would be the recovery of others from the strata destroyed by Sennacherib's army in 701 B.C.E. Statistics may reveal interesting facts about ancient Hebrew seals, most significantly the far greater number that are known (711 seals, bullae, and jar stamps in the *Corpus*) in contrast to the number for neighbouring states (107 Aramaic, 38 Phoenician, 149 Ammonite). Even if half the Hebrew seals were proved to be forgeries, the remainder far outnumber the

---

6. André Lemaire, "Leonard Wolfe's Assessment of Unprovenanced Seals," *Kusatu* 8 (2008): 195–218, see 200 n.11.

7. See my essay "Why do we have the Texts we do? Survival of the Latest?" in *Writing and Ancient Near Eastern Society: Papers in Honour of Alan R. Millard* (ed. P. Bienkowski, C. B. Mee and E. A. Slater; London: T&T Clark, 2005), 301–19.

Aramaic, Phoenician and others, a factor that is relevant to the question of literacy in ancient Israel and Judah. It is likely that administration required for the payment of tribute to Assyria by Menahem and his successors and by Ahaz and his successors was a factor in the production of inscribed seals from the latter part of the eighth century B.C.E. onward. However, this analysis indictaes that statistics cannot yet answer the question of authenticity; that will remain dependent upon the experienced eye.

Bibliography

Deutsch, Robert. *Biblical Period Hebrew Bullae: The Josef Chaim Kaufman Collection.* Tel Aviv: Archaeological Center Publications, 2003.

Deutsch, Robert, and André Lemaire. *Biblical Period Personal Seals in the Shlomo Moussaieff Collection.* Tel Aviv: Archaeological Center Publications, 1997.

Diringer, David. *Le iscrizioni antico-ebraiche palestinesi.* Florence: Le Monnier, 1934.

Lemaire, André. "Leonard Wolfe's Assessment of Unprovenanced Seals." *Kusatu* 8 (2008): 195–218.

Millard, Alan. "Why do we have the Texts we do? Survival of the Latest?" Pages 301–19 in *Writing and Ancient Near Eastern Society: Papers in Honour of Alan R. Millard.* Edited by Piotr Bienkowski, Christopher B. Mee and Elizabeth A. Slater. London: T&T Clark, 2005.

Vaughn, Andrew G., and Carolyn P. Dobler. "A Provenance Study of Hebrew Seals and Seal Impressions: A Statistical Analysis." Pages 757–71 in *"I Will Speak the Riddle of Ancient Times": Archeological and Historical Studies in Honor of Amihai Mazar on the Occasion of His Sixtieth Birthday.* Edited by Aren M. Maeir and Pierre de Miroschedji. Winona Lake, Ind.: Eisenbrauns, 2006.

Chapter Fifteen
The Moabitica and Their Aftermath: How to Handle a Forgery Affair with an International Impact

*Martin Heide**

In the nineteenth century, large numbers of ancient artifacts were unearthed and eagerly acquired for public and private collections. As a side effect, the very same collections were at times deluged by fakes and forgeries. Moses Shapira (1830–1884), born to a traditional Jewish family in Kamjanez-Podilskyj (Ukraine), who later converted to Christianity and added "Wilhelm" to his name, emigrated to Palestine in 1855–1856 and became in 1861 an antiquities dealer in Jerusalem. He is known for the shrewdness with which he sold an entire forged culture, known also as the "Moabitica," to the Royal Museum of Berlin, and for his attempt to sell the "earliest scroll of Deuteronomy ever found" for one million pounds Sterling to the British Museum.

In 1868, the famous Mesha Inscription[1] was seen *in situ* by the missionary Friedrich August Klein,[2] and arrangements were made to buy the stone for the

---

* This is a revised and enlarged version of the paper "What we can learn form the Shapira Forgeries," which I gave at the 2009 SBL conference in Rome. I want to thank Prof. André Lemaire for his helpful comments, and Prof. Meir Lubetski for editing and publishing the volume.

1. For details of the find of this important inscription see M. Patrick Graham, "The Discovery and Reconstruction of the Mesha Inscription," in *Studies in the Mesha Inscription and Moab* (ed. A. Dearman; Atlanta: Scholars Press, 1989), 41–92. For an overview of the more recent literature, see Erasmus Gass, *Die Moabiter—Geschichte und Kultur eines ostjordanischen Volkes im 1. Jahrtausend v. Chr.* (Abhandlungen des deutschen Palästina-Vereins Band 38; Wiesbaden: Harrassowitz, 2009), 6.

2. Klein grew up in the French city of Strassburg. He was a missionary of the Anglican Christian Missionary Society in Jerusalem. After the French-German war in 1870–71, Strassburg was given to Germany and Klein became a German. Klein's relationship to three nations is

Royal Museum in Berlin. The following year, the French dragoman to the Consulate at Jerusalem, Charles Clermont-Ganneau, had a partial copy made of it before the Arabs broke it for mainly political reasons. In 1870 he obtained possession of most of the remaining fragments for transmission to the Louvre, where it was reassembled, the missing parts being reproduced mainly from his copy and a squeeze made by Salim al-Khouri,[3] Shapira's associate. In the same year, Clermont-Ganneau published a preliminary edition of the Mesha Inscription. The subject was taken up by various scholars in Europe.[4] The Mesha Inscription is today on display in the Louvre.

The Moabitica

Not very long after the sensational find of the Mesha Inscription, Professor Konstantin Schlottmann from the university of Halle, a member of the editorial board of the *Zeitschrift der Deutschen Morgenländischen Gesellschaft* (ZDMG) and the only member of the managing board of the *Deutsche Morgenländische Gesellschaft* (DMG) competent in Northwest Semitics,[5] announced the discovery of inscriptions written on stone and clay figurines.[6] These inscribed artifacts had been brought to his attention by Hermann Weser, a pastor of the German protestant church in Jerusalem and former student of Schlottmann. Weser had seen them in Shapira's antiquities shop. He had sent sketches and drawings of some

---

symbolical and may in part be considered as the cause for the quarrels that these nations had when their ambitions were roused to possess the Mesha Inscription. See Friedrich A. Klein "The Original Discovery of the Moabite Stone," *PEQS* 1870: 281–83; H. Petermann, "Ueber die Auffindung der Moabitischen Inschrift des Königs Mesa," *ZDMG* 24 (1870): 640–44.

3. In the various reports, his personal name is mostly spelled as Selim, while his second name is variously spelled as al-Qari, al-Kari, el-Kary and al-Gari; for the spelling used here, see Gusta Lehrer-Jacobson, *Fakes and Forgeries from Collections in Israel* (Tel Aviv: Eretz Israel Museum, 1989), 11*; cf. also Andreas Reichert, "Julius Euting, die Pseudo-Moabitica und 'La petite fille de Jérusalem.' Neue Funde zu einer alten Affäre," in *Exegese vor Ort. Festschrift für Peter Welten zum 65. Geburtstag* (ed. Christl Maier et al.; Leipzig: Evangelische Verlagsanstalt, 2001), 342 n. 21.

4. In Germany, most prominently by Konstantin Schlottmann, "Die Inschrift Mesa's. Transscription und Uebersetzung revidirt nach Ganneau's und Warren's letzten Textdarstellungen," *ZDMG* 24 (1870): 253–60; cf. also his remarks in *ZDMG* 24 (1870): 438–60, 645–64, and *ZDMG* 25 (1871): 463–83, and his monograph *Oster-Programm der Universität Halle-Wittenberg, enthaltend eine Abhandlung über Die Siegessäule Mesa's, Königs der Moabiter* (Halle: Buchhandlung des Waisenhauses, 1870).

5. Theodor Nöldeke, "Die moabitischen Fälschungen," *Deutsche Rundschau* 6 (1876): 448.

6. Konstantin Schlottmann, "Neue Moabitische Funde und Räthsel: Erster Bericht," *ZDMG* 26 (1872): 393–407.

of the artifacts and their inscriptions to Schlottmann and promised to produce further evidence if these were considered to be scientifically acceptable. Schlottmann pointed to the fact that when the Mesha Inscription had been found, he[7] and others had already hoped for similar finds from Moab. These inscriptions later became known under the title "Moabitica." Schlottmann immediately began to publish them on the basis of the drawings that Weser had sent to him.[8] He emphasized that with the publication he intended to communicate the news to his colleagues, anticipating the scholarly assessment of these mysterious finds.[9] Although Schlottmann had learned of warnings against forgeries on the antiquities market, he was optimistic. After the Mesha Inscription itself had been suspected by some to be a forgery[10] and finally had been vindicated, he expected a similar procedure to take place again.

The Moabitica consisted of some human heads, carved from stone, and of many clay figures of various shapes, such as vessels, pitchers, human bodies and body parts, or abstractions of body parts. The shape of the Moabitica is very clumsy and odd; they consist of "ziellos verschrobene und doch rohe, entsetzlich dumm aussehende Gestalten."[11] Schlottmann used to see the ugly shapes of the Moabitica as a vivid expression of "abominations" (שקוצים) mentioned in the Hebrew Bible, but he seems to have ignored that שקוץ denotes *every* idol, not only the gross and disgusting ones.[12] The sheer number of these items—hundreds of figurines were offered for sale in Shapira's shop—roused suspicions: Why had so many items not been found before, with so many people in search for antiquities? Some argued, however, that finds of Punic inscriptions in Carthage had reached similar numbers.[13]

---

7. Ibid. 393.

8. Schlottmann, "Neue Moabitische Funde und Räthsel: Erster Bericht;" "Zweiter Bericht," *ZDMG* 26 (1872): 408–16; "Dritter Bericht. Inschrift des Bildes einer Göttin," *ZDMG* 26 (1872): 786–97.

9. In Schlottmann's own words, he hurried to inform his colleagues of the new finds and to lay his conclusions open to their evaluation ("um über die wichtigen Entdeckungen den Fachgenossen einige Mittheilungen zu machen und ihnen meine Bemerkungen darüber zur Prüfung vorzulegen"), Schlottmann, "Neue Moabitische Funde und Räthsel: Erster Bericht," 393–94.

10. Schlottmann, *Oster-Programm der Universität Halle-Wittenberg, enthaltend eine Abhandlung über Die Siegessäule Mesa's, Königs der Moabiter*, 4–6.

11. Nöldeke, "Die moabitischen Fälschungen," 450.

12. Neubauer, letter to *The Academy*, 102.

13. O. Blau, "Karthagische Inschriften," *ZDMG* 29 (1875): 644; L. Diestel, "Die moabitischen Altertümer," *Jahrbücher für Deutsche Theologie* 21 (1876): 462.

The inscriptions on the various clay figurines are likewise clumsy, although they more or less resemble the script of the Mesha Inscription. The forms of the letters are very unstable and appear at times shifted by 90 degrees, mirrored or upside down. Some letters could not be assigned to any known form. It is amazing that these irregularities rarely moved Schlottmann to question the authenticity of the objects under scrutiny. He tried to see every letter form as evidence of a special Moabite script. In addition, he had discovered specimens of South Arabian and Nabataean scripts. Although these letters were not created to make sense in a word, let alone in a sentence or in a larger syntactical structure, Schlottmann tried to read as much as possible into them. Assuming many irregularities in script, orthography, morphology, and grammar, Schlottmann was happy to read at least some lines.[14] He fell prey to speculation, which even today may repeat itself when puzzling inscriptions with contradicting features are investigated, thereby excluding himself from any further critical assessment. According to Schlottmann, the inscriptions looked too special and too sophisticated to have been made by a cunning forger,[15] although he admitted that at times he did not look at them without a certain amount of scepticism.

In 1872, the British journal *The Academy* printed a warning against inscriptions from Jerusalem. The warning was issued by Albert Socin[16] who pointed to the fact that Jerusalem obviously had become home to a "flourishing manufactory of inscriptions." A Nabataean inscription, which had passed through the hands of Shapira, had been acquired by a certain Mr. Henry Lumley and subsequently been published by him in the *Times*. He realized later that the very item in question was a bad and enlarged copy of a genuine Nabataean sepulchral inscription published in 1870 by Warren and later deciphered by Levy.[17] Another forged artifact that had been "discovered" by Shapira was a Greek inscription, forbidding non-

---

14. K. Schlottmann, "Ueber die Aechtheit der Moabitischen Altertümer," *ZDMG* 28 (1874): 178.

15. "Eben so werden diejenigen, welche meiner Darstellung aufmerksam gefolgt sind, mir darin beistimmen, dass bei den Vasen und ihren Inschriften an schlaue Antiquitäten-Fabrikate jerusalemitanischer Industrie-Ritter (denn die Möglichkeit solcher Productionen bei den Beduinen der Wüste fällt von selbst weg) nicht gedacht werden kann." (Schlottmann, "Zweiter Bericht," 412). Regarding the palaeography and script, Schlottmann claimed that nobody would be able to create a script like that: "Dergleichen erfindet kein Fälscher"; see idem, review of E. Kautzsch and A. Socin, *Die Aechtheit der moabitischen Altertümer geprüft* (Strassburg and London: Trübner, 1876) and of A. Koch, *Moabitisch oder Selimisch? Die Frage der moabitischen Altertümer* (Stuttgart: Schweizerbart, 1876) in *Jenaer Literaturzeitung* 3 (1876): 237a.

16. Albert Socin, "The Manufacture of Inscriptions," *The Academy* 3 (1872): 179–80.

17. Jacob Levy, "Eine neue nabathäische Inschrift aus Ammonitis," *ZDMG* 25 (1871): 429–34, esp. 429.

Israelites to enter the inner court of the Temple (and thus harmonizing beautifully with Josephus). In addition, Shapira had gained possession of a stone with Psalm 117 in Moabite letters (which he later himself debunked as a forgery),[18] and more was to come … Socin reasoned that "Bedouins go in quest of inscriptions; then pashas extort them from them out of avarice, and play the part of harem-guardians of Semitic monuments; and the last part is now before us—the convenient though clumsy system of forgery." Later, Socin admitted that Shapira should not be seen as the deceiver but as the deceived,[19] relying on the "testimony of reputable persons," but Socin nevertheless hoped "that people in Jerusalem will bestir themselves to find out the real forgers." Socin had also published his concerns in German.[20]

Schlottmann, however, and several members of the DMG[21] remained unmoved by these first signs of a coming catastrophe, although he admitted it as perceivable that some items may not be authentic.[22] In September 1872, Weser sent a report to Schlottmann,[23] giving an account of his expedition to Moab together with Shapira and Wilhelm Duisberg, the German Consul from Khartoum. This expedition, led by the aforementioned Salim al-Khouri, had been made to investigate the assumed locations where the Moabitica had been unearthed. Although many of the conclusions Weser himself had already drawn from his observations were begging the question (he repeatedly called any fraudulent action of the Bedouins in regard to the Moabitica as unimaginable), and although Weser was fully aware of the possibility that Salim al-Khouri, who had provided Shapira with the Moabitica and who was well acquainted with the surroundings of the find-place and with the local Bedouins, could have arranged this expedition into the area of Moab and that his accomplices could have "salted" the location in advance, he disregarded it as completely out of question and unthinkable.[24] An additional assertion of Weser, namely, that the special kind of pottery known as the Moabitica could not have been made in Jerusalem or Palestine,[25]

---

18. Hermann Weser, "Ueber die neuesten Moabitischen Funde. Reisebericht von Lic. Weser in Jerusalem, eingesandt von K. Schlottmann," ZDMG 26 (1872): 722–34, esp. 723.

19. A. Socin, "The Manufacture of Inscriptions," 260.

20. At first, in the *Augsburger Allgemeine Zeitung* (March 20, 1872); later, in the ZDMG ("Ueber Inschriftenfälschungen," ZDMG 27 [1873]: 133–35).

21. K. Schlottmann, "Zur Verständigung in der moabitischen Streitfrage," Anzeiger Nr. 14 zur *Jenaer Literaturzeitung* (1876): 57.

22. Schlottmann, "Zweiter Bericht," 413–16; idem, "Nachschrift," ZDMG 27 (1873): 135–36.

23. Weser, "Ueber die neuesten Moabitischen Funde. Reisebericht," 722–34.

24. Ibid. 729.

25. Ibid. 725.

was evidently wrong.²⁶ Weser's report, however, convinced Schlottmann of the Moabitica's authenticity beyond any doubt.

After Schlottmann had come to a firm conclusion, the DMG, at their convention in September 1872,²⁷ assented to further the publication of those Moabitica which were readily available and to recommend to the Royal Prussian minister for education the acquisition of the Moabitica. It seems that the German authorities in Berlin did not want to lose the academic battle for antiquities from Palestine a second time. This time, they would not allow a smart Frenchman like Clermont-Ganneau to interfere and win the day, as he had done in the case of the Mesha Inscription. So they hurried to buy the first Moabitica collection of 911 pieces, which shortly afterwards would be joined by the second Moabitica collection of more than seven hundred pieces,²⁸ for the Royal Museum in Berlin in 1873²⁹ and paid to Shapira the immense sum of more than 20,000 Taler, partly donated by the German Kaiser himself. Only one year later, however, the DMG, which was responsible for the acquisition of the Moabitica, took precautions against any uncritical publication of the material. It was decided that the Moabitica should be published for the disclosure of the material and its assessment, without involving any opinion of the DMG. Meanwhile, Shapira began to build up his third collection.

In the meantime, the general opinion about the Moabitica in Germany had changed, and most scholars regarded the Moabitica as modern fabrications. It is the way this conclusion was finally reached in Germany, Switzerland, England, and France that still is very intriguing to investigate, and that might help us today to form our opinion of questionable objects that are offered on the market.

---

26. Diestel, "Die moabitischen Altertümer," 469–70; Nöldeke, "Die moabitischen Fälschungen," 448.

27. For discussions and decisions regarding the Moabitica made at the regular conferences of the DMG and referred to in this paragraph, see the "Nachrichten über Angelegenheiten der Deutschen morgenländischen Gesellschaft" in *ZDMG* 27 (1873): VI; *ZDMG* 29 (1875): VII, and *ZDMG* 31 (1877): XV.

28. But cf. a short note in *PEQS* 1874: 206–7, which probably gives the number of the Moabitica according to the enumeration used by Shapira. At that time, the number of the Moabitica was increasing continually. "The first collection contains 911 pieces, of which 465 bear inscriptions. The second collection contains 493 pieces, of which 60 only are inscribed. The third collection contains 410 pieces, of which 68 are inscribed." For further data see Kautzsch and Socin, *Die Aechtheit der moabitischen Altertümer geprüft*, 2:26, and Koch, *Moabitisch oder Selimisch?*, 3–21.

29. Eugen Prym, review of Kautzsch and Socin, *Die Aechtheit der moabitischen Altertümer geprüft* and Koch, *Moabitisch oder Selimisch?*, 238b.

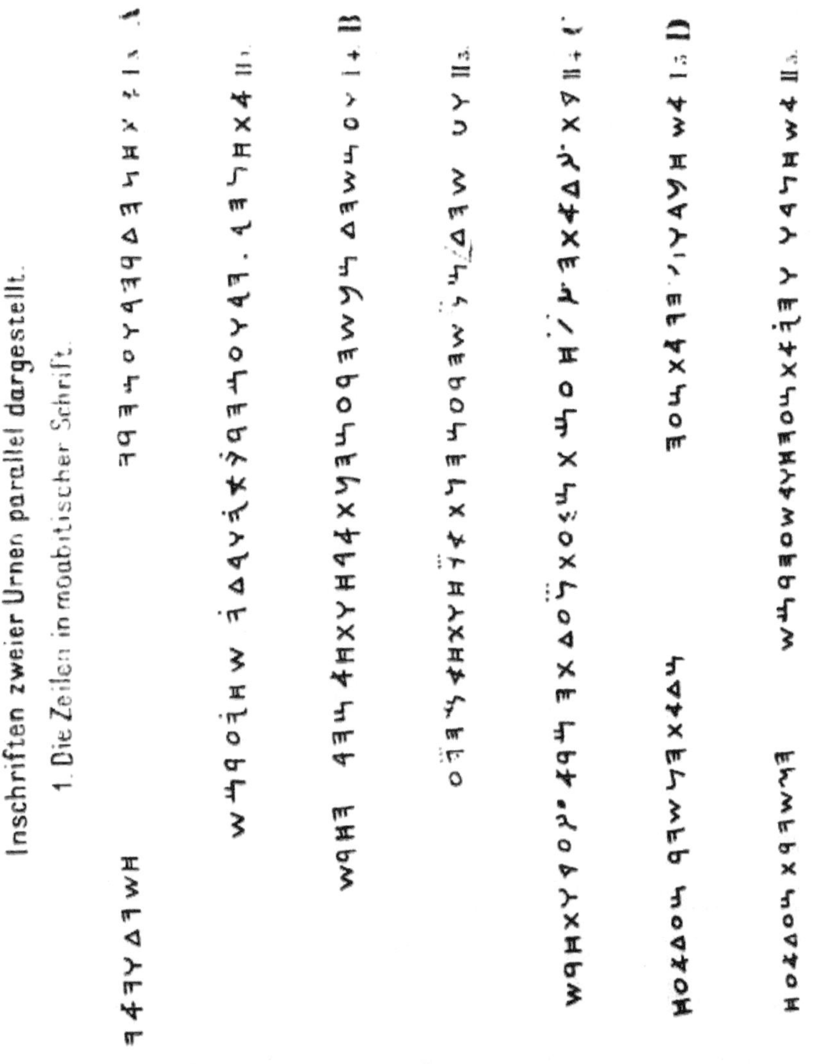

HEIDE: THE MOABITICA AND THEIR AFTERMATH 199

Fig. 1. Script charts of the inscribed objects published by Schlottmann ("Neue Moabitische Funde und Räthsel: Erster Bericht," plate before p. 393).

In 1873, drawings of two hundred Moabitica objects were sent from Jerusalem to the Palestine Exploration Fund by Lieut. Conder and Mr. Tyrwhitt Drake.[30] Both had seen these objects at Shapira's shop and had initially had no

---

30. Claude R. Conder and Charles F. Tyrwhitt Drake, "Notes on the Drawings and Copies

suspicions. Scholars from England and America, however, became increasingly alarmed by the ever increasing number of artifacts, of which not a single item had been seen or found before 1872.[31] The Palestine Exploration Fund reported in 1873 that the Moabitica were "warmly supported by Professor Schlottmann" while "the opinions of English scholars have as yet been unfavourable."[32]

In the same year, the aforementioned French epigrapher Clermont-Ganneau went to London. At that time, nobody knew the Mesha Inscription better than Clermont-Ganneau. When he had learned of Schlottmann's publication and had viewed the script specimens,[33] Clermont-Ganneau had formed his opinion right "at the outset."[34] His suspicions were confirmed when he looked in London at the drawings that had been sent to the Palestine Exploration Fund. Clermont-Ganneau had recognized the letters of the Moabitica script immediately as belonging to the writing style of Salim, Shapira's business-partner,

> a painter by trade [...] I had to do with him at the commencement of the Moabite Stone business. He had copied a few lines from the original seen by him at Diban, and I have always kept this copy [...] which at least enabled me to detect from the very first, in the fantastic script of the Shapira Collection, the characteristic and peculiar manner in which our artist sees, understands, and designs the Moabite letters; among other things, there being a certain manner of drawing the *mim* peculiar to him [...] Selim's copies [...] show us the *mim* several times drawn in a variation of form essentially peculiar to Selim, and not existing *at all* in the original.[35]

Clermont-Ganneau's observations become comprehensible when figures 1 and 2 are compared. The *mem* of fig. 1 is found in fig. 2, line 2 (first letter) and line 3 (last letter). The very same form of the *mem* had been triumphantly "found" by Hermann Weser inscribed on a vessel during his expedition to Moab.[36] Schlottmann knew very well that in terms of palaeography this kind of *mem* was

---

of Inscriptions from the 'Shapira Collection' Sent Home by Lieut. Conder and Mr. Drake," *PEQS* 1873: 79–80.

31. Charles Clermont-Ganneau, "The Shapira Collection" (and various letters from different authors), *PEQS* 1874: 114–24. 201–7, esp. 118–19; Kautzsch and Socin, *Die Aechtheit der moabitischen Altertümer geprüft*, 8.

32. Conder and Tyrwhitt Drake, "Notes on the Drawings and Copies of Inscriptions from the 'Shapira Collection' Sent Home by Lieut. Conder and Mr. Drake," 80.

33. Ibid.

34. Clermont-Ganneau, "The Shapira Collection," 114.

35. Ibid., 115. 204.

36. Weser, "Ueber die neuesten moabitischen Funde. Reisebericht," 729.

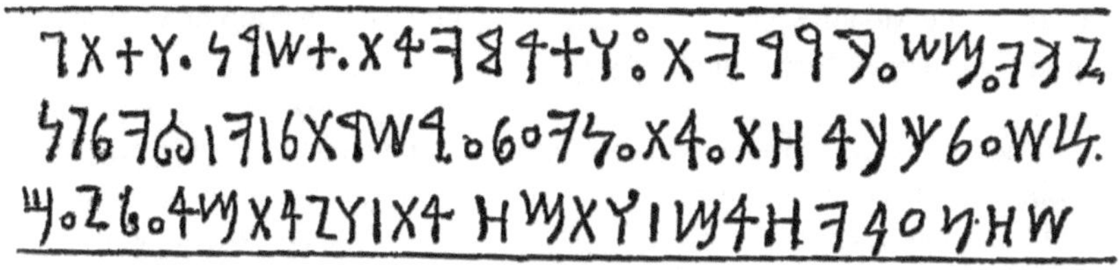

[inscription image]

N° 16. Copie partielle de la stèle de Mesa, par Selim.

Fig. 2. Salim's left-to-right copy, with some missing letters (cf. Schlottmann, review of Kautzsch and Socin, and Koch, 328), of lines 13–15 of the Mesha Inscription. (Clermont-Ganneau, *Les fraudes archéologiques en Palestine, suivies de quelques monuments phéniciens apocryphes* [Paris: Ernest Leroux, 1885], 159).

younger than the *mem* of the Mesha Inscription[37] and younger than the assumed age of the Moabitica, but he seems to have ignored it. There are further examples of letters common to figures 1 and 2, but totally absent from the Mesha Inscription: The *waw* in figures 1 and 2 exhibits a large head and a short vertical down stroke. The tail of the *yod* and the third bar of the *he* are often missing. Thereby both letters are virtually merged into one, a feature also obvious in additional Moabitica vessels investigated by Kautzsch (fig. 6). The *nun* appears often as a simple rectangular hook in both figures, removed of its elaborated angular shape on the Mesha Inscription. The head of the *qof* is never drawn correctly in both figures and appears with only half of its head on the left side of the vertical shaft. The forms of the letters, however, increased in variation as more and more Moabitica were available at Shapira's (cf. fig. 6), which made it difficult for Clermont-Ganneau to generalize his initial persuasion. Besides Salim's few notes, more publications of inscriptional material must have been used to produce such a large number of vessels with increasingly varying script styles.[38]

In addition, Clermont-Ganneau wondered how hundreds of objects were inscribed with letters evidently meant to be Moabite, while the very texts they belonged to—in opposition to the Mesha Inscription—were totally unintelligible. He dismissed any reading efforts as contradictory and impossible.

During an official archaeological expedition to Jerusalem on behalf of the Palestine Exploration Fund in 1873, Clermont-Ganneau hoped also to clarify the

---

37. K. Schlottmann, "Zur semitischen Epigraphik," *ZDMG* 24 (1870): 403–14, esp. 413.

38. Prym, review of Kautzsch and Socin, *Die Aechtheit der moabitischen Altertümer geprüft* and Koch, *Moabitisch oder Selimisch?*, 240a.

question of the Moabite pottery. He visited the famous collection of Shapira in his shop in Jerusalem, which contained

> statues and vases, covered with inscriptions, supposed to be Moabite, lavished in suspicious profusion. [...] I at once recognized, in these models of badly baked earth, the manner and style of our artist, of whom I already possess certain drawings [...] The clay is absolutely identical with that used now by Jerusalem potters [...] I have also seen on some of the specimens the famous deposits of saltpetre, which play so great a part in the question, and which have been produced by the partisans of authenticity as proofs of their extreme antiquity. These saltpetre deposits are only superficial, and must have been obtained, as I have always said, by plunging the things in a solution of nitre.[39]

Clermont-Ganneau's suspicions were substantiated when he learned that the Moabite pottery had been delivered by none other than Salim al-Khouri to Shapira. Subsequently, Clermont-Ganneau managed to extract confessions from some Jerusalemite pottery workers. One of them admitted that he had assisted Salim in his forgery business. He told how the objects were minutely counted when they were brought into the potter's workshop to be burnt, and carefully picked up again; how they were dipped in a caldron filled with water to make them look old. Another man, 'Abd al-Baki, who gave to Clermont-Ganneau only some general hints that he had worked for Salim, made a confession some weeks later, officially confirmed at the British Consulate, to the aforementioned Tyrwhitt Drake that he had worked for Salim and had burnt clay vessels for him.[40] Tyrwhitt Drake later suggested that genuine artifacts had probably been found in the beginning, and that Salim used these as models for his own creations, so that "genuine and forged [Moabitica] are inextricably mixed up in the Berlin Museum."[41] When Schlottmann heard of that, he admitted the possibility that some items were probably inauthentic and that he was going to apply for a physical investigation of the Moabitica at the Prussian ministry of education.[42] Weser himself, however, was totally unmoved by these incidents. He tried to refute Clermont-Ganneau's

---

39. Clermont-Ganneau, "The Shapira Collection," 116.
40. Ibid., 119.
41. Ibid., 120.
42. H. Weser, "Eine antiquarische Consular-Untersuchung in Jerusalem. Bericht die behauptete Fälschung der Moabitischen Thonsachen betreffend, von Lic. Weser. Eingesandt von Konst. Schlottmann," *ZDMG* 28 (1874): 460–80, esp. 461; K. Schlottmann, "Die neuen Beweise für die Ächtheit der moabitischen Altertümer," *Deutsch-evangelische Blätter* 2 (1877): 466–70, esp. 467–68.

inquiry into the potters' business and suggested that Clermont-Ganneau had bullied these men and had extracted manipulated reports.[43]

Some months later, Weser and Duisberg arrived again in Jerusalem for the very same reason as Clermont-Ganneau before, although with different presuppositions. To try to find out the truth of the statements made by the pottery workers of Jerusalem, an inquiry was held at the German Consulate for four days, in presence of Weser, Duisberg, Clermont-Ganneau, Tyrwhitt Drake, Salim al-Khouri and the Jerusalemite pottery workers.[44] The pottery workers declared unanimously that they knew nothing of the matter. One pottery worker, the young apprentice Hassan ibn al-Bitar, from whom Clermont-Ganneau had received most of his information, declared that Clermont-Ganneau had forced him to his confession. Salim topped all that by claiming that Clermont-Ganneau had promised him one hundred pounds if he would affirm that the Moabitica were forgeries. Shapira scented gain in the wake of Clermont-Ganneau's embarrassment and wrote a letter to the *Athenaeum*, claiming that by this inquiry not the "slightest evidence against the genuineness of my collection" had been brought forward.[45]

Clermont-Ganneau appealed to the public to make a definite decision either in favor of or against his honesty, and commented on the whole affair that either he had truly "devised this black plot, or these men are hardened scoundrels, or else poor devils telling their story from fear of interest."[46] Clermont-Ganneau's latter suggestion came very near to the truth; it is corroborated by the fact that one of the potters, 'Abd al-Baki, claimed that he never had said anything of what Clermont-Ganneau had accused him—while (un)fortunately, his report had been recorded before at the British Consulate. In the eyes of Weser and Schlottmann, however, this inquiry substantiated that the accusations of Clermont-Ganneau were unfounded. But academics in Europe felt increasingly suspicious about the Moabitica. Besides Schlottmann, no scholar seemed to have been convinced of the Moabitica's authenticity.[47]

In Switzerland, thorough investigations of the Moabitica were made by Albert Socin, who had already issued warnings against the Jerusalemite antiquities market (see above), and Emil Kautzsch. In 1876, they published the results of their investigation in a monograph entitled *Die Aechtheit der moabitischen Altertümer geprüft* ("The authenticity of the Moabite antiquities investigated").

---

43. Weser, "Eine antiquarische Consular-Untersuchung in Jerusalem," 463.
44. Ibid., 460–80.
45. Wilhelm Moses Shapira, letter to the editor of the *Athenaeum*, PEQS (1874): 121.
46. Clermont-Ganneau, "The Shapira Collection," 123.
47. Nöldeke, "Die moabitischen Fälschungen," 448.

Both were at that time professors at the University of Basel. Socin emphasized the importance of his investigation into the external circumstances of the "find" of the Moabitica, and knew from his own experience that Jerusalemite forgeries were nothing unusual.

The internal characteristics were discussed by Emil Kautzsch who today is still known for his revised edition of Gesenius's *Hebrew Grammar*.[48] Weser had hoped that the internal investigation of the Moabitica by Kautzsch "should support the external arguments" and could refute the criticism raised by Socin and Clermont-Ganneau.[49] These investigations were carried through in the field of archaeology, history of religion, and palaeography. Remarkably, most of the Moabitica showed no indication of weathering or decay.[50] None of the vessels seemed to have had contained any liquid, such as water, oil, or wine.[51] To repudiate the argument that the Moabitica should be seen as unique pottery artifacts, Kautzsch copied some of the Moabitica in a Basel pottery workshop,[52] not without success. The most important arguments were, however, based on palaeography,[53] an opinion expressed also by Theodor Nöldeke: "[The Moabitica] can be identified as forgeries for palaeographical reasons alone."[54] It is the science of palaeography that today is considered to be of utmost importance when investigating any unprovenanced inscription.

Let us take a look at the steps Kautzsch took when dealing with the question of palaeography, always keeping in mind that in the 1870s only a few stratified Northwest Semitic inscriptions were available for comparison. Kautzsch first of all did not claim infallibility.[55] He even admitted that the Moabitica should be regarded as genuine as long as there was no compulsive evidence to the contrary. On the other hand, he claimed the right to keep up his scientific scepticism, as

---

48. *Wilhelm Gesenius' Hebräische Grammatik, völlig umgearbeitet von E. Kautzsch* (28th ed.; Leipzig: Vogel, 1909); *Gesenius' Hebrew Grammar: As Edited and Enlarged by the Late E. Kautzsch* (2nd Eng. ed.; Oxford: Oxford University Press, 1963).

49. Weser, "Eine antiquarische Consular-Untersuchung in Jerusalem," 480.

50. Kautzsch and Socin, *Die Aechtheit der moabitischen Altertümer geprüft*, 162.

51. Diestel, "Die moabitischen Altertümer," 454.

52. Kautzsch and Socin, *Die Aechtheit der moabitischen Altertümer geprüft*, 175. Kautzsch was aided by another well-known scholar of Semitics, Julius Euting from Strassburg. Every reader of *Gesenius' Hebrew Grammar as Edited and Enlarged by the Late E. Kautzsch* knows of Euting's facsimile of the Siloam inscription. For Eutings involvement in the Moabitica discussion, see Reichert, "Julius Euting, die Pseudo-Moabitica und 'La petite fille de Jérusalem,'" 347–67.

53. Ibid., 465.

54. Nöldeke, "Die moabitischen Fälschungen," 450.

55. Kautzsch and Socin, *Die Aechtheit der moabitischen Altertümer geprüft*, 66.

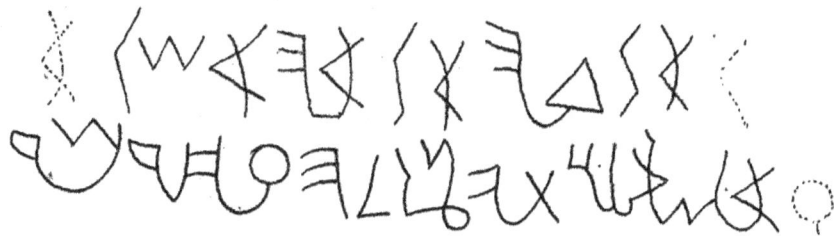

Probe aus Inschrift 26ᵇ Zeile 1.2.

Fig. 3. Ligatures in the script of the Moabitica according to the table in Kautzsch and Socin's monograph (*Die Aechtheit der moabitischen Altertümer geprüft*) characterized later by Delitzsch as the "Gickelgackel von allerlei närrischen Lautverbindungen" (Franz Delitzsch, "Schapira's Pseudo-Deuteronomium," *Allgemeine Evangelisch-Lutherische Kirchenzeitung* 1883: 870–72).

long as the objections against their authenticity could not be removed with well-founded reasons.

While some of Kautzsch's criticisms were not based on enough evidence,[56] most of his arguments hit the mark and were received as the final word on the Moabitica. Even in the 1870s, with only few inscriptions for comparison at hand, the strange and suspicious features of the Moabitica's script were detected very soon. Some of the letters were combined as ligatures.[57] Could it be that a forger had invented new letter forms? On the one side, anyone forging an inscription is not supposed to take the extra pains to invent ligatures. On the other hand, the awkward forms, especially of ד ה in fig. 3, line 1, and the groups אלשאלם, עחר, and שר in line 2 roused suspicions. But how should these ligatures be evaluated, with no comparisons at hand?

The decisive argument was drawn from a comparison of various script developments known at that time. In Greek and Latin, ligatures came into being after the script had advanced to various progressive stages. Despite the small amount

---

56. Kautzsch claimed that according to the Hebrew Bible, we should not expect any other deity besides Chemosh in Moab. Therefore he dismissed Schlottmann's reading אלעמת "goddess of unification" on one of the Moabitica for religio-historical reasons, and criticized his equation of אלעמת with עשתרת (which criticism certainly was justified), but negated even the possibility of a combined deity in the divine names עשתר כמש in the Mesha Inscription, line 17 (Kautzsch and Socin, *Die Aechtheit der moabitischen Altertümer geprüft*, 68–86). For Kautzsch's suggestions regarding the South Arabian script, see below.

57. Cf. Adolf Koch, *Moabitisch oder Selimisch? Die Frage der moabitischen Altertümer* (Stuttgart: Schweizerbart, 1876), 6.

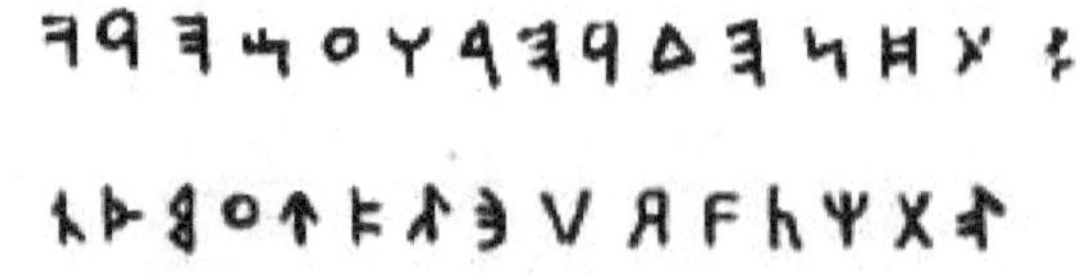

NEW INSCRIPTIONS AND SEALS

Fig. 4. Alleged Moabite (line 1) and South Arabian scripts (line 2) on figurine no 1, assumed by Schlottmann to give the same words in two different writing systems ("Neue Moabitische Funde und Räthsel: Erster Bericht," plate before page 393).

of stratified inscriptions available in the nineteenth century, it was an established fact that the cursive styles of the Syriac and Arabic scripts with their idiosyncratic ligatures had emerged from the noncursive Aramaic script after a long period of time. Quite to the contrary, the script of the Moabitica provided no evidence of any development, but represented letter shapes that were well-known from the Mesha Inscription, albeit linking these by superfluous lines and thereby creating a unique scribal fussiness. In other words, the ligatures of the Moabitica could only be interpreted as a palaeographic anachronism.[58]

Another argument adduced by Kautzsch referred to the South Arabian shape of some letters on two clay vessels of which drawings had been sent to Schlottmann by Weser.[59] These letters appeared side-by-side with Moabite letters on the same vessels, thereby creating the impression of bilingual inscriptions.

Kautzsch observed that there are certainly some characters that seem to resemble South Arabian letters,[60] yet there are many irregularities: Only letters no 5 and 10 are nearly identical, the remaining characters differ from each other, and letter no 9 resembles closely a mirrored form of letter no 15. Most characters were seen by Kautzsch and Socin as bizarre variants of the Moabite *yod* (cf. letters no 1, 5, 8, 10) and *resh*.[61] According to Kautzsch, those few letters which seemed to have a South Arabian shape had probably been created by accident in the squeeze that Salim al-Khouri, Shapira's associate, had made for Clermont-Ganneau (see fig. 4, line 2 with fig. 2, line 1, for a "South Arabian" *mem*), but this observation was regarded as too speculative.[62] At that time, various script charts with pre-Islamic Arabian characters had already been published that could have served as

---

58. Kautzsch and Socin, *Die Aechtheit der moabitischen Altertümer geprüft*, 88–89.
59. Schlottmann, "Neue Moabitische Funde und Räthsel: Erster Bericht," 395.
60. In fig. 4, line 2, the second, third, twelfth and thirteenth letters, counted from right to left.
61. Kautzsch and Socin, *Die Aechtheit der moabitischen Altertümer geprüft*, 92–93.
62. Prym, review of Kautzsch and Socin, *Die Aechtheit der moabitischen Altertümer geprüft* and Koch, *Moabitisch oder Selimisch?*, 239.

a kind of *Vorlage*. Of these,[63] some characters had entered the Moabitica, as Hoffmann could demonstrate.[64]

Schlottmann had tried hard to read as much as possible, but except for a few lines, most of the Moabitica resisted his reading efforts. He admitted that many lines were not decipherable and suggested (but rejected that idea again) that the Moabitica may be post-Christian fabrications inscribed with Gnostic incantations.[65] Following are two examples of his very strained proposed readings.

Schlottmann tried to read the first four letters in both lines (fig. 4) as the personal name אתחך,[66] but these few letters must definitely be read as אתחן. Letter 4 of line 2 may be read as a South Arabian *kaf*, but letter 1 of line 2 seems not to be of South Arabian origin. Schlottmann then proceeded to read הדרהר (line 1), which he interpreted as a surname of אתחך. Alternatively, he divided the first nine letters of line 1 as reading אתחך הדר הר, meaning something like "אתחך, the ornament of Hor" (cf. Dan 11:20).

To read the inscription on a very clumsy "goddess," Schlottmann proposed that some of the letters in fig. 5, lines 1–2 should be read as אל אדמן, but could also be read as אל אדמת, because the *nun* appeared to form a ligature with the *taw* of another word in line 3 below (!). Disregarding this conjecture as too speculative, Schlottmann finally admitted that only אל אדמן should be read, which in turn could be a variant for אל אמת, a certain "Erdengottheit," female in character and depiction, while grammatically of the masculine gender.[67]

Kautzsch questioned also some Nabataean letters which Schlottmann had described in detail.[68] Kautzsch did not deny the Nabataean character of these signs, but wondered why Schlottmann never pointed to the epigraphical anachronism implicated by this fact. How could the Nabataean writing style, which did not come into use before the second century B.C.E. and had its *floruit* in the second and third centuries C.E., turn up in a Moabite inscription believed to date to the ninth century B.C.E.? Script-charts of the Nabataean writing system were

---

63. Cf. Johann Gottfried Wetzstein, *Reisebericht über Hauran und die Trachonen nebst einem Anhange über die sabäischen Denkmäler in Ostsyrien* (Berlin: Dietrich Reimer, 1860), 67, 75, 151; Cyril C. Graham, "Notiz des Herrn Cyril C. Graham zu den von ihm copirten Inschriften," *ZDMG* 12 (1858): 713–14.

64. G. Hoffmann, review of Kautzsch and Socin, *Die Aechtheit der moabitischen Altertümer geprüft*, and of Koch, *Moabitisch oder Selimisch?* in *Göttingische gelehrte Anzeigen* 1876: 494–99.

65. Schlottmann, "Neue Moabitische Funde und Räthsel" 412.

66. Ibid. 400.

67. K. Schlottmann, "Neue Moabitische Funde und Räthsel. Dritter Bericht. Inschrift des Bildes einer Göttin," *ZDMG* 26 (1872): 786–97, esp. 788. For further details see Kautzsch and Socin, *Die Aechtheit der moabitischen Altertümer geprüft*, 152–53.

68. Schlottmann, "Neue Moabitische Funde und Räthsel," 406.

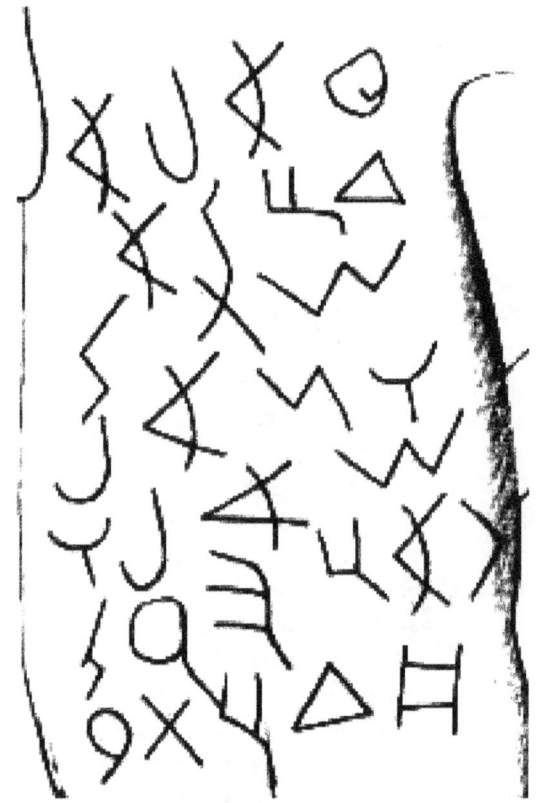

Fig. 5. Inscription on the back of a "goddess." Schlottmann, "Neue Moabitische Funde und Räthsel. Dritter Bericht. Inschrift des Bildes einer Göttin," 786–87.

available in the 1870s in Jerusalem and could easily have been utilized by the alleged forger,[69] who seems to have copied some of these letters while others had been slightly modified to delude the eye.[70]

Kautzsch also investigated the frequency of letters in the Moabitica. As none of the letter clusters made any sense without considerable strain, an investigation of the distribution of the various letters promised to give further insight into their creation and intention. Kautzsch compared the distribution of the consonants

---

69. M. A. Levy, "Uber die nabathäischen Inschriften von Petra, Hauran, vornehmlich der Sinai-Halbinsel und über die Münzlegenden nabathäischer Könige," *ZDMG* 14 (1860): 363–484; cf. Socin, "Ueber Inschriftenfälschungen," *ZDMG* 27 (1873): 133–35.

70. Kautzsch and Socin, *Die Aechtheit der moabitischen Altertümer geprüft*, 99–101.

in the Hebrew Bible with that of the Mesha Inscription according to Clermont-Ganneau's edition and with that of the Moabitica. To take a particular example: The letter *alef* accounts for 5 percent of all consonants in the Hebrew Bible. In the Mesha Inscription, this letter comprises about 10 percent of the sum total of all letters. King Mesha had written the Mesha Inscription in first person, often adding the pronoun אנך, and he had used the *nota accusativi* את frequently. In the Moabitica, however, with its more than one thousand letters, no reason is discernible which would account for as high a percentage of the letter *alef* as 12 percent. Any reasoning comparing these statistics with the Aramaic script and its many *alef* letters in final position, has to realize that the language of the Moabitica is not Aramaic and that the general style of the script resembles the Moabite script of the Mesha Inscription. In addition, the sum of the gutturals אהחע in relation to the sum total of all consonants amounts in the Hebrew Bible to 16 percent, in the Mesha Inscription to 24 percent, but in the Moabitica to 32 percent! Schlottmann had argued that the large amount of gutturals may be due to some magic formula,[71] which, however, sounds rather makeshift. Moreover, the letter *bet*, one of the most frequent letters in all Northwest Semitic inscriptions, is very rare in the Moabitica.

A further suspicious fact was seen in the awkward variations, which become obvious when letter charts are drawn and the various letter forms are compared. Variations with that intensity are unknown from any lapidary or clay inscription, even today. Particularly conspicuous are letter forms that seem to have borrowed idiosyncratic features from each other (cf. ה and י in fig. 6). On the other hand, some patterns were repeated quite uniformly on different objects, which led Schlottmann to speculate that "the characters have undoubtedly been formed by the application of stamps or types, presenting the earliest evidence of a reproducible script which later evolved into the art of printing."[72]

Kautzsch's observations (of which the most important ones have been presented here) led to a damning verdict. It was not the one or the other point by itself which convincingly denounced the Moabitica as forgeries, but the accumulation of evidence. While the results of the inquiry at the German Consulate in Jerusalem could with some strain be interpreted either way (as even Clermont-Ganneau admitted), the internal criteria (in terms of palaeography, orthography, and morphology) were increasingly regarded as decisive. Clermont-Ganneau's observations (see above, fig. 2) were still valid, even if they could not be applied to every item of the Moabitica, and Kautzsch's observations on the script and its

---

71. Schlottmann, "Zweiter Bericht," 412.
72. Schlottmann, "Der Chauvinismus in der Alterthumswissenschaft," cited according to the translation in *The Academy*, 498.

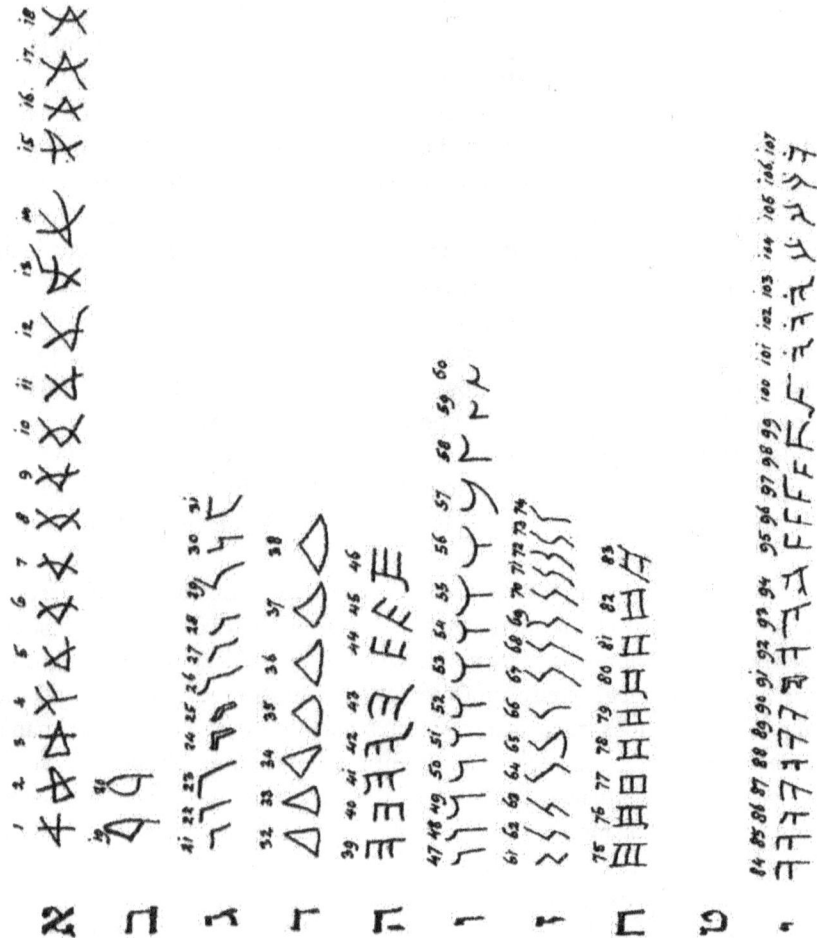

Fig. 6. Table of Moabitica letters (Kautzsch and Socin, *Die Aechtheit der moabitischen Altertümer geprüft*, plates).

awkward features were a death blow to the belief in their authenticity. In 1876, after a fierce debate in the Prussian government, where, among others, Theodor Mommsen admitted the error that had been made with the acquisition of the Moabitica and lamented the international scandal they had generated,[73] the

---

73. Clermont-Ganneau, *Les fraudes archéologiques en Palestine, suivies de quelques monuments phéniciens apocryphes*, 179–81.

Moabitica were declared to be forgeries—at least most of them. The DMG, which had consented to their acquisition on the recommendation of Schlottmann, gave up its plans to publish the material.[74]

The same year, however, saw the publication of another monograph on the Moabitica by Adolf Koch. From the outset, Koch had suspected the Moabitica to be forgeries, but later became convinced to the contrary. For his investigation, Koch, being a professor at the "Kantonsgymnasium" in Schaffhausen, could not only resort to the Moabitica from Berlin but also to his own investigations made in 1875 in Jerusalem. Shapira provided him insight into his own notebook with most of the correspondence he had had in the last few years, and unlimited access to his third Moabitica collection. From Shapira's notebook, Koch learned that the first Moabitica delivery to Shapira had been made on the day after All Fools' day, 1872.[75] In his monograph, Koch tried to answer Kautzsch and Socin's refutation, on which Socin gave in turn another comment in the same year.[76] Koch declared all artifacts and inscriptions made of stone as forgeries.[77] They seem to have been made by Martin Boulos, a stonecutter and engraver of tombstones by profession

---

74. Adolf Erman, the director of the Egyptian Museum, reports that after the "disgusting treasure" arrived in Berlin in 1873, everybody seems to have lost interest in the Moabitica and they were shelved in the basement of the ministry of education ("Kultusministerium"). Neubauer reported in 1883 their whereabouts at the Foreign Office ("Auswärtiges Amt"), the Municipal Museum ("Stadtmuseum") of Berlin having refused their acceptance (Adolf Neubauer, "Correspondence: The Shapira MS. of Deuteronomy," *The Academy* 24 [1883]: 116). In or after 1884, Erman was commissioned to transfer them to the depots of the Egyptian Collection (Adolf Erman, *Mein Werden und mein Wirken. Erinnerungen eines alten Berliner Gelehrten* [Leipzig: Quelle & Meyer, 1929], 247–48). At that time, they showed already signs of decay. Today, only some twenty of the Moabitica are left in the "Vorderasiatisches Museum" in Berlin, and eleven pieces are stocked in the library of the DMG in Halle (Budde and Lewy, *Von Halle nach Jerusalem*, 108–9; Budde, "Die Affäre um die 'Moabitischen Altertümer,'" 111). According to Jerome M. Eisenberg ("A 19th Century Forger in Palestine: Wilhelm Moses Shapira," *Minerva* 12 [2001]: 25), some pottery items of this genre are housed in the Franciscan Archaeological Museum in Jerusalem and in the collections of the Archaeological Institute of the Hebrew University. The École Biblique et Archéologique Française (EBAF) in Jerusalem has also a few Moabitica (personal communication by André Lemaire). Five Moabitica vessels of Julius Euting's estate could be located in the "Bibliothèque nationale et universitaire de Strasbourg" (Reichert, "Julius Euting, die Pseudo-Moabitica und 'La petite fille de Jérusalem,'" 349), and there are certainly additional pieces, some of them forgotten long ago and covered with dust, stacked in the basements of various public and private collections.

75. Koch, *Moabitisch oder Selimisch? Die Frage der moabitischen Altertümer*, 67.

76. Albert Socin, "Die pseudomoabitischen Steininschriften und Thonwaaren," *Das Ausland* 13 (1876): 252–54.

77. Koch, *Moabitisch oder Selimisch? Die Frage der moabitischen Altertümer*, 67–97.

and a friend and accomplice of Salim.[78] Regarding the clay artifacts, Koch admitted that they could have been forged in Jerusalem, but pointed to the fact that various experts had investigated the clay of the Moabitica and had found it to be different from clay vessels made in Jerusalem today.[79] It was also argued that Muslims would not dare to manufacture human forms and deities. Besides these easily refutable arguments, another objection raised by Koch against the forgery charge was the great diversity of the Moabitica in forms.

Koch regarded the palaeographical discussion as decisive, but unfortunately defended his point with very weak arguments. As more and more Moabitica were coming up, Koch had difficulties explaining why Shapira's third collection bore closer analogies to the letter forms of the Mesha Inscription, and why some letters on the Moabitica, which rarely ever were seen before, such as *pe*, suddenly turned up more frequently, while others were rarely used (*qof*) or never (*samek*), or seemed to have undergone some change at a certain point of time (*lamed*). If these new letter forms had to be explained as belonging to some evolutional stage of the Moabite alphabet, why did this progress suddenly turn up *now* in Shapira's third collection?[80] Although Koch made very accurate script charts of hundreds of Moabitica, he was not a very good epigrapher and had no eye for the essential forms of the Moabite script (which in part was due to the scarcity of the material in his time). He could not adequately explain why those letters which he identified as *resh* and *bet* or *gimel* and *kaf* respectively had nearly identical letter forms. He argued that a mélange of letter forms or (seemingly) palaeographical anachronisms were not impossible or unthinkable because they were common in Nabataean and Greek inscriptions.[81] He surmised that a Moabite *yod* with no tail was possible for the reason that it was found on Aramaic coins,[82] and tried to explain the Moabitica *alef* with the *alef* of Maccabaean coins.[83] From Koch's point of view, palaeographical anachronisms in the Moabitica should be seen as part of the Moabite religious syncretism.[84] He also tried to refute Clermont-Ganneau's argument that Salim used his own copy of the Mesha Inscription when he inscribed the Moabitica, but, as we have already seen, Salim's copy served him only partly as a *Vorlage* for the material. Ligatures of letters in lapidary inscrip-

---

78. Ibid., 80; cf. Lehrer-Jacobson, *Fakes and Forgeries from Collections in Israel*, 20*.
79. Ibid., 28–31.
80. Socin, "Die pseudomoabitischen Steininschriften und Thonwaaren," 253.
81. Koch, *Moabitisch oder Selimisch? Die Frage der moabitischen Altertümer*, 57–58.
82. Ibid., 41.
83. Ibid., 45.
84. Diestel, "Die moabitischen Altertümer," 466.

tions were according to Koch likewise possible and are sometimes made "by force."[85] All these arguments, of course, were criticized as begging the question.

In various articles, most prominently in the *ZDMG*, Schlottmann had continued to defend the authenticity of the Moabitica against suspicions raised foremost by Socin and Clermont-Ganneau. On the other hand, Schlottmann was an open-minded and serious scholar. Already in 1870, he had defended the authenticity of the Mesha Inscription against various forgery suspicions.[86] In 1874, while still holding fast to the authenticity of the Moabitica, Schlottmann published the newly "discovered" Parahyba Inscription and raised considerable concerns over its authenticity for internal reasons.[87] He judged, though with some hesitation, that the accumulation of evidence, based foremost on orthography and morphology, was enough to denounce the Parahyba Inscription a forgery. A more rigorous evaluation[88] would have probably convinced him beyond a reasonable doubt. Two years later, he published another fragment of the Mesha Inscription brought to his attention by Dr. von Niemeyer (fig. 7), who in turn had received it as a gift from a Bedouin-sheik. Kautzsch had suspected it initially to be a forgery, but later admitted its authenticity.[89] Schlottmann weighed the pros and cons of this tiny unprovenanced fragment and finally came to the conclusion that it should be regarded as a genuine fragment of the Mesha Inscription.[90] Both assessments of Schlottmann were later vindicated.[91]

Nevertheless, the debate about the authenticity of the Moabitica continued. It is important that Kautzsch, Socin, and Schlottmann did not publish their papers and books as enemies but regarded their investigations as a "mutual search for truth." Kautzsch and Socin did not portray Schlottmann as a pitiful scholar who

---

85. Koch, *Moabitisch oder Selimisch?*, 64.

86. Schlottmann, *Oster-Programm der Universität Halle-Wittenberg*, 4–6.

87. K. Schlottmann, "Ladisloao Netto, Die Phönizier in Brasilien (Os Phenicios no Brazil). Ein Brief in dem zu Rio de Janeiro erscheinenden ilustrirten Journal O novo mondo vom 23. April 1874. Mit dem Facsimile einer achtzeiligen phönizischen Inschrift und beigefügten Bemerkungen des Redacteurs," *Jenaer Literaturzeitung* 30 (1874): 459–61; idem, "Notizen und Correspondenzen. Die sogenannte Inschrift von Parahyba," *ZDMG* 28 (1874): 481–86.

88. Cf. Julius Euting, "The Phoenicians in Brazil," *The Academy* 5 (1874): 664.

89. Friedrich von Hellwald, "Der Streit über die moabitischen Funde," *Das Ausland* 51 (1878): 378.

90. K. Schlottmann, "Ein neugefundenes kleines Fragment des Mesasteines. Aus einem Briefe des Kais. Deutschen Dragoman Dr. von Niemeyer an Prof. Schlottmann," *ZDMG* 30 (1876): 325–28.

91. Mark Lidzbarski, *Handbuch der nordsemitischen Epigraphik* (2 vols.; Weimar: Felber, 1898), 1:132; for the Mesha fragment, cf. Rudolf Smend and Albert Socin, *Die Inschrift des Königs Mesa von Moab. Für akademische Vorlesungen herausgegeben* (2 vols.; Freiburg: Mohr, 1886), 1:10.

Fig. 7. Fragment of the Mesha Inscription (Schlottmann, "Ein neugefundenes kleines Fragment des Mesasteines").

had fallen prey to a primitive fraud. Despite all their suspicions they did not claim to have proven the forgery of the Moabitica beyond any doubt.[92] Nöldeke and Hoffmann, however, criticized Kautzsch and Socin's approach as too cautious. From their point of view, Kautzsch and Socin had virtually *proven* that the Moabitica were nothing else than a modern concoction and scientifically of no value.[93] More problematic was the relationship between Clermont-Ganneau and Schlottmann, which in part must be seen against the background of the Franco-German conflicts of the nineteenth century. Moreover, the Germans could not forget Clermont-Ganneau's role in acquiring the Mesha Inscription for the Louvre after they had already laid their hands on it.[94] Schlottmann treated Clermont-Ganneau's indications that the Moabitica are forgeries as a threat. He took no pains to answer the palaeographic observations of Clermont-Ganneau in detail and accused him of chauvinism and misdirected patriotism. "There was more than one script style on the Moabitica, so they cannot have been made

---

92. Schlottmann, review of Kautzsch and Socin, *Die Aechtheit der moabitischen Altertümer geprüft* and Koch, *Moabitisch oder Selimisch?*, 236.

93. Nöldeke, "Die moabitischen Fälschungen," 451; Hoffmann, review of Kautzsch and Socin, *Die Aechtheit der moabitischen Altertümer geprüft* and Koch, *Moabitisch oder Selimisch?*, 490; cf. Clermont-Ganneau, *La stèle de Dhiban ou stèle de Mesa, roi de Moab 896 avant J.C.*, 148–49.

94. Cf. Petermann, "Ueber die Auffindung der Moabitischen Inschrift des Königs Mesa;" Schlottmann, "Der Chauvinismus in der Alterthumswissenschaft," cited according to its translation in *The Academy*, 499.

by Salim (who knew only the Mesha Inscription) and his accomplices," was his repeated argument.[95] Schlottmann viewed Shapira and Salim as being beyond suspicion.

In 1876, Schlottmann published a review of Kautzsch and Socin's monograph in the journal *Jenaer Literaturzeitung* in which he, however, did not go into much detail. He pointed to Koch's monograph instead, which, from his point of view, had disposed of Kautzsch and Socin's criticisms once and for all. A more appropriate review of both books appeared in the same volume of the *Jenaer Literaturzeitung* by Eugen Prym.

In 1876, after Kautzsch and Socin had published their monograph, Kautzsch visited Jerusalem. There he learned that those who believed in the authenticity of the Moabitica were mainly members of the German Colony, who did it for personal reasons. No one had investigated the Moabitica by himself. For them, it was unthinkable that these experts who had sold or bought the Moabitica should have been duped. Further research revealed that virtually every "Moabite" vessel had passed through Salim's hands, which pointed, besides additional evidence, to the existence of a forgery workshop in Jerusalem.[96]

In 1877, the German Consul in Jerusalem, Freiherr von Münchhausen, wrote a letter to Shapira, which was subsequently published in the *Athenaeum* and in the *Palestine Exploration Quarterly Statement*. Münchhausen declared that up to the end of 1876, the question of the authenticity of the Moabitica was, from his point of view, still open: Neither Kautzsch and Socin, nor Schlottmann and Weser had proven their assumptions. "All of a sudden this state of things was altered by the expedition of Dr. Almkvist" (a Swedish Orientalist from Uppsala), who, driven by curiosity, and being generally suspicious of the Moabitica, had found a jar with a Moabite inscription, resembling the type of pottery known from Berlin, beneath a rock in a cave of the Moabite mountains. But, as Münchhausen admitted, Salim was again present.[97] Later, Münchhausen himself went into the Moabite mountains, accompanied by some gentlemen who according to him were totally disinterested in the Moabitica question, and discovered some Moabite pottery in a cave, in the soft earth beneath a rock. These two events together seemed to prove the authenticity of the material found and, consequently, the authenticity of the Moabitica,[98] which was immediately echoed in

---

95. Ibid., 499.
96. E. Kautzsch, Beilage zur *Augsburger Allgemeinen Zeitung* no 193, July 11, 1876; Hellwald, "Der Streit über die moabitischen Funde," 376–77.
97. Freiherr von Münchhausen, letters to Mr. Shapira, subsumed under the title "The Moabite Pottery," *PEQS* 1878: 41–44, 95–98, esp. 42.
98. Schlottmann, "Die neuen Beweise für die Ächtheit der moabitischen Altertümer," 467.

some of the media. Some doubts remained, however, as it seemed impossible to bring together that most of these vessels on earlier "expeditions" had been dug up from the ground (amazingly often unbroken), while the very same type of Moabitica was now unearthed in caves, *after* Kautzsch and Socin had opined that pottery in such a good condition as the Moabitica could have survived in hollows only.[99]

Meanwhile, Schlottmann had entrusted two independent specialists in clay vessels with the physical and technical analysis of the Moabitica. This close inspection seemed to confirm their authenticity. These vessels

> have many distinguished and different signs of aging. A forger would have had to overcome many financial and technical challenges to fabricate them. From that I concluded that this kind of pottery, which had been manufactured at different times, can only be understood as the produce of a whole nation, but not as that of a forger.[100]

The examination also seemed to substantiate Schlottmann's suggestions that some of the vessels had been incised, while others had been imprinted by a stamp. In addition, a close inspection of the artifacts revealed that every inscribed object was made from one lump of clay and not cobbled together from various chunks. The vessels and their script seemed to have been made together in antiquity.[101] Schlottmann emphasized that he laid very great stress on the physical analysis, but admitted that he had not yet answered the palaeographical objections raised by Kautzsch.[102]

But the facts which Clermont-Ganneau, Kautzsch, Socin, Nöldeke, Hoffmann, and others had already established were now virtually accepted by everyone. After all, the report of a German Consul and the physical investigation with its limited informative value would not shake the convictions reached unanimously by scholars in England, France, Switzerland, and Germany.

---

99. Kautzsch and Socin, *Die Aechtheit der moabitischen Altertümer geprüft*, 168–69.

100. Schlottmann, "Die neuen Beweise für die Ächtheit der moabitischen Altertümer," 468. Similar speculations were embraced by A. L. Rawson, who classified the Moabitica inscriptions into four or five systems of writing that had derived from an equal number of historical periods. He seriously stated that the "several systems are so distinct and consistent in themselves that any one of them may be determined from an examination of a few of the peculiar forms of the letters, and there is not one of the inscriptions that mingles any two of the systems" (Albert Leighton Rawson, "Moabite Inscriptions," *The Nation* 19 [1874]: 397–98).

101. Hellwald, "Der Streit über die moabitischen Funde," 384.

102. Schlottmann, "Die neuen Beweise für die Ächtheit der moabitischen Altertümer," 468–69.

After further discussions, Clermont-Ganneau replied in December 1877.[103] First of all, he pointed to the fact that Münchhausen obviously was not impartial but had definite presuppositions in the matter. In addition, Münchhausen himself had declared that the newly found pottery was of the same type as the Berlin Moabitica; what Almkvist and Münchhausen had found added absolutely nothing to the state of the matter. In the same month, however, the *Athenaeum* reported that Lieut. Kitchener, successor to Lieut. Conder in the Palestine Exploration Fund, could verify that two Moabite pottery idols had been made by Salim al-Khouri, resembling the type of earthenware known from the Moabitica in Berlin.[104] Immediately thereafter, Shapira and Münchhausen arranged another investigation into Salim's workshop. In his house a newly made unburnt clay idol and four small iron chisels were identified that evidently had been used in the Moabitica production before. After this exposure of Salim's workshop, not only Shapira,[105] but also Münchhausen[106] admitted that Salim definitely was a forger but denied that consequently all of the Moabitica should be regarded as forgeries, let alone Mr. Shapira's large collections, sold and unsold. Schlottmann, Koch, and Münchhausen, however, and the German Colony in Jerusalem, stubbornly kept their belief in the authenticity of the Moabitica.[107]

Meanwhile, Salim had made his escape to Alexandria in Egypt. Some twenty years later, A. S. Yahuda met an old Arab guide in Jerusalem, who offered him several pieces of Moabite pottery and identified himself as Salim al-Khouri. He seems to have given Yahuda a short, but very frank (and probably also not very reliable) account of his adventurous involvement in the Moabitica forgeries.[108]

---

103. These letters, written between December 1877 and February 1878, had been published in the *Athenaeum*. Extracts of these letters appeared in the *PEQS* of 1878.

104. Horatio H. Kitchener ("Lieut. Kitchener"), letter subsumed under the title "The Moabite Pottery," *PEQS* (1878): 94–95.

105. Moses W. Shapira, letter subsumed under the title "The Moabite Pottery," *PEQS* (1878): 95.

106. Münchhausen, letters to Mr. Shapira, subsumed under the title "The Moabite Pottery," *PEQS* (1878): 95–98.

107. Hellwald, "Der Streit über die moabitischen Funde," 387. When in 1884 the *Handwörterbuch des Biblischen Altertums für gebildete Bibelleser* (ed. by Eduard K. A. Riehm; Bielefeld: Velhagen & Klasing, 1884) was published, various articles written by Schlottmann treated the Moabitica still as genuine. Schlottmann's article on "Moab" (pp. 1007–9) seriously defended the authenticity of the Moabitica by pointing to the "expedition" of Münchhausen. The second edition of the *Handwörterbuch*, which appeared in 1894, after Schlottmann's death, seems to have been cleansed of all references to the Moabitica material.

108. Abraham Shalom Yahuda, "The Story of a Forgery and the Mēša Inscription," *JQR* 35 (1944): 139–64.

If some of the facts presented in this essay are deliberately brought together, we get a strange assemblage of data: The Moabitica affair started with the day after All Fools' Day in Jerusalem and with 911 pieces in Berlin, and ended with the name of Freiherr von Münchhausen, whose name is reminiscent of Karl Friedrich Hieronymus Freiherr von Münchhausen (1720–1797), known for his fantasy stories, most notably that he allegedly pulled himself out of a swamp by his own hair.

In 1885, Clermont-Ganneau published a book on forgeries.[109] In the first chapter, he pointed to the fact that there are fewer archaeological finds in Palestine than might be expected. Then he exposed some of the most intriguing forgeries, such as an alleged seal of King David, an ossuary with Moabite script, a sarcophagus of Samson and various other niceties. The third chapter he devoted soleley to the "Berlin Moabitica." When Mark Lidzbarski published his *Handbuch der nordsemitischen Epigraphik* at the end of the nineteenth century, Lidzbarski not only dealt briefly with the Moabitica, but devoted one chapter to the issue of forgeries.[110] The crisis at the beginning of the twenty-first century, which culminated in the forgery trial in Jerusalem, is at least in part due to negligence: the important introductions to Northwest Semitic inscriptions of the twentieth century rarely discuss the issue of forgeries, although forgeries were known to be around.[111] In 1968, Joseph Naveh stated that,

> allegations of forgery are not the scholarly fashion of the moment. In earlier times, at the beginning of the century, they were much more frequent, a not unusual reaction to surprising and unexpected objects appearing on the antiquities market. Often such allegations proved to be without foundation, and as a result scholars at present are rightly wary of such hasty conclusions. Nevertheless, forgeries do occur. It is therefore legitimate to raise questions concerning forgeries, but, needless to say, with the necessary reservation and caution.[112]

---

109. *Les fraudes archéologiques en Palestine, suivies de quelques monuments phéniciens apocryphes* (Paris: Ernest Leroux, 1885).

110. Lidzbarski, *Handbuch der nordsemitischen Epigraphik*, 1:104–5, 129–32.

111. Joseph Naveh, "Aramaica Dubiosa," *JNES* 27 (1968): 317–25; idem, "Some Recently Forged Inscriptions," *BASOR* 247 (1982): 53–58; Nahman Avigad, *Corpus of West Semitic Stamp Seals* (Jerusalem: The Israel Academy of Sciences and Humanities, 1997), 453–60.

112. Naveh, "Aramaica Dubiosa," 317.

A Moabite Version of the Ten Commandments

Shapira had meanwhile modified his business, turning towards the merchandising of ancient Hebrew manuscripts. He sold various Hebrew scrolls he had obtained in remote parts of the Arabian Peninsula to the British Museum and to the Berlin Museum, thereby gaining virtually the official status of a reliable antiquities dealer. A sign at his Jerusalem shop proudly recommended him as "Correspondent to the British Museum." In July 1882,[113] he could sell 145 Karaite Hebrew manuscripts to the British Museum, thereby greatly enhancing the wealthy British collection of oriental manuscripts. In September 1878, Shapira aimed for the stars. He wrote a letter to Schlottmann, who some years earlier had been on Shapira's side, announcing the find of very old Hebrew manuscript strips in Phoenician letters. Schlottmann had continued to defend the Moabitica while most of his colleagues had acknowledged their error and had declared them to be forgeries. His scholarly reputation had suffered and he was now hardly ready to listen to the Jerusalem antiquities dealer's story of another fabulous discovery. After Schlottmann had received Shapira's letter with a transliteration of the text in Hebrew square script, he declared the strips to be forgeries and warned Shapira to continue his game. Schlottmann had presented Shapira's letter with its script specimens to the famous Hebrew scholar Franz Delitzsch who immediately had perceived them as forgeries.[114] But Schlottmann and Delitzsch did not go into further detail. Shapira thought it best to let the matter rest and set the fragments aside in the safety vaults of a Jerusalem bank until Easter 1883. At that time, the German Consul Dr. Schroeder came for a visit from Beirut to Jerusalem. On learning about the leather fragments, he looked at them carefully and believed and declared them to be genuine, which in turn encouraged Shapira to go to Europe and to take the fragments along.

Prior to his departure, Shapira had written a letter to the Hebrew scholar Hermann L. Strack in Germany, telling him about his very old Hebrew manuscript strips. He told him how the German Consul had expressed his opinion and he complained about Schlottmann who had declared them to be forgeries. According to Shapira, these leather strips should be seen as a short and unorthodox version of the "last speech of Moses in the plains of Moab." He claimed that they had been found somewhere in a cave near the Dead Sea by Bedouins. But

---

113. The details of the visits Shapira made in Europe, his correspondence with Schlottmann and Strack and later with the British scholars and the trustees of the British Museum are all well documented in Fred N. Reiner, "C. D. Ginsburg and the Shapira Affair," *The British Library Journal* 21 (1995): 109–27.

114. Delitzsch, "Schapira's Pseudo-Deuteronomium," 844–45.

Strack had made up his mind that these leather strips should not be regarded as genuine,[115] and dissuaded him from his intended visit to Germany. Inspite of that, Shapira visited Berlin and presented the strips to Strack, but Strack remained unconvinced. Shapira then took the fragments to Halle and Leipzig. In Halle, he met Hermann Guthe, a gifted scholar of the Hebrew Bible, who was ready to scrutinize the strips carefully. After Guthe had finished his investigation, he published a book, in content and thoroughness comparable to the monograph that had been published by Albert Socin and Emil Kautzsch on the Moabitica six years earlier. Guthe's monograph is entitled *Fragmente einer Lederhandschrift enthaltend Mose's letzte Worte an die Kinder Israel, mitgeteilt und geprüft von Hermann Guthe* ("Fragments of a parchment manuscript, containing Mose's final words to the children of Israel, disclosed and investigated by Hermann Guthe"). Franz Delitzsch joined Guthe in his endeavor and published several articles on the Shapira fragments in the *Allgemeine Evangelisch-Lutherische Sonntagszeitung*.

The aftermath of the Moabitica had been a more critical attitude towards inscriptions of any kind. Even the Mesha Inscription itself was viewed with suspicion, not only shortly after its find for various reasons,[116] but also in later times because of its connection with Salim or the Moabitica respectively.[117] The famous Egyptologist Georg Ebers coined the notable saying: "Die Moabitica sind Vogelscheuchen, welche auch kluge Spatzen von den guten Früchten fern halten" ("The Moabitica are scarecrows which keep you clever sparrows away from the good fruits").[118] Ebers had heard about Shapira's manuscript from his student Eduard Meyer, one of the foremost historians in Germany. Meyer had attended Guthe in his investigation and reported the news to Ebers. Unfortunately, Ebers had uttered his reply to Meyer's suspicions a little bit too early.

Guthe begins his report by explaining the general condition of the leather strips, which he could study on five subsequent days, seven to eight hours each

---

115. Hermann L. Strack and O. O. Fletcher, "Writing among the Hebrews," *Hebraica* 2 (1886): 212–13.

116. Schlottmann, *Oster-Programm der Universität Halle-Wittenberg*, 4–6; Diestel, "Die moabitischen Altertümer," 452.

117. Hoffmann, review of Kautzsch and Socin, *Die Aechtheit der moabitischen Altertümer geprüft* and Koch, *Moabitisch oder Selimisch?*, 502–4, 506*; Albert Löwy, "The Apocryphal Character of the Moabite Stone," *The Scottish Review* 9 (1887): 215–45; Gustav Jahn, *Das Buch Daniel nach der Septuaginta hergestellt, mit einem Anhang: Die Mesha-Inschrift aufs Neue untersucht* (Leipzig: Pfeiffer, 1904), 122–37; Eduard König, "Ist die Mesa-Inschrift ein Falsifikat?," *ZDMG* 59 (1905): 233–51; Abraham Shalom Yahuda, "The Story of a Forgery and the Mēša Inscription," *JQR* 35 (1944): 147–63; cf. William Foxwell Albright, "Is the Mesha Inscription a Forgery?," *JQR* 35 (1945): 247–50.

118. Eduard Meyer: Nachlaß von Eduard Meyer. Letter from Georg Ebers, Tutzing to Eduard Meyer, July 10, Berlin-Brandenburgische Akademie der Wissenschaften, Akademiearchiv: Nachlaß, 1883.

day, beginning on Monday, June 30, 1883. On the general background of the Shapira-strips, and how they must have been created by cutting the edges off old Torah scrolls, several extensive publications have been published.[119] "These external findings were important, but it was on the internal evidence that the Shapira fragments were finally proclaimed a forgery without any shred of doubt."[120] The physical examination of the strips, carried out by several natural scientists in Leipzig, produced a positive result. According to their scrutiny, the ink in the strips looked very old, and rips and fissures visible in the leather had certainly come into being after it had been inscribed.[121]

Some of the inner criteria, such as the palaeography, orthography, and grammar of the Shapira strips have been covered by Oskar K. Rabinowicz[122] and André Lemaire.[123] So I will confine myself to those observations of Delitzsch and Guthe on the palaeography and orthography, which have not been dealt with in the last decades, but that are still worthwhile to consider.

Guthe made a complete and very careful transcript of the text found in Shapira's leather fragments. He published them side by side with the text of the Hebrew Bible, and with a German translation of both the fragments and of the parallel sections from the Hebrew Bible. Transcripts and translations alone covered about forty pages in his monograph. For comparison, Guthe could in 1883 not only resort to the Mesha Inscription, but also to the Siloam Inscription, which had been discovered in June 1880, and on which Guthe himself had published an article.[124] Compared, however, to the wealth of inscriptions that is at our fingertips today, Guthe had to look very carefully at the strips to pass an adequate judgment on them.

Guthe observed the following features: In terms of palaeography, the general character of the letters made a uniform impression. It seemed that two scribes had worked on the fragments. The shape of the letters closely resembled those known from the Mesha Inscription (in part), from some seals of the First Temple period and especially from coins printed during the Second Temple period and later. Compared to the Siloam inscription, the letters seemed to be particularly

---

119. John Marco Allegro, *The Shapira Affair* (New York: Doubleday, 1965); Lehrer-Jacobson, *Fakes and Forgeries from Collections in Israel*; Reiner, "C. D. Ginsburg and the Shapira Affair."
120. Oskar K. Rabinowicz, "The Shapira Forgery Mystery," *JQR* 47 (1956): 173.
121. Erman, *Mein Werden und mein Wirken*, 248. Erman, who for thirty years had been the director of the Egyptian Museum in Berlin, did not appreciate physical investigations very much: "Niemand ist so leichtherzig und ungeschickt im Beurteilen von Altertümern wie die Männer der 'exakten Wissenschaften' und die 'sachkundigen' Techniker" (ibid.).
122. Rabinowicz, "The Shapira Forgery Mystery," 170–82.
123. André Lemaire, "Paleography's Verdict: They're Fakes!," *BAR* 23/3 (1997): 36–39.
124. Herrmann Guthe, "Die Siloahinschrift," *ZDMG* 36 (1882): 725–50.

edgy, without any flourishing and without those tiny ticks and strokes that can be seen on the Siloam inscription. Guthe speculated that it would have been quite easy for him to take a pen and write the very same letters on a smooth leather surface. Some letters shapes were unknown at Guthe's time and they are still unknown today (ק ב ט).[125]

When Guthe proceeded to the investigation of the fragments' orthography, more inconsistencies came up. Shapira had held the leather fragments to have been written early in the First Temple period, so that from our knowledge today the consistent writing of the 3rd masc. suffix with ו instead of ה was very questionable. But Guthe had besides the Mesha stone only recourse to the Siloam Inscription and some Hebrew seals. Although the Mesha Inscription employs constantly ה for this personal pronoun, the Siloam inscription's only instance of a 3rd masc. sg. pronoun suffixed to a noun is רעו "his neighbor,"[126] which in Guthe's estimation was evidence enough to find nothing suspicious in the fragments' consistent use of ו as suffix of the 3rd masc. sg.[127]

A serious problem presented itself by the internal *matres lectionis* in Shapira's fragments. Evidently, these strips were believed to be very old. Consequently, only some internal *matres lectionis* should be visible for specific reasons. When Guthe compared the orthography of Shapira's fragments with the Siloam inscription, he missed *matres lectionis* in nouns having diphthongs. The Shapira strips never employ בית, but בת; never לילה, but ללה; never עיר, but ער. While these forms would be tolerable in respect to the Mesha Inscription, he found on the other hand often יום "day" in Shapira's manuscript, which is always spelled defective (ים) in the Mesha Inscription *and* in the Siloam Inscription, and מול "over, against," of which the internal *waw* likewise had not emerged from a diphthong. The same applies to איש "man" in respect to its internal *yod*. In addition, some

---

125. Herrmann Guthe, *Fragmente einer Lederhandschrift* (Leipzig: Breitkopf & Härtel, 1883), 64–68. Colette Sirat ("Le Fragments Shapira," *Revue des Études juives* 143 [1984]: 95–111) reassessed the verdict that was issued in 1883 and came to the conclusion that, from the point "de la paléographie hébraique moderne," it seems that "la majorité des arguments avancés contre l'authenticité des fragments Shapira ne peuvent plus être retenues" (111). Sirat's palaeographical arguments, however, are superficial and cannot prove what was later postulated. Sirat claimed that our knowledge of the Shapira strips is bound to Ginsburg's drawings, the originals being lost, but she did not deal with Ginsburg's and especially Guthe's detailed conclusions after they had investigated the script (Guthe, *Fragmente einer Lederhandschrift*, 64–68. 95). Guthe did not investigate the drawing of Ginsburg, but the original, independently of Ginsburg, and had come to a balanced assessment.

126. See Jo Ann Hackett, Frank Moore Cross et al., "Defusing Pseudo-Scholarship. The Siloam Inscription Ain't Hasmonean," *BAR* 23 (1997): 41–50, esp. 44.

127. Guthe, *Fragmente einer Lederhandschrift*, 73.

words were written at times plene, at times defective, such as בן and בין, or הא and הוא. According to Guthe, the strips were written by someone who had not been thinking in Biblical, but in Late or Modern Hebrew, and who had not succeeded in adjusting the vocabulary and orthography to fit the ancient language.[128] From our point of view today, Guthe's opinion on the proper orthography of an eighth-century B.C.E. inscription may be considered all too restrictive.[129] Even the Mesha Inscription varies, though on a small scale, in plene and defective writing.[130] Yet, the general condition of the orthography of the Shapira strips with its conspicuous late features and its manifold variations would still be considered to be highly questionable.

Some forms and expressions betrayed more than ever the hand of a modern forger. In one of the fragment's version of the Ten Commandments (Exod 20:16), we read,[131] לא תענו באחך עדת שקר אנך אלהם אלהך, which was meant to say: "You shall not attest false testimony against your brother. I am Elohim, your God."

On the orthographical and morphological level there are some very problematic forms. The Shapira version of the ninth commandment has לא תענו in the sense of "you shall not attest," 2nd masc. sg. In the biblical parallel (Exod 20:16) we have the expression לא תענה. Guthe observed that the final *waw* in the Shapira strips' תענו could not function as a personal pronoun in the context לא תענו באחך עדת שקר. It definitely was meant to represent the final consonant, which in Biblical Hebrew would be written with *he*. In Epigraphic Hebrew, we do not have many examples of verbs III *w/y* in the Imperfect, but from all what we know, the morphology of those verbs in the Imperfect is the same in Epigraphic Hebrew as it is in Biblical Hebrew.[132] That is our knowledge today; but even more than 120 years ago, Guthe pointed to the fact that the only parallel to Shapira's fragments is found in the Mesha Inscription where we have the form יענו in line 5 and the form אענו in line 6.[133] Dictionaries of Biblical Hebrew usually have four entries (I–IV) to the verb ענה. Two of these entries are very common. They are based on two different Semitic roots: *'ny* means "to answer, to respond, to attest" (this root is to be expected in Exod 20:16), while *'nw*, used in lines 5 and 6 of the

---

128. Ibid., 76.
129. Cf. the discussion in Sandra L. Gogel, *A Grammar of Epigraphic Hebrew* (Atlanta: Scholars Press, 1998), 49–74.
130. Kent P. Jackson, "The Language of the Mesha Inscription," in *Studies in the Mesha Inscription and Moab* (ed. by Andrew Dearman; Atlanta: Scholars Press, 1989), 119.
131. Guthe, *Fragmente einer Lederhandschrift*, 38.
132. Johannes Renz and Wolfgang Röllig, *Handbuch der Althebräischen Epigraphik* (4 vols.; Wiesbaden: Wissenschaftliche Buchgesellschaft, 1995–2003), 2/2:58–59.
133. Guthe, *Fragmente einer Lederhandschrift*, 72–73.

Mesha Inscription, means "to be bowed down, to be afflicted."[134] The reading תענו was an indisputable sign of forgery. The faker wanted to present his text with an authentic orthography and, in pursuing this aim, took counsel with the Mesha Inscription, adapted the 2nd masc. sg. of his text to the form ואענו that he had found in the Mesha Inscription and finally created the monstrosity לא תענו באחך עדת שקר, which literally means "you shall not oppress false witness against your brother."

Besides Guthe, Delitzsch pointed to various anachronisms of vocabulary and style. Often Shapira's strips present the strange expressions "I am Elohim, your God" or "whose God is Elohim" respectively, as in the final words of the ninth commandment cited above. As Delitzsch observed, the stylistic device אנך אלהם אלהך is only known from the "elohistic" Psalms (Pss 42–84; cf. Pss 45:7; 50:7) and constitutes an anachronism of style in a text supposed to belong to the Pentateuch.[135] The introduction to Shapira's version of Deut 6 provides another very strange anachronism. The text reads אנך אלהם אלהך אשר החרתך מארץ מצרם and was believed to mean "I am Elohim, your God, who has liberated you from the land of Egypt,"[136] as against the biblical "who brought you out of the Land of Egypt." The verb חרר, however, in the meaning "to free; to liberate," is only used in Late Hebrew and in Aramaic, and even then we would not expect the Hiphil-form החרתך, but rather the Piel חרתך, which in addition would never be employed with the preposition מן.[137]

After Guthe had finished his investigation, which was published only six weeks later(!), Shapira went to Berlin to present the leather strips to a royal committee on the 10th of July. This committee consisted of the most learned men of Oriental languages in the late-nineteenth century, scholars such as Eduard Sachau, August Dillmann, Adolf Erman, and Moritz Steinschneider. After ninety minutes of close inspection the committee declared unanimously the Shapira goat-skin strips to be a forgery. Again, the committee was satisfied with the impressive internal evidence, and they deemed it unnecessary to call for further proof.

But Shapira did not give up. He played his last card and went to London, only two weeks after his Berlin disaster, where he arrived on July 26, 1883. Mean-

---

134. Cf. Shmuel Aḥituv, *Echoes from the Past. Hebrew and Cognate Inscriptions from the Biblical Period* (Jerusalem: Carta, 2008), 399.

135. Delitzsch, "Schapira's Pseudo-Deuteronomium," 845.

136. Guthe, *Fragmente einer Lederhandschrift*, 34; A. Neubauer, "Correspondence: The Shapira MS. of Deuteronomy," *The Academy* 24 (1883): 116.

137. Jacob Levy, *Wörterbuch über die Talmudim und Midraschim* (4 vols.; 2d ed.; Berlin: Harz, 1924), 2:116.

while, information from Germany had not made its way to London very fast. This delay in information forced the scholars from Britain to form their own opinion independently from the German decision. And again, as Rabinowicz has pointed out,[138] it was the internal evidence that brought the learned Englishmen to their decision. In England, the fragments were not treated as forgeries right from the beginning. Instead, Christian D. Ginsburg from London published all he could learn from the strips, and their texts in Hebrew and English, in the journals *The Times*, the *Athenaeum*, and the *Jewish Chronicle*.

Ginsburg was very reluctant to pass judgment on the strips. His own publication of the Hebrew texts and their English translation in the *Athenaeum* during more than three weeks, without formulating any verdict, led to increasing media hype in Britain. Any news from Germany about Shapira's leather strips seems to have been either ignored or withheld, although Delitzsch informed his "English friends" as soon as he had learned that Shapira had left for London.[139] It seems that Ginsburg wanted to reach his own firm conclusion on the matter. Only when Clermont-Ganneau, who so ably had debunked the Moabitica a decade before, arrived in London to inspect the Shapira manuscript and declared it at once to be a forgery, Ginsburg felt compelled to express and publish his initial suspicions, which now had come to a firm conclusion. Clermont-Ganneau could explain how the scraps had been made by cutting them off an old Torah scroll. The original divisions of the scroll were still visible, but had been ignored by the counterfeiter, who wrote over these lines. In addition, Adolf Neubauer had published in August 1883 an account of his opinion on the Shapira "Moabite Deuteronomy" in *The Academy*, declaring that he had held those strips a forgery "right from the outset." In his final report to the British Museum, Ginsburg joined in his judgment with those who had already investigated the strips in Germany.[140]

Of those forms that Guthe and Ginsburg debunked as anachronisms, there is one that made its way into the critical apparatus of the Hebrew Bible, and which would appear again on a very famous inscription that came up some years ago. It is the form עדת (in the Hebrew Bible usually written עדות) in the aforementioned version of the ninth commandment from the Shapira strips: לא תענו באחד עדת שקר, as against the biblical עד in עד שקר עד ברעך תענה לא (Exod 20:16). This form had already been detected as anachronistic by Guthe, who observed that עדות in Biblical Hebrew does not have the meaning "testimony / evidence of / for something or someone," which emerged only later. In the Pentateuch, עדות refers exclusively to the "covenant," that means, to the testimony of

---

138. Rabinowicz, "The Shapira Forgery Mystery," 173.
139. Delitzsch, "Schapira's Pseudo-Deuteronomium," 846.
140. Rabinowicz, "The Shapira Forgery Mystery," 179.

the stone tablets of law (Exod 25:16.21; 31:18 etc), in the Psalms also to the law itself (Pss 19:8; 78:5 etc), and in the historical books also to the testimony as a royal protocol, given to the king at his coronation (2 Kgs 11:12).[141] עדות in the general meaning of "evidence" or "testimony" occurs for the first time in post-biblical Hebrew, such as Sirach utters the invitation תן עדות למראש מעשיך "give evidence of your deeds of old" (Sir 36:15).[142]

The primary versions of the Hebrew Bible translate Exod 20:16 שקר עד, verbally translated "[answer] as a witness of deceit," in similar fashion as modern English translations ("[bear] false witness"), with μαρτυρίαν ψευδῆ (LXX), *falsum testimonium* (Vulgate), סהדותא דשקרא (Targum Onqelos) and ܣܗܕܘܬܐ ܕܓܠܬܐ (Peshitta). All versions unanimously carry the meaning "[to give] false evidence." Delitzsch had already pointed to these readings[143] and suggested that in Exod 20:16, עד could denote the witness (subject) as well as the object attested. In the latter sense, it could be a synonym for עדות or עדה. These considerations, however, had been known before. In his extensive commentary on Exodus, Abraham ibn Ezra (1089–1164)[144] writes that for many years he had been moved by the question of why Exod 20:16 reads עד שקר and not עדות שקר.[145] Neither Ibn Ezra nor Delitzsch, however, had pointed to the fact that only in post-biblical Hebrew,[146] not in Biblical Hebrew, עדות could be regarded as an alternate reading for עד. The suggestions of Abraham ibn Ezra or Delitzsch seemed to have led Kittel in his edition of the *Biblia Hebraica*[147] to

---

141. For further discussions see J. A. Thompson, "Expansions of the '*d* root," *JSS* 10 (1965): 222–40, esp. 226; B. Volkwein, "Masoretisches *ʿēdūt*, *ʿēdwāt*, *ʿēdōt* – 'Zeugnis' oder 'Bundesbestimmungen'?" *BZ* 13 (1969): 8–40; N. Lohfink, "'*d(w)t* im Deuteronomium und in den Königsbüchern," *BZ* 35 (1991): 86–93.

142. Cf. also Sir 31:23–24 עדות טובו נאמנה "the testimony to his goodness is lasting" and עדות רועו נאמנה "the testimony to his stinginess is lasting." The references to Sirach are cited according to the verse numbering used in Pancratius C. Beentjes, *The Book of Ben Sira in Hebrew: A Text Edition of All Extant Hebrew Manuscripts and a Synopsis of All Parallel Hebrew Ben Sira Texts* (Leiden: Brill, 1997). עדות in Sir 31:24 is a marginal reading of manuscript B for דעת. Hebrew Dictionaries generally use another verse numbering system and refer to Sir 36:20 and 34:23–24 respectively.

143. Franz Delitzsch, "Urmosaisches im Pentateuch. III. Der Dekalog in Exodus und Deuteronomium," *Zeitschrift für Kirche und Wissenschaft* 3 (1882): 284.

144. From the fifteenth century onwards ibn Ezra's longer commentary on Exodus (ספר ואלה שמות) has been available in printed form. For a modern annotated translation of his longer commentary on Exodus see Dirk U. Rottzoll, *Abraham Ibn Esras langer Kommentar zum Buch Exodus* (2 vols.; Berlin: de Gruyter, 2000).

145. Ibid., 613.

146. Levy, *Wörterbuch über die Talmudim und Midraschim*, 3:620.

147. Rudolf Kittel, *Biblia Hebraica* (Leipzig: Hinrichs, 1905); cf. Johann Weiss, *Das Buch*

propose the emendation עדות in place of the original reading עד in Exod 20:16. A similar consideration may have led the forger of the Shapira strips, who tried to place as much sensational variants as he could get hold of in his text, to exchange עד for עד[ו]ת. Moreover, the expression עדות שקר "false evidence; perjury" is common in Modern Hebrew.[148]

The Jehoash Inscription, the "Three Shekels" Ostracon and the "Widow's Plea" Ostracon

In the discussion about the authenticity of the so-called Jehoash inscription, most scholars realized that the form עדת of line 15 has to be viewed as anachronistic: והיה הים הזה לעדת "and this day shall be unto a testimony,"[149] or "and may [this inscribed stone] become this day a witness."[150] While we do find עדת in post-biblical Hebrew and in Shapira's Decalogue with the general meaning of "testimony; evidence; witness" (see above), that meaning would be anachronistic for Biblical Hebrew.[151] As a Biblical parallel to the expression והיה לעדת, we may compare both Gen 31:44 "and let it be a witness" והיה לעד and Isa 19:19–20 "and in that day there will be an altar [...] and a pillar to YHWH near its border, and it will become a sign and a witness to YHWH" והיה לאות ולעד ליהוה. In both instances, the Hebrew scribe did not employ עדות, but עד. Isaiah 30:8–9, which also implicates a written tablet, provides a further parallel to the Jehoash inscription, if the Masoretic Text is vocalized according to the Hebrew *Vorlage* required by the versions (Targum, Vulgate, Greek, Syriac): ותהי ליום אחרון לעד עד עולם "that [the inscribed tablet] may be for the time to come a witness forever." Again, עד, not עדות, is the appropriate term for "witness" or "testimony," which in many manuscripts of the LXX is μαρτυρίον, in the Vulgate *testimonium* etc. Sasson pointed

---

Exodus (Wien: Styria, 1911), 164.

148. Reuben Alcalay, *The Complete Hebrew-English Dictionary: New Enlarged Edition* (2 vols.; Tel-Aviv: Chemed Books, 2000), 1855.

149. David Noel Freedman, "Don't Rush to Judgment: Jehoash Inscription may be Authentic," *BAR* 30, no. 2 (2004): 49–50.

150. Chaim Cohen, "Biblical Hebrew Philology in the Light of Research on the New Yeho'ash Royal Building Inscription," in *New Seals and Inscriptions, Hebrew, Idumean and Cuneiform* (ed. by Meir Lubetski; Hebrew Bible Monographs 8; Sheffield: Phoenix, 2007), 224.

151. Some might suppose עדת to be a variant form of עדה "witness" (Stig Norin, "Die sogenannte Joasinschrift—echt oder falsch?," *VT* 55 [2005]: 67). עדה is known from Gen 21:30; 31:52 and Josh 24:27. To suppose another noun עדה, however, based on עדה, but in the sense of the late attested meaning of עדות in the context of the object under scrutiny (Jehoash inscription), is begging the question.

to the religious connotation of עדות to explain and justify its use in the Jehoash Inscription,[152] but Isa 19:20 and Isa 30:8-9 have a religious connotation as well without using עדות.[153]

Notwithstanding, an expression coming very near to lines 14-15 of the Jehoash inscription (והיה הים הזה לעדת) is found in Franz Delitzsch's translation of the New Testament into Hebrew.[154] This edition was composed before the modern revival of Hebrew, to be utilized for proselytization among Jews.[155] Delitzsch translated Luke 21:13, καὶ ἀποβήσεται δὲ ὑμῖν εἰς μαρτύριον ("and it will turn to you for a testimony"), with והיתה זאת לכם לעדות ("and this will be for you unto a testimony").[156] He rendered μαρτυρίον "testimony" with the Hebrew expression עדות, thereby implicating the late meaning and connotation of עדות. In his translation, Delitzsch aimed at restoring the Hebrew idiom of the late Second Temple and early Mishnaic periods, which justifies his use of עדות.[157]

עד[ו]ת is a lexical anachronism, in the Shapira strips as well as in the Jehoash inscription. The search for variants on the forger's side may be the explanation for עדת in the Shapira strips.[158] Simple ignorance or carelessness, however, probably accounts for the intrusion of עדת in the Jehoash inscription.

The connection between these two fabrication errors may suggest a connection between the Jehoash Inscription and the Shapira forgery. Lemaire even opined, as one alternative among four, that the Jehoash Inscription may be "a modern forgery connected with the Shapira affair (ca. 1870-1884). More precisely, it would have been the work of the association Shapira-Selim el Qari [...] and Martin Boulos."[159] But the Jehoash inscription has, compared with the Shap-

---

152. Victor Sasson, "Philological and Textual Observations on the Controversial King Jehoash Inscription," *UF* 35 (2004): 582.

153. For further uses of עד in the sense of "testimony; witness" cf. Gen 31:48; 21:30; Deut 31:19.26; Josh 24:27; Micah 1:2; cf. also עדה in Gen 21:30.

154. Franz Delitzsch, ספרי הברית החדשה נעתקים מלשון יון ללשון עברית (London: The Trinitarian Bible Society, 1885).

155. Gustav Dalman, "Das Hebräische Neue Testament von Franz Delitzsch," *Hebraica* 9 (1893): 226-31.

156. The text cited here is from the 1875 edition (London). Delitzsch continuously revised his translation, starting with the first edition in 1877, which was translated from the Received Text of the New Testament; cf. Dalman, "Das Hebräische Neue Testament von Franz Delitzsch."

157. Ibid., 228-29.

158. C. D. Ginsburg ("The Shapira Manuscripts," *PEQS* [1883]: 207-9) had suggested that the fragments, an inaccurate critical recension of the text of Deuteronomy, had, due to some idiosyncratic spelling errors, probably been concocted by a Jew from Germany, Poland, or Russia.

159. A. Lemaire, "Jerusalem Forgery Conference" in the "Appendix" of *Jerusalem Forgery Conference* (ed. Hershel Shanks; Biblical Archaeology Society: Special Report, 2007), 27.

ira strips, only a small amount of orthographical, morphologiocal, and syntactical errors. In addition, the physical condition of the Jehoash Inscription seems to exclude a *recent* fabrication and to call for a considerable amount of time between its creation and its discovery.¹⁶⁰

Dwelling on the Jehoash Inscription is worth some further remarks. Rollston pointed to the fact that *two* suspicious inscriptions, the Jehoash Inscription and the "Three Shekels" ostracon,¹⁶¹ refer to donations to the temple of YHWH, under the auspices of the monarchy. Both refer to a king with a similar name, or might even have been intended to refer to the same monarch (Jehoash of Judah), and both share certain palaeographic "anomalies," such as are visible in the Old Hebrew letters *šin* and *samek*.¹⁶² I want to add a few observations that have probably not been made before. Common to both inscriptions is the expression כאשר...לתת...כסף. Both inscriptions employ a verbal form in the perfect tense after the introductory particle כאשר,¹⁶³ followed by the subject. In both inscriptions, a genitive noun qualifies the silver donated, and in both inscriptions the amount and purpose of the money collected is given. In contrast to the "Three Shekels" ostracon (1), the Jehoash Inscription (2) continues with a *wayyiqtol*-form (ואעש), some additional phrases and a final blessing. The כאשר ... ואעש sequence is interpreted as a temporal "when—then" sentence by F. M. Cross and C. Cohen,¹⁶⁴ but in face of the parallel, it is questionable whether it was created

---

160. Cf. the most recent assessments of Shimon Ilani, Amnon Rosenfeld et al., "Archaeometric Analysis of the 'Jehoash Inscription' Tablet," *Journal of Archaeological Science* 35 (2008): 2966–72; Amnon Rosenfeld, Shimon Ilani et al., "Archaeometric Evidence for the Authenticity of the Jehoash Inscription Tablet," *Antiguo Oriente* 7 (2009): 57–73; and of E. Ganor et al., "Environmental Dust: A Tool to Study the Patina of Ancient Artifacts," *Journal of Arid Environments* 73 (2009): 1170–76.

161. For the "Three Shekels" ostracon, see Pierre Bordreuil, Felice Israel, and Dennis Pardee, "Deux ostraca paléo-hébreux de la collection Sh. Moussaïeff: I) Contribution financière obligatoire pour le temple de YHWH; II) Réclamation d'une veuve auprès d'un fonctionnaire," *Sem* 46 (1996): 49–76; idem, "King's Command and Widow's Plea: Two New Hebrew Ostraca of the Biblical Period," *NEA* 61 (1998): 2–13.

162. Christopher Rollston, "Non-Provenanced Epigraphs I," *Maarav* 10 (2003): 179–80.

163. The "Three Shekels" ostracon commences with the particle כאשר. In the Jehoash inscription, the body text begins with כאשר (line 4) subsequently to the fragmental introductory lines 1–3.

164. Frank Moore Cross, "Notes on the Forged Plaque Recording Repairs to the Temple," *IEJ* 53 (2003): 119; Cohen, "Biblical Hebrew Philology in the Light of Research on the New Yeho'ash Royal Building Inscription," 227.

with that intention. The passages following כאשר of both inscriptions are given here, with two minor rearrangements to make the parallels visible:

	{qualifier}	לתת	{adv. expr.}	{subject}	{verbal f.}	כאשר
(1)	תרשש	לתת כסף165	ביד [ז]כריהו	אשיהו המלך	צוך	כאשר
(2)	הקדשם	לתת כסף	בארץ ובמדבר166	נדבת לב אש	נמלאה	כאשר

			{given for what}		{amount}
(1)			לבית יהוה167		ש 3
(2)			לקנת אבן מחצב וברשם ונחשת אדם לעשת במלאכה באמנה		לרב

The final blessing of the Jehoash Inscription ("may YHWH ordain his people with blessing," line 16) is remotely reminiscent of the introductory blessing of another suspicious inscription, the "Widow's Plea" ostracon. This ostracon is of the same quality as the "Three Shekels" ostracon and was published together with the latter. The first line of the "Widow's Plea" ostracon (1) has a similar structure as the last line of the Jehoash Inscription (2); both constructions are related to the blessing of Ps 29:11 (3).

	{adverbial expr.}	{object}	{subject}	{verb}
(1)	בשלם		יהוה	יברכך
(2)	בברכה	את עמו168	יהוה	יצו
(3)	בשלום	את עמו	יהוה169	יברך

The term ברכה (Jehoash Inscription line 16), constructed with the preposition ב, and in addition to a direct object, is only known from a marginal reading in Sir 45:7 (וישרתהו בברכה) "and he ministered unto him with blessing").[170]

---

165. In the "Three Shekels" ostracon, the exact order is לתת ביד [ז]כריהו כסף.

166. The adverbial expression (giving the domain) of the Jehoash Inscription continues: ובכל ערי יהדה.

167. In the "Three Shekels" ostracon, {amount} follows on {purpose}: לבית יהוה ש 3.

168. In the "Widow's Plea" ostracon, the object is suffixed to the verb; in the Jehoash inscription and in Ps 29:11, it is introduced with את.

169. In Ps 29:11, the order is יהוה יברך.

170. Cf. A. E. Cowley and A. Neubauer, *The Original Hebrew of a Portion of Ecclesiasticus (XXXIX. 15 to XLIX. 11)* (Oxford: Clarendon, 1897), 24. Uses of ברכה with the preposition ב in Biblical Hebrew are instrumental, as in Ps 109:17 and Prov 11:11. In Biblical Hebrew, YHWH's blessing is always the *direct* object of צוה, such as in Lev 25:21, Deut 28:8, and Ps 133:3, while a preposition introduces those who are blessed.

Conclusion

The exposure of the Moabitica, the debunking of the Shapira strips as well as the rejection to renew these discussions after the Qumran scrolls had been found,[171] the debunking of the Parahyba Inscription as well as the rejection to rehabilitate it[172] and the denunciation of various clumsy forgeries[173] all have one thing in common: In the end, decisive arguments have always been based on the palaeography, orthography, morphology, and grammar of the inscribed texts. It is intriguing, by the way, that the latter forgeries denounced by J. Naveh "fit so well into the pattern established by Selim al-Khouri."[174] It has to be admitted, however, that these observations apply primarily to inscriptions with a relatively large amount of text. Forgeries of small objects, such as seals and bullae, are more difficult to detect.[175]

The way in which the final conclusions were reached on these unprovenanced artifacts can be of considerable help today. Of course, as has been pointed out time and again, provenaced inscriptions are always preferable and unprovenanced inscriptions lack the proper context to come to firm conclusions as to their archaeological and historical relevance. Nevertheless, unprovenanced inscriptions need to be handled properly. Here are some recommendations to consider:

1. Non-provenanced antiquities cannot be ignored; they must be published and assessed. They should be clearly indicated as "non-provenanced," but otherwise dealt with adequately.[176] The script, orthography, mor-

---

171. Oskar K. Rabinowicz, "The Shapira Forgery Mystery," *JQR* 47 (1956): 170–82; idem, "The Shapira Scroll: A Nineteenth-Century Forgery," *JQR* 56 (1965): 1–21; Menahem Mansoor, "The Case of Shapira's Dead Sea (Deuteronomy) Scrolls of 1883," *Transactions of the Wisconsin Academy of Sciences, Arts and Letters* 47 (1958): 183–229; Allegro, *The Shapira Affair*.

172. Cyrus H. Gordon, "The Authenticity of the Phoenician Text from Parahyba," *Or* ns 37 (1968): 75–80; Frank Moore Cross, "The Phoenician Inscription from Brazil: A Nineteenth-Century Forgery," *Or* ns 37 (1968): 437–60.

173. Joseph Naveh, "Aramaica Dubiosa," *JNES* 27 (1968): 317–25; idem, "Some Recently Forged Inscriptions," *BASOR* 247 (1982): 53–58.

174. Lehrer-Jacobson, *Fakes and Forgeries from Collections in Israel*, 23*.

175. Benjamin Sass, "Summing Up: How Many Seals?"; Avigad, *Corpus of West Semitic Stamp Seals*, 547–52.

176. Cf. the ostraca flagged with an asterisk (*) in Aḥituv, *Echoes from the Past. Hebrew and Cognate Inscriptions from the Biblical Period*; cf. also the remarks in Stefan Wimmer, *Palästinisches Hieratisch. Die Zahl- und Sonderzeichen in der althebräischen Schrift* (Wiesbaden: Harrassowitz, 2008), 7.

phology, and syntax must be evaluated in the context of material found *in situ*. The best way to deal with unprovenanced artifacts is to publish them and to wait for comments, reviews, and additional publications where applicable. Time will tell.

2. Some dangers, pitfalls, and biases to avoid in assessing unprovenanced inscriptions: 2.1 There is always the danger that new objects turn up when they are expected to.[177] 2.2 We should never speculate that a forger would be unable to fabricate such a complicated artifact, as Schlottmann did[178] and as has been done again and again.[179] 2.3 We should never speculate that an artifact looks too good to be true. Objections like that have been raised in connection with the Mesha Inscription, the Qumran Scrolls and the Tel Dan Inscription. 2.4 We should avoid the logical error of *petitio principii* ("begging the question") when a new inscription is under scrutiny. One of the main logical errors in dealing with the Moabitica ran as follows: 2.4.1 Our knowledge of the Moabite culture depends on the Moabitica. 2.4.2 These could be forgeries. 2.4.3 They must, however, be genuine, because all individual artifacts of that culture are consistent with what we know from the Moabitica.[180]

3. Forgeries may create forgery hysteria and paralyze the sober investigation of any further unprovenanced material, or may lead to suspicions of objects which are genuine.[181] In 1883, when not only the Moabitica but also the Shapira strips had been denounced, it was none other than Franz Delitzsch who affirmed that "not all manuscripts which have come through [Shapira's] hands into German and English public and private collections are suspicious."[182] Some, if not most of the ostraca that were suspected at (or in the wake of) the Antiquities Forgery Indictment of 2004 to be modern fabrications will in the end be considered as genuine. On the other hand, if there *seem* to be no forgeries around, we are in great danger of accepting every unprovenanced inscription at face

---

177. Schlottmann, "Neue Moabitische Funde und Räthsel: Erster Bericht," 393.
178. Schlottmann, review of Kautzsch and Socin, *Die Aechtheit der moabitischen Altertümer geprüft* and Koch, *Moabitisch oder Selimisch?*, 237a.
179. Cf. D. Pardee, "The Widow's Plea" *COS*, 3:86.
180. Kautzsch and Socin, *Die Aechtheit der moabitischen Altertümer geprüft*, 68 (footnote).
181. Hoffmann, review of Kautzsch and Socin, *Die Aechtheit der moabitischen Altertümer geprüft* and Koch, *Moabitisch oder Selimisch?*, 502–4; Jahn, *Das Buch Daniel nach der Septuaginta hergestellt, mit einem Anhang: Die Mesha-Inschrift aufs Neue untersucht*, 122–37; Löwy, "The Apocryphal Character of the Moabite Stone;" idem, *Die Echtheit der Moabitischen Inschrift im Louvre aufs Neue geprüft* (Wien: Holzhauser, 1903).
182. Delitzsch, "Schapira's Pseudo-Deuteronomium," 893.

value. In a way, the awareness of forgeries being around is helpful for the careful scrutiny of every inscription. Forgeries are commonplace in every field of archaeology. As long as there are public and private collections, there will be forgeries.[183]

4. New script styles have to be analyzed carefully: do they fit into the general development of the script, or do they represent something totally illogic—such as the ligatures on the Moabitica? When I published the Moussaieff alphabet ostracon, I realized that a peculiar script was visible at the concave side of the ostracon, a very developed Hebrew script of the First Temple period that had been unknown before. The special features of this script, however, do fit nicely into the script patterns of the First Temple period and cannot therefore be regarded as evidence against the authenticity of the alphabet ostracon.[184] In general, however, forgeries are not unique creations. Forgers tend to use a *Vorlage* to give their fabrication an air of authenticity, at the same time modifying it to divert the specialist from its recognition.

5. Modern forgeries are much more elaborate than those of the nineteenth century, but the means of identifying forgeries have also become more sophisticated. Nevertheless, our limited knowledge (objective or subjective) of Northwest Semitic inscriptions can lead us either to accept an inscription or reading that was fabricated,[185] or to reject an inscription, form, or reading that is genuine,[186] or to mismatch an inscription or reading.[187] It is a challenge to stay ahead of the forgers in profound knowledge, but even if we do, it will not always be possible to determine with certainty if an unprovenanced object is fabricated or authentic.[188]

---

183. Eckhard Unger, "Fälschungen," in *Reallexikon der Assyriologie* (10 vols.; Berlin: de Gruyter, 1928–), 3:5–9.

184. Martin Heide, "Impressions from a New Alphabetic Ostracon in the Context of (Un)provenanced Inscriptions: Idiosyncrasy of a Genius Forger or a Master Scribe?" in *New Seals and Inscriptions, Hebrew, Idumean and Cuneiform* (ed. Meir Lubetski; Hebrew Bible Monographs 8; Sheffield: Phoenix, 2007), 159–63.

185. See Guthe's comment on the orthography of the 3rd masc. sg. pronoun in the Shapira strips (see above).

186. Cf. the repeated challenge of the authenticity of the Mesha Inscription.

187. See John Rogerson and Philip R. Davies ("Was the Siloam Tunnel Built by Hezekiah?" *BA* 59 [1996]: 138–49), who assigned the Siloam inscription to post-exilic times and who mistakenly asserted that "paleography itself is not decisive for dating the [Siloam] inscription" (145); cf. the response from Hackett, Cross, et al., "Defusing Pseudo-Scholarship. The Siloam Inscription Ain't Hasmonean."

188. Aḥituv, *Echoes from the Past*, 9.

6. Are there scribal anachronisms? Cf. the Nabataean letters in the Moabitica, and the Moabite script in the Shapira strips, which were assumed to represent early Hebrew documents. Some anachronisms may not be easy to detect, as those on the famous "Three Shekels" and "Widow's Plea"-ostraca.[189] The script of both pieces could also be interpreted as belonging to an apprentice,[190] but additional evidence seems to point to a forgery.[191]
7. Are there orthographical abnormalities? See especially the missing diphthongs in the Shapira strips, while at the same time various words appeared in plene writing. Also, some words in the Jehoash Inscription do not meet the orthography expected to have been used in monumental inscription of the ninth–eighth centuries B.C.E.[192]
8. Are there lexical anachronisms? See the reading עדות for עדת in Shapira's Decalogue and in the Jehoash Inscription.
9. Are there syntactical or stylistic anachronisms? See the reading אנך אלהם אלהך in the Shapira strips and the reading יצו יהוה את עמו בברכה in the Jehoash Inscription.
10. Do suspicious objects bear resemblances to other unprovenanced objects which are likewise problematic? See the similarities between the script of the Moabitica and the script of the Shapira strips, and see the strange parallels between the Jehoash Inscription and the "Three Shekels" and "Widow's Plea" ostraca.[193]
11. Investigations of a judicious character are usually not very helpful. The inquiry in 1874 did not bring out the truth in the Moabitica affair, nor

---

189. Cf. the analysis in Rollston, "Non-Provenanced Epigraphs I," 158–73. It is important to have an eye for the decisive features which identify a script as belonging to a certain horizon. On the other hand, we have to acknowledge that handwriting is subject to a large measure of fluctuation. Both factors together are not always easy to combine. Moreover, that a certain letter has anomalous features in a presumed horizon is nothing special. Forgeries usually provide an accumulation of evidence, with many letters, especially those that are known to carry evidentiary value for a certain horizon, deviating from their normal shape.

190. A. Lemaire, "Veuve sans enfants dans le royaume de Juda," *ZAR* 5 (1999): 6.

191. Yuval Goren, Avner Ayalon et al., "Authenticity Examination of Two Iron Age Ostraca from the Moussaieff Collection," *IEJ* 55 (2005): 20–34; Aḥituv, *Echoes from the Past*, 9–10.

192. Frank M. Cross, "Notes on the Forged Plaque Recording Repairs to the Temple," *IEJ* 53 (2003): 119–22.

193. We need to be careful, however, not to overstretch these comparisons; cf. Heide, "Impressions from a New Alphabetic Ostracon in the Context of (Un)provenanced Inscriptions: Idiosyncrasy of a Genius Forger or a Master Scribe?," 175 with idem, "Ein 27-zeiliges Listenostrakon aus der Sammlung Shlomo Moussaieff," *UF* 39 (2008): 406 n. 3.

has the "Forgery Trial of the Century" in Jerusalem, though commenced with much confidence in 2004, given any new insights in the matter of the Jehoash Inscription, James Ossuary, and Moussaieff Ostraca to justify the enormous amounts of money and time the trial has devoured.

12. Physical investigations can be extremely helpful. Except for a few cases, however, where the matter is very clear from the outset,[194] they are rarely decisive and can at times be contradictory.[195] Cf. the various assessments of the two famous Moussaieff ostraca,[196] where the latter investigation seems to settle the matter. The physical investigation of the Jehoash Inscription, however, has not yet come to a satisfactory conclusion.[197]

13. Investigations in suspicious artifacts may lead to *ad hominem* arguments and may even create hatred, or ruin the reputation of highly qualified scholars. We need to keep up an ethic of the "mutual search for truth" to beware of these pitfalls.

Bibliography

Albright, William Foxwell. "Is the Mesha Inscription a Forgery?" *JQR* 35 (1945): 247–50.
Alcalay, Reuben. *The Complete Hebrew–English Dictionary: New Enlarged Edition*, vols. 1–2. Tel-Aviv: Chemed, 2000.
Aḥituv, Shmuel. *Echoes from the Past: Hebrew and Cognate Inscriptions from the Biblical Period*. Jerusalem: Carta, 2008.
Allegro, John Marco. *The Shapira Affair*. New York: Doubleday, 1965.
Avigad, Nahman, and Benjamin Sass. *Corpus of West Semitic Stamp Seals*. Jerusalem: The Israel Academy of Sciences and Humanities, 1997.
Beentjes, Pancratius C. *The Book of Ben Sira in Hebrew: A Text Edition of All Extant*

---

194. Cf. Clermont-Ganneau, "The Shapira Manuscripts," *PEQS* 1883: 201–5.
195. Cf. Schlottmann, "Die neuen Beweise für die Ächtheit der moabitischen Altertümer," 468.
196. Rollston, "Laboratory Analysis of the Moussaïeff Ostraca using the Scanning Electron Microscope (SEM) with an Energy Dispersive X-Ray Microanalyzer (EDS);" Goren, Ayalon et al., "Authenticity Examination of Two Iron Age Ostraca from the Moussaieff Collection."
197. Cf. the various assessments and interpretations in Shimon Ilani, Amnon Rosenfeld, et al., "Archaeometry of a stone tablet with Hebrew inscription referring to repair of the House," *Israel Geological Survey Current Research* 13 (2002): 109–16; Yuval Goren, Avner Ayalon, et al., "Authenticity Examination of the Jehoash Inscription," *TA* (2004) 31: 3–16; Shimon Ilani, Amnon Rosenfeld, et al., "Archaeometric Analysis of the 'Jehoash Inscription' Tablet," *Journal of Archaeological Science* 35 (2008): 2966–72; Amnon Rosenfeld, Shimon Ilani, et al., "Archaeometric Evidence for the Authenticity of the Jehoash Inscription Tablet," *Antiguo Oriente* 7 (2009): 57–73; Ganor et al., "Environmental Dust," 1170–76 .

Hebrew Manuscripts and a Synopsis of All Parallel Hebrew Ben Sira Texts. VTSup. Leiden: Brill, 1997.

Be'er, Haim. "Reflections on the Elusive Charm of the Shapira Affair." Pages 11–13 in *Truly Fake: Moses Wilhelm Shapira, Master Forger.* Edited by Efrat Karmon. Jerusalem: The Israel Museum, 2000.

Blau, O. "Karthagische Inschriften," *ZDMG* 29 (1875): 644–45.

Bordreuil, Pierre, Felice Israel and Dennis Pardee. "Deux ostraca paléo-hébreux de la collection Sh. Moussaïeff: I) Contribution financière obligatoire pour le temple de YHWH; II) Réclamation d'une veuve auprès d'un fonctionnaire." *Sem* 46 (1996): 49–76.

———. "King's Command and Widow's Plea: Two New Hebrew Ostraca of the Biblical Period." *NEA* 61 (1998): 2–13.

Budde, Hendrik. "Die Affäre um die 'Moabitischen Altertümer.'" Pages 111–16 in *Von Halle nach Jerusalem. Halle—Zentrum der Palästinakunde im 18. und 19. Jahrhundert.* Edited by H. Budde and M. Lewy. Halle: Union Druck, 1994.

———, and Mordechay Lewy, eds. *Von Halle nach Jerusalem. Halle—Zentrum der Palästinakunde im 18. und 19. Jahrhundert.* Halle: Union Druck, 1994.

Clermont-Ganneau, Charles. *Les fraudes archéologiques en Palestine, suivies de quelques monuments phéniciens apocryphes.* Paris: Ernest Leroux, 1885.

———. "The Shapira Collection" (and various letters from different authors). *PEQS* (1874): 114–24, 201–7.

———. "The Shapira Manuscripts." *PEQS* (1883): 201–5.

———. *La stèle de Dhiban ou stèle de Mesa, roi de Moab 896 avant J.C. Lettres à M. le Cte de Vogué.* Paris: Baudry, 1870.

———. Two Letters to Mr. Shapira, Subsumed under the Title "The Moabite Pottery," *PEQS* (1878): 91–94.

Cohen, Chaim. "Biblical Hebrew Philology in the Light of Research on the New Yeho'ash Royal Building Inscription." Pages 222–86 in *New Seals and Inscriptions, Hebrew, Idumean and Cuneiform.* Edited by Meir Lubetski. Hebrew Bible Monographs 8. Sheffield: Phoenix, 2007.

Conder, Claude R. ("Lieut. Conder"). "Explorations in Jerusalem." *PEQS* (1873): 13–22.

———, Drake Tyrwhitt, and Frederick Charles. "Notes on the Drawings and Copies of Inscriptions from the 'Shapira Collection' Sent Home by Lieut. Conder and Mr. Drake." *PEQS* (1873): 79–80.

Cowley, A. E., and Adolf Neubauer. *The Original Hebrew of a Portion of Ecclesiasticus (XXXIX. 15 to XLIX. 11).* Oxford: Clarendon, 1897.

Cross, Frank Moore. "Notes on the Forged Plaque Recording Repairs to the Temple." *IEJ* 53 (2003): 119–22.

———. "The Phoenician Inscription from Brazil: A Nineteenth-Century Forgery." *Or* NS 37 (1968): 437–60.

Dalman, Gustav. "Das Hebräische Neue Testament von Franz Delitzsch." *Hebraica* 9 (1893): 226–31.

Delitzsch, Franz. "Schapira's Pseudo-Deuteronomium." *Allgemeine Evangelisch-Lutherische Kirchenzeitung* (1883): 843–46, 870–72, 894, 915–16.

———. "Urmosaisches im Pentateuch. III. Der Dekalog in Exodus und Deuteronomium." *Zeitschrift für Kirche und Wissenschaft* 3 (1882): 284.

———. ספרי הברית החדשה נעתקים מלשון יון ללשון עברית. London: The Trinitarian Bible Society, 1885.
Diestel, L. "Die moabitischen Altertümer." *Jahrbücher für Deutsche Theologie* 21 (1876): 451–73.
Donner, Herbert, and Wolfgang Röllig. *Kanaanäische und Aramäische Inschriften*. 3 vols. Wiesbaden: Harrassowitz, 1962–64.
Eisenberg, Jerome M. "A 19th Century Forger in Palestine: Wilhelm Moses Shapira." *Minerva: The International Review of Ancient Art & Archaeology* 12 (2001): 21–25.
Erman, Adolf. *Mein Werden und mein Wirken. Erinnerungen eines alten Berliner Gelehrten*. Leipzig: Quelle & Meyer, 1929.
Euting, Julius. "The Phoenicians in Brazil." *The Academy* 5 (1874): 664.
Freedman, David Noel. "Don't Rush to Judgment. Jehoash Inscription may be Authentic." *BAR* 30, no. 2 (2004): 48–50.
Ganor, E., and J. Kronfeld, H. R. Feldman, A. Rosenfeld, and S. Ilani. "Environmental Dust: A Tool to Study the Patina of Ancient Artifacts." *Journal of Arid Environments* 73 (2009): 1170–76.
Gass, Erasmus. *Die Moabiter—Geschichte und Kultur eines ostjordanischen Volkes im 1. Jahrtausend v. Chr.* = Abhandlungen des deutschen Palästina-Vereins Band 38. Wiesbaden: Harrassowitz. 2009.
Ginsburg, Christian D. "The Shapira Manuscripts." *PEQS* (1883): 207–9.
Gogel, Sandra Landis. *A Grammar of Epigraphic Hebrew*. SBL Resources for Biblical Study 23. Atlanta: Scholars Press, 1998.
Gordon, Cyrus H. "The Authenticity of the Phoenician Text from Parahyba." *Or* NS 37 (1968): 75–80.
Goren, Yuval, Avner Ayalon, Miryam Bar-Matthews, and Bettina Schilman. "Authenticity Examination of the Jehoash Inscription." *TA* (2004) 31: 3–16.
———. "Authenticity Examination of Two Iron Age Ostraca from the Moussaieff Collection." *IEJ* 55 (2005): 20–34.
Goshen-Gottstein, Moshe H. "The Shapira Forgery and the Qumran Scrolls." *Journal of Jewish Studies* 7 (1956): 187–93.
Graham, Cyril C. "Notiz des Herrn Cyril C. Graham zu den von ihm copirten Inschriften." *ZDMG* 12 (1858): 713–14.
Graham, M. Patrick. "The Discovery and Reconstruction of the Mesha Inscription." Pages 41–92 in *Studies in the Mesha Inscription and Moab*. Edited by Andrew Dearman. Atlanta: Scholars Press, 1989.
Guthe, Herrmann. "Die Siloahinschrift." *ZDMG* 36 (1882): 725–50.
———. *Fragmente einer Lederhandschrift*. Leipzig: Breitkopf & Härtel. 1883
Hackett, Jo Ann, Frank Moore Cross, P. Kyle McCarter, Ada Yardeni, André Lemaire, Esther Eshel, and Avi Hurvitz. "Defusing Pseudo-Scholarship: The Siloam Inscription Ain't Hasmonean." *BAR* 23/2 (1997): 41–50.
Heide, Martin. "Impressions from a New Alphabetic Ostracon in the Context of (Un)provenanced Inscriptions: Idiosyncrasy of a Genius Forger or a Master Scribe?" Pages 148–82 in *New Seals and Inscriptions, Hebrew, Idumean and Cuneiform*. Edited by Meir Lubetski. Hebrew Bible Monographs 8. Sheffield: Phoenix, 2007.
———. "Ein 27-zeiliges Listenostrakon aus der Sammlung Shlomo Moussaieff." *UF* 39 (2008): 399–412.
Hellwald, Friedrich von. "Die moabitischen Altertümer." *Das Ausland* 49 (1876): 113–14.

———. "Der Streit über die moabitischen Funde." *Das Ausland* 51 (1878): 375–79, 384–87.

Hoffmann, G. Review of Kautzsch and Socin (*Die Aechtheit der moabitischen Altertümer geprüft*, Strassburg: Trübner, 1876) and Koch (*Moabitisch oder Selimisch? Die Frage der moabitischen Altertümer*, Stuttgart: Schweizerbart, 1876). *Göttingische gelehrte Anzeigen* (1876): 481–507.

Ilani, Shimon, Amnon Rosenfeld, and Michael Dvorachek. "Archaeometry of a Stone Tablet with Hebrew Inscription Referring to Repair of the House." *Israel Geological Survey Current Research* 13 (2002): 109–16.

Ilani, Shimon, Amnon Rosenfeld, H. R. Feldman, W. E. Krumbein, and J. Kronfeld. "Archaeometric Analysis of the 'Jehoash Inscription' Tablet." *Journal of Archaeological Science* 35 (2008): 2966–72.

Jackson, Kent. P. "The Language of the Mesha Inscription." Pages 96–130 in *Studies in the Mesha Inscription and Moab*. Edited by Andrew Dearman. Atlanta: Scholars Press, 1989.

Jahn, Gustav. *Das Buch Daniel nach der Septuaginta hergestellt, mit einem Anhang: Die Mesha-Inschrift aufs Neue untersucht*. Leipzig: Pfeiffer, 1904.

Kautzsch, Emil. Beilage zur *Augsburger Allgemeinen Zeitung*. No 193. July 11, 1876.

———. *Wilhelm Gesenius' Hebräische Grammatik, völlig umgearbeitet von E. Kautzsch*. 28th ed. Leipzig: Vogel, 1909.

———. *Gesenius' Hebrew Grammar: As Edited and Enlarged by the Late E. Kautzsch*. 2nd Eng. ed. Oxford: Oxford University Press, 1963.

Kautzsch, Emil, and Albert Socin. *Die Aechtheit der moabitischen Altertümer geprüft*. Strassburg: Trübner, 1876.

Kitchener, Horatio Herbert ("Lieut. Kitchener"). Letter subsumed under the title "The Moabite Pottery." *PEQS* (1878): 94–95.

Kittel, Rudolf. *Biblia Hebraica* (1. Auflage). Leipzig: Hinrichs, 1905.

Klein, Friedrich August. "The Original Discovery of the Moabite Stone." *PEQS* (1870): 281–83.

Koch, Adolf. *Moabitisch oder Selimisch? Die Frage der moabitischen Altertümer*. Stuttgart: Schweizerbart, 1876.

König, Eduard. "Ist die Mesa-Inschrift ein Falsifikat?" *ZDMG* 59 (1905): 233–51.

Lehrer-Jacobson, Gusta. *Fakes and Forgeries from Collections in Israel*. Tel Aviv: Eretz Israel Museum. 1989.

———. "Fake! The Many Faces of the Forger's Art." *BAR* 23/2 (1997): 36–38, 67.

Lemaire, André. *Inscriptions Hébraïques. Tome I: Les Ostraca*. Paris: Cerf, 1977.

———. "Jerusalem Forgery Conference." Pages 24–30 in the "Appendix" of *Jerusalem Forgery Conference*. Hershel Shanks. Biblical Archaeology Society: Special Report. Washington, 2007.

———. "Paleography's Verdict: They're Fakes!" *BAR* 23/3 (1997): 36–39.

———. "Veuve sans enfants dans le royaume de Juda." *Zeitschrift für Altorientalische und Biblische Rechtsgeschichte* 5 (1999): 1–14.

Levy, Jacob. *Wörterbuch über die Talmudim und Midraschim*. 4 vols. 2nd ed. Berlin: Harz. 1924.

Levy, M. A. "Eine neue nabathäische Inschrift aus Ammonitis." *ZDMG* 25 (1871): 429–34.

———. "Über die nabathäischen Inschriften von Petra, Hauran, vornehmlich der Sinai-Halbinsel und über die Münzlegenden nabathäischer Könige." *ZDMG* 14 (1860): 363–484.

Lidzbarski, Mark. *Handbuch der nordsemitischen Epigraphik.* 2 vols. Part I (Text) and II (Tafeln). Weimar: Felber, 1898.
Lohfink, N. "*d(w)t* im Deuteronomium und in den Königsbüchern." *BZ* 35 (1991): 86–93.
Löwy, Albert. "The Apocryphal Character of the Moabite Stone." *The Scottish Review* 9 (1887): 215–45.
———. *Die Echtheit der Moabitischen Inschrift im Louvre aufs Neue geprüft.* Wien: Holzhauser, 1903.
Mansoor, Menahem. "The Case of Shapira's Dead Sea (Deuteronomy) Scrolls of 1883." *Transactions of the Wisconsin Academy of Sciences, Arts and Letters* 47 (1958): 183–229.
Meshorer, Ya'akov. "On the Forging of Antiquities." Pages 9–10 in *Truly Fake: Moses Wilhelm Shapira, Master Forger.* Edited by Efrat Karmon. Jerusalem: The Israel Museum, 2000.
Meyer, Eduard. Nachlaß von Eduard Meyer. Brief von Georg Ebers aus Tutzing an Eduard Meyer vom 10. Juli 1883. Berlin-Brandenburgische Akademie der Wissenschaften. Akademiearchiv. Nachlaß, 1883.
Münchhausen, Freiherr von. Letters to Mr. Shapira subsumed under the title "The Moabite Pottery." *PEQS* (1878): 41–44, 95–98.
Naveh, Joseph. "Aramaica Dubiosa." *JNES* 27 (1968): 317–25.
———. "Some Recently Forged Inscriptions." *BASOR* 247 (1982): 53–58.
Neubauer, Adolf. Letter to *The Academy. PEQS* (1878): 44–45.
———. Letter to *The Academy. PEQS* (1878): 101–2.
———. "Correspondence: The Shapira MS. of Deuteronomy." *The Academy* 24 (1883): 116.
Nöldeke, Theodor. "Die moabitischen Fälschungen." *Deutsche Rundschau* 6 (1876): 447–51.
Norin, Stig. "Die sogenannte Joasinschrift—echt oder falsch?" *VT* 55 (2005): 61–74.
Pardee, Dennis. "The Widow's Plea." *COS* 3:86–87.
Petermann, H. "Ueber die Auffindung der Moabitischen Inschrift des Königs Mesa." *ZDMG* 24 (1870): 640–44.
Prym, Eugen. Review of Kautzsch and Socin (*Die Aechtheit der moabitischen Altertümer geprüft*, Strassburg and London: Trübner, 1876) and Koch (*Moabitisch oder Selimisch? Die Frage der moabitischen Altertümer*, Stuttgart: Schweizerbart, 1876). *Jenaer Literaturzeitung* 3 (1876): 238–40.
Rabinowicz, Oskar K. "The Shapira Forgery Mystery." *JQR* 47 (1956): 170–82.
———. "The Shapira Scroll: A Nineteenth-Century Forgery." *JQR* 56 (1965): 1–21.
Rawson, Albert Leighton. "Moabite Inscriptions." *The Nation* 19 (1874): 397–98.
Reichert, Andreas. "Julius Euting, die Pseudo-Moabitica und 'La petite fille de Jérusalem.' Neue Funde zu einer alten Affäre." Pages 335–67 in *Exegese vor Ort. Festschrift für Peter Welten zum 65. Geburtstag.* Edited by Christl Maier, Klaus-Peter Jörns and Rüdiger Liwak. Leipzig: Evangelische Verlagsanstalt, 2001.
Reiner, Fred N. "C. D. Ginsburg and the Shapira Affair." *The British Library Journal* 21 (1995): 109–27.
———. "Tracking the Shapira Case: A Biblical Scandal Revisited." *BAR* 23 (1997): 32–41.
Renz, Johannes, and Wolfgang Röllig. *Handbuch der Althebräischen Epigraphik.* 4 vols. Wiesbaden: Wissenschaftliche Buchgesellschaft, 1995–2003.
Riehm, Eduard Karl August, ed. *Handwörterbuch des biblischen Altertums für gebildete Bibelleser.* 2 vols. 1st ed. Bielefeld: Velhagen & Klasing, 1884. 2nd ed. Besorgt von

Friedrich Baethgen. Bielefeld: Velhagen & Klasing, 1894.

Rogerson, John, and Philip R. Davies. "Was the Siloam Tunnel Built by Hezekiah?" *BA* 59 (1996): 138–49.

Rollston, Christopher A. "Laboratory Analysis of the Moussaïeff Ostraca using the Scanning Electron Microscope (SEM) with an Energy Dispersive X-Ray Microanalyzer (EDS)." *NEA* 61 (1998): 8–9.

———. "Non-Provenanced Epigraphs I." *Maarav* 10 (2003): 135–93.

———. "Non-Provenanced Epigraphs II." *Maarav* 11 (2004): 57–79.

Rosenfeld, Amnon, Shimon Ilani, Howard R. Feldman, Wolfgang E. Krumbein, and Joel Kronfeld. "Archaeometric Evidence for the Authenticity of the Jehoash Inscription Tablet." *Antiguo Oriente* 7 (2009): 57–73.

Rottzoll, Dirk U. *Abraham Ibn Esras langer Kommentar zum Buch Exodus*, vols. 1 (Ex 1–17) and 2 (Ex 18–40). Berlin: de Gruyter, 2000.

Salmon, Ira. "The Life and Times of Moses Wilhelm Shapira." Pages 4–8 in *Truly Fake: Moses Wilhelm Shapira, Master Forger*. Edited by Efrat Karmon. Jerusalem: The Israel Museum. 2000.

Sass, Benjamin. "Summing Up: How Many Seals?" Pages 547–52 in *Corpus of West Semitic Stamp Seals*. N. Avigad and B. Sass. Jerusalem: The Israel Academy of Sciences and Humanities, 1997.

Sasson, Victor. "Philological and Textual Observations on the Controversial King Jehoash Inscription." *UF* 35 (2004): 573–87.

Schlottmann, Konstantin. "Astarte." "Götzendienst." "Moab." Pages 112–15, 520–24, 1007–9 in *Handwörterbuch des biblischen Altertums für gebildete Bibelleser*. Edited by Eduard Karl August Riehm. 2 vols. 1st ed. Bielefeld: Velhagen & Klasing, 1884. 2d ed. besorgt von Friedrich Baethgen. Bielefeld: Velhagen & Klasing, 1894.

———. "Der Chauvinismus in der Alterthumswissenschaft." Sonntagsbeilage zur *Norddeutschen Allgemeinen Zeitung*, April 12, 1874. Cited according to the translation in *The Academy* 5 (1874): 498–99.

———. "Die Inschrift Mesa's. Transscription und Uebersetzung revidirt nach Ganneau's und Warren's letzten Textdarstellungen." *ZDMG* 24 (1870): 253–60; cf. *ZDMG* 24 (1870): 438–60, 645–64; *ZDMG* 25 (1871): 463–83.

———. "Ladislaoa Netto, Die Phönizier in Brasilien (Os Phenicios no Brazil). Ein Brief in dem zu Rio de Janeiro erscheinenden ilustrirten Journal O novo mondo vom 23. April 1874. Mit dem Facsimile einer achtzeiligen phönizischen Inschrift und beigefügten Bemerkungen des Redacteurs." *Jenaer Literaturzeitung* 30 (1874): 459–61.

———. "Nachschrift." *ZDMG* 27 (1873): 135–36.

———. "Neue Moabitische Funde und Räthsel: Erster Bericht." *ZDMG* 26 (1872): 393–407.

———. "Neue Moabitische Funde und Räthsel. Dritter Bericht. Inschrift des Bildes einer Göttin." *ZDMG* 26 (1872): 786–97.

———. "Die neuen Beweise für die Ächtheit der moabitischen Altertümer." *Deutsch-evangelische Blätter* 2 (1877): 466–70.

———. "Ein neugefundenes kleines Fragment des Mesasteines. Aus einem Briefe des Kais. Deutschen Dragoman Dr. von Niemeyer an Prof. Schlottmann." *ZDMG* 30 (1876): 325–28.

———. "Notizen und Correspondenzen. Die sogenannte Inschrift von Parahyba." *ZDMG* 28 (1874): 481–86.

———. *Oster-Programm der Universität Halle-Wittenberg, enthaltend eine Abhandlung über*

Die Siegessäule Mesa's, Königs der Moabiter. Halle: Verlag der Buchhandlung des Waisenhauses, 1870.

———. Review of Kautzsch and Socin (*Die Aechtheit der moabitischen Altertümer geprüft,* Strassburg and London: Trübner, 1876) and Koch (*Moabitisch oder Selimisch? Die Frage der moabitischen Altertümer,* Stuttgart: Schweizerbart, 1876). *Jenaer Literaturzeitung* 3 (1876): 236–38.

———. "Ueber die Aechtheit der Moabitischen Altertümer." *ZDMG* 28 (1874): 171–84.

———. "Zur semitischen Epigraphik." *ZDMG* 24 (1870): 403–14.

———. "Zur Verständigung in der moabitischen Streitfrage." Anzeiger Nr. 14 zur *Jenaer Literaturzeitung* 3 (1876): 57–58.

———. "Zweiter Bericht." *ZDMG* 26 (1872): 408–16.

Shanks, Hershel. "Fakes! How Moses Shapira Forged an Entire Civilization." *Odyssey* 9/10 (2002): 33–41.

Shapira, Wilhelm Moses. Letter to the editor of the *Athenaeum*. *PEQS* (1874): 121.

———. Letter subsumed under the title "The Moabite Pottery." *PEQS* (1878): 95.

Sirat, Colette. "Le Fragments Shapira." *Revue des Études juives* 143 (1984): 95–111.

Smend, Rudolf, and Albert Socin. *Die Inschrift des Königs Mesa von Moab. Für akademische Vorlesungen herausgegeben.* 2 vols. Freiburg: Mohr, 1886.

Socin, Albert. "The Manufacture of Inscriptions." *The Academy* 3 (1872): 179–80.

———. "The Manufacture of Inscriptions: To the Editor of the Academy." *The Academy* 3 (1872): 260.

———. "Die pseudomoabitischen Steininschriften und Thonwaaren." *Das Ausland* 13 (1876): 252–54.

———. "Ueber Inschriftenfälschungen." *ZDMG* 27 (1873): 133–35.

Strack, Hermann L., and O. O. Fletcher. "Writing among the Hebrews." *Hebraica* 2 (1886): 209–17.

Thompson, J. A. "Expansions of the '*d* root." *JSS* 10 (1965): 222–40.

Unger, Eckhard. "Fälschungen." Pages 5–9 in vol. 3 of *Reallexikon der Assyriologie.* 10 vols. Berlin: de Gruyter, 1928–.

Volkwein, B. "Masoretisches *'ēdūt, 'ēdwāt, 'ēdōt*—'Zeugnis' oder 'Bundesbestimmungen'?" *BZ* 13 (1969): 8–40.

Weiss, Johann. *Das Buch Exodus.* Wien: Styria, 1911.

Weser, Hermann. "Eine antiquarische Consular-Untersuchung in Jerusalem. Bericht die behauptete Fälschung der Moabitischen Thonsachen betreffend, von Lic. Weser. Eingesandt von Konst. Schlottmann." *ZDMG* 28 (1874): 460–80.

———. "Ueber die neuesten Moabitischen Funde. Reisebericht von Lic. Weser in Jerusalem, eingesandt von K. Schlottmann." *ZDMG* 26 (1872): 722–34.

Wetzstein, Johann Gottfried. *Reisebericht über Hauran und die Trachonen nebst einem Anhange über die sabäischen Denkmäler in Ostsyrien.* Berlin: Dietrich Reimer, 1860.

Wimmer, Stefan. *Palästinisches Hieratisch. Die Zahl- und Sonderzeichen in der althebräischen Schrift.* Ägypten und Altes Testament 75. Wiesbaden: Harrassowitz, 2008.

Yahuda, Abraham Shalom. "The Story of a Forgery and the Mēša Inscription." *JQR* 35 (1944): 139–64.

Chapter Sixteen
Biblical Hebrew Philology in Light of the Last Three Lines of the Yeho'ash Royal Building Inscription (YI: lines 14–16)

Chaim Cohen

In continuation of my previous article "Biblical Hebrew Philology in the Light of Research on the New Yeho'ash Royal Building Inscription,"[1] which dealt with the first thirteen lines of the YI, the present article concludes this research by suggesting another six philological contributions: the first one based on a change in translation of lines 4–5, while the other five suggestions are based on the final lines 14–16 of the YI. The present article thus begins with section IIA, a revision of my provisional translation of the YI in section II of my previous article, and then continues with section IIIA. Another Six Philological Contributions to BH, as outlined above.

§IIA. Revised Translation of the YI

English Translation	The YI
I. Prologue (lines 1–4) [I am Yeho'ash, son of A]hazyahu, k[ing over Ju]dah, and I executed the re[pai]rs.	1) א[נכי יהואש בן א] 2) חזיהו.מ[ל]ך על י 3) הדה.ואעש.את.הב[דק]

---

1. My previous article was published in M. Lubetski, ed., *New Seals and Inscriptions* (Sheffield: Sheffield Phoenix, 2007), 222–84. §I of course remains unchanged.

II. Body of the YI (lines 4–14) When people in the (densely populated) land and in the (sparsely populated) steppe, and in all the cities of Judah, enthusiastically volunteered to donate silver for the sacred contributions abundantly, in order to acquire quarry stone and juniper wood and Edomite copper / copper from (the city of) ʿAdam, (and) in order to perform the work faithfully (=without corruption), --- (Then) I renovated the breach(es) of the Temple and of the surrounding walls, and the storied structure, and the meshwork, and the winding staircases, and the recesses, and the doors.	(4) ה.כאשר.נמלאה.נ⌈ד⌉ (5) בת.לבאש.בארץ.ובמד (6) בר.ובכל.ערי.יהדה.ל (7) תת.כסף.הקדשם.לרב (8) לקנת.אבן.מחצב.ובר (9) שם.ונחשת.אדם.לעשת (10) במלאכה.באמנה.ואעש (11) את.בדק.הבית.והקרת.ס (12) בב.ואת.היצע.והשבכ (13) ם.והלולם.והגרעת.וה
III. Epilogue (lines 14–16) May (this inscribed tablet) become this day a witness that the work has succeeded, (and) may God (thus) ordain His people with a blessing.	(14) דלתת.והיה.הים.הזה (15) לעדת.כי.תצלח.המלאכה (16) יצו.יהוה.את.עמו.בברכה

§IIIA. Another Six Philological Contributions to Biblical Hebrew[2]

1. Change in Translation of YI, Lines 4–5

כאשר נמלאה נ⌈ד⌉בת לבאש ... לתת

Old Translation: "When men's hearts became replete with generosity ... to donate"
New Translation: "When people ... enthusiastically volunteered to donate"

---

2. All six of these previously unpublished contributions were presented together in a preliminary version in my lecture in Lisbon on August 8, 2008 as part of the European Association of Biblical Studies (EABS) 2008 Conference. I hereby thank all of the participants of that session

This contribution is in accordance with the suggestion of Y. Blau[3] that YI: lines 4–5 is based on the BH idiom נדב לב meaning "to volunteer" and should therefore *not* be translated literally (as in my previous translation) but rather idiomatically (as in my new translation above). The philological evidence from BH and Akk. discussed below leads to the following conclusion (which stands whether or not the YI is authentic): BH ... ל אוֹתוֹ לְבּוֹ נָשָׂא = ... ל אוֹתוֹ לְבּוֹ נָדַב = ... ל אוֹתוֹ לִבּוֹ מָלֵא = Akk. *ana X libbašu našīšu* "he enthusiastically desired/volunteered to do X" (lit. *libbašu* = לבו "his heart" as the grammatical subject in both BH [in all three semantically related idioms] and Akk.) with the perpetrator(s) of the action as the grammatical direct object (object pronoun or pronominal object suffix) of the verb in all of the cases below:

1a) BH Evidence[4]

Exod 35:29—

כָּל אִישׁ וְאִשָּׁה אֲשֶׁר נָדַב לִבָּם אֹתָם לְהָבִיא לְכָל הַמְּלָאכָה אֲשֶׁר צִוָּה
ה' לַעֲשׂוֹת בְּיַד מֹשֶׁה הֵבִיאוּ בְנֵי יִשְׂרָאֵל נְדָבָה לַה'

---

for their worthy comments concerning my lecture (and especially Profs. Lambert, Lubetski, and Millard, and Dr. Morgenstern, all of whose comments will be specifically acknowledged below).

3. Personal communication from Prof. Yehoshua Blau. In fact, after reading my previous 2007 article (see n. 1 above), Prof. Blau informed me orally that he accepted everything in my paper except for this (my aforementioned "old") translation of lines 4–5. I am indebted to my good friend and colleague Prof. Blau for his most generous assistance. I was previously influenced by the initial translation of F. M. Cross, "Notes on the Forged Plaque Recording Repairs to the Temple," *IEJ* 53 (2003): 119, who translated YI: line 4 as follows: "When men's generosity was full." His comment (p. 120) was as follows: "*ndbt lb* is a post-biblical expression meaning 'generosity'. It is construed here with *nmlʾh* with the meaning, presumably, 'to be full'. In biblical Hebrew, the *nipʿal* has the meaning 'to be filled', the *qal* having the meaning 'to be full'. This distinction, however, seems to have been lost in later Hebrew. Clearly we are not dealing in these instances with ninth-century Hebrew. We judge that the biblical expression *lbʾyš* (2 Kgs 12:5) has inspired the curious composition of the forger." Each one of these claims is dealt with in the present section and seen to be completely unjustified philologically, based on a total misunderstanding of the clearly intended idiomatic usage. Some of these claims were already correctly addressed by V. Sasson, "Philological and Textual Observations on the Controversial King Jehoash Inscription," *UF* 35 (2003): 581–82. He, too, however, understood נדבת לב in this inscription incorrectly as "heartfelt generosity" (see his translation on p. 575).

4. The YI seems to contain here a passive hendiadys form combining such expressions as נְדִיב לֵב "enthusiastic volunteer" (lit. "one volunteered by [his] heart") in Exod 35:22 (see below) and מָלְאוֹ לִבּוֹ "who has enthusiastically desired" (Est 7:5—see below). One additional passage, where the MT is however in disarray, should be slightly emended and read approximately as follows (2 Kgs 14:10 = 2 Chr 25:19):

"All the men and women who enthusiastically volunteered to bring anything for the work that the Lord, through Moses, had commanded to be done, brought it as a donation to the Lord."

Exod 36:2—

וַיִּקְרָא מֹשֶׁה אֶל בְּצַלְאֵל וְאֶל אָהֳלִיאָב וְאֶל כָּל אִישׁ חֲכַם לֵב אֲשֶׁר נָתַן ה' חָכְמָה בְּלִבּוֹ כֹּל אֲשֶׁר נְשָׂאוֹ לִבּוֹ לְקָרְבָה אֶל הַמְּלָאכָה לַעֲשֹׂת אֹתָהּ

"Moses then called upon Bezalel and Oholiab and upon every skilled person whom the Lord had endowed with skill, all who had enthusiastically volunteered to undertake the task and carry it out."[5]

Est 7:5—

וַיֹּאמֶר הַמֶּלֶךְ אֲחַשְׁוֵרוֹשׁ וַיֹּאמֶר לְאֶסְתֵּר הַמַּלְכָּה מִי הוּא זֶה וְאֵי זֶה הוּא אֲשֶׁר מְלָאוֹ לִבּוֹ לַעֲשׂוֹת כֵּן

"Thereupon King Ahasuerus demanded of Queen Esther, who is he and where is he who has enthusiastically desired to do such a thing (i.e., to annihilate the Jewish people)?"

Finally, consider the following additional passages, which are also relevant:

Exod 25:2 (כֹּל אִישׁ אֲשֶׁר יִדְּבֶנּוּ לִבּוֹ) "every person who enthusiastically volunteers"); 35:5 (כֹּל נְדִיב לִבּוֹ) "every enthusiastic volunteer"), 21 (כָּל-אִישׁ אֲשֶׁר נְשָׂאוֹ לִבּוֹ // וְכֹל אֲשֶׁר נָדְבָה רוּחוֹ אֹתוֹ) "everyone who had enthusiastically volunteered"), 22 (כֹּל נְדִיב לֵב) "every enthusiastic volunteer"), 26 (וְכָל-הַנָּשִׁים אֲשֶׁר נָשָׂא לִבָּן אֹתָנָה) "and all those [skilled] women who had enthusiastically volunteered").[6]

---

*הִכֵּה הִכִּיתָ אֶת אֱדוֹם וּנְשָׂאֲךָ לִבְּךָ לְהִכָּבֵד וְעַתָּה שְׁבָה בְּבֵיתֶךָ לָמָּה תִתְגָּרֶה בְּרָעָה וְנָפַלְתָּ אַתָּה וִיהוּדָה עִמָּךְ

"Because you (King Amaziah) have defeated Edom, you (now) enthusiastically desire to become more glorified (i.e., militarily); but now, stay at home lest, provoking disaster, you fall, you and Judah with you."

5. The Akk. evidence above (see also n. 6) demonstrates the semantic correspondence of the three BH idioms מָלֵא לִבּוֹ אוֹתוֹ ל... = נָשָׂא לִבּוֹ אוֹתוֹ ל... = נָדַב לִבּוֹ אוֹתוֹ ל... together with the Akk. idiom *ana X libbašu našīšu* meaning "he enthusiastically volunteered / desired to do X." This is the basis of the translation above of such verses as Exod 35:21, 26; 36:2; Est 7:5. Cf. also 2 Kgs 14:10 = 2 Chr 25:19 as translated in the previous note. In Exod 35:26, the placement of the אתנחתא should be transferred to the word אֹתָנָה (cf. 36:2). Contrast, e.g., NJPS, 141–42, 589, 1605–6.

6. Cf. also the much later formulation (without the infinitive of purpose) in Sir

1b) Akkadian Evidence[7]

VAB 4 126 iii 18–19: *ana epēšu Esagil našânni libbī*
"I (Nabû-kudurra-uṣur) enthusiastically desired to rebuild Esagil."

וְגַם פִּינְחָס [ב]ֶן אֶלְעָזָר ... אֲשֶׁר נִדְּבוּ לִבּוֹ וַיְכַפֵּר עַל בְּנֵי יִשְׂרָאֵל—45:23 "There was also Pinechas son of Eleazar ... who enthusiastically volunteered and atoned for the people of Israel."

7. For several additional examples of this idiomatic usage, see CAD N/2, 105. Here I wish to especially thank my friend and colleague, Prof. W. G. Lambert, for informing me of the many cases of this idiom in his recently published edition of the *tamītu* texts. See W. G. Lambert, *Babylonian Oracle Questions* (Mesopotamian Civilizations Series; Winona Lake, Ind.: Eisenbrauns, 2007), 52–53: lines 2–5; 56–57: lines 30–32; 68–69: lines 1–2; 84–85: lines 10–12. In all four cases, the I/1 stative verbal form must be read *našûšu* with subjunctive *-u* (**naši'ušu > našûšu*). One additional case may be found in SAA 4, #81: lines 4–5 (page 94), where however the correct restoration in line 5 would almost surely be [*a-šar* ŠÀ]-*ba-šú na-š*[*ú-šú* ...], in accordance with the four previously mentioned cases (rather than merely the sign *-u* reconstructed in the SAA edition as the final sign of the verbal form omitting the required 3ms. pronominal object suffix of the verb *-šú*). Note that while in BH there are three separate idioms all meaning "enthusiastically desired/volunteered to do X" (see in the text above and in the previous note) *for which* לֵב "heart" *serves as grammatical subject and which refer to the perpetrator of the action as the grammatical direct object of the verb* (object pronoun or pronominal object suffix), in Akk. only the idiom *ana X libbašu našīšu* (cognate to BH ...לְ אוֹתוֹ לִבּוֹ נָשָׂא) is both relatively well-attested and has the same meaning and usage. There are several other semantically related idioms in Akk. for which *libbu* "heart" serves as grammatical subject. For a convenient listing of all such idioms in general, see CAD L, 172, section 3c, 3', a'. Those which are closest semantically are the following: a) *ana X libbašu ubla* "he desired to do X" (cf. CAD A/1, 21–22, section 5d, 1'; e.g., OIP 2 137:28—*ana epēš bīt akīti libbī ublannīma* "I desired to build an Akītu temple" [cf. the similar context quoted in section 1b above; this is one of only a few examples of this well-attested idiom including the pronominal object suffix]); b) *ana X libbašu erissu* "he desired to do X" (only Cagni Erra I:6 [pp. 58–59—reading I/1 stative 3ms. form of *erēšu* with ms. B and with commentary on pp. 141–42]—*erissūma libbašu epēš tāḫazi* "he (Erra) desired to do battle" [cf. CAD E, 283]); c) *ana X libbašu iḫšuḫ / iḫaššaḫ* "he desired / desires to do X" (e.g., TCL 3, 110—*ittīya ana mitḫuṣ tūšāri libbašu iḫšuḫ* "He desired to engage in battle with me" [cf. CAD M/2, 138]; for a few more examples, cf. CAD Ḫ, 135 and *AHw*, 333). Note that of these three additional Akk. idioms, idiom a (as opposed to the somewhat atypical example quoted here for semantic reasons) usually does not include the pronominal object suffix, while idiom b (as read above) does include this suffix, but is unattested elsewhere. Finally, note that the nominal phrase *nīš libbi* (for many examples, see CAD N/2, 296) in its less common general usage meaning "desire" (as opposed to the better attested technical meaning "male sexual desire, libido, ability to obtain and maintain an erection" especially in the *šaziga* corpus of incantations—cf. Biggs, Šaziga, 2–3 for discussion) may be seen as derived from the idiom *ana X libbašu našīšu*. In fact, the latter verbal idiom does occur with its regular general meaning at least once in this corpus. See Biggs Šaziga, 40 (#21): lines 13–14 (composite text based on the different versions in texts A and B presented there): *zikaru u šinništu* UR.BI (*mitḫāriš / ištūniš*) *libbaš*[*unu*] *našīšunūti ul inuḫḫ*[*ū*] "the man and the woman both have an enthusiastic (sexual) desire but they cannot find (sexual) satisfaction."

This example is particularly parallel semantically to the YI usage.[8]

1c) Final Conclusion

For the main conclusion of this section, see the end of the introductory paragraph (before section 1a) above. Furthermore, in light of the above discussion demonstrating the centrality of the bonafide BH idioms נדב / מלא לבו ... אותו ל as the basis for lines 4–5 of the YI, it seems much more likely that YI: lines 4–7 (כאשר נמלאה נדבת לבאש ... לתת כסף הקדשם לרב) served as the source of the expression in 2 Kgs 12:5 (כל כֶּסֶף הַקֳּדָשִׁים ... אֲשֶׁר יַעֲלֶה עַל לֶב-אִישׁ[9] לְהָבִיא בֵית ה׳) rather than vice-versa. Both verbal roots נדב and

---

8. Note that in the phrase כאשר נמלאה נ[ד]בת לבאש in YI: lines 4–5, there is no difference in meaning between passive *nifʿal* נמלאה and the active verbal form מָלֵא in the idiom מָלְאוֹ לִבּוֹ "who has enthusiastically desired" (Est 7:5). For this case of verbal suppletion, see my previous extensive discussion in Cohen, "New Yehoʾash Inscription," 229–33. See also nn. 3 and 4 above.

9. The usage of the relatively rare phrase לֶב-אִישׁ in both YI: line 5 and 2 Kgs 12:5 is certainly clear evidence of some degree of dependence between the two. See already I. Ephal, "The 'Jehoash Inscription': A Forgery," *IEJ* 53 (2003): 124–25 (for the present author's position that in this context there is clear evidence for the dependence of 2 Kgs 12:5 on YI:lines 4–5 rather than vice versa, see at the beginning of section 1c above and in the next note below). Here it should be noted that the phrase (בְּ)לֶב-אִישׁ "lit. (in) the heart of man" occurs only six times in the MT: 2 Sam 15:13; 2 Kgs 12:5; Prov 12:25; 18:12 (with A; L apparently reads here לְב-אִישׁ [cf. BHS] although the ink is somewhat faded at this point in the ms.); 19:21; 20:5. In all six cases, the special construct form לֶב- is used (of a total of sixteen occurrences both construct and absolute but always with *maqqef*) as opposed to the regular unchanged construct form לֵב (altogether approximately one hundred occurrences usually without *maqqef*). This special construct form is a result of vowel reduction (לֵ>לֶ) which is a known feature of Tiberian Hebrew and of the MT, both as regards certain construct forms in general (e.g., בֶּן "the son of" as construct form of בֵּן "son") and especially as a result of the use of *maqqef* (e.g., almost always: אֶת- without cantillation sign but followed by *maqqef*; אֵת with cantillation sign not followed by *maqqef*). For the former, see, e.g., P. Joüon and T. Muraoka, *A Grammar of Biblical Hebrew* (2nd ed.; Rome: Biblical Institute, 2006), 284–85 (§96E*b*) and 292–93 (98*c*); for the latter, see especially I. Yeivin, *The Biblical Masorah* (Jerusalem, 2003), 200 (§§339–340), 201–2 (§343), and 204 (§349) [in Hebrew]. All sixteen cases of the form לֶב- (in both construct and absolute states) occur when the next word is accented on the first syllable (six of the seven following words for all sixteen occurrences are טוֹב, אִישׁ, מֶלֶךְ, רָע, יָם, נַעַר) in order to prevent the undesirable phenomenon of two consecutive accented syllables (this is one of the main linguistic reasons for the *maqqef*—see Yeivin, *Masorah*, 201–2 [§343] and 204 [§349]). [The only apparent exception is Prov 12:20 (מִרְמָה בְּלֶב-חֹרְשֵׁי רָע) where, however, as clearly indicated by the cantillation signs, the plural construct form חֹרְשֵׁי is indeed accented on the first syllable according to the Masoretic principle of נסוג אחור "retraction of the accent"—see Yeivin, *Masorah*, 206–8.] It should be noted that this is precisely the same situation with respect to the six occurrences of the special construct form שֶׁם- "the name of" in Gen 16:15; 21:3; 1 Sam 8:2; 1 Kgs 16:24; Ezek 39:16; Prov 30:4 (always with

מלא occur in the YI but are lacking in 2 Kgs 12:5, while the expression עָלָה עַל לֵב, which replaces them in 2 Kgs 12:5 means merely "to come to mind, to occur to someone, to realize" (without any nuance of enthusiastic volunteering or free-will desire)[10] and may thus be considered a very general paraphrase of the YI on the part of the author of 2 Kgs 12:5.

2. YI: Lines 14–15

והיה הים הזה לעדת כי ...

"May (this inscribed tablet) become this day a witness that ..."

---

maqqef) as opposed to the regular unchanged construct form שֵׁם (altogether approximately three hundred occurrences both with and without *maqqef*). All six cases of the special construct form שֶׁם- likewise occur when the next word is accented on the first syllable (the three following words for all six occurrences are עִיר, שָׁמַר, בְּנוֹ). This is also the case with respect to certain MT verbal forms such as the special imperative form לֶךְ-(וּ) "go" (altogether nine times always with *maqqef* and always followed by a word accented on its first syllable) as opposed to the regular imperative form לֵךְ(וּ) (altogether approximately one hundred occurrences almost always without *maqqef*). Now it is further noted by Yeivin (*Masorah*, 200 [§339]) that on occasion instead of inserting the *maqqef*, the scribe simply left no space between the two words (e.g., in A, אֶתְעַנֵּי [Ps 31:8]). Thus, theoretically, the biblical phrase לֵב-אִישׁ (occurring only with *maqqef*) could also have been written in the MT לְבאִישׁ*. As first suggested to me by my friend Ziyyon Yas'ur, it cannot be a mere coincidence that in the entire YI, the only case of two consecutive words occurring in the same line which are not separated by a dot is in fact the phrase לבאיש in YI: line 5. I hereby thank Prof. Yosef Ofer from Bar-Ilan University for kindly discussing this issue with me.

10. The expression עָלָה עַל לֵב / לֵבָב occurs in eight additional contexts in the MT (half of them with God as subject): Isa 65:17 (// תִזָּכַרְנָה); Jer 3:16 (+ יִזְכְּרוּ בוֹ); 7:31, 19:5, and 32:35 (אֲשֶׁר לֹא צִוִּיתִי / צִוִּיתִים וְלֹא עָלְתָה עַל לִבִּי); 44:21 (// זָכַר); 51:50 (// זִכְרוּ); Ezek 38:10 (+ וְחָשַׁבְתָּ מַחֲשֶׁבֶת רָעָה). The correct meaning as stated in BDB, 523, 524–25 (where this expression is listed within both articles on the words לֵבָב and לֵב in section "3d. *memory*" rather than in section "4. spec. ref. to *inclinations, resolutions and determinations of the will*") is "*come upon the mind / come into mind* (occur to one)." It is interesting that although the sign indicating that all references of this expression (with the term לֵב) have been cited is present on p. 524, 2 Kgs 12:5 is *not* listed. Cf. the complete listing in *DCH* 6:402 (which does include 2 Kgs 12:5). Perhaps the author of 2 Kgs 12:5, after detailing (from another, perhaps priestly, source) "the silver of the census tax and the silver from the valuation of persons" (which are both obligatory priestly levies—see the translation of 2 Kgs 12:5a and the detailed discussion in M. Cogan and H. Tadmor, *II Kings* [AB; New York: Doubleday, 1988], 135, 137), sought to emphasize here that donations were also made which were *not* obligatory and were made as it were when people just happened to think about it. This, however, is quite a different nuance from the enthusiastic voluntary donations referred to in YI: lines 4–7, which is much more fitting in the wider context.

2a) BH Evidence

Isa 30:8–9—

עַתָּה בּוֹא כָתְבָהּ עַל לוּחַ אִתָּם וְעַל סֵפֶר חֻקָּהּ וּתְהִי לְיוֹם אַחֲרוֹן לְעֵד![11] עַד עוֹלָם: כִּי...

"Now, go write it down on a tablet and inscribe it in a record, and may (this inscribed prophecy) be for future days a witness(!) forever that..."

The following translation of 2 Kgs 12:5b by Cogan and Tadmor (*II Kings*, 135) is in fact more appropriate as a paraphrase of YI: lines 4–7: "or any silver that a man may voluntarily bring to the House of YHWH."

11. This emendation of the MT vocalization (לָעַד "forever") in Isa 30:8 is reflected in almost all ancient biblical translations (except for LXX) and accepted by almost all modern scholars. See, e.g., *BHS*, 719, n. 8b; *HALOT*, 788; H. Wildberger, *Isaiah 28–39* (A Continental Commentary; Minneapolis: Fortress, 2002), 139, 140 n. 8e, 142–43; W. A. M. Beuken, *Isaiah II* (HCOT; Leuven: Peeters, 2000), 131, 135; W. H. Irwin, *Isaiah 28–33: Translation with Philological Notes* (Rome: Biblical Institute, 1977), 78–80 (correctly emphasizing the same usage in covenant language of the root כחש "deny, betray" in verse 9 as in Josh 24:27—וְהָיְתָה בָכֶם לְעֵדָה פֶּן תְּכַחֲשׁוּן בֵּאלֹהֵיכֶם "it shall be a witness against you lest you betray your God." See also especially I. Rabinowitz, *A Witness Forever* (Bethesda: CDL, 1993), 44 (the name of this book is based on the emended text of Isa 30:8—see page ix). Note also that the same emended reading לְעֵד! for MT לָעַד is also the generally accepted reading in Zeph 3:8. See, e.g., *BHS*, 1058, n. 8b; *HALOT*, 788; J. Vlaardingerbroek, *Zephaniah* (HCOT; Leuven: Peeters, 1999), 185–86. Against this reading, see, e.g., A. Berlin, *Zephaniah* (AB; New York: Doubleday, 1994), 133 (reading לָעַד and translating "once and for all"). Decisive here in favor of the reading לְעֵד! (besides the evidence from the LXX and the Peshitta—see *BHS*, 1058 n. 8b) are the many other verses in which God serves as a witness against individuals and nations as a precursor to the meting out of Divine punishment. See especially Jer 29:23; Micah 1:2 (MT: לְעֵד); Mal 3:5. See already BDB, 729. Note finally the very clear case of Hab 2:3, where the MT עוֹד חָזוֹן לַמּוֹעֵד (despite the identical reading in 1QpHab 7,5) must surely be emended to עֵד! חָזוֹן לַמּוֹעֵד "the prophecy is a witness for the appointed time" in light of the parallel clause וְיָפֵחַ לַקֵּץ וְלֹא יְכַזֵּב "a witness for future time that does not lie," where the BH substantive יָפֵחַ / יָפִיחַ "witness" is a Poetic Semantically Equivalent (PSE) B-Word to the BH A-Word עֵד "witness" which is cognate to the Ug. substantive *yph*, the regular everyday Ugaritic term for "witness" (cf. G. del Olmo Lete and J. Sanmartín, *A Dictionary of the Ugaritic Language in the Alphabetic Tradition* [Leiden: Brill, 2003], 974 and the bibliography listed there). BH יָפֵחַ / יָפִיחַ "witness" occurs altogether seven additional times (Ps 27:12 [based on the separate construct form יְפֵחַ* proving that the initial *yod* must be understood as the first root letter]; Prov 6:19; 12:17; 14:5, 25; 19:5, 9). *In all seven verses* יָפֵחַ / יָפִיחַ *occurs together with it's A-Word* עֵד *either in parallelism or in hendiadys.* For the usage of BH PSE B-Words in general and for the specific case of BH יָפֵחַ / יָפִיחַ "witness," see most recently C. Cohen, "New Directions in Modern Biblical Hebrew Lexicography," in *Birkat Shalom: Studies in the Bible, Ancient Near Eastern Literature and Postbiblical Judaism Presented to Shalom M. Paul* (ed. C. Cohen et al.; Winona Lake: Eisenbrauns, 2008), 458–461 and especially Table 2, example 2g and note d on p. 459 together with the basic bibliography listed there. For the correct interpretation

2b) Syntactic Comment

Just as in YI: lines 14–15, the inscribed tablet (presumably referring to masc. לוּחַ) itself is the unexpressed, but clearly self-understood, subject of the verb היה "to be, become," such is the case in Isa 30:8–9 as well with respect to the inscribed prophecy for the future (presumably referring to fem. נְבוּאָה).[12] This syntactic parallel is the key to understanding the syntax of YI: 14–15, namely that הים הזה "this day" in YI: line 14 is *not* the subject of the sentence, but rather simply an adverbial time phrase as it usually is in BH (syntactically parallel to the usage of לְיוֹם אַחֲרוֹן "for future days" in Isa 30:8 above). Besides the 83 occurrences of עד היום הזה and the 18 occurrences of בְּ/עַד עֶצֶם הַיּוֹם הַזֶּה cf. especially 1 Sam 12:5 וַיֹּאמֶר אֲלֵיהֶם- עֵד ה' בָּכֶם וְעֵד מְשִׁיחוֹ הַיּוֹם הַזֶּה כִּי לֹא מְצָאתֶם בְּיָדִי מְאוּמָה ... "He (Samuel) said to them, 'the Lord then is witness and his anointed one is witness, against you this day, that you have found nothing in my possession' ...."

2c) Akkadian Evidence

There are also several cases in Akk. inscriptions where the inscription itself (or the object upon which the inscription is written, e.g., the clay tablet or statue) is the unexpressed, but clearly implied subject or object of a verb in that inscription.[13] Perhaps the most celebrated case is in the ninth century B.C.E. bilingual Akk.–Aram. inscription from Tel Fekhereye,[14] where both lines 14–15 of the

---

of Hab 2:3, see especially J. J. M. Roberts, *Nahum, Habakkuk, and Zephaniah* (OTL; Louisville, Ky.: Westminster John Knox, 1991), 105, 106 nn. 5 and 6; Y. Avishur in *'Olam Ha-Tanakh: The Twelve Minor Prophets, Part Two* (Tel-Aviv: Davidson-Attai, 1994 [Hebrew]), 100, 102 (on Hab 2:3); NJPS, 1065, n. c-c. Contrast, e.g., the completely unacceptable convoluted suggestions made in F. I. Andersen, *Habakkuk* (AB; New York: Doubleday, 2001), 205–7. Once this verse is correctly understood, Hab 2:2-3 serves as an excellent semantic parallel to Isa 30:8.

12. While not specifically noted in most modern commentaries to Isaiah, the masc. nouns לוּחַ "tablet" and סֵפֶר "record" obviously can not be the subject of the verb וּתְהִי "and may it (fem.) be." The correct subject can only be the unexpressed, self-understood antecedent of the verbal 3fs. object suffix ־הָ "it (fem.)" at the end of the imperative verbal forms כָּתְבָהּ "write it down" and חֻקָּהּ "inscribe it," namely the inscribed prophecy itself (fem. נְבוּאָה—cf. esp. 2 Chr 9:29). This prophecy will serve as a witness against the people in the future just as the written Song of Moses and the written Book of Tora serve precisely the same function in Deut 31:19, 21, 26. This is also the function of the written חָזוֹן "prophecy" according to the correct understanding of Hab 2:2-3 (see the previous note). See especially Roberts, *Nahum, Habakkuk, and Zephaniah*, 110.

13. For several examples, see CAD Q, 157–58 (sub *qâšu*—section 1d).

14. For this inscription, see most recently the translation of the Aramaic version by A. R. Millard in *COS* 2.34: 153–54 with a listing of all major bibliography.

Akk. inscription and line 10 of the Aram. counterpart are lacking the Akk. term *ṣalmu* and its Aram. equivalent term דמותא or צלמא (all meaning "statue" and all occurring elsewhere in this bilingual inscription referring to the statue of Hadad-yisʿī upon which both versions of the inscription were written) as follows:[15] Akk. version, lines 1…8…14–15: *ana Adad … bēli rabî bēlišu Adad-idʾī šakinmāti Guzani … ikrumma iqīš* "To Adad, …, the great lord, his lord, did Adad-idʾī, governor of Guzan … dedicate (this statue) as a gift."[16]

2d) Final Conclusion

Neither is it correct to consider the above phrase from YI: lines 14–15 as evidence of forgery because "we have not found in the ancient near east a custom that the building or restoration of a temple is celebrated periodically"[17] or any textual precedent for "a particular day serving as a witness";[18] nor is it appropriate to attempt to answer these claims by comparing the very different usage in Siloam Tunnel Inscription: line 3 of the term ובים "lit. and on the day of (but better translated 'and at the time of')",[19] which does not serve syntactically as either subject or object, is not indicated in the text as a witness to any event, and is devoid of any contextual evidence which would imply that such a day should be celebrated by future generations (contrast, e.g., Exod 12:14). As shown above, both of these claims and the answer to them are based on a complete misinterpretation of YI:

---

15. Here I am indebted to my friend and colleague Prof. Alan Millard, who kindly informed me that this feature had already been noted by Prof. F. M. Fales as one of the original Akk. features in the first part of the inscription (Part A = Akk. lines 1–18; Aram. lines 1–12) which is lacking in the second part (Part B = Akk. lines 19–38; Aram. lines 12–23) and was used as part of Fales's evidence that in the first part (as summarized by Millard in the introduction to his translation in *COS* 2.34: 153) "the Assyrian text is clearly primary, containing many stock phrases from the Assyrian scribal repertoire." For all the relevant evidence justifying this claim, see F. M. Fales, "Le double bilinguisme de la statue de Tell Fekherye," *Syria* 60 (1983): 233–50 and especially 237, 246.

16. Millard translates the somewhat different parallel version in line 10 of the Aramaic text as follows: "set up and gave (the statue) to him." See Millard in *COS* 2.34: 154. The term "statue" is also placed in parentheses in the composite translation of J. C. Greenfield and A. Shaffer, "Notes on the Akkadian-Aramaic Bilingual Statue from Tell Fekherye," *Iraq* 45 (1983): 112–13 (composite line 18).

17. See V. A. Hurowitz, "The Jehoash Inscription," page 8 [cited 19 August 2003]. Online: http://www.bibleinterp.com/articles/Report9.htm. See also in Hebrew, idem, "The Jehoash Inscription under a Magnifying Glass," *Bet Miqra* 176 (2004): 97.

18. See D. Talshir, "The Jehoash Inscription: A Philological Angle," *Leshonenu Laʿam* 54 (2004): 9 [Hebrew].

19. See Sasson, "King Jehoash Inscription," 585.

lines 14–15. The phrase היום הזה "this day" has here its regular BH meaning and usage as an adverbial time phrase. As further demonstrated above, the subject of this sentence is the unexpressed (but self-understood) term לוח "inscribed tablet" referring to the Yeho'ash inscribed tablet itself. Such a literary practice where the inscription itself (or the object upon which it is written) is the unexpressed, but clearly implied subject or object of a verb in that inscription has precedents in BH (Isa 30:8–9) and ninth century Akk. and Aram. (the bilingual inscription from Tel Fekhereye). Surely the inclusion of this bonafide ancient feature in the YI (with precedents from both classical BH and from ancient Near Eastern inscriptions from the historical period of King Yeho'ash) should be looked upon as another indication of possible authenticity, rather than as evidence of forgery.

3. YI: Line 15: עדת "witness, testimony, evidence"

3a) Philological Comment.

As regards the usage of the term עדת "witness, testimony, evidence" in YI: line 15 instead of the BH exclusive usage of the terms עֵד / עֵדָה in similar contexts referring to inanimate objects,[20] it should be noted that while it is true that the BH term עֵדוּת does have specialized usages and meanings especially in covenantal terminology (e.g., שְׁנֵי לֻחֹת הָעֵדֻת "the two Tablets of the Pact" [Exod 31:18; 32:15; 34:29] // לוּחֹת הַבְּרִית (שְׁנֵי) "the (two) Tablets of the Covenant [Deut 9:9, 11, 15]), its basic meaning and derivation is as an abstract noun meaning "testimony" or the like, derived from the BH noun עֵד "witness."[21] This derivation

---

20. See, e.g., Isa 30:8–9 above and see Gen 31:44, 47, 48, 52 below. The other passages are as follows: עֵד (referring to a masculine antecedent)—Exod 22:12; Deut 31:26; Josh 22:27, 28, 34; Isa 19:20; Hab 2:3 (see n. 11 above); Job 16:8; Ps 89:38; עֵדָה (referring to a feminine antecedent)—Gen 21:30 (... בַּעֲבוּר תִּהְיֶה לִּי לְעֵדָה כִּי "in order that it should be for me a witness that ..." referring to fem. שֶׁבַע כְּבָשֹׂת "seven ewes"); Josh 24:27 (see n. 11 above for the BH text and translation—referring to הָאֶבֶן הַזֹּאת "this stone"). Only in the two contexts of Isa 30:8 (see above) and Deut 31:19, 21 (referring to the feminine שִׁירָה "poem") does the masculine עֵד refer to a feminine antecedent. See already BDB, 729. Here I wish to thank my friend and colleague Meir Lubetski for discussing this entire matter with me especially as regards Gen 21:30.

21. See, e.g., the detailed discussion in H. Simian-Yofre, "'wd; 'ēd; 'ēdût; te'ûda," TDOT 10 (1999): 495–98, 510–15 with extensive bibliography on pp. 495–96. Contrast most recently D. Talshir, "אָחוֹת and עֵדוּת in Ancient Hebrew," ZAH 15–16 (2002–2003): 108, 115–22. Note that Prof. Talshir relates there to the usage of עדת in the YI: line 15 as follows (page 117): "To my mind, the usage of עדות in the late meaning of "testimony" is the main philological proof that Joash Inscription is a forgery." As regards the key semantic issue of the interchanging of the meanings "witness" and "testimony" in Akkadian, Aramaic, and BH, especially with respect to inanimate antecedents, see the discussion in the text above and below. As regards the proper

finds its precedent in both of the regular Akkad. terms for "testimony," šībūtu[22] and mukinnūtu,[23] both abstract nouns derived respectively from the two regular terms for "witness," šību[24] and mukinnu.[25] Such is also the case in Aramaic, where ש/סהדותא "testimony" (already in BA—see Gen 31:47 quoted below) is derived from ש/סהדא "witness."[26] What is most important is that especially with

---

etymology of BH עֵדוּת, let me quote here part of what I wrote on this subject in 1978 (long before the YI was first published) in response to B. Volkwein, "Masoretisches ʿēdūt, ʿēdwōt, ʿēdōt— 'Zeugnis' oder 'Bundesbestimmungen'?," BZ 13 (1969): 18–40, in H. R. (C.) Cohen, *Biblical Hapax Legomena in the Light of Akkadian and Ugaritic* (SBLDS; Missoula: Scholars Press, 1978), 79–80 n. 170: "There is absolutely no justification for the assumption that ʿēdūt 'testimony' must be a late word (i.e., 'Aramaism') because of its construction with the abstract ending -ūt. While this ending is common in Aramaic, it is just as common in Akkadian (-ūtu), where not only many of the concepts which are attested with this ending in Hebrew occur (e.g., Heb. מלכות— Akk. šarrūtu 'kingship'; Heb. עבדות—Akk. ardūtu 'slavery'), but many are also cognate (e.g., Heb. רפאות—Akk. ripūtu [Amarna] 'health'; Heb. אלמנות—Akk. almanūtu 'widowhood'...; Heb. כבדות—Akk. kabtūtu 'heaviness, majesty'). Therefore, the occurrence of šībūtu (= šību 'witness' + -ūtu) as the regular word for 'testimony' in Akkadian (AHw, 1229–30) clearly demonstrates that Hebrew ʿēdūt 'testimony' should indeed be analyzed as ʿēd 'witness' + -ūt, and that there is no valid reason for considering either this word or its construction as late due to Aramaic influence. As for Volkwein's contextual evidence…, there can be no doubt that ʿēdūt and ʿēdwōt / ʿēdōt must approach the meaning 'treaty' and 'treaty stipulations' in the passages he cites. This, however, has been noted before, and has been generally explained as a semantic development of ʿēdūt 'testimony'. Since the treaties and laws are by definition testified (i.e., sworn) to, they may themselves be called ʿēdūt or ʿēdōt / ʿēdwōt as 'a testimony of God' [i.e., treaty] or 'of laws as divine testimonies or solemn charges' [i.e., 'treaty stipulations'] (see BDB, 730). Evidence for this development comes from the usage of שבועה 'oath'. For just as ברית 'treaty' can alternate freely with ʿēdūt 'testimony' …, so it can alternate with שבועה 'oath' (compare e.g., Gen 26:3 [והקמתי את השבועה] with Gen 17:7 [והקמתי את בריתי] and Exod 6:4 [וגם הקמתי את בריתי] where both ברית and שבועה must be taken to mean "treaty"). Just as שבועה can mean 'treaty' by extension because it is sworn to, so ʿēdūt can mean 'treaty' because it is testified to (compare also the usage and semantic range of māmītu 'oath' in Akkadian treaty contexts)." For the correct comparison between the technical terms for "vassal treaty," Akk. adû and Aram. (Sefîre) עדן, with the BH *hapax legomenon* technical term עָדִים ׄ "vassal treaty" (Isa 33:8) rather than with the unrelated terms עֵדֻת and עֵדוֹת / עֵדֹת, see the detailed discussion in Cohen, *Hapax Legomena*, 42–44, 75–81 nn. 152–73 (esp. notes 158, 162, 169, and 170).

22. See CAD Š/2, 400–402; CDA, 371.
23. See CAD M/2, 186–87; CDA, 215.
24. See CAD Š/2, 394–98; CDA, 370.
25. See CAD M/2, 185–86; CDA, 215.
26. Note that instead of correctly using the occurrence of BA שָׁהֲדוּתָא "testimony" (Gen 31:47—clearly the abstract term derived from the regular Aram. term סהדא "witness") as an Aram. precedent for the original usage and derivation of the BH term עֵדוּת meaning "testimony" as derived from BH עֵד "witness" (like the Akk. abstract term šībūtu "testimony" derived from šību "witness"—see above), those scholars who assume that the YI is a modern-day forgery

respect to inanimate antecedents, the respective terms for "witness" also come to mean "testimony" (as is the case for the Akkadian and Aramaic terms mentioned above—see below) and are used in addition to the regular terms for "testimony." This is the reason for the masc. / fem. usage of עֵד / עֵדָה "witness" in BH with the additional meaning "testimony." This is not a matter of עֵד / עֵדָה independently being understood as an abstract noun (abstract nouns do not generally occur in both masculine and feminine forms), but rather a semantic development of the primary meaning "witness." See already BDB, 729 (`ed and `eda, both "of things") and especially Gen 31:47, 52 (see below). Such is also the usage of the English term 'witness' and the modern Hebrew term עֵד to this day. Therefore, the usage of עדת "witness, testimony" in YI: line 15 (as an abstract noun derived from the regular term עֵד "witness") should be considered as a perfectly acceptable equivalent to the regular usage of BH עֵד / עֵדָה with respect to inanimate objects (as is also the case in Akk. and Aram. in the examples presented below). Under no circumstances should this usage be considered as valid evidence in favor of forgery.

3b) BH / BA Evidence (BH עֵד = BA שָׂהֲדוּתָא):

Gen 31:47—

וַיִּקְרָא לוֹ לָבָן יְגַר שָׂהֲדוּתָא וְיַעֲקֹב קָרָא לוֹ גַּלְעֵד

"Laban called it (the mound) 'mound of שָׂהֲדוּתָא', while Jacob called it 'mound of עֵד'."[27]

---

ignore this important evidence and point out only that the BH equivalent in Gen 31:47 is not עֵדוּת, but rather עֵד. They then see this and the other aforementioned occurrences of BH עֵד / עֵדָה meaning "testimony" with respect to inanimate objects (see n. 20 above) as proof that the latter is the term for "testimony" in BH rather than עֵדוּת. See, e.g., Talshir, "The Jehoash Inscription," 8–9 (Hebrew); Hurowitz, "The Jehoash Inscription," 8; idem, "Magnifying Glass," 98 (Hebrew); E. Greenstein, "Hebrew Philology Spells Fake," *BAR* 29/3 (2003): 29. As clearly demonstrated here (see in the text above and below), BH עֵד / עֵדָה are *not* at all independent abstract terms meaning "testimony, evidence," but rather the regular BH masc. and fem. terms meaning primarily "witness," which through a semantic development (for which there are also precedents in Akk. and Aram.) come to mean "testimony, evidence" as well. As in Akk. and Aram., this must be considered *another means* to express the meaning "testimony, evidence" in addition to the assumed original usage of the abstract noun עֵדוּת. Here it may be added that of the scholars cited above in the present note, only Prof. Greenstein correctly notes that the usage of BH עֵד meaning "testimony" (he doesn't mention the feminine עֵדָה) is a semantic development from the regular meaning "witness," but he still claims that this is the only possible way to express that concept ("never עֵדוּת"—p. 29).

27. Note that it is quite possible in this context that the term עֵד was deemed necessary here

Gen 31:52—

עֵד הַגַּל הַזֶּה וְעֵדָה הַמַּצֵּבָה

"This mound is witness (masc.) and the pillar is witness (fem.)."[28]

3c) Akkadian Evidence (interchange of *mukinnu / mukinnūtu*)[29]

YOS 3 135:20, CT 22 84:23–24 etc.: *šipirtâ lū* ˡúˊ*mukinniya*
"Let my letter be my witness."

YOS 3 44:23–24: *šipirtâ ana* ˡúˊ*mukinnūtu paqdakka*
"My letter is entrusted to you as a witness (for your case)."

3d) Aramaic Evidence (usage of סהדא "witness" meaning "evidence/testimony")[30]

Šab 65b // *Ned* 40a // *Bek* 55b (שהדא): מיטרא במערבא סהדא רבה פרת

---

rather than עֵדוּת because of the assumed aetiological connection between גִּלְעָד and הַר הַגִּלְעָד (see vv. 23, 25, 54).

28. As already noted above, Abstract nouns generally do not occur in separate masc. / fem. forms. Cf. also verses 44 (indirectly) and 48 where עֵד likewise refers to גַּל.

29. Cf. *CAD* M/2, 186, 187. For the usage of Akk. *mukinnu* as the main term for "witness" in NB documents (at that time replacing the regular Akk. term *šību* even though *mukinnu* was already being used together with *šību* in the OB period—see *CAD* M/2, 186), see especially E. von Dassow, "Introducing the Witnesses in Neo-Babylonian Documents," in *Ki Baruch Hu— Ancient Near Eastern, Biblical, and Judaic Studies in Honor of Baruch A. Levine* (ed. R. Chazan et al.; Winona Lake: Eisenbrauns, 1999), 3–22.

30. Besides the Aramaic evidence cited above, my friend and colleague Dr. Matthew Morgenstern kindly informed me of another interesting example found in five Geniza manuscripts of Palestinian Targumim dating from the ninth to the sixteenth centuries and relating to a midrashic addition to Gen 38:25: הוּא מוּצֵאת וְהִיא שָׁלְחָה אֶל חָמִיהָ לֵאמֹר לְאִישׁ אֲשֶׁר אֵלֶּה לּוֹ אָנֹכִי הָרָה וַתֹּאמֶר הַכֶּר נָא לְמִי הַחֹתֶמֶת וְהַפְּתִילִים וְהַמַּטֶּה הָאֵלֶּה "As she was being brought out, she sent the following message to her father-in-law: 'I am pregnant to the man to whom these belong', and she further stated, 'Examine these: whose seal and cord and staff are these?'". According to this midrashic addition, Tamar, as she was being taken out to be executed, was unable at first to locate the three pieces of evidence, namely the seal, the cord and the staff. Only through Divine intervention in answer to her desparate prayers did God send one of the angels (some manuscripts have Gabriel, others have Michael) to find them for her. The phrase "(three) pieces of evidence" occurs in the five Palesinian Targumim manuscripts as follows: תלתי שהדייה / תלתֵּי שָׁהֲדָיָיה / תלתא סהדי / תלתה סהדין / לסהדיא. In all five manuscripts, the regular Aramaic term for "witness" is being used here with the meaning "evidence" in accordance with the aforementioned semantic development common to BH, Akk., and Aram. For all details concerning these five manuscripts and the midrashic addition to Gen 38:25, see the important article of M. Morgenstern, "Secondary

"(A rise in the level of the) Euphrates is great evidence for rain in Eretz Yisraʾel."[31]

3e) Final Conclusion

Just as the regular abstract term for "testimony, evidence" is derived from the regular term for "witness" in both Akk. (*šību / mukinnu* "witness"; *šībūtu / mukinnūtu* "testimony, evidence") and Aram. (ש/סהדא "witness"; ש/סהדותא "testimony, evidence"), so it may be assumed that this was the original meaning of BH עֵדוּת (as derived from the regular BH term עֵד "witness") as well. In all three cases, the abstract term for "testimony, evidence" is formed by adding the cognate abstract endings Akk. -ūtu and BH / Aram. -וּת to the regular term for "witness." Likewise, in accordance with a common semantic development, the regular terms for "witness" in all three languages (especially when used with respect to inanimate antecedents) take on the additional abstract meaning of "testimony, evidence" (the same semantic development is still found with respect to both modern English 'witness' and modern Hebrew עֵד), but this usage does *not replace* the usage of the aforementioned regular abstract terms, but is rather *used in addition* to them. Thus the usage of the term עדת "testimony, evidence" in YI: line 13, in addition to the same usage of the regular masc. and fem. terms עֵד / עֵדָה "witness, testimony, evidence" in BH, is by no means evidence in favor of forgery of the YI, but rather is precisely what is expected in Classical BH according to the aforementioned precedents in Akk. and Aram., whether or not the YI is authentic.

4. YI: LINE 15: כי תצלח המלאכה "THAT THE WORK HAS SUCCEEDED"

4a) Philological Comment

This usage of the BH verb צלח (in the הפעיל conjugation—see the precedents below) with מלאכה "work" as its subject is implied both by the BA הַפְעֵל usage in Ezra 5:8 (with reference to the rebuilding of the Second Temple in a context similar to the YI—cf. also Ezra 6:14) and by the BH הפעיל usage in Gen 39:2–3, 23 (for the implied object מלאכה, see v. 11). This phrase in the YI is the first explicit case of this BH usage. There are also some excellent Akkadian semantic paral-

---

Editing in Jewish Aramaic Texts and the Creation of a Mixed Literary Aramaic," in *Late Aramaic: The Literary and Linguistic Context of the Zohar* (ed. A. Rapoport Albert; Studies in Judaica; Leiden: Brill, forthcoming).

31. Cf. M. Sokoloff, *A Dictionary of Jewish Babylonian Aramaic* (Ramat-Gan: Bar-Ilan University Press, 2002), 790.

lels from the Neo-Assyrian annals of Sennacherib using the Akkadian equivalent terms *šutēšuru* "to succeed" and *šipru* "work." This corresponding feature in the YI surely should not be considered evidence in favor of forgery.³²

4b) BA Evidence³³

Ezra 5:8—

יְדִיעַ לֶהֱוֵא לְמַלְכָּא דִּי אֲזַלְנָא לִיהוּד מְדִינְתָּא לְבֵית אֱלָהָא רַבָּא וְהוּא מִתְבְּנֵא אֶבֶן גְּלָל וְאָע מִתְּשָׂם בְּכֻתְלַיָּא וַעֲבִידְתָּא דָךְ אָסְפַּרְנָא מִתְעַבְדָא וּמַצְלַח בְּיֶדְהֹם׃

"May it be known to the king that we went to the province of Judah to the Temple of the great God. It is being rebuilt with hewn stone and wood is being set in the walls. This work is being done precisely and is succeeding in their hands."

---

32. Contrast the opposite claims of, e.g., both Profs. V. A. Hurowitz and E. Greenstein. Hurowitz maintains that while there are BH precedents for the use of הצלחה "success" in building contexts (he cites Neh 2:20; 1 Chr 22:11-13; 2 Chr 7:11; 14:6), there are no extant BH contexts in which מלאכה "work" occurs as the subject of the verb תִּצְלַח or תַּצְלִיחַ. On the other hand, Hurowitz then cites a precise semantically equivalent parallel usage in Akk. (which I have referred to above in sections 4a and 4d together with the bibliography cited by Hurowitz). Instead of considering this Akk. parallel as evidence in favor of possible authenticity of the YI, Hurowitz simply assumes that in this case "the author [of the YI—C.C.] 'got lucky' and succeeding (sic!) in inventing an expression with an Akkadian parallel." See Hurowitz, "The Jehoash Inscription," 8–9 (quote is from p. 9); idem, "Magnifying Glass," 98 (Hebrew). Greenstein maintains as follows: "In early Biblical Hebrew a person succeeds (literally 'makes one's path smooth') in one's work. The 'work' itself does not succeed. Only in later Hebrew (compare, for example the post-Exilic Ps 1:3) can a person's action succeed." See Greenstein, "Hebrew Philology Spells Fake," 29. Against this attempt to limit the First Temple usage of this verb to human subjects alone, note the following very clear contrary example in Num 14:41: וַיֹּאמֶר מֹשֶׁה לָמָּה זֶּה אַתֶּם עֹבְרִים אֶת פִּי ה' וְהִוא לֹא תִצְלָח׃ "But Moses said, 'Why do you transgress the Lord's command? This will not succeed!'" Contrast the post-Exilic 2 Chr 24:20 where in a similar context the people do not succeed—exactly the opposite chronologically of what Greenstein maintains. Neither Hurowitz nor Greenstein even mention the crucial positive evidence from BA and BH discussed above in sections 4b and 4c, which renders the precise Akk. semantic parallel in section 4d as additional evidence in the present case.

33. Surely this precise BA parallel from Ezra 5:8 is the most important positive evidence for accepting the possible authenticity of YI: line 15—כי תצלח המלאכה "that the work has succeeded" (reading the verb in the הפעיל conjugation as in Gen 39:2-3 quoted in section 4b above and especially corresponding to the Aramaic הפעל conjugation in Ezra 5:8 and cf. also both Ezra 6:14 quoted above and the parallel usage of the Št [III/2] causative conjugation of the Akk. verb *šutēšuru* "to succeed" in section 4d below). Yet, Ezra 5:8 has never been previously mentioned in any discussion of this line of the YI.

[cf. Ezra 6:14—

וְשָׂבֵי יְהוּדָיֵא בָּנַיִן וּמַצְלְחִין

"So the elders of the Jews rebuild successfully..."]

4c) BH Evidence[34]

Gen 39:2–3—

וַיְהִי ה' אֶת יוֹסֵף וַיְהִי אִישׁ מַצְלִיחַ וַיְהִי בְּבֵית אֲדֹנָיו הַמִּצְרִי׃
וַיַּרְא אֲדֹנָיו כִּי ה' אִתּוֹ וְכֹל אֲשֶׁר הוּא עֹשֶׂה ה' מַצְלִיחַ בְּיָדוֹ

"The Lord was with Joseph and he was a successful man, staying in the house of his Egyptian master. His master realized that the Lord was with him and all that he did the Lord made succeed in his hand.

[Gen 39:11 informs us exactly what Joseph did in his master's house:

וַיְהִי כְּהַיּוֹם הַזֶּה וַיָּבֹא הַבַּיְתָה לַעֲשׂוֹת מְלַאכְתּוֹ ...

"One such day he came into the house to do his work..."

Thus what Joseph was successful (מַצְלִיחַ) in doing was his work (מְלָאכָה), the same two terms used in line 15 of the YI.]

4d) Akkadian Evidence[35]

OIP 2 107 vi 45–46: aššu šipri ēkalliya šutēšuri u lipit qātēya šullume
"in order to make the construction work of my (Sennacherib's) palace succeed, and (in order) to complete my handiwork."

[= a precise semantic parallel to YI: line 15]

---

34. For this evidence, see section 4a above.
35. For this context and other similar Neo-Assyrian contexts especially from the eighth century B.C.E. Annals of Sennacherib, cf. CAD E, 359. As noted above in n. 32, it was Prof. V. A. Hurowitz who first suggested this precise Akk. parallel to the YI, citing also the general discussion of Dr. H. Tawil concerning the Akk. usage. See Hurowitz, "'The Jehoash Inscription,'" 9; idem, "Magnifying Glass," 98 (in Hebrew); H. Tawil, "Hebrew הצלח / צלח, Akkadian ešēru / šūšuru: A Lexicographical Note," JBL 95 (1976): 405–13 (especially p. 407 and n. 17).

5. YI: Line 16:

יצו ה' את עמו בברכה

"(and) may God (thus) ordain His people with a blessing"

5a) Philological Comment

The key to understanding this rare syntactic structure is the equivalence *יְצַו אֶת הַבְּרָכָה "may He ordain the blessing" (see, e.g., Lev 25:21 below) = יְבָרֵךְ "may He bless." Thus, וְצִוִּיתִי אֶת בִּרְכָתִי לָכֶם "I will ordain My blessing for you" (Lev 25:21) = יצו את עמו בברכה "May He ordain His people with a blessing" (YI: line 16) in the same way that וְנָתַתִּי שָׁלוֹם בָּאָרֶץ "I will grant well-being in the land" (Lev 26:6) = יְבָרֵךְ אֶת עַמּוֹ בַשָּׁלוֹם "May He bless His people with well-being" (Ps 29:11). Cf. also MO2:1— יברכך ה' בשלם "May God bless you with well-being."[36]

5b) BH Evidence

Lev 25:21—

וְצִוִּיתִי אֶת בִּרְכָתִי לָכֶם בַּשָּׁנָה הַשִּׁשִּׁית וְעָשָׂת אֶת הַתְּבוּאָה לִשְׁלֹשׁ הַשָּׁנִים

"I will ordain my blessing for you in the sixth year, so that it shall yield a crop sufficient for three years.'

---

36. Many scholars have claimed that the syntax of the YI in this line (and especially the form בברכה with prepositional prefix ב) is unacceptable BH syntax for the First Temple period. Note for example the following claims with regard to this context: "Cf. Lev 25:21, and especially Deut 28:8. However, the line is awkward, and would read more smoothly if it were changed to ‹to ordain blessings for his people›." (Cross); "a deviation from the Biblical idiom and nonsensical" (Greenstein); "בברכה prefixed with the preposition bet is a very rare form ... It is never used as a direct object as required here." (Hurowitz' English article); "The author should have written ה' יצו ברכה בעמו" (Hurowitz' Hebrew article); "One could seemingly solve the problem of the double ב [at the beginning of the word בברכה—C. C.] as dittography, i.e., unintentionally doubling the ב ..., but isn't it more likely that the author in his haste to conclude his inscription was led astray by the modern Hebrew custom of ending letters with the concluding term בברכה?" (Talshir). Cf. Cross, "Notes on the Forged Plaque," 121; Greenstein, "Hebrew Philology Spells Fake," 30; Hurowitz, "The Jehoash Inscription," 10; idem, "Magnifying Glass," 99 (Hebrew); Talshir, "The Jehoash Inscription," 10 (Hebrew). None of these scholars considered the important syntactical evidence provided by Ps 29:11 and MO2:1 as discussed above.

Lev 26:6—

וְנָתַתִּי שָׁלוֹם בָּאָרֶץ וּשְׁכַבְתֶּם וְאֵין מַחֲרִיד וְהִשְׁבַּתִּי חַיָּה רָעָה מִן הָאָרֶץ וְחֶרֶב בְּאַרְצְכֶם לֹא תַעֲבֹר

"I will grant well-being in the land, and you shall lie down untroubled by anyone; I will give the land respite from vicious beasts, and no sword shall cross your land."

Ps 29:11—

ה' עֹז לְעַמּוֹ יִתֵּן ה' יְבָרֵךְ אֶת עַמּוֹ בַשָּׁלוֹם

"May the Lord grant strength to His people, may the Lord bless His people with well-being."

5c) Epigraphic Evidence

MO2:1—

יברכך יהוה בשלם

"May God bless you with well-being." [37]

---

37. This First Temple Hebrew inscription was first published in P. Bordreuil, F. Israel, and D. Pardee, "Deux ostraca paléo-hébreux de la Collection Sh. Moussaïeff," *Sem* 46 (1996): 49–76, especially 62–76. For MO2: line 1, cf. especially pp. 62–63. Like the YI, both inscriptions MO1 and MO2 were suspected of being forgeries. Cf. especially I. Eph'al and J. Naveh, "Remarks on the Recently Published Moussaieff Ostraca," *IEJ* 48 (1998): 269–73. For the present author's negative opinion regarding the claim of forgery, see C. Cohen, "Once Again: The Two Meanings of the Parallel Terms שפחה / אמה in Biblical Hebrew," in קול ליעקב—*The Yaakov Bentolila Jubilee Volume* (ed. D. Sivan et al.; Beer-Sheva: Ben-Gurion University Press, 2003), 239–40, especially n. 4 (in Hebrew). For an updated bibliography concerning this issue, see most recently S. Aḥituv, *Echoes from the Past: Hebrew and Cognate Inscriptions from the Biblical Period* (Jerusalem: Carta, 2008), 9–10. Note that this epigraphic evidence from MO2: line 1 is in addition to the very clear BH syntactical evidence, especially from Ps 29:11 (see paragraph 5b above). Note finally that when MO2 was first published, the following was incorrectly stated with respect to MO2: line 1: "l'expression *brk bšlm* est nouvelle en paléo-hébreu épigraphique etelle n'est pas attestée dans la Bible." See Bordreuil, Israel, and Pardee, "Deux ostraca," 62. This claim was then repeated in S. L. Gogel, *A Grammar of Epigraphic Hebrew* (Atlanta: Scholars Press, 1998), 287, n. 49. Obviously, Ps 29:11 was overlooked in both of these studies.

6. YI: Line 16: עמו "His people" = BH עמיו < *עמהו

Phonologically BH *עַמְהוּ > עַמּוּ just as רֵעֵהוּ > רֵעוּ in the Siloam Tunnel Inscription: lines 2, 3, 4.[38] The letter 'ה (as 3ms. pronominal suffix) elides when in an intervocalic position resulting in such BH forms as פִּיו, אָחִיו, אָבִיו deriving respectively from פִּיהוּ, אָחִיהוּ, אָבִיהוּ (see the chart immediately below).[39] This phenomenon is extant also in Phoenician (Byblian and Standard Phoenician)[40] in such forms as אדתו "his lady" (KAI 5, 6, 7),[41] ארנו "his coffin" (KAI 9b:4)[42], and זרעו "his seed" (KAI 10:15) [see also in the chart immediately below], demonstrating that it is not restricted to either final weak stems or to long i vowels.[43] Therefore, under no circumstances should it be necessarily assumed that the 3ms. pronominal suffix at the end of the form עמו in YI: line 16 represents the vowel letter o, which of course would be clear evidence of forgery in an inscription presumably dating from the ninth century B.C.E.

Consonantal ו as 3ms Pronominal Suffix on Singular Noun Form	= Same Form with Consonantal ה	Additional Equivalent Forms in the MT
עמו (YI: line 16)	עמה / לעמ[ה] (2× in Deir `Alla' Inscr.: I:4; II:17)[44]	עַמּוֹ (Gen 49:16 + 124×); עַמָּיו (Gen 25:8 + 13×)[45]

---

38. See most recently Ahituv, *Echoes from the Past*, 22–23 and the comprehensive bibliography on p. 25. Surely, this unexpected form רעו (occurring three times in this seventh century B.C.E. inscription instead of the expected form *רעה) must be considered an important precedent for the equally unexpected form עמו (instead of the expected form *עמה in YI: line 16).

39. I hereby thank my friend and colleague Prof. Daniel Sivan for first suggesting this solution to me; it was subsequently also adopted by the late Prof. D. N. Freedman. See D. N. Freedman, "Don't Rush to Judgment: Jehoash Inscription May Be Authentic," *BAR* 30/2 (2004): 51. Note that Prof. Sivan had previously analyzed the Ug. form *bbtw* "in his house" (*KTU*² 3.9:4) as a similar case of elision of the 3ms Ug. intervocalic pronominal suffix *-h* [*bi-bêtiw*] (< *bi-bêtihu*). See D. Sivan, *A Grammar of the Ugaritic Language* (Leiden: Brill, 2001), 33–34.

40. See especially C. Krahmalkov, *A Phoenician–Punic Grammar* (Leiden: Brill, 2001), 55, 57. Note that while Krahmalkov notes that the Phoenician attested examples are all in the genitive, the examples cited in the table below demonstrate that no such restriction exists in BH.

41. Cf. the form אדתה in line 3 of the new Eqron inscription in Ahituv, *Echoes from the Past*, 335.

42. This is according to Krahmalkov's reading and reconstruction of this line (based especially on *KAI* 9A:2). See C. Krahmalkov, *Phoenician–Punic Dictionary* (Leuven: Peeters, 2000), 374 (inadvertently omitted from p. 73—article 'rn); idem, *A Phoenician–Punic Grammar*, 282 (slightly corrected reconstruction).

43. Contrast especially Talshir, "The Jehoash Inscription," 10 and n. 21.

רֵעוֹ (3× in Siloam Tunnel Inscription: lines 2,3,4)⁴⁶	רֵעֵהוּ (Gen 11:3 + 116×)	וְרֵעוֹ (Jer 6:21)
אָבִיו (Gen 2:24 + 220×)	אֲבִיהוּ (Judg 14:19 + 6×)	-
אָחִיו (Gen 4:2 + 112×)	אֲחִיהוּ (Jer 34:9 + 3×)	-
בְּעֵ֫שָׂיו (Ps 149:2)	עֹשֵׂהוּ (Isa 17:7 + 6×)	הָעֹשׂוֹ (Job 40:19)
פִּיו (Gen 25:28 + 54×)	פִּיהוּ (Exod 4:15 + 21×)	-
Phoen. לאדנו "for his lord"⁴⁷	Ug. ʾadnh (KTU² 1.24:33)⁴⁸	אֲדֹנָיו (Gen 24:9 + 41×)⁴⁹
Phoen. אדתו (3× in KAI 5:2; 6:2; 7:4)	אדתה (Eqron inscription: line 3)⁵⁰	-
Phoen. ארנו (KAI 9B:4)⁵¹	-	-
Phoen. זרעו (KAI 10:15)	-	זַרְעוֹ (Gen 1:11 + 37×)

---

44. See conveniently Aḥituv, *Echoes from the Past*, 438–39, 454–55. For the correct phonological analysis, see J. A. Hackett, *The Balaam Text from Deir ʿAlla* (HSM; Chico: Scholars Press, 1980), 23, 37 and n. 17. It is here assumed (together with Prof. J. Heuhnergard) that the (apparently) eighth-century B.C.E. Deir ʿAlla' text is not written in Aramaic, but rather represents an independent branch of Northwest Semitic. See most recently Aḥituv, *Echoes from the Past*, 434–35.

45. See sections 6b–6d and 6f below.

46. See most recently G. A. Rendsburg and W. M. Schniedewind, "The Siloam Tunnel Inscription: Historical and Linguistic Perspectives," *IEJ* 60 (2010): 192–93.

47. For this form with 3ms pronominal suffix ו- in a tenth-century B.C.E. fragmentary inscription found 10 km from ancient Byblos and first published in 1977, see P. Bordreuil, "Une inscription Phénicienne champlevée des environs de Byblos," *Sem* 27 (1977): 23–27. See most recently T. N. D. Mettinger, "Amarna Letter No. 84: Damu, Adonis, and 'The Living God' at Byblos," in *Sefer Moshe—The Moshe Weinfeld Jubilee Volume* (ed. C. Cohen et al.; Winona Lake: Eisenbrauns, 2004), 365–66.

48. For this text, see, e.g., D. Marcus in *UNP*, 217. For the Ug. term ʾadn "lord, master, father," see del Olmo Lete and Sanmartín, *Dictionary*, 18–19.

49. The usage of BH אֲדֹנָיו (always with singular meaning despite the suffix with י) must be considered semantically analogous to BH עָמָיו (always with singular meaning as demonstrated below). The only difference is that the analogy to other pronominal suffixed forms (e.g., אֲדֹנֶיךָ / עַמֶּיךָ and עַמֶּיהָ / אֲדֹנֶיהָ always with singular meaning) sometimes extends in the case of אָדוֹן to the non-suffixed plural form אֲדֹנִים / אֲדוֹנִים (1 Kgs 22:17 [=2 Chr 18:16], Isa 19:4, and Mal 1:6 with singular meaning; Deut 10:17, Isa 26:13, and Ps 136:3 with plural meaning). All cases of עַמִּים have only plural force. Prof. D. Sivan has kindly reminded me of the opposite case in Isa 9:1 where the singular form עַם has plural force: הָעָם הַהֹלְכִים בַּחֹשֶׁךְ רָאוּ אוֹר גָּדוֹל "The people who were walking in darkness have seen a brilliant light."

50. Cf. n. 41 above.

51. See n. 42 above.

6a) All 28 Occurrences of BH עַמָּיו / עַמֶּיהָ / עַמֶּיךָ. Generally Understood as Plural Forms and Translated "his / her / your kinsmen" (Although עַם in Singular Never Means "kinsman, relative"!):[52]

I understand twenty-seven of these twenty-eight occurrences in the singular according to the regular meaning of עַם "people" (i.e., "his / her / your people") and according to the same phonological analysis discussed above regarding the form עמו in YI: line 16 (and via analogy with respect to the other two forms).[53]

---

52. The major BH dictionaries all deal with this alleged second meaning of עַם "relative, kinsman" in one of two ways: a) as the primary meaning and usage of the regular term עַם "people"—A. R. Hulst, "עם / גוי," TLOT, 896–919; HALOT, 837; b) as a homonym II עַם—BDB, 769; DBH, 805 (Hebrew); DCH 6:448. It is here maintained that there is not a single occurrence of the term עַם "people" in BH which *semantically* requires assuming either an additional meaning "relative, kinsman" or a homonym with that meaning. The main problem which led to these assumptions was *not* semantic, but rather grammatical. Because of the misunderstanding of the aforementioned 27/28 occurrences as *plural forms* (see section 6a above), it was incorrectly concluded that the regular meaning of עַם "people, nation" was impossible in these contexts. Abundant semantic evidence has been provided in the present study below which demonstrates through precise textual precedents exactly how semantically appropriate the *regular singular usage* of the term עַם is in each of these contexts. It is especially telling that there is not one case of the BH term עַם in the regular singular form in which contextual semantic evidence demonstrates that the regular usage is inappropriate (as already correctly noted in BDB, 769 and DBH, 805; proper names such as בֶּן־עַמִּי [Gen 19:38] are of course devoid of contextual semantic evidence). Such regular singular contexts as 2 Kgs 4:13; Jer 37:12; Job 18:19; Ruth 1:10, 16 [all cited in HALOT, 837 with the additional meaning "(paternal) relationship, clan, kin"] are all easily understood in accordance with the regular meaning "people, nation" as convincingly translated, e.g., in the NJPS translation. Finally, note that the main etymological evidence for this additional usage is Arabic ʿamm meaning specifically "father's brother, paternal uncle," a meaning which has *never* been specifically suggested for any occurrence of BH עַם. It is, however, also used more generally in the widest sense to denote any "paternal agnate." See E. Lipínski, "עַם," TDOT 11 (2001): 169.

53. I know of only one previous attempt by Prof. A. Sperber to analyze at least some of these 27/28 occurrences as singular forms. This pioneering attempt (although not in agreement with the phonological reconstruction accepted in the present study—see the beginning of section 6 and n. 39 above) deserves to be quoted in full: "The evidence listed in the preceding paragraphs 220–222 may serve as additional proof for the correctness of my statement in the prefatory note to chapter 'F. Nominal and Verbal Suffixes' in HPT [= A. Sperber, "Hebrew Based upon Biblical Passages in Parallel Transmission," HUCA 14 (1939)—C. C.], p. 210: 'The pronominal suffixes to the noun in the singular and the plural are the same. י is merely a helping vowel and does not indicate the number of the noun.' Perhaps the most frequently recurring phenomenon of this kind in MT is עַם with suffixes in phrases like (ויאסף אל עַמָּיו) Gen 49:33. Such forms were hitherto erroneously taken for plural-forms; and this error led to further misconceptions, as, e.g., the emendation of R. Kittel to Gen 49:29: עַמִּי (אני נאסף אל), which he 'corrects' into עַמִּי with reference to v. 33 עַמָּיו (which he mistook to be a plural)." See A. Sperber, *A Grammar of Masoretic Hebrew* (Copenhagen: Ejnar Munksgaard, 1959), 185. I hereby thank my former student, Dr.

All the contextual evidence for the analysis of these twenty-seven attestations is presented below in sections 6b–6f. The twenty-eighth occurrence is discussed separately in section 6g.

6b) First Context

The Divine Punishment of כָּרֵת "Cutting-Off (=Extirpation of Descendants)"—12 Occurrences.[54] This punishment is best understood through the parallelism in Ps. 109:13:

יְהִי אַחֲרִיתוֹ לְהַכְרִית // בְּדוֹר אַחֵר יִמַּח שְׁמָם:

"May his posterity be cut off; // May their names be blotted out in the next generation."

1. Exod 30:33, 38; Lev 17:9 (=3 occs.)—ונכרת (האיש ההוא) מֵעַמָּיו
2. Gen 17:14; Lev 7:20, 21, 27; 19:8; 23:29; Num 9:13 (=7 occs.)—ונכרתה (הנפש ההיא) מֵעַמֶּיהָ
3. Exod 31:14 (=1 occ.)—ונכרתה הנפש ההיא מקרב עַמֶּיהָ
4. Lev 7:25 (=1 occ.)—ונכרתה הנפש האכלת מֵעַמֶּיהָ

Compare on the one hand the same context with regular singular forms—10 occurrences:

5. Lev 17:4 (=1 occ.)—ונכרת האיש ההוא מקרב עַמּוֹ
6. Lev 20:3,6 (=2 occs.)—והכרתי אתו מקרב עַמּוֹ
7. Num 15:30 (=1 occ.)—ונכרתה הנפש ההיא מקרב עַמָּהּ
8. Lev 17:10 (=1 occ.)—והכרתי אתה מקרב עַמָּהּ
9. Lev 18:29 (=1 occ.)—ונכרתו הנפשות העשת מקרב עַמָּם
10. Lev 20:5 (=1 occ.)—והכרתי אתו וְאֵת כל הזנים אחריו ... מקרב עַמָּם
11. Lev 20:17 (=1 occ.)—ונכרתו לעיני בני עַמָּם
12. Lev 20:18 (=1 occ.)—ונכרתו שניהם מקרב עַמָּם
13. Ezek 14:8 (=1 occ.)—והכרתיו מתוך עַמִּי וידעתם כי אני ה'

Alexey (Eliyahu) Yuditsky, for kindly calling my attention to this interesting suggestion. On Gen 49:29, see also n. 57 below.

54. On this Divine punishment and the evidence from parallelism in Ps 109:13, see especially J. Milgrom, *Leviticus 1–16* (AB; New York: Doubleday, 1991), 457–60.

Are these precise parallels not clear evidence that it is the regular meaning of עַם, the entire people of Israel, which is the correct meaning of this term in all the above 12 occurrences of this idiom, and *not* the individual's relatives?

Compare also the one case of a bonafide plural form, but in a different context:

14. Ezek 25:7 (=1 occ.) –

לָכֵן הִנְנִי נָטִיתִי אֶת-יָדִי עָלֶיךָ וּנְתַתִּיךָ לְבַז (=קרי) לַגּוֹיִם וְהִכְרַתִּיךָ מִן הָעַמִּים וְהַאֲבַדְתִּיךָ מִן הָאֲרָצוֹת אַשְׁמִידְךָ וְיָדַעְתָּ כִּי אֲנִי ה':

"Assuredly, I will stretch out My hand against you and give you as booty to the nations; *I will cut you off from among the peoples*[55] and wipe you out from among the countries and destroy you. And you shall now that I am the Lord."

Compare on the other hand in semantically parallel contexts—4 occurrences:[56]

15. Exod 12:15; Num 19:13 (=2 occs.)—ונכרתה הנפש ההיא מישראל
16. Exod 12:19 (=1 occ.)—ונכרתה הנפש ההיא מעדת ישראל בגר ובאזרח הארץ
17. Num 19:20 (=1 occ.)—ונכרתה הנפש ההיא מתוך הקהל

6c) Second Context

Idiom for the Death of Israel's Forefathers and Heroes Emphasizing Both Their Own Connection and the Connection of Their Descendants to the People (and Their Ancestors) [= the Opposite of כָּרֵת]—9 Occurrences:

1. Gen 25:8, 17; 35:29; 49:33 (= 4 occs.)— וַיִּגְוַע ... (וַיָּמָת) ... וַיֵּאָסֶף אֶל עַמָּיו
   [Referring to the deaths of Abraham, Ishmael, Isaac, and Jacob]
2. Num 20:24 (=1 occ.—Aaron)—יֵאָסֵף אַהֲרֹן אֶל עַמָּיו
3. Num 27:13 (=1 occ.—Moses)—וְנֶאֱסַפְתָּ אֶל עַמֶּיךָ גַּם אָתָּה כַּאֲשֶׁר נֶאֱסַף אַהֲרֹן אָחִיךָ:
4. Num 31:2 (=1 occ.—Moses)— אַחַר תֵּאָסֵף אֶל עַמֶּיךָ:
5. Deut 32:50 (=2 occ.—Moses and Aaron)—
   וּמֻת ... וְהֵאָסֵף אֶל עַמֶּיךָ כַּאֲשֶׁר מֵת אַהֲרֹן אָחִיךָ ... וַיֵּאָסֶף אֶל עַמָּיו:

---

55. Note that in this context הָעַמִּים refers to "all the peoples on earth." On this entire verse, see M. Greenberg, *Ezekiel 21–37* (AB; New York: Doubleday, 1997), 519–20.

56. Contrast the treatment of this same evidence in, e.g., J. Joosten, *People and Land in the Holiness Code* (VTSup; Leiden: Brill, 1996), 79–82.

Compare especially in the regular singular form—1 occurrence:

6. Gen 49:29 (=1 occ.—Jacob)—
    וַיְצַו אוֹתָם וַיֹּאמֶר אֲלֵהֶם אֲנִי נֶאֱסָף אֶל עַמִּי[57] קִבְרוּ אֹתִי אֶל אֲבֹתָי
    אֶל הַמְּעָרָה אֲשֶׁר בִּשְׂדֵה עֶפְרוֹן הַחִתִּי:

    "Then he instructed them, saying to them, '*I am about to be gathered to my people*. Bury me with my ancestors in the cave which is in the field of Ephron the Hittite.'"

6d) Third Context—Laws Concerning the Priests (Lev 21)—4 Occurrences.

Attention should be paid especially to the parallels between the laws concerning the regular priests and the laws concerning the high priest.

1. Lev 21:1–3 (=1 occ.)—
    וַיֹּאמֶר ה' אֶל מֹשֶׁה אֱמֹר אֶל הַכֹּהֲנִים בְּנֵי אַהֲרֹן וְאָמַרְתָּ אֲלֵהֶם לְנֶפֶשׁ לֹא יִטַּמָּא בְּעַמָּיו:
    כִּי אִם לִשְׁאֵרוֹ הַקָּרֹב אֵלָיו לְאִמּוֹ וּלְאָבִיו וְלִבְנוֹ וּלְבִתּוֹ וּלְאָחִיו:
    וְלַאֲחֹתוֹ הַבְּתוּלָה הַקְּרוֹבָה אֵלָיו אֲשֶׁר לֹא הָיְתָה לְאִישׁ לָהּ יִטַּמָּא:

    "The Lord said to Moses: Speak to the priests, the sons of Aaron, and say to them: None shall defile himself for any (dead) person among his people, except for his relatives who are closest to him: his mother, his father, his son, his daughter, and his brother; also for a virgin sister, close to him because she hasn't married, for her he may defile himself."

It is clear that the term בְּעַמָּיו in verse 1 can not refer to the priest's relatives because the relatives are first referred to in verses 2–3 in the phrase כִּי אִם לִשְׁאֵרוֹ "except for his relatives," the purpose of which is *to limit the exceptions only to those relatives*. Therefore, once again בְּעַמָּיו must simply be taken as a singular form meaning "his people" (i.e., all of Israel) as was understood by virtually all the ancient translations, the Samaritan Tora, the Jewish Halakha, and virtually all the Jewish medieval commentators. In verse 11, there is a similar law regarding the high priest: וְעַל כָּל־נַפְשֹׁת מֵת לֹא יָבֹא לְאָבִיו וּלְאִמּוֹ לֹא יִטַּמָּא "He shall not enter where there is any dead body; he shall not defile himself (even) for his father

---

57. Compare especially Gen 49:33 (see #1 above). In order to resolve the apparent contradiction, the vocalization here should *not* be changed from עַמִּי to עָמָי* (contra *BHS*, p. 84, n. 29a), but rather the form עַמָּיו in verse 33 should be understood (as in all the verses under discussion) as reflecting the singular form עַמּוֹ in accordance with the above phonological explanation. See also n. 53 above.

and his mother." Clearly, the purpose of בְּעַמָּיו ... לְנֶפֶשׁ "for any (dead) person among his people" in verse 1 must be the same as that of the phrase וְעַל כָּל־ נַפְשֹׁת מֵת "where there is any dead body," namely to state the general prohibition for the priest to be in contact with any dead body among his people. Thus the only difference between the two laws is the granting of the exceptions for the closest relatives as regards the regular priests, while these exceptions do not apply for the high priest.[58]

2. Lev 21:4 (=1 occ.)—

לֹא יִטַּמָּא בַּעַל בְּעַמָּיו לְהֵחַלּוֹ:

This verse is a well-known crux, which is still incomprehensible. Perhaps compare the discussion immediately below concerning verse 15 (ולא יחלל זרעו בעמיו). If the singular meaning "his people" is accepted there for the term בְּעַמָּיו, then it is logical to assume that meaning in this verse as well.[59]

3. Lev 21:13–15 (=2 occ.)—

וְהוּא אִשָּׁה בִבְתוּלֶיהָ יִקָּח: אַלְמָנָה וּגְרוּשָׁה וַחֲלָלָה זֹנָה אֶת־אֵלֶּה לֹא יִקָּח כִּי אִם בְּתוּלָה מֵעַמָּיו יִקַּח אִשָּׁה: וְלֹא יְחַלֵּל זַרְעוֹ בְּעַמָּיו כִּי אֲנִי ה' מְקַדְּשׁוֹ:

"He may marry only a woman who is a virgin. A widow or a divorced woman, or one who is degraded by harlotry—such he may not marry, but only a virgin from among his own people may he take to wife. And thus he will not profane his offspring among his own people, for I the Lord have sanctified him."

This law concerns the high priest. The parallel law for the regular priests is in verse 7:

---

58. Here it should be noted that the usual modern interpretation of Lev 21:1–3 (e.g., J. Milgrom, *Leviticus 17–22* [AB; New York: Doubleday, 2000], 1791, 1798–99) according to the incorrect understanding that עַמָּיו means "his relatives, his kin" leads to the absurd conclusion that the regular priest may not have contact with the corpses of his regular, more distant relatives, but may have contact with the corpses of his closest relatives and *the corpses of all in Israel who were not his relatives.*

59. The most interesting suggestion for understanding this verse was that of M. Paran, *Forms of the Priestly Style in the Pentateuch* (Jerusalem: Magnes, 1989), 216–17 (Hebrew). Paran suggested to delete the word בעל (as a result of partial dittography with the following word בְּעַמָּיו) and then to look upon verses 1–4 as an *inclusio* which opens with verse 1 (לנפש לא יטמא בעמיו) and closes with the emended verse 4 (לא יטמא בעמיו להחלו). This makes good stylistic sense, but is difficult because of the emendation.

אִשָּׁה זֹנָה וַחֲלָלָה לֹא יִקָּחוּ וְאִשָּׁה גְּרוּשָׁה מֵאִישָׁהּ לֹא יִקָּחוּ כִּי קָדֹשׁ הוּא לֵאלֹהָיו:

"They shall not marry a woman defiled by harlotry, nor shall they marry one divorced from her husband, for they are holy to their God."

The only difference between the two laws would appear to be the prohibition for the high priest to marry a widow, while this is not prohibited for the regular priests. This difference is further emphasized by the positive commandment (only for the high priest): "He may marry only a woman who is a virgin." There is no further limitation on whom the high priest may marry. Yet this same limitation is found twice more in this law, once positively—"but only a virgin from among his own people (בְּתוּלָה מֵעַמָּיו) may he take to wife"; and once negatively—וְלֹא יְחַלֵּל זַרְעוֹ בְּעַמָּיו "And thus he will not profane his offspring among his own people." In both cases, the term עַמָּיו is present. If עַמָּיו is translated here "his relatives," this would substantially change the meaning of this law. Such an interpretation is extremely unlikely for the following two reasons: a) The parallel law for the regular priests (which differs from the present law only with respect to the widow) does not include the term עַמָּיו. b) The selective paraphrase of this law in Ezek 44:22 (albeit with respect to the regular priest rather than the high priest) reads instead of the phrase כִּי אִם בְּתוּלָה מֵעַמָּיו the parallel phrase כִּי אִם בְּתוּלֹת מִזֶּרַע בֵּית יִשְׂרָאֵל "but only virgins of the stock of the House of Israel." For these two reasons, it seems much more likely to interpret עַמָּיו as a singular form meaning "his own people" in this context as well.

6e) *Fourth Context—Lev 19:16—1 Occurrence*

לֹא תֵלֵךְ רָכִיל בְּעַמֶּיךָ לֹא תַעֲמֹד עַל דַּם רֵעֶךָ אֲנִי ה':

"Do not act as a slanderer / gossiper among your own people. Do not profit by (?) the blood of your fellow. I am the Lord."

This verse is also not completely clear especially because of the usage of the phrase תֵלֵךְ רָכִיל (but cf. the clearer contexts and parallelism in Jer 6:28; 9:3; Prov 11:13; 20:19;—the first two favor "slanderer," the latter two favor "gossiper"). Whether "slanderer" or "gossiper," it is difficult to understand why this law would be limited to infractions against "relatives." In the wider context, the pair of terms עַמֶּיךָ—רֵעֶךָ "your own people—your fellow" is replaced in verse 18 by the similar pair בְּנֵי עַמֶּךָ—רֵעֶךָ "your countrymen—your fellow." In the paraphrase of Ezek 22:9, instead of בְּעַמֶּיךָ "among your own people," the text simply reads בָּךְ "among you": ... אַנְשֵׁי רָכִיל הָיוּ בָךְ "Slanderers / gossipers were among you ...."

6f) Fifth Context—Ezek 18:18—1 Occurrence

אָבִיו כִּי עָשַׁק עֹשֶׁק גָּזַל גֵּזֶל אָח וַאֲשֶׁר לֹא טוֹב עָשָׂה בְּתוֹךְ עַמָּיו וְהִנֵּה מֵת בַּעֲוֹנוֹ׃

"His father (to be sure), because he practiced fraud, robbed his brother, and acted wickedly among his own people, did die for his iniquity."

While within this specific verse, the victim could actually be a relative (אָח), the wider context specifies the crimes involved in the context of the doctrine of personal retribution, and these specified crimes are surely not limited to crimes committed against relatives (cf. vv. 5–9, 11–13, 15–17, 20). Therefore, interpreting עַמָּיו here as a singular form meaning "his own people" surely best fits this context as well.[60]

6g) Sixth Context—Hos 10:14—The 28th Occurrence

וְקָאם שָׁאוֹן בְּעַמֶּיךָ / בְּעַמֶּךָ ...

"But the din of war shall arise against your own people ..."

Here the interpretation "relatives, kin" is absolutely impossible.[61] The reading with or without *yod* in this verse, however, does not reflect any grammatical distinction, but is rather a matter of controversy between the major sources of the Masoretic Text and simply reflects a Masoretic variant. From the following sources, we also learn in general how the two forms עַמֶּיךָ and בְּעַמֶּיךָ (both with *yod*) were treated by the Masoretes—namely *not* as plural forms, but as (singular) *plene* (כתיב מלא) writing. The first source is the Leningrad codex itself[62] in which the word in question in Hos 10:14 is written "בְּעַמֶּ ךָ" with a space indicating that a letter (presumably the *yod*) has been erased in between the letters *mem* and final *kaph*.[63] The reading with *yod* is according to מקראות גדולות and its Masora Magna and

---

60. On this verse, see especially M. Greenberg, *Ezekiel 1–20* (AB; New York: Doubleday, 1983), 332.

61. Neither does the meaning "against / amongst your tribes" make any sense in this context. For this meaning, see already the commentary of R. David Qimchi (Radaq) to Hos 10:14 and more recently its correct rejection in A. A. Macintosh, *Hosea* (ICC; Edinburgh: T&T Clark, 1997), 428, 430.

62. See D. N. Freedman, ed., *The Leningrad Codex: A Facsimile Edition* (Grand Rapids: Eerdmans; Leiden: Brill, 1998), 624 (Folio 306 verso).

63. See M. Breuer, "The Version of the Text and Its Sources," in *The Twelve Minor Prophets—Part One* (Daʿat Miqraʾ; Jerusalem: Mossad Harav Kook, 1971), xv, n. 10 (Hebrew).

also Ms. Sassoon 1053 and its Masora Parva.[64] The reading without *yod* is according to the Aleppo Codex, and the corrected Leningrad Codex.[65] The second source is the Masora Parva of the Leningrad Codex to the word בַּעֲמֶיךָ in Lev 19:16: 'ל מל' "(occurring) nowhere else (in BH) as *plene* writing."[66] This of course is in agreement with the aforementioned *corrected* Leningrad Codex (without the *yod* in Hos 10:14). The third source is the Masora Magna and Masora Parva of the Leningrad Codex to the word עַמֶיךָ in Num 27:13, 31:2, and Deut 32:50: 'מל ג' בתור' "(occurring) 3x as *plene* writing in the Tora" (with the Masora Magna in each case listing the three verses—Num 27:13; 31:2; Deut 32:50).[67] These sources clearly imply that the Masoretes understood the two forms בַּעֲמֶיךָ / עַמֶיךָ *not* as plural forms meaning "against / among your relatives" or the like, but rather as a variant (singular) form meaning "against your (own) people" with additional *yod* (*plene* writing). Thus it may be assumed that this *yod* was copied by the Masoretes in the 27/28 aforementioned cases as a variant *plene* writing *not* as an indication of a plural form, but rather in order to preserve the oral reading tradition which, just in these cases, happened to include a final consonantal *waw*.

§IVA. Conclusion

As opposed to the philological summary concluding my first paper regarding the YI,[68] I will end the present article with a brief discussion of two additional issues having to do with proper method and my agreement with a previously suggested possible solution to the paleographical anomalies of the YI.

One of the most common contentions against the historicity of the YI is that "it is too good to be true."[69] Now in order for the YI to be authentic, 2 Kgs 12 would have to be historically accurate as well. There is one major element in 2 Kgs 12 which does not appear in the YI, namely the occurrence twice of an אָרוֹן "collection box" (2 Kgs 12:10, 11; cf. 2 Chr 24:8, 10, 11[2×]). Of the 201 BH attes-

---

64. See ibid., XV and n. 11.
65. See ibid., XV and n. 9.
66. The Masora Parva to Lev 19:16 is quoted from *BHS*, 190.
67. The Masora Parva to Num 27:13, 31:2, and Deut 32:50 is quoted from *BHS*, 265, 270, 349. For the corresponding Masora Magna, see G. E. Weil, *Massorah Gedolah*, vol. 1 (Rome: Pontificium Istitutum Biblicum, 1971), 124 (list #1010).
68. Cohen, "Yeho'ash," 268–70.
69. See the discussion of this principle, e.g., in H. Shanks, ed., *Jerusalem Forgery Conference* (Washington, D.C.: Biblical Archaeology Society, 2007), ch. 1: 7–8 (H. Shanks); ch. 2: 36 (A. Millard); ch. 2: 80 (G. Barkay).

tations of this term, this usage and meaning occurs nowhere else.[70] When we turn to Akk. documents, however, especially from the Neo-Babylonian period, we find numerous parallels for such usage of both *arānu*[71] and its synonym *quppu*,[72] both used in the meaning "collection box" set up at the various temple gates where silver donated to the temple was deposited and eventually melted down and utilized in different ways including for the purposes of renovation and reconstruction.[73] Note particularly the following NB text referring to the Ebabbar Temple at Sippar:[74] 3 GÍN *kaspu ultu quppu ša Gula ana Ebabbar ana dullu ša ziqqurratu* "3 sheqels of silver from the collection box of (the temple of) Gula (to be used) for Ebabbar for the purpose of (construction) work on the temple tower." Thus, like all the aforementioned textual parallels to elements in the YI, the one major unique element in 2 Kgs 12 not occurring in the YI likewise finds its precise parallel in ancient Near Eastern literature. Is this also "too good to be true"?

Finally, while the present study does not deal with problems of paleography, it is here accepted that such problems do exist with regard to the YI and the determination of its possible authenticity. One suggestion, made originally

---

70. Note that besides the regular usage and meaning of this term as "the Ark of the Lord," there is one other rare usage and meaning of ארון, namely "coffin, sarcophagus" which occurs only in Gen 50:26. The Akk. interdialectal equivalent term *arānu* (on this term see further below) also occurs but once in this meaning. Among the ancient Semitic languages of the First Temple period, only in Phoenician does the term ארן occur regularly with the meaning "coffin, sarcophagus." On this usage, see D. Marcus, "The Term 'Coffin' in the Semitic Languages," *JANES* 7 (1975): 85–94; C. Cohen and M. Weinfeld, "וישם בארון במצרים," *'Olam Ha-tanakh: Genesis* (Ramat-Gan: Bar-Ilan University Press, 1982), 255 (Hebrew). For the latest edition of the Akk. text including the sole occurrence of *arānu* meaning "coffin," see now T. Kwasman, "A Neo-Assyrian Royal Funerary Text," in *Of God(s), Trees, Kings, and Scholars* (ed. M. Luukko et al.; Helsinki: Finnish Oriental Society, 2009), 111–25.

71. See CAD A/2, 231, meaning c.

72. See CAD Q, 308–10, meaning 3b. Cf. RH קוּפָּה / קֻפָּה "basket, large vessel; the communal fund for dispensing sustenance to the poor every Friday." See, e.g., M. Jastrow, *A Dictionary of the Targumim, the Talmud Babli and Yerushalmi, and the Midrashic Lierature* (New York: Pardes, 1950), 1338.

73. See the classic study by A. L. Oppenheim, "A Fiscal Practice of the Ancient Near East," *JNES* 6 (1947): 116–20 (with reference to BH ארון on pp. 117–18, n. 6). This study is now updated considerably in A. C. V. M. Bongenaar, *The Neo-Babylonian Ebabbar Temple at Sippar: Its Administration and Its Prosopography* (Istanbul: Nederlands Historisch—Archaeologisch Instituut te Istanbul, 1997), 104–12. See also most recently O. Lipschits, "On Cash-Boxes and Finding or Not Finding Books: Jehoash's and Josiah's Decisions to Repair the Temple," in *Essays on Ancient Israel in Its Near Eastern Context – A Tribute to Nadav Na'aman* (ed. Y. Amit et al.; Winona Lake, Ind.: Eisenbrauns, 2006), 243–49 and the additional bibliography cited there.

74. See CAD Q, 308, meaning 3b. Cf. Bongenaar, *Ebabbar Temple at Sippar*, 390.

by Dr. Victor Sasson, could potentially solve these problems and should be seriously considered especially by those (like the present author) who are convinced that all the philological problems are indeed open to reasonable resolution. In 2003, Sasson suggested as follows:[75] "The sandstone inscription needs [sic] not be the first and original record. If the *stone* itself cannot be dated to late-ninth century B.C.E., then it could be a copy of an original inscription." Elsewhere, in the same article, this suggestion was phrased slightly differently:[76] "… the *text* of this inscription could be an *ancient* copy of an original one—and hence the so-called 'mixed' script forms—…." Such a possibility has also been theoretically postulated in print by both Prof. A. R. Millard[77] and Prof. A. Lemaire[78] and was very positively considered during the public discussion following the presentation of the preliminary version of this study.[79] It will once again be mentioned in the new edition of the YI being currently prepared by the present author together with the two geologists, Dr. Shim'on Ilani and Dr. Amnon Rosenfeld.[80]

Bibliography[81]

Aḥituv, S. *Echoes from the Past: Hebrew and Cognate Inscriptions from the Biblical Period*. Jerusalem: Carta, 2008.
Andersen, F. I. *Habakkuk*. Anchor Bible. New York: Doubleday, 2001.
Avishur, Y. "Habakkuk." Pages 87–115 in *'Olam Ha-Tanakh: The Twelve Minor Prophets*. Part Two. Edited by Z. Weissman. Tel-Aviv: Davidson-Attai, 1994 (in Hebrew).
Berlin, A. *Zephaniah*. Anchor Bible. New York: Doubleday, 1994.
Beuken, W. A. M. *Isaiah II*. Vol. 2. Historical Commentary on the Old Testament. Leuven: Peeters, 2000.
Bongenaar, A. C. V. M. *The Neo-Babylonian Ebabbar Temple at Sippar: Its Administration and Its Prosopography*. Istanbul: Nederlands Historisch—Archaeologisch Instituut te Istanbul, 1997.
Bordreuil, P. "Une inscription Phénicienne champlevée des environs de Byblos." *Sem* 27 (1977): 23–27.
Bordreuil, P., F. Israel, and D. Pardee. "Deux ostraca paléo-hébreux de la Collection Sh. Moussaïeff." *Sem* 46 (1996): 49–76.
Breuer, M. "The Version of the Text and Its Sources." Pages xii–xvii in *The Twelve Minor*

---

75. Sasson, "King Jehoash Inscription," 584.
76. Ibid., 576.
77. See Shanks, ed., *Jerusalem Forgery Conference*, ch. 2, 34 (possible explanation #4).
78. Ibid., Chapter 2, 27 (possible answer #2).
79. See n. 2 above.
80. See Cohen, "Yeho'ash," 222, preliminary note.
81. Excluding primary Akkadian and Ugaritic sources, for which see respectively CAD U/W, vii–xxix; del Olmo Lete and Sanmartín, *A Dictionary of the Ugaritic Language*, xxi–xliv.

Prophets—Part One. Daʿat Miqraʾ. Jerusalem: Mossad Harav Kook, 1971 (Hebrew).
Cogan, M., and H. Tadmor. *II Kings*. Anchor Bible. New York: Doubleday, 1988.
Cohen, C. (H. R.). *Biblical Hapax Legomena in the Light of Akkadian and Ugaritic*. SBLDS. Missoula, Mont.: Society of Biblical Literature, 1978.
———. "Once Again: The Two Meanings of the Parallel Terms אמה / שפחה in Biblical Hebrew." Pages 239–57 in קול ליעקב—*The Yaakov Bentolila Jubilee Volume*. Edited by D. Sivan et al. Beer-Sheva: Ben-Gurion University Press, 2003.
———. "Biblical Hebrew Philology in the Light of Research on the New Yehoʾash Royal Building Inscription." Pages 222–84 in *New Seals and Inscriptions*. Edited by M. Lubetski. Sheffield: Sheffield Phoenix, 2007.
———. "New Directions in Modern Biblical Hebrew Lexicography." Pages 441–73 in *Birkat Shalom: Studies in the Bible, Ancient Near Eastern Literature and Postbiblical Judaism Presented to Shalom M. Paul*. Edited by C. Cohen et al. Winona Lake, Ind.: Eisenbrauns, 2008.
Cohen, C. (H. R.), and M. Weinfeld. "וייׄשם בארון במצרים." Page 255 in ʿ*Olam Ha-tanakh - Genesis*. Ramat-Gan: Revivim, 1982 (Hebrew).
Cross, F. M. "Notes on the Forged Plaque Recording Repairs to the Temple." *IEJ* 53 (2003): 119–22.
von Dassow, E. "Introducing the Witnesses in Neo-Babylonian Documents." Pages 3–22 in *Ki Baruch Hu: Ancient Near Eastern, Biblical, and Judaic Studies in Honor of Baruch A. Levine*. Edited by R. Chazan et al. Winona Lake, Ind.: Eisenbrauns, 1999.
Ephʾal, I. "The 'Jehoash Inscription': A Forgery." *IEJ* 53 (2003): 124–28.
Ephʾal, I., and J. Naveh. "Remarks on the Recently Published Moussaieff Ostraca." *IEJ* 48 (1998): 269–73.
Fales, F. M. "Le double bilinguisme de la statue de Tell Fekherye." *Syria* 60 (1983): 233–50.
Freedman, D. N., ed. *The Leningrad Codex: A Facsimile Edition*. Grand Rapids: Eerdmans. Leiden: Brill, 1998.
———. "Don't Rush to Judgment: Jehoash Inscription May Be Authentic," *BAR* 30/2 (2004): 48–51.
Gogel, S. *A Grammar of Epigraphic Hebrew*. Atlanta: Scholars Press, 1998.
Greenberg, M. *Ezekiel 1–20*. AB. New York: Doubleday, 1983.
———. *Ezekiel 21–37*. AB. New York: Doubleday, 1997.
Greenfield, J. C., and A. Shaffer. "Notes on the Akkadian-Aramaic Bilingual Statue from Tell Fekherye." *Iraq* 45 (1983): 109–16.
Greenstein, E. L. "Hebrew Philology Spells Fake." *BAR* 29/3 (May/June 2003): 28–30.
Hackett, J. A. *The Balaam Text from Deir ʿAlla*. HSM. Chico: Scholars Press, 1980.
Hurowitz, V. A. "The Jehoash Inscription." Pages 1–12. Cited 19 August 2003. Online: http://www.bibleinterp.com/articles/Report9.htm.
———. "The Jehoash Inscription under a Magnifying Glass." *Bet Miqra* 176 (2004): 89–102 (Hebrew).
Irwin, W. H. *Isaiah 28–33: Translation with Philological Notes*. Rome: Biblical Institute, 1977.
Jastrow, M. *A Dictionary of the Targumim, the Talmud Babli and Yerushalmi, and the Midrashic Lierature*. New York: Pardes, 1950.
Joosten, J. *People and Land in the Holiness Code*. VTSup. Leiden: Brill, 1996.
Joüon, P., and T. Muraoka. *A Grammar of Biblical Hebrew*. 2nd ed. Rome: Biblical Institute, 2006.

Kaddari, M. Z. *A Dictionary of Biblical Hebrew*. Ramat-Gan: Bar-Ilan University Press, 2006.
Krahmalkov, C. *A Phoenician–Punic Grammar*. Leiden: Brill, 2001.
———. *Phoenician–Punic Dictionary*. Leuven: Peeters, 2000.
Kwasman, T. "A Neo-Assyrian Royal Funerary Text." Pages 111–25 in *Of God(s), Trees, Kings, and Scholars*. Edited by M. Luukko et al. Helsinki: Finnish Oriental Society, 2009.
Lambert, W. G. *Babylonian Oracle Questions*. Mesopotamian Civilization Series. Winona Lake, Ind.: Eisenbrauns, 2007.
Lipschits, O. "On Cash-Boxes and Finding or Not Finding Books: Jehoash's and Josiah's Decisions to Repair the Temple." Pages 243–49 in *Essays on Ancient Israel in Its Near Eastern Context – A Tribute to Nadav Na'aman*. Edited by Y. Amit et al. Winona Lake, Ind.: Eisenbrauns, 2006.
Macintosh, A. A. *Hosea*. ICC. Edinburgh: T&T Clark, 1997.
Marcus, D. "The Term 'Coffin' in the Semitic Languages." *JANES* 7 (1975): 85–94.
Mettinger, T. N. D. "Amarna Letter No. 84: Damu, Adonis, and 'The Living God' at Byblos." Pages 361–71 in *Sefer Moshe: The Moshe Weinfeld Jubilee Volume*. Edited by C. Cohen et al. Winona Lake: Eisenbrauns, 2004.
Milgrom, J. *Leviticus 1–16*. AB. New York: Doubleday, 1991.
———. *Leviticus 17–22*. AB. New York: Doubleday, 2000.
Morgenstern, M. "Secondary Editing in Jewish Aramaic Texts and the Creation of a Mixed Literary Aramaic." In *Late Aramaic: The Literary and Linguistic Context of the Zohar*. Edited by A. Rapoport Albert. Studies in Judaica. Leiden: Brill (forthcoming).
del Olmo Lete, G., and J. Sanmartín. *A Dictionary of the Ugaritic Language in the Alphabetic Tradition*. Leiden: Brill, 2003.
Oppenheim, A. L. "A Fiscal Practice of the Ancient Near East." *JNES* 6 (1947): 116–20.
Paran, M. *Forms of the Priestly Style in the Pentateuch*. Jerusalem: Magnes, 1989 (Hebrew).
Rabinowitz, I. *A Witness Forever*. Bethesda: CDL, 1993.
Rendsburg, G. A., and W. M. Schniedewind. "The Siloam Tunnel Inscription: Historical and Linguistic Perspectives." *IEJ* 60 (2010): 188–203.
Roberts, J. J. M. *Nahum, Habakkuk, and Zephaniah*. OTL. Louisville, Ky.: Westminster John Knox, 1991.
Sasson, V. "Philological and Textual Observations on the Controversial King Jehoash Inscription." *UF* 35 (2003): 573–87.
Shanks, H. ed. *Jerusalem Forgery Conference*. Washington, D.C.: Biblical Archaeology Society, 2007.
Simian-Yofre, H. "ʿwd; ʿēd; ʿēdût; teʿûda." *TDOT* 10 (1999): 495–515.
Sivan, D. *A Grammar of the Ugaritic Language*. Leiden: Brill, 2001.
Sokoloff, M. *A Dictionary of Jewish Babylonian Aramaic*. Ramat-Gan: Bar-Ilan University Press, 2002.
Sperber, A. "Hebrew Based upon Biblical Passages in Parallel Transmission." *HUCA* 14 (1939): 153–249.
———. *A Grammar of Masoretic Hebrew*. Copenhagen: Ejnar Munksgaard, 1959.
Talshir, D. "אֲחֹות and עֵדוֹת in Ancient Hebrew." *ZAH* 15–16 (2002–2003): 108–23.
———. "The Jehoash Inscription: A Philological Angle." *Leshonenu La`am* 54 (2004): 3–10 (Hebrew).

Tawil, H. "Hebrew הצלח / צלח, Akkadian *ešēru* / *šūšuru*: A Lexicographical Note." *JBL* 95 (1976): 405–13.
Vlaardingerbroek, J. *Zephaniah*. HCOT. Leuven: Peeters, 1999.
Volkwein, B. "Masoretisches ʿēdût, ʿēdwōt, ʿēdōt—'Zeugnis' oder 'Bundesbestimmungen'?" *BZ* 13 (1969): 18–40.
Weil, G. E. *Massorah Gedolah*. Vol. 1. Rome: Pontificium Istitutum Biblicum, 1971.
Wildberger, H. *Isaiah 28–39*. A Continental Commentary. Minneapolis: Fortress, 2002.
Yeivin, I. *The Biblical Masorah*. Jerusalem: Hebrew Language Academy, 2003 (Hebrew).

Chapter Seventeen
Dr. Shlomo Moussaieff's View of the Nerva Coin

Meir Lubetski*

> *Praeter ceteros Iudaicus fiscus acerbissime actus est*
> Besides other taxes, that on the Jews
> was levied with the utmost rigor.[1]

Was It Annulled during the Time of Nerva?

The epigraphical session at the International Meeting of the Society of Biblical Literature in Rome, 2009, culminated with a paper presented by Dr. Shlomo Moussaieff, who graciously provided the artifacts on which most of the papers were based. He discussed a coin from his collection that was struck by Marcus Cocceius Nerva, the Roman Emperor who ruled sixteen months from September 96–January 98 C.E. This coin apparently commemorates the change in attitude toward the *fiscus Iudaicus,* a special poll tax of two *dinarii* per annum required from Jews after the rebellion of 66–70 C.E. Jews all over the Empire had to pay it to the Temple of Jupiter Capitolinus in Rome as formerly they had paid it to the Temple in Jerusalem.[2]

Jewish sources make reference to the tax. Rabbi Yohanan ben Zakai (first century C.E.) chastises his people:

---

* Shlomo Moussaieff and I discussed the Nerva coin during our meeting in January 2010. The article reflects his additional thoughts. I wish to thank Aran Patinkin for providing the pictures of the coin and the original draft of Shlomo Moussaieff's paper.

1. Gaius Tranquillus Suetonius, *De vita Caesarum. Dom.* 12:2 (ed. and trans. J. C. Rolfe; LCL; Cambridg, Mass.: Harvard University Press, 1950).

2. Josephus, *War* 7.218.

Fig. 1 The Nerva coin, obverse and reverse. Courtesy of Dr. Shlomo Moussaieff.

You were unwilling to pay to Heaven (the Temple of God) a *beka* per one head, now you have to pay 15 shekels to the Kingdom of your enemies.[3]

This tax was levied in the most humiliating manner and under circumstances of peculiar severity especially during the time of Domitian, the last of the Flavian emperors.[4] Nerva, his successor, was strikingly different. Wise, humane, and just, the emperor, without delay, put an end to the abuse suffered by the Jews. He struck a coin to validate his ordinance.

The description of the coin is as follows: Obverse: head of Nerva to the right with his full face and coiffure laureate. The rim carries the legend:

IMP NERVA CAES AUG P M TR P COS III PP
Imperator Nerva Caesar Augustus Pontifex Maximus Tribunicia Potestas Consul III[5] Pater Patriae.

Reverse: a branched palm tree with fruits on both sides flanked by the letters S C. The inscription on the rim reads:

---

3. *Mekhilta d'Rabbi Ishmael* (ed. Horvitz-Rabin; Jerusalem: Bamberger & Wahrman, 1960), ba-hodesh, parasha 1 Exod 19:1. It should be noted that this same sage was the one who negotiated with Vespasian to save Yavneh and its sages; *b. Giṭ.* 56b. For a similar view about the shekel tax, although expressed by a later Amora, see *b. B. Bat.* 9a.

4. Suetonius, *Dom.* 12:2.

5. In the short period that Nerva reigned, the coin was minted at least three times. This is indicated by the Roman numerals, I, II, III on respective mintings.

FISCI IUDAICI CALVMNIA SVBLATA
The unjust charges [on account] of the *fiscus Iudaicus*[6] are removed [with the agreement of] *Senatus Consultum*.

The engraving of the palm tree generally was a symbol for Judaea on Roman coins.[7] In contrast to the coins issued by the Flavians who celebrated victories over the Jews,[8] the Nerva coin, in its more than one exemplar, must have been a most pleasant respite for the Jewish community. However, modern scholars do not agree as to whom the promulgation was directed. Some believe that Nerva's coin did not represent the rescinding of the tax for all. Rather, it was thought that it was directed to non-practicing Jews and non-Jewish god-fearing people drawn to the synagogue. Only such individuals were exempted from paying the Jews tax. Practicing Jews, however, had to continue to pay the *fiscus Iudaicus* if they wanted to strictly observe the Torah and its interpretation according to the rabbis.[9] If this is indeed so then Nerva's coin did not change the tax levied on the Jewish community and it remained the same as it was when Vespasian issued his original decree.

Shlomo Moussaieff rejects that assumption because of the following: Rabbinic literature discusses voyages of rabbis to Rome during the very same period of Domitian's demise and Nerva's rise to power. They had every intention of influencing a policy change. He suggests that the visiting rabbis voiced their opposition to the unjust accusations against the Jewish community and thus succeeded in convincing those in power to promulgate monetary relief specifically for those adhering to the commandments.[10] The Jewish "lobbying" should therefore be credited for shaping the positive outcome. It is clear that four Tannaim were in Rome at the time that Flavius Clemens was executed.[11] The Roman senator, who was also a former consul and a relative of Domitian, was condemned to death by this emperor because of his affinity to Judaism. The rabbis, who came to plead his

---

6. For a thorough explanation see Menahem Stern, *Greek and Latin Authors on Jews and Judaism* (2 vols.; Jerusalem: Academy of Science and Humanities, 1980), 2:129–31.

7. Ibid., 1:490–95, esp. Stern's comments on the palm tree's symbolism.

8. For example, there is a coin with Vespasian (69–79 C.E.) on the obverse and the goddess of victory, standing on the prow of a ship, on the Reverse. On her left shoulder there is a palm branch and in her right hand a wreath with the legend Victoria Navalis (commemorating the triumph over the Judean navy). *Sefunim* 3 (1969–71), 34, pl. VI, #7. See also #8; there is also a coin showing an engraving of a mourning woman sitting under a palm tree on a heap of arms taken from the vanquished Jews with the inscription *iudaea capta*. Y. Meshorer, *Coins of the Ancient World* (Jerusalem: Keter, 1979), 46–47 (Hebrew).

9. Marius Heemstra, *The Fiscus Judaicus and the Parting of the Ways* (Tübingen: Mohr Siebeck, 2010).

10. See *Deut. Rab.* 2:15.; b. '*Abod. Zar.* 10b; m. '*Erub.* 4:1.

11. b.'*Abod. Zar.* 10b.

case, unfortunately failed and he was executed in 95 C.E. Domitian met his death a short time later and the new emperor, Nerva, ascended to the throne in 96 C.E. It is quite possible that the rabbis, while they were in Rome, made contact with Nerva and his administration and achieved a positive outcome. The coin survived as proof that indeed a more benevolent attitude was instituted.

Moussaieff also suggests that Agrippa, and principally Berenice, the remaining members of Herod's family, who were veteran advocates of Jewish causes, appear to have assisted in alleviating the pressure on the Jewish community. Berenice, the oldest daughter of Agrippa I, was close to Flavius Vespasianus, emperor 69–79 C.E. and had intimate relations with his son Titus, who later became emperor of Rome, 79–81 C.E. The prejudice of the ruling classes in Rome put an end to the marriage plans and under pressure of Vespasian, his father, Titus was forced to send Berenice away. When she returned to Rome her influence on the Flavian family waned[12] but it would be interesting to know if she still held sway in court when the emperors changed. Moussaieff believes that this powerful woman played a role in forging the new approach toward the Jews. He delineates his reasons in a paper that was published in *Biblical Archaeology Review*,[13] yet he admits his assumption is a conjecture. He would be delighted to hear from anyone who would be able to solve this puzzle definitively.

Finally, Moussaieff believes that the emperor's measure primarily benefited the authentic Jewish community.[14] There is no question in his mind that the unique coin annulled the tax for all those living a Jewish life and it illustrates an indisputable change for all practicing Jews under the Roman government. Lamentably, the reign of Nerva ended too quickly and it seems that the tax benefits were abolished by his successors, Trajan and Hadrian, who stirred up the old hatred between Rome and the Jews.[15]

Shlomo Moussaieff has a passion for acquiring any artifact that will illuminate Jewish antiquity. He has amassed a significant collection of important materials and he invites competent scholars to interpret them, thereby enriching our understanding of the Bible and ancient Jewish life immeasurably.

---

12. Abraham Schalit, "Berenice," in *Encyclopaedia Judaica* (ed. Fred Skolnik and Michael Berenbaum; 2nd ed.; Detroit: Macmillan Reference USA in Association with the Keter Pub. House, 2007), 3:410–11. See also Heinrich Graetz, *History of the Jews* (Philadelphia: JPS, 1893), 2:299–300, 332–33, 388.

13. Shlomo Moussaieff, "The 'New Cleopatra' and the Jewish Tax," *BAR* 36 (2010): 47–49.

14. The only other scholar who agrees is Martin Goodman, *Judaism in the Roman World* (Leiden: Brill, 2007), 54.

15. Later sources, however, report that the levy of the tax existed, for example, in Egypt. See *CPJ* 2 (1960), 111 and *CPJ* 3 (1964) 17–18 n. 460 line 7.

Fig. 2 Dr. Shlomo Moussaieff holding the Nerva coin. Photo by Aron Patinkin.

Bibliography

Goodman, Martin. *Judaism in the Roman World*. Leiden: Brill, 2007.
Graetz, Heinrich. *History of the Jews*. Philadelphia: JPS, 1893.
Heemstra, Marius. *The Fiscus Judaicus and the Parting of the Ways*. Tübingen: Mohr Siebeck, 2010.
Mekhilta d'Rabbi Ishmael. Edited by Horvitz-Rabin. Jerusalem: Bamberger & Wahrman, 1960.
Meshorer, Yaakov. *Coins of the Ancient World*. Jerusalem: Keter, 1979 [Hebrew].
Moussaieff, Shlomo. "The 'New Cleopatra' and the Jewish Tax." *BAR* 36 (2010): 47–49.
Schalit, Abraham. "Berenice." Pages 3:410–11 in *Encyclopaedia Judaica*. Edited by Fred Skolnik and Michael Berenbaum. 2nd ed. Detroit: Macmillan Reference USA in Association with the Keter Publishing House, 2007.
Stern, Menahem. *Greek and Latin Authors on Jews and Judaism*. 2 vols. Jerusalem: Academy of Science and Humanities, 1980.
Suetonius, Gaius Tranquillus. *De vita Caesarum. Dom.* Edited and translated by J. C. Rolfe. Loeb Classical Library. Cambridge, Mass.: Harvard University Press, 1950.

A Teacher, A Colleague, A Friend: Wilfred G. Lambert, 1926-2011

Meir Lubetski

> "So sad, so strange, the days that are no more"
> *Morte d'Arthur* Alfred Lord Tennyson

The passing of Wilfred G. Lambert brings to a close a chapter in Near Eastern Assyriology research. His discoveries of ancient sources at the British museum were legion and his expertise in deciphering them brought him world recognition.

As a faculty member of the University of Birmingham, Lambert was the sole Assyriologist and concentrated on Sumerian and Akkadian arts and literature. Acclaimed as a leading scholar in the field, his brilliant research was chronicled in many publications. Every article of his, is a book, each note, a paper. I had to read his works more than once in order to grasp their full meaning. As a responsible scholar he never confused secondary or antiquated bibliography with original texts. He dedicated his life to seeking the absolute truth. A prolific author, Lambert's elegant style of writing never bored the reader; on the contrary, it left him wishing for more.

While Lambert's prominence was a result of his contributions in Assyriology, his methodology is worthy of emulation. His article, "Leviathan in Ancient Art," is an example of what a thorough scholar should produce while controlling a variety of art sources and different scripts. He was loath to accept other scholars' innovations when "the textual basis is weak and doubtful" and ... when the art historical basis is equally weak." The specialist provided sound guidelines in the above article:

> The principle we follow is that in such matters a single example is never certain proof ... To us half a dozen ordinary and mediocre examples of one

motif are much stronger proof than one staggering monument which could form the front piece of coffee-table books.

Lambert was not only a scholar par excellence, he was a consummate speaker. In an age when mediocrity is on the rise, it was a privilege to listen to an authentic scholar, one who had been educated from childhood on, in the best of the English classic tradition. Wilfred, the student, and later the teacher, mastered the original texts of the ancient Near East and with great ease communicated his insights. At the many lectures I heard him deliver, it always amazed me that he would hold a tiny piece of paper in front of him with a few notes jotted down and then present a most coherent, engaging, and meaningful speech. Unfailingly, his eloquence was spiced with humor.

Even though age took its toll, he still managed to continue working energetically at the British Museum every Thursday, reading inscriptions and cataloging the West Asiatic collection of seals. Despite his illness these past two years, he managed to proofread some of his forthcoming articles. These achievements brought him great satisfaction.

My wife Edith and I spent a few days each summer with Prof. Lambert at different conferences. The last time I met with him was in July 2011 at the Society of Biblical Literature conference at Kings College, London. After the session, we walked along the street in the late afternoon as the rays of sunlight finally broke through London's overcast skies. Strolling along to the underground station that would take him home to Birmingham, I asked him how it felt to be known as a leading Assyriology expert. To which he gave me the following humble assessment: I am a scholar who has been fortunate to have had the correct comprehension in deciphering cuneiform and intuitively guessing the missing lacunae. In all other respects I am no different than any simple person walking in the street. Now, after four score and five I am gratified that I was able to decipher some artifacts from the enormous archaeological warehouse waiting for future scholars to decode. And with that he bade us farewell and disappeared among the multitudes of the underground crowd. His words were genuine and came straight from his profound belief. We were awed by this gentleman who recognized his accomplishments yet remained a modest, unassuming individual.

A great man, a wise man left us. Rav Lia, eulogizing a talmudic sage, captures the feelings of so many of us who knew Lambert:

ארבעה דברים תשמישו של עולם וכולן אם אבדו יש להן חליפין (איוב כח)
כי יש לכסף מוצא ומקום לזהב יזוקו ברזל מעפר יוקח ואבן יצוק נחושה. אילו
אם אבדו יש להן חליפין אבל תלמיד חכם שמת מי מביא לנו חליפתו מי מביא
לנו תמורתו.

Four things are in use in the world and if they are lost, they are replaceable. "There is a mine for silver, and a place where gold is refined; iron is taken out of the earth, and copper smelted from rock"*(Job* 28:1, 2). If they are lost, they can be replaced. But a scholar who died, who can bring us his replacement, who can bring us his substitute? (y. *Ber.*, 2:8)

Subject Index

Abbai, 161
Abdi-Heba, 59
Abibaal, 3
Abraham, 79
Achaemenid, 104, 111, 115
Adab (Bismaya), 129–31
Adad-apla-iddina, 140, 142, 144
Adalat?, 8, 9
Adonijah, 179–80
Agrippa, 280
Ahaz (king), 38, 66, 185, 191
Ahaziah, 178
Ahiqam, 21, 24, 31
Ahiram, 64
Aḫu-nūrī, 113, 116, 119, 121, 125
Akkadian, 3, 37, 45, 47, 54, 96, 111, 112, 115, 120, 124, 130, 165, 177, 247, 251, 253–59, 273, 283
Al-Baydâ', 94
aliyn.b'l, 73
alphabet/alphabetic writing, 1–4, 17, 111–14, 123–26, 130, 212, 233–24
Al-'Ula, 105
Amēl-Marduk (Evil-Merodach), 122, 125
Amenophis III, 87
Amenophis IV, 74, 84
Ammon(ite), 52, 100
    seal(s), 191
'Ammshafaq, 94
Amorites, 79
Amurru, 74, 79, 143
Anatolian, 4, 9, 171
Anu, 141
Apheqah, 64, 66

Appuashu, 97
Arab, Arabic, Arabia, Arabian, 3, 12–14, 59, 66, 71, 73, 75, **93–110**, 151, 165, 196, 205–7, 217, 219, 264
Arad, 103, 190
Arad-Ea, 142, 144–46
AraxSamnu, 142
Aram, 43–44, 100
Aramaic, 13, 42, 45–46, 103, 111–12, 114–15, 120, 123–26, 165, 168, 173, 191, 206, 209, 212, 224, 251–59, 263
    grammar, 167–69
    seals, 191
Arameans, 79
Archives, survival of, 190
Aroer, 102
Arrowhead, 6–11, 17
Arubboth, 66
'Ashna', 38
Ashur ostracon (*KAI* 233), 41, 44–45
Assyria(n), 41, 42, 44–46, 54, 61, 66, 85, 96, 103, 114–15, 129, 173, 252
axe, 11, 14, 17
Azekah, 65, 100
Aziru, 74
b'r, "Bu'ur," (in *brb'r*), 52
Ba'alâ, 10, 11
Baal, 73
Baal Cycle, 174
Baalis, king of the Ammonites, 52
Babylon, 98, 142
Babylonia(n), 31, 47, 62, 87 96, 146, 161, 165–66, 168–69
Balaam, son of Beor, 52–53

banquet, 153
Bar izi, 161
Bar Rekub inscriptions 1 (*KAI* 216, Istanbul) and 8 (*KAI* 217, Berlin), 45
Bastet, 76
bed/bod, 14
Beersheba, 61, 101–3
beetle, 77
Bēlet-ilî, 141
Benjamin, 100
Beor, father of Balaam, 52–53
Berenice, 280
Berlin, 3, 45, **193–224**
Bes (god), 13
Bes(i), 13
BH philology, **243–76**
Bible, 8, 10, 36, 42–43, 46–49, 53–54, 74, 76–77, 79, 83–87, 89–90, 93, 105, 172–73, 178, 195, 205, 209, 220–21, 225–26, 280
Bithiah, 87
Bôlḫâ, 148
Boundary Stones, 137–46
bowl, 4, 120, 147–48, 151–54, 157–69
bread, 175–76
bricks, **129–36**
Bubastis, 76
building inscriptions, 130, 174, **234–76**
Byblus/Byblian inscriptions 3, 7, 262
Canaan(ite), 11–12, 15–16, 79–80
Carchemish, 97, 171–72, 175–77, 179–80
Chaldea(n), 32, 94, 96, 97, 111
chronology, 4, 26, 93, 95, 103–4, 130
Cilicia(n), 96–99, 101
City of David seals and bullae, 22–24, 26–29, 31–32, 48–51, 185
collection box, 271–72
crater, 152
curses, 137, 141, 173
Cyprus, 97
Damal, 71
Dana Adasi, 98
David (king), 41–43, 59, 63, 66, 175,
179–80, 183, 218
Dedan, 94, 102, 105
Deir ʿAlla' inscription, 52–53, 262–63
Deutsche Morgenländische Gesellschaft (DMG), 194, 197–98, 211
Dionysos, 147, 153
dm, 70, 72–74
dmlʾ, **69–82**
dmlʾl, 69, 71, 72
dmlʾl/dmlyhw, 69, 70
dmlyhw, 70–72
dmm, 70
Domitian, 278–80
drinking, 153, 154
Ea, 141
ʿebed (Heb., Amm.), "minister" only of a king or a deity, 46, 52
Edom(ite), 86, 100, 101, 244, 246
Egypt(ian), 1, 3, 4, 13, 16, 37, 43, 45, 54, 60, 73–78, 84–89, 98, 104, 115, 211
Ekron/Tel Miqneh, 99
ʾl, 71–72, 74, 151
ʾlh(y)ʾ, 151
El, 73
El Amarna, 59, 73–79, 80, 84, 86–87, 254, 263
Ela Valley, 65
Elephantine, 153
Elibaal, 3
Elisha (Cyprus), 97
Elisha (prophet), 10, 174
Eltolad, 66
Enlil, 141
Enlil-mudammiq, 142
Enlil-zākir-Sumi, 142
Eqron inscription, 262–63
Eshtamoa, 65
Ethiopia, 85
ʿEzer (in *brʿzr*), 47–48
Fadak, 105
fakes, xii–xiii, 37, **183–92**, 193. *See also* forgery
farmer (*ikkaru*), 116–18, 123

SUBJECT INDEX

fighting cock, on seal, 190
fiscal bullae, 59–66
Fiscus Iudaicus, 277, 279
Flavians, 279
Flavius Clemens, 279
Flavius Vespasianus, 280
forgery, xii–xiii, 32, 38, **183–92, 193–242**, 245, 252–55, 257–58, 261, 262, 272–73. *See also* fakes
Gath, 4-6. *See* Tell eṣ-Ṣafi
Gaza, 94, 101, 103
Gebim, 66
German Kaiser, 198
Gezer 5, 11, 14, 86
Gibeah, 60-61, 66
Gibeon, 78-80, 190
Goliath, 66
Greek, 3, 4, 13, 63, 69, 96, 103, 177, 196, 205, 212, 227
Hadad, 86, 103
Hadad-Yith'l, 73
Hadadezer, 36, 44, 47–48
Ḥaḍramawt, 93, 94
Halakha, 267
Hathor, 60, 63, 64
Hatti/u, 99, 100
Hazael, 36, 43–44
Hebrew/palaeo-Hebrew 8, 10, 11, 103
Hebron, 59-60, 64–66, 78–79, 100
Hellenistic, 74, 153
Herod, 280
Hezekiah, 25, 41, 44, 59, 60, 63, 66, 185, 191
Ḥilqiyahu, 49
Hiram, 64
Hittite, 16, 79, 175–77
Horse bridle from Umqi/Unqi, 43–44
Ḥume 97–99
Ibn Ezra, Abraham 226
Ilum, 71
Incense road, 94, 102, 104, 105
Inscriptions
 ('A)pheqah, to/belonging to the king, 64, 66
 ʿbd hmlk, 21, 25–26, 28–29
 'DLT?, 8
 ʿebed hammelek (Heb.), "the king's minister," 51–52
 ʿEzer (in brʿzr), 47–48
 ʿL, 148, 150
 ªšer ʿal habbāyit (Heb.), "who is over the palace," 51
 ʾšr ʿl hbyt, who is over the palace", 51
 Abanda Gušnaṣ son of Pidardost, 162
 Abbai son of Eboi, 161
 Abiyaw, minister of Uziyaw, 46
 Aḫu-nūrī (ᵐŠEŠ-ZALAG₂), 113
 Asmandad son of Marta, 159
 Azaryahu ben Ḥilqiyahu, 24, 46, 48–50
 Azyazdan Khwast-Bindad son of Madukh, 161
 B'L, 9
 bʿr, "Buʿur," (in brbʿr), 52
 B<N?>'NT, 7
 Bar-hadad, son of Ezer (br [.] h /dd brʿzr [.] dmšqy[ʾ], 47–48
 Bar-hadad, son of Hadadezer, 48
 Bar-hadad, son of Hazael (brhdd brḥz'l mlk 'rm), 36, 43–44
 Bar-Izi (?) son of Eboi, 161
 ʿbd yhw dwd mlk, 183
 BD/BS?, 13–14
 ʿbdyhw, 185
 blʿm, "Balaam," 52
 BLḤ, 148, 150, 151
 BN, 7–9
 BR/BN(WHY),148, 150–52
 br mlk, 113
 brhdd br ḥz'l mlk 'rm, 36, 44
 bt[d]wd, "the house of [Da]vid," 41
 Buhksra son of Bhrtuia, 161
 bytdwd, "the house of David," 41
 Dād-Manda son of Eboi, 161
 Dād-Manda son of Iboi, 159

Inscriptions, cont'd
  derashyahu son of X, 190
  DM/MD?, 14
  dml' bn pqHyw, 69, 77
  É ᵈInanna, 130
  Ebabbar (É ᵈUTU), 132
  Esagil, 131
  Ezida, 131
  'bdyhw 185
  ḎR 94
  Gedaliah ben Ahiqam 21, 31
  Gedaliah/,Gedalyahu, son of [P]
    ashḥur, 21–22, 24, 28–29, 31, 50
  GN'(Y') 148, 150–52
  hadabiyat-dawit, "the heights of
    David," 43
  Hazael (*ḥz'l mlk 'rm*), 43
  ḥāzē(h) ilāhīn (Can. dialect or
    Aram.), "a seer of (the) gods," 53
  HGR 94, 100
  ḤṢ, 7–9
  ḤY(WHY)/ḤY(Y), 148, 150–52
  ikkaru (ˡúENGAR), 113
  *In the 13th year, Gibeah, to/belonging
    to the king,* 60
  *In the 20th year, 'Adullam, to/belong-
    ing to the king,* 63
  *In the 21st year, Lachish, to/belonging
    to the king,* 61
  *In the third year, Socoh, to/belonging
    to the king,* 65
  Ištar (ᵈINANNA), 130
  J(eh)ucal ben Shelemiah, 50, 51
  Koniyahu son of Hodiyahu, 190
  KŠDM, 94
  L, 148, 150
  l'zryhw b/n ḥlqyhw, "belonging to
    ᵃzaryāhû, so / n of *Ḥilqiyāhû*," 49
  l'byw 'bd l'zyw, "belonging to ᵃ*bi-
    yaw*, minister of / *'Uziyaw*," 46
  Larsa (UD.UNUGᵏⁱ), 133
  lgdlyhw/bn [p]šḥwr, "belonging to
    Gᵃdalyāhû, / son of [*P*]*ašḥûr*,"
  22, 50
  lgmryhw/[b]n špn, "belonging to
    Gᵃmaryāhû, / [so]n of Šāfān," 48
  lmlkm'wr 'b/d b'lyš', "belonging
    to Milkom'ur, the minister of
    Ba'alyiša'/ Ba'alîša'," 52
  lšbnyw, "belonging to *Shubnayaw*"
    (obv.), (rev.) *lšbnyw '/ bd 'zyw*,
    "belonging to *Shubnayaw*, mi/
    nister of *'Uziyaw*," 46
  lšm'/'bd yrb'm, "belonging to Šema', /
    minister of *Yārob'am*," 46
  ly'znyhw/'bd hmlk, "belonging to
    Yaᵃzanyāhû, the king's minister,"
    51
  lyhwkl b/[n] šlmyhw /bn šby, "be-
    longing to *Yᵃhûkal*, so / [n] of
    Šelemyāhû, / son of Šōbî," 23, 24,
    31, 50
  ma'adana, 190
  Marduk (ᵈAMAR.UTU), 132
  Marduk-nādin-aḫi (ᵐᵈAMAR.UTU-
    na-din-ŠEŠ), son of Nebuchadne-
    zzar II, 113
  mrdkndn'ḥ, 113
  Nabû-kudurri-uṣur (=Nebuchadnez-
    zar II, ᵐᵈAG-*ku-dúr-ri-ú-ṣu-úr*),
    132
  Nabû-kudurri-uṣur (=Nebuchadnez-
    zar II, ᵐᵈAG-NÍG.DU-URÙ), 113
  Narām-Sîn (ᵈ*na-ra-am*-ᵈEN.ZU),
    130
  Omri, king of Israel (*'mr/y mlk yśr'l*),
    42–43
  PḤK?, 16
  qaqqara ṣabātu, 113
  QRB, 148, 150–51
  rab ša-rēši (Bab. Akk.), "(military?)
    chief of staff," 47
  Šamaš (ᵈUTU), 133
  Sarkon (*srkwn*), 45
  Sennacherib ([*sn*]*ḥrb*), 44
  SKR(Y'), 148, 150–52

SUBJECT INDEX

ŠNT, 148, 150–51
ŠPṬ, 9
ṬB(Y'), 148, 150–51
Tiglath-pileser III (*tgltplsr* and variants), 44–45
TRKRŠYN, 8
turtānu/tartānu (Assyr. Akk.), Heb. *tartān*, "army general," 45
Tzaʾananim, to/belonging to the king, 64
'Ushna', *see* 'Ashna'
W, 148, 150–51
WHBY, 148, 150–51
yaʾazanyahu son of the king, 190
Yayai son of Emmoi, 159
YDN, 7, 8
yehoʾahaz son of the king, 190
Yehoʾash Inscription, 227–30, 234–35, **243–76**
YHD, 94
Yehukal. *See* J(eh)ucal.
YWN, 94
Ionia(n)/Iawan 94, 96–99
Isis-Hathor, 76
Ištar (^{d}INANNA) 129–31, 141
i-ti-lum, 71
itti-(I)lum, 71
itti-Šamaš- balāṭ, 118
ivories from Arslān Tash (Hadattah) and Nimrud (Calah), 44
ivy leaf, 147
Izbet Ṣarṭah, 5, 16
jar, impression on, 186–90
jar lid, 120, 122, 125
Jehoash Inscription, *see* Inscriptions, Yehoʾash
Jeremiah, 24, 31, 40, 49, 85, 101, 153, 178,
Jeroboam I, 46
Jeroboam II, 180
Jerusalem, 6, 7, 69, 78–79, 100, 102
  bullae hoards, 185, 190
Jewish, 153, 157, 193, 246, 267, 277, 279, 280
Jewish community, 279–80

Jezebel, 38, 46, 177–78
Jinn, 148, 153
Josiah, 48
Judah(ite)/Judean, 5, 6, 21–22, 24, 27–29, 31–32, 38–39, 41–43, 46, 48, 51, 59–60, 63–64, 66, **93–110**, 114, 121, 183, 185, 191, 229, 244, 246, 258
Karkhemish, *see* Carchemish
Kassite Dynasty, 137
Katuwas (king), 171–82
Kefar Veradim, 4
Keilah, 59, 62, 63, 66
Khaybar, 105
Khirbet Qeiyafa, 5
kings in inscriptions, **41–48**
Kiribiti-Enlil, 142
Kirshu, 98
Kition, 94, 103
Kittim/Kittiyim, 97, 103
Krt, 73
Kunzumpiya, 96
Kush, 85
Lachish/Lakish, 5, 21, 25–28, 31–32, 48–49, 54, 61, 62, 65, 66, 100
  bullae hoards, 185, 190
Lambert, Wilfred G., 245, 247, **283–85**
Lan, 73
Larsa (Tell es-Senkereh), 118, 126, 129, 131–35
ldmlʾ, 70
Lebanon, 6, 13
Leia, 73–74, 79–80
Lemaire, André, 35, 41–42, 70, 184, 190, 193, 211, 221, 228, 273
Levant, 3, 13, 17, 102, 130, 178, 181
Leya, 73
li-e-ia (leia), 73–74
lmlk stamps 65, 77–78, 190
London, 200, 224–25, 284
Lubetski, Meir, 35, 83, 193, 245, 253
Lum, 71
Luwian, 9, 79, 96, 171–72, 174–75, 177–79

l'y, 73
Lydia(n), 98
l'y/lan, l'yl/yan, 72
lyre on seal, 190
Ma'in, 94
Maon, 66
Maqqef, 248–49
mār šarri, 115, 122
Mār-Sapin son of Eboi, 161
Marduk, 119, 132, 135, 144
Marduk-nādin-aḫi, son of Nebuchadnezzar II, 113–14, 116, 120–21, 124–25
Mareshah, 59, 100
Marriage, 85–87, 89, 280
marzeah, xi, 153–54
mašīḫu, 121–22
Masora, 248, 270–71
Mater lectionis, 151–52
measuring vessels 121
Melqart stele, 47–48
Menahem, 191
Mered, 87
Mesha Inscription, 39, 41–43, 54, 115, **193–233**
Meydancikkale, 98
Millard, Alan, 2, 245, 251, 273
Millo, 22
Milton, John, 77
Minaeans, 93, 104, 105
Mizpah (Tell en-Nasbeh), 31–32, 51, 100–101
Moab(ite), 11, 100
Morgenstern, Matthew, 256
Morphology, 196, 209, 213, 223, 231
Moussaieff
    alphabet ostracon, 233
    bowl, 151–52, 159–60, 164
    brick, 130–35
    bullae, 24, 26–29, 31–32
    clay lid, 125
    ostraca, 233–35
    parallel, 163
    seal, **69–82**
    stone, 137–40
Moussaieff Collection, 7, 21, 25–26, 11–112, 129, 135, 137, 147, 157, 159–60, 169, 184
Moussaieff, Shlomo, 26, 111, 129, 138–40, **277–81**
Mt, 73
MU.NAG.TU, 142
Munnabittu, 142
mušḫuš, 141
Nabataean script, 196, 207, 212, 234
Nabatea, 153
Nabonidus 97, 98, 104, 105
Nabû, 119, 141, 167
Nabuch, 62, 99
Nabû sharrussu-ukin, *rab ša-rēši* of Nebuchadnezzar II, 39–40, 47
Nabû-šuma-iddina, 142
NapSiru, 142
Narām-Sîn, 129–31
Nashq, 94, 95
Nasib, 66
Nazi-Marduk, 142
Nb, 78
Nebuchadnezzar, 47, 62, 98–100, 102, 111–13, 117–18, 121–26, 129, 131–35, 176
Negev, 100, 103
Nehemiah, 22
Neo-Assyrian, 96, 117, 119–20, 258–59, 272
Neo-Babylonian, 97–102, 104
Neo-Babylonian history (Nebuchadnezzar II's successor), 21–22, 24, 97–102, 104, 116–17, 119–24
Neo-Hittite, 9
Neo-Mandaic, 165, 168
Neriglissar, 97, 98
Nerva, **277–80**
New Kingdom, 73, 84
Nineveh, 61, 114–15
North Arabia(n), 105
North Arabic, 13

SUBJECT INDEX

Northwest Semitic, **35–58**, 73–74, 79, 204, 209, 218, 233, 263. *See also* West Semitic
Nuzi, 16
officials in inscriptions, 39–40, 45–47, 51–53
Orthography, 152, 161–62, 196, 209, 213, 221–24, 231, 233–34
  Mandaic, 162–63
Osorkon 3, 85
Paxxaru, 142
Paleographical dating, 6, 152
Paleography, 5, 14, 26, 38, 125–26, 196, 200, 204, 209, 221, 231
Pallula, 142
Palm tree, 278–79
Palmyra/Palmyrene, **147–56**
Panamu/ Panamuwa, 45, 173
Pashhur, 21–24, 28, 31, 50
Persia(n), 22, 36, 37, 53, 54, 59, 104–5, 165
Pharaoh. *See also* Shishak
  Hophra, 85
  Necho, 85
Philistia(n) Philistine, 4–6, 65–66
Phoenicia(n), 6–7, 10, 16, 45, 103, 126, 153, 175, 191, 219, 262–63, 272
Pirindu, 97–99
Pitusu/Pityoussa, 98
pqHyw, 69, 77
priests, 175, 267–69
pronominal suffix 3ms., 262–64
prophet, 10, 154
proto-Arabic, 14
proto-Sinaitic inscriptions, 11, 13, 14, 16
Punic, 6, 10, 195
Qila, 59
Raamah, 102
Ramses II, 73
Rashi, 76
Rashwân, 94
Rehoboam, 63, 66, 180
Rodanim, 97
Roman
  coins, 279
  government, 280
royal inscriptions, 129–30, **243–76**
royal officials in inscriptions, **46–52**
rw-Abw, 73
Sabaean, 94–95, 97, 99, 101, 102, 104, 105
Ṣabaḥḥumû, 94
Safaitic, 16
Saxirtu Canal, 142–44
Sakhmet, 75, 76
Samaria, 11, 71, 174, 178
  bullae hoards, 191
Šamaš, 141 173, 176, 179
Sargon I, 130
Sargon II, 36, 45–46, 96
Sarkon (*srkwn*), 46
Sasson bulla, 26, 28–30, 32
Saul (king), 43, 59, 63
scriptio continua, 147
Second Isin Dynasty, 137, 140, 142
Second Temple, 221, 228, 257–59
Seleucid era, 152
Sennacherib, 36, 41, 44, 61, 191, 258–59
Šerin daughter of Mama, 159
Šetqt, 73
Shalmaneser III, 44
Shaphan the scribe, 48–49
Shaphat, 10
Shapira, **193–242**
Sheba, 93–94, 101–2
Shebanyahu, 62
Shebna, overseer of the palace, 51
Shebnayahu, 25–26
Shelemiah, father of J(eh)ucal, 50–51
Shephelah, 5, 100
Sheshonq, *see* Shishak
Shishak, 3, 43, 63, 79, 84–85
Sxm, 76
Shobai, father of Shelemyahu, 50
Shoshenk, *see* Shishak
Shuwaikah, 65
Silifkeh, 97

Siloam Tunnel inscription, 204, 221, 222, 233, 262–63
Silwan epitaph, 51
Sîn, 144
Sîn-nāṣir, 142, 144
So, King of Egypt, 85
Socoh, 63, 65–66
Solomon (king), 3, 79, 83, 85–90, 93, 175–76, 179–80
South Arabia(n), 93-95, 100–103, 105, 196, 205–7
South Arabic, 102
Statistics, Aramaic Hebrew seals, **183–91**
Šuranu, 142
Tamar, 256
Tannaim, 279
Tāribu, 142
Tarku/Tarḫu(nt), 9
Tarkurashyan, 8, 9
Tarshish, 97
Tarsus, 97
Tašmag son of Eboi, 161
Teima(nite), 104–5
Tel Arad, 25
Tel Fekhereye (Tell Fekheriye), 173, 251, 253
Tel Rehov, 4
Tell ed-Duweir, 61
Tell en-Nasbeh, 28–29, 51, 100, 190,
Tell esh Sheikh Madhkur, 63
Tell eṣ-Ṣafi. *See* Gath, 4
Tell Zayit, 5
Temple in Jerusalem, 277
Temple of Jupiter Capitolinus, 277
Tesserae, 153
Testimony, 42, 197, 223, 225-28, 253–57
Thiases, 153
Three shekels ostracon, 227–35
Tiglath-pileser III, 36, 38, 44–45
Tirhaka, 85
Titus, 280
toponyms, Babylonian, 161, 164
Trade, 93, 94, 102
Trajan, 280

Tunna, 144
turtānu/tartānu (Assyr. Akk.), Heb. *tartān*, "army general," 45
Tuthmosis III, 84
Twenty-Fifth Dynasty, 85
Twenty-Sixth Dynasty, 85
Tyre, 102
Tzaʾananim, 64–66
Ugarit, 3, 16, 153
Ugaritic, 8, 14, 72–74, 77, 174, 250–51, 263, 273
unprovenanced, xi--iii, 14, 17, 21, 25, 37–39, 46, 59, 69 94, 135, 184–85, 189–90, 229, 231–32, 234, 240
Ur, 14
Ura, 97
Uzib-Suqab, 142, 146
Uzziah, 39, 46
Vale of Elah, 5
Van der Veen, Peter, 35
Vespasian, 278–80
Volunteering, 244–49
Wadi el-Ḥôl inscriptions, 2, 4
Wahabay, 148
War, 70, 79, 94, 96–97, 193, 270
West Semitic, 15–16, 38, 74 103, 111, 114, 153, 172, 173–76, 181
Widow's plea ostracon, 227–35
Wine, 78, 80, 153–54, 204
witness, 137, 140, 145, 161, 168–69, 224, 226–28, 244–47, 249–57
Yadaʿil Bayin, 94, 95, 101
Yadiʿ, 105
Yadin, 7
Yatrib/medine, 105
Yehud, 101
Yithaʿamar, 94–95, 101
Yohanan ben Zakai, 277
Zakkur stele (*KAI* 202), 43–44
Zeanan, 65
Zedekiah, 21, 24, 31–32
Zenjirli-area inscriptions, 45
Ziph, 66

Index of Sources

Hebrew Bible

Genesis

Reference	Page
1:11	263
1:29	74
2:24	263
4:2	263
6:14–19	87
10:7	93
10:26	93
10:28	93
11:3	263
13	88
14	88
14:14	88
15:3	88
16:11	71, 73
16:15	248
17:7	254
17:14	265
17:23	88
17:27	88
18	87
19:38	264
21:3	248
21:30	227, 228, 253
23:1–20	79
24:9	263
25:3	93
25:8	262, 266
25:17	266
25:28	263
26:3	254
31:23	256
31:25	256
31:44	227, 253, 256
31:47	253–55
31:48	228, 253, 256
31:52	227, 253, 255, 256
31:54	256
35:29	266
38:25	256
39:2–3	257–59
39:11	257, 259
39:23	257
39–41	88
41:41–43	77
49:16	262
49:29	264, 265, 267
49:33	264, 266, 267
50:26	272

Exodus

Reference	Page
1:8	84
1:11	84
1:15	84
1:17	84
1:18	84
1:19	84
1:22	84
2	83
2:1–9	87
2:5	87
4:15	263
12:14	252
12:15	266

Exodus, cont'd
12:19	266
19:1	278
20:2	76
20:16	223, 225–27
22:12	253
25:2	246
25:16	226
25:21	226
30:33	265
30:38	265
31:14	265
31:18	226, 253
32:15	253
34:29	253
35:5	246
35:21	246
35:22	245, 246
35:26	246
35:29	245
36:2	246

Leviticus
7:20	265
7:21	265
7:25	265
7:27	265
17:4	265
17:9	265
17:10	265
18:29	265
19:8	265
19:16	269, 271
19:18	269
20:3	265
20:5	265
20:6	265
20:17	265
20:18	265
21	267
21:1–4	268
21:1–3	267, 268
21:1	267, 268
21:2–3	267
21:4	268
21:7	268
21:11	267
21:13–15	268
22:11	88
23:29	265
24:5–9	175
25:21	230, 260
26:6	260, 261

Numbers
9:13	265
12:8	83
13:5	10
13:29	79
14:41	258
15:30	265
19:13	266
19:20	266
20:24	266
22–24	53
23:24	74
27:13	266, 271
31:2	266, 271

Deuteronomy
9:9	253
9:11	253
9:15	253
10:17	263
28:8	230, 260
28:15–68	173
28:18	173
28:31	173
28:51	173
31:19	228, 251, 253
31:21	251, 253
31:26	228, 251, 253
32:50	266, 271

Joshua
1:11	65
10:4	172
12:15	63
15:35	63, 65
15:44	59

INDEX OF SOURCES

15:53	64	8:12–13	175
15:57	61	8:13	175
16:37	65	9:16	86
22:27	253	9:20–22	79
22:28	253	9:24	86
22:34	253	10	93
24:27	227, 228, 250, 253	10:1	93
		10:4	93
Judges		10:10	93
3:20–24	178	10:13	93
3:31	8	11:1–3	86
5:6	8	11:14–20	86
14:19	263	11:33	180
		11:40	85
1 Samuel		12	180
8:2	248	12:22–24	180
12:5	251	14:25–26	79
16:13	41	14:25	85
17:1	66	16:13	41
21:6	175	16:16	43
		16:24	248
2 Samuel		16:31	38, 85
15:13	248	17:19	178
17:25	85	19:15	43
23:1–13	59	19:16	10
		19:19	10
1 Kings		22:4	4, 44, 47
1–10	93	22:17	263
1:9	180	22:31	47
1:19	180		
1:25	180	*2 Kings*	
1:47–48	180	1:2	178
3–11	3	3:4	43
3	83	3:11	10
3:1	85, 87	4:13	264
3:11	180	5	47
3:28	180	6:8–23	47
4:7–13	89	6:23	44
5–9	175	6:24–8:15	44
6–7	176	6:24	47
7:1–12	176	6:31	10
7:8	85	7	174
7:13–51	176	7:1	174
7:48	175	7:6	79
		7:16	174

2 Kings, *cont'd*		60:6	93
7:18	174	65:17	249
8:7–15	47		
8:8	43	*Jeremiah*	
9:30–33	178	1:15	101
11:12	226	3:16	249
12	271, 272	4:16	101
12:5	245, 248–50	4:26	101
12:10	271	6:20	93
12:11	271	6:21	263
13:3	43, 44	6:28	269
13:13	46	7:17	101
14:10	245, 246	7:31	249
14:21	46	7:34	101
15:19	44	9:3	269
15:29	45	9:10	101
17:4	85	10:22	101
18:13	44, 101	11:6	101
18:18	51	11:12	101
19:9	85	16:5	153, 154
22:3	48, 49	19:5	249
22:4	49	25:18	101
23	85	29:23	250
23:29	85	32:35	249
23:33–35	85	33:10	101
24:2	100	34:7	100
25:23	31, 51	34:9	263
		34:22	101
Isaiah		36:10	24, 48
1:8	90	37:3	24, 50
9:1	263	37:12	264
19:4	263	38:1	24, 50
19:19–20	227	39:3	47
19:20	228, 253	40:8	31, 51
20:1	45	40:14	52
22:15–19	51	44:6	101
22:15	51	44:21	249
26:13	263	44:30	85
28:7–8	154	46:11	90
30:8–9	227, 228, 250, 251, 253	46:24	90
30:8	250, 251	51:50	249
30:9	250	52:30	100
33:8	254		
36:1	101	*Ezekiel*	
37:9	85	14:8	265

16:3	79	*Zephaniah*	
16:45	79	3:8	250
18:5–9	270		
18:11–13	270	*Malachi*	
18:15–17	270	1:6	263
18:18	270	3:5	250
18:20	270		
22:9	269	*Job*	
24:17	72	1:15	93
25:7	266	6:19	93
27	102	13:15	74
27:21–22	102	16:8	253
27:22	93	18:19	264
27:23	93	28:1	285
30:17	76	28:2	285
38:10	249		
38:13	93	*Proverbs*	
39:16	248	6:19	250
39:17–20	154	1:6	83
44:22	269	11:11	230
		11:13	269
Hosea		12:17	250
3:2	173	12:20	248
4:16–19	154	12:25	248
10:14	270, 271	14:5	250
		14:25	250
Joel		18:12	248
4:8	93	19:5	250
		19:9	250
Amos		19:21	248
2:7–8	154	20:5	248
4:1	154	20:19	269
6:4–7	154	21:17	154
6:7	ix, 153	23:20–21	154
		30:4	248
Micah		31:4	154
1:2	228, 250		
1:15	63	*Psalms*	
		1:3	258
Habakkuk		17:8	76
2:2–3	251	19:8	226
2:3	250, 251, 253	22:30	73
		27:12	250
		29:11	230, 260, 261

Psalms, *cont'd.*		11:3	101
31:8	249	11:30	63
36:8	76		
37:7	70, 72	*1 Chronicles*	
42–84	224	1:9	93
45:7	224	1:20	93
50:7	224	1:22	93
57:2	76	1:32	93
61:5	76	3:22	10
72:10	93	4:18	87, 89
72:15	93	4:41	93, 105
78:5	226	5:6	45
89:38	253	5:12	10
104:14–15	154	5:39–41	49
109:13	265	5:39	24, 49
109:17	230	6:13–15	49
117	197	6:13–14	24
133:3	230	9:11	49
136:3	263	22:11–13	258
137:6	166	27:29	10
Ruth		*2 Chronicles*	
1:10	264	7:11	258
1:16	264	9:1	93
		9:3	93
Esther		9:9	93
2:40	93	9:12	93
6:6–10	77	9:29	251
7:5	245, 246, 248	11:7	63, 66
		12:2–9	79
Daniel		12:2	85
1:6	71	12:5	85
11:20	207	12:9	85
		14:6	258
Ezra		16:7	105
2:49	13	18:16	263
2:50	105	24:8	271
5:8	257, 258	24:10	271
6:14	257–59	24:11	271
7:1	49	24:20	258
		25:19	245, 246
		26:7	93
Nehemiah		28:18	66
2:20	258	35:20	85
7:52	13, 93, 105	35:22	85

INDEX OF SOURCES

36:4	85

DEUTEROCANONICAL BOOKS

Sirach
31:23–24	226
31:24	226
34:23–24	226
36:15	226
36:20	226
45:7	230
45:23	247

NEW TESTAMENT

Hebrews
21:7	175
22:1	63

Luke
21:13	228

DEAD SEA SCROLLS

1QpHab 7,5	250

ANCIENT JEWISH LITERATURE

Josephus
Antiquities
X, 181–182	100

War
VII, 218	277

Mishnah
Bekhorot
55b	256

Eruvin
4:1	279

Nedarim
40a	256

Shabbat
65b	256

Babylonian Talmud
Avodah Zarah
10b	279

Bava Batra
9a	278

Baba Metzi'a
84a	168

Gittin
56b	278

Sanhedrin
94b	168

Sotah
27b	74

Jerusalem Talmud
Berakhot
2:8	285

Mo'ed Qatan
3:5	72

Midrashim
Leviticus Rabbah
5:3	xi

Deuteronomy Rabbah
2:15	279

Sipre Numbers
131	xi

GRECO-ROMAN LITERATURE

De vita Caesarum. Dom.
12:2	277, 278

OSTRACA, PAPYRI, AND TABLETS

Papyrus Anastasi II
18.9, 3	78

El Amarna tablet
162 line 70	73, 74

NEW INSCRIPTIONS AND SEALS

Hebrew Samaria ostraca
1,7	11
3,3	11
27,3	11
28,3	11
31a,3	11

Moussaïeff Ostracon
2:1	260, 261

BULLAE. See also Subject index

City of David bullae
B7	27, 28
B9	26
B15	28
B17	28
B20–21	27, 28
B23	28
B25	28
B27	27
B29	26
B30	26
B31	26
B33	28
B35	27
B36	26
B37	28
B45	27

Fiscal bullae	59–66
Sasson bulla	26, 28–30, 32

INSCRIPTIONS

BE 1/1
plate 3	130
plate II	130
plate II/3	131

Babylonian Boundary Stone
1–18 rev.	142
1–4 rev.	141
5–19 rev.	142
19–20 rev.	143
19 rev.	145
20 rev.	143
1–7	144
6	145

British Museum collection (BM)
90275	132
90695	132
91715	161
91775	159, 161
91779	161
91780	161
114789	47
115036	132
115036 10	133
115036 13	133
115036 15	133
115036 18	133
117880	160
132947	164

Cagni Erra
I:6	247

Calah Annal
18, lines 3'–7'	45
24, lines 3'–11'	45

Collection of the Babylonian Section Philadelphia (CBS)
8754	130
8755	130
16034	161

COS
2.34: 153	252
2.34: 153–54	251
2:118A:294	45
2:118E:296-7	45
2:119B:302-3	44
2:159	173
2:308–9	132

INDEX OF SOURCES

2:306–14	136	*Khorsabad Summary Inscription*	
3: 86	232	lines 90–109	45
3: 86–87	239		

CT

22 84:23–24	256

CUSAS

17	24, 131

Dakhleh stela

line 2	84

Elephantine legal document

C 15:2	114

Eqron inscription

3	263

Hilprecht Collection (HS)

3021	161
3025	161

Jehoash. See Yeho'ash

KAI

5	262
6	262
7	262
10:15	262, 263
5:2	263
6:2	263
7:4	263
9A:2	262
9B:4	262, 263
181:23	115
202	44
215	45
216	45
217	45
222A:6	115
233	41, 44–46

Lambert, Tamitu texts

52–53: lines 2–5	247
56–57: lines 30–32	247
68–69: lines 1–2	247
84–85: lines 10–12	247

Larsa Bricks

Brique A	132–34
Brique B	134
L. 70.86	134 135
L. 70.87	134
L. 74.9	134

Luwian text of King Katuwas

§1	171
§2	178
§3	178
§4	178
§5	179
§6	179
§7	179
§8	179
§10	172
§§11–12	176
§11	174
§13	176
§14	176
§§15–16	176
§§18–19	177

Melqart stele

lines 1–2	48
line 2	47 48

Mesha Inscription

line 1	43
lines 4–5	43
line 5	223
line 6	223
line 7	223
lines 13–15	20

Mesha Inscription, *cont'd.*
    line 23   115
    line 31   41, 42

Moabitica script
    line 1   205–7
    line 2   200, 205–7
    line 3   200

Moussaieff Magic Bowls
    M23   159
    4   166
    10–11   166
    M24   159
    12   166
    M25i   159
    M26   161
    7   163
    M45   161
    12   167
    13   167
    M139   161
    M154   161
    4–6   164
    5   165

Neo-Babylonian archival texts
    Nbk 382   124

Panamu/Panamuwa inscription (KAI 215)
    line 6b   173
    line 9   173
    line 11a   173
    line 13   45
    line 15   45
    line 16   45

Pohl 1934 no. from Uruk1
    lines 1–2   117
    line 4   117
    line 100   117
    line 97   117

proto-Arabic Or inscription
    2   14

proto-Sinaitic inscriptions
    346   11
    350–357   11
    352   11
    353   16
    355   16
    357   12 16
    358   12
    359–365   11
    362   16
    374–376   11
    375   12
    376   12

RIME
    2 nos 15–17   131

Sabaean inscription
    lines 1–2   94
    lines 5–9   94
    lines 13–16   94
    lines 17–22   101
    lines 17–18   94

Schøyen Collection
    1927/11:5   169
    1928/25   160
    2054/2:10   167
    2054/20: 53–54   167
    2054/34   159
    2054/59   163
    2054/122   161

Sefire text I.A
    14b–42   173
    21b–22a   173

Siloam Tunnel Inscription
    line 2   262 263
    line 3   262 263
    line 4   262 263

INDEX OF SOURCES

Silwan epitaph
    line 1   51

Tamitu texts, see Lambert, Tamitu texts

TCL
    3, 110   247
    12, 56   121

Tel Dan Stele
    line 9 (A9)   41 42

Tel Fekhereye Biblingual inscription
  Akkadian
    1–18   252
    1   252
    8   252
    14–15   251, 252
    19–38   252
  Aramaic
    1–12   252
    10   252
    12–23   252
  Assyrian-Aramaic
    18–19   173

Tell Deir 'Allā
    I:2   52
    I: 3–4   52
    I:4   262
    II:17   262

Tell Fekhariye, see Tel Fekhereye
  Bilingual inscription
    VS 6 255+
      obv. line 1   117
      rev. lines 4–5   117

WSS
    2   46
    3   46
    4   46
    5   38

8   52, 190
12   183
13   190
30   190
132   190
137   75
180   184
220   195
279   184
293   24
326   24
405   26
409   26, 28
470   48 114
596   49
740   38
762   125
772   125
860   52
898   8
1195-1215   183
1210   190

Yale Babylonian Collection (YBC)
    3449   124
    3526   118
    15334   161

Yeho'ash Royal Building inscription
    lines 1–16   244
    lines 1–3   229
    lines 1–4   243
    lines 4–14   244
    lines 4–7   248–50
    lines 4–5   243–45, 248
    line 4   245
    line 4-5   248 249
    line 13   257
    lines 14–15   228, 249, 251–53, 255, 258–59
    lines 14–16   243–76
    line 16   230, 252, 260, 262, 264

YOS
  3 44:23–24   256
  3 135:20   256

Index of Authors

Abraham, Kathleen 112, 126
Achtemeier, Paul J. 85, 90
Aharoni, Yohanan 103, 105
Ahituv, Shmuel 6, 103, 105, 224, 231, 233–35, 261–63, 273
Ahlström, Gösta 46, 54
Aisleitner, Joseph 73, 80
Al-As'ad, Khaled 147, 153–55
Al-Said, Said F. 105
Albright, William F. 3, 12, 13, 17, 73, 79, 80, 220, 235
Alcalay, Reuben 227, 235
Alexandre, Yardenna 4, 17
Allegro, John M. 221, 231, 235
Alonso Corral, Martin 99, 105
Amadasi Guzzo, Maria G. 7, 18
Andersen, Francis I. 251, 273
Anderson, Arnold A. 85, 90
Arie, Eran 48, 49, 54
Arnaud, Daniel 124, **131–36**
Athas, George 42, 54
Avigad, Nahman (+WSS) 8, 17, 24, 26, 28, 32, 38, 46, 52, 55, 60, 67, 70, 71, 75, 80, 114, 125, 183, 184, 190, 195, 218, 231, 235, 236
Avishur, Yitshak 251, 273
Ayalon, Avner 234, 235, 237
Balkan, Kemal 146
Banks, Edgar J. 130, 136
Bar-Matthews, Miryam 237
Barkay, Gavriel 77, 80, 271
Be'er, Haim 236
Bearman, Greg 6
Beaulieu, Paul-Alain 112, 118, 124–26, 131, 132, 136
Becking, Bob 21, 40, 47, 55, 153, 155
Beentjes, Pancratius C. 226, 236
Beeston, A. F. L. 100, 105
Benz, Frank L. 10, 14, 17
Berger, Paul-Richard 122, 126, 129, 134, 136
Berlin, Adele 250, 273
Beuken, W. A. M. 250, 273
Biran, Avraham 41, 55
Birot, Maurice 134–35
Blau, O. 195, 236
Bongenaar, A. C. V. M. 272, 273
Bordreuil, Pierre 42, 46, 55, 229, 236, 261, 263, 273
Breuer, M. 270, 273
Brewer, Douglas J. 76, 80
Brinkman, J. A. 96, 97, 105
Briquel-Chatonnet, Françoise 97, 106, 147, 151–53, 155
Brockelmann, Carl 165, 169
Bron, François 14, 17, 18, 94, 102, 103, 106
Brunner, Hellmut 76, 80
Budde, Hendrik 211, 236
Budge, E. A. Wallis 75, 80
Burstein, Stanley M. 125, 126
Burtea, Bogdan 162, 169
Buttrick, George A. 85, 90
Byrne, Ryan 1, 2, 18
Cardahi, P. 165, 169
Caubet, Annie 103, 104, 106

Christens-Berry, William A. 6
Clermont-Ganneau, Charles 200, 202, 203, 210, 214, 218, 235, 236
Cocquerillat, Denise 117, 126
Cogan, Mordechai 45, 55, 86, 90, 249, 250, 273
Cohen, Chaim (Harold R.) 227, 229, 236, 243, 248, 250, 254, 261, 271–73, 274
Cole, Steven 117, 127
Collins, Billie Jean xi
Conder, Claude R. 199, 200, 236
Cowley, A. E. 230, 236
Cross, Frank M. 3, 5, 8, 10, 13, 15, 16, 18, 38, 47, 55, 60, 67, 111, 127, 130, 136, 222, 229, 231, 233, 234, 236, 237, 245, 260, 274
Currid, John D. 79, 80, 84–86, 90
D'Agostino, Franco 71, 80
Da Riva, Rocio 117, 127, 129, 134–35
Dahood, Mitchell J. 73
Dalley, Stephanie 96, 106
Dalman, Gustav 228, 236
Dandamaev, Muhammad A. 124, 127
Darnell, John C. 2, 4, 18
Dassow, Eva von 256, 274
Davesne, Alain 98, 106
Davies, Graham I. 8, 10, 13, 14, 18
Davies, Philip R. 233, 240
DeVries, Simon J. 85, 90
Delitzsch, Franz 219, 224–26, 228, 232, 236, 237
Demsky, Aaron 4, 6
Deshayes, Jean 11, 18
Desideri, Paolo 99, 106
Deutsch, Robert 6, 18, 22, 24–26, 32, 59, 60, 62, 66, 67, 69, 71, 75, 80, 184, 185, 191
Diakonoff, Igor M. 102, 106
Diestel, L. 195, 198, 204, 212, 220, 237
Diringer, David 36, 55, 72, 80, 183, 191
Dobbs-Alsopp, F. W. 69, 80
Dobler, Carolyn P. **183–91**
Donner, Herbert 55, 173, 181, 237
Dothan, Trude 99, 106
Drower, Ethel S. 162, 166, 169
Dubberstein, Waldo H. 113, 128
Dvorachek, Michael 238
Eisenberg, Jerome M. 211, 237
Elayi, Josette 6, 18, 96, 106
Eph'al, Israel 261, 274
Epstein, J. N. 168, 169
Erman, Adolf 211, 221, 237
Eshel, Esther 237
Euting, Julius 213, 237
Fales, Frederick M. 111, 114, 115, 120, 127, 252, 274
Faulkner, Raymond O. 76, 81, 87, 90
Feldman, Howard R. 237, 238, 240
Feldman, Louis H. 176, 181
Ferioli, Piera 120, 127
Fiandra, Enrica 120, 127
Fiechter, Jean-Jacques xiii
Finkel, Irving L. 125, 127
Finkelstein, Israel 5, 18, 24, 32, 94, 101, 106
Fletcher, O. O. 220, 241
Folmer, Margaretha L. 115, 127
Ford, James N. 157, 158, 161, 166, 169
Fowler, Jeaneane D. 69, 81
Fox, Nili S. 32, 37, 55
Franklin, Norma 45, 55
Frayne, Douglas R. (RIME 2) 130, 131
Freedman, David N. 227, 237, 262, 270, 274
Freud, Liorah 26, 33
Friedrich, Johannes 7, 18
Fuchs, Andreas 96, 106
Gadd, Cyril J. 105, 106
Gajda, Iwona 103, 104, 106
Ganor, Eli 229
Ganor, Saar 5, 6, 235, 237
Garbini, Giovanni 104
Gardiner, Alan H. 74, 76, 78, 81, 84, 90
Garfinkel, Yosef 5, 6, 77, 81
Gass, Erasmus 193, 237
Gawlikowski, Michał 147, 154, 155

INDEX OF AUTHORS

Gelb, Ignace J.	16, 18	Hellwald, Friedrich von	213, 215–17, 238
Geller, Mark	111, 127	Heltzer, Michael	6, 8, 18, 69, 71, 80, 105, 107
George, Athas R.	131, 136		
Geraty, Lawrence T.	52, 55	Herbordt, Suzanne	119, 120, 127
Geus, C. H. J. de	35, 40, 56	Herr, Larry G.	52, 56
Gibson, J. C. L.	72, 81	Hess, Richard S.	74, 81, 172, 181
Ginsburg, Christian D.	228, 237	Hoch, James E.	73, 74, 81
Gitin, Seymour	99, 106	Hoffmann, G.	207, 214, 220, 232, 238
Glassner, Jean-Jacques	99, 106	Hoffmeier, James K.	88, 90
Gnoli, Gherardo	104, 106	Höfner, Maria	103, 107
Goetze, Albrecht	96, 106	Hoftijzer, J. (*DNWSI*)	115
Gogel, Sandra L.	223, 237, 261, 274	Horn, Siegfried H.	72, 81
Goldwasser, Orly	2, 18	Houtman, Cornelis	84, 90
Goodman, Martin	280, 281	Houwink ten Cate, P. H. J.	96, 97, 107
Gordon, Cyrus H. (+ *UT*)	xii, xiv, 72, 73, 231, 237	Hubbard, Robert L. Jr.	47, 56
		Huehnergard, John	111
Goren, Yuval	48, 49, 54, 234, 235, 237	Hulst, A. R.	264
Goshen-Gottstein, Moshe H.	237	Huot, Jean-Louis	134, 136
Graetz, Heinrich	280, 281	Hurowitz, Victor	174, 181, 252, 255, 258–60, 274
Graham, Cyril C.	207, 237		
Graham, M. Patrick	193, 237	Hurvitz, Avi	237
Grayson, A. Kirk	44, 56, 99, 100	Ilani, Shimon	229, 235, 237, 238, 240
Greenberg, Moshe	266, 270, 274	Irwin, William H.	250, 274
Greenfield, Jonas C.	252, 274	Israel, Felice	229, 236, 261, 273
Greenstein, E.	255, 258, 260, 274	Jackson, Kent P.	223, 238
Greer, Jonathan S.	154, 155	Jahn, Gustav	220, 232, 238
Grenfell, Alice	75, 81	James, Peter J.	24, 33
Gröndahl, Frauke	8, 14, 16, 18, 73, 81	Jamme, Albert	102, 103, 107, 130, 136
Grundfest, Yaakov	105, 107	Jasink, Anna M.	96, 99, 106, 107
Gurney, Oliver R. (+ *UET* VII)	145, 146	Jasmin, Michael	94, 107
Guthe, Hermann	221–24, 237	Jastrow, Marcus	272, 274
Häberl, Charles G.	168, 170	Joannès, Francis	96, 97, 107, 117, 118, 121, 122, 127
Hackett, Jo A.	52, 56, 222, 233, 237, 263, 274		
		Jongeling, K. (*DNWSI*)	115
Hallo, William	56	Joosten, Jan	266, 274
Hamilton, Gordon J.	2, 18	Joüon, Paul	248, 274
Harding, G. Lancaster	13, 16, 18	Junker, Hermann	76, 81
Hawkins, J. David	79, 81, 171, 174, 175, 177–79, 181	Jursa, Michael	47, 56, 116, 117, 125, 127
		Kaddari, Menachem Z.	275
Hayajneh, Hani	105, 107	Kaiser, Otto	56
Hayes, William C.	89, 90	Kaufman, Stephen A.	173, 181
Heemstra, Marius	279, 281	Kautzsch, Emil	196, 198, 200, 204–8, 215, 216, 232, 238
Heide, Martin	233, 234, 237		

Kessler, Karlheinz	164, 170	Liverani, Mario	93, 102, 108
Keulen, Percy S. F. van	176, 181	Livingstone, Alasdair	97, 108
Kitchen, Kenneth A.	42, 43, 56, 76, 81, 85, 90	Lohfink, Norbert	226, 239
		Löwy, Albert	220, 232, 239
Kitchener, Horatio H.	217, 238	Lozachmeur, Hélène	98, 106, 108
Kittel, Rudolf	226, 238	Lubetski, Meir	ix
Klein, Friedrich A.	194, 238	Lundberg, Marilyn J.	5
Klein, Jacob	130, 136	Macia, L. Miralles	153, 155, 168
Knapp, A. Bernard	88, 91	Macintosh, Andrew A.	270, 275
Koch, Adolf	196, 198, 205–7, 211–14, 220, 238	Macuch, Rudolf	165, 166, 169, 170
		Maeir, Aren M.	4, 19
König, Eduard	220, 238	Mansoor, Menahem	231, 239
Kornfeld, Walter	8, 9, 13, 18, 97, 107	Marcus, David	263, 272, 275
Korpel, Marjo C. A.	38, 56	Margalit, Baruch	42, 56
Krahmalkov, Charles	262, 275	Margueron, Jean	131, 136
Kronfeld, Joel	237, 238, 240	Mayer, Walter	96, 108
Krumbein, Wolfgang E.	238, 240	Mazar, Amihai	4, 19
Kutscher, Eduard Y.	79, 81	Mazar, Eilat	22, 33, 37, 50, 56
Kwasman, Theodore	272, 275	McCarter, P. Kyle Jr.	5, 52, 56, 237
Lackenbacher, Sylvie	3, 19	McLaughlin, John L.	153–55
Lambdin, Thomas O.	15, 84, 91	Melville, Sarah C.	173, 181
Lambert, W. G.	98, 107, 145, 146, 247, 275	Mercer, Samuel A. B.	73, 74, 79, 81
Lanfranchi, Giovanni B.	96	Meshorer, Ya'akov	239, 279, 281
Langdon, Stephen	135, 136	Mettinger, Tryggve N. D.	263, 275
Lansing, Ambrose	75, 81	Meyer, Eduard	220, 239
Laroche, Emmanuel	177, 181	Milgrom, Jacob	176, 182, 265, 268, 275
Lehmann, Manfred R.	79, 81	Milik, Jósef T.	152, 155
Lehrer-Jacobson, Gustav	194, 212, 221, 231, 238	Millard, Alan	2, 19, 190, 191, 251, 252
		Miller, J. Maxwell	39, 56
Lemaire, André	1–3, 5, 6, 8, 11, 14, 19, 41, 56, 71, 75, 80, 93, 94, 97, 98, 100, 103, 104, 106–8, 111, 118, 121, 122, 151, 155, 184, 190, 191, 221, 228, 234, 237, 238	Miller, Patrick D., Jr.	39, 56
		Misgav, Haggai	5, 6
		Montgomery, James A.	87, 91
		Moortgat-Correns, U.	120, 127
		Moran, William L.	73, 81, 86, 91
Lenormont, François	103, 108	Morenz, Siegfried	76, 81
Lesko, Leonard H.	74, 77, 81, 87, 91	Morgenstern, Matthew	157, 158, 166, 168–70, 256–57, 275
Levene, Dan	157, 170		
Levy, Jacob	196, 224, 226, 238	Moussaieff, Shlomo	280, 281
Levy, Moritz A.	208, 238, 239	Muchiki, Yoshiyuki	73, 74, 81, 84, 87, 91
Lichtheim, Miriam	88, 91	Müller, Walter W.	102, 105, 108
Lidzbarski, Mark	103, 108, 213, 218, 239	Müller-Kessler, Christa	111, 128, 158, 159, 161, 163, 164, 170
Lipiński, Edward	93, 102, 108, 111, 264		
Lipschits, Oded	100, 108, 272–73, 275	Münchhausen, Freiherr von	215, 239

INDEX OF AUTHORS

Muraoka, Takamitsu   115, 128, 248, 274
Mykytiuk, Lawrence J. (+ *IBP*) 36–54, 57, 71, 82
Na'aman, Nadav   99, 101, 108
Nadelman, Yonatan   103, 108, 109
Naveh, Joesph   xii–xiii, 12–14, 16, 19, 41, 55, 125, 128, 218, 231, 239, 261, 283
Nebes, Norbert   104, 109
Neubauer, Adolf   211, 224, 230, 236, 239
Noegel, Scott   173, 181
Nöldeke, Theodor   167, 168, 170, 194, 195, 203, 204, 214, 239
Norin, Stig   227, 239
O'Connor, Michael   52, 57
Olmo Lete, Gregorio del   72, 82, 250, 263, 273, 275
Oppenheim, A. Leo   105, 109, 272, 275
Otzen, B.   114, 128
Padilla Monge, Aurelio   97, 109
Paran, Meir   268, 275
Pardee, Denis   229, 232, 236, 239, 261, 273
Parker, Richard A.   113, 128
Parker, Simon B. (*UNP*)   263
Pedersén, Olof   122, 124, 128
Petermann, Heinrich   194, 214, 239
Pirenne, Jacqueline   95, 103, 109
Pitard, Wayne T.   47, 57
Porten, Bezalel   9, 19, 71, 82, 115
Postgate, J. N.   120, 127
Potts, Dan T.   104, 109
Powell, M. A.   122, 128
Pritchard, James B.   57, 70, 78, 79, 82
Prym, Eugen   198, 201, 206, 239
Puech, Émile   8, 12, 16, 19, 20, 52, 57
Quirke, Stephen   75, 76, 82, 89, 91
Rabinowicz, Oskar K.   221, 225, 231, 239
Rabinowitz, Isaac   250, 275
Radner, Karen   120, 128
Rainey, Anson F.   41, 57
Ranke, Hermann   73, 74, 78, 82
Ravn, Otto E.   146
Rawson, Albert L.   216, 239
Redford, Donald B.   86, 91
Reichel, Clemens D.   120, 128
Reichert, Andreas   194, 211, 239
Reiner, Fred N.   219, 221, 239
Reinhold, Gotthard G. G.   47, 57
Rendsburg, Gary A.   42, 57, 263, 275
Renz, Johannes   103, 109, 223, 239
Riehm, Eduard K. A.   217, 239, 240
Ries, Gerhard   116, 128
Rin, Shifra   72, 73, 82
Rin, Svi   72, 73, 82
Ritner, Robert K.   84, 91
Roberts, J. J. M.   251, 275
Robin, Christian   104, 109
Robins, Gay   86, 91, 109
Rogerson, John   233, 240
Röllig, Wolgang   7, 18, 55, 105, 109, 173, 181, 223, 237, 239
Rollinger, Robert   96, 97, 109
Rollston, Christopher A.   3, 20, 37, 38, 46, 57, 229, 234, 240
Rosenfeld, Amnon   229, 235, 237, 238, 240
Rottzoll, Dirk U.   226, 240
Sack, Ronald H.   131, 136
Salmon, Ira   240
Salonen, Armas   121, 128
Samet, Inbal   48, 49, 54
Sanders, Seth   2, 20
Sanmartín, Joaquin   72, 250, 263, 273, 275
Sarna, Nahum M.   79, 82
Sass, Benjamin (+ *WSS*)   2, 3, 5, 8, 11–16, 18, 20, 24, 26, 28, 32, 38, 46, 48, 49, 51, 52, 55, 70, 71, 75, 103, 109, 114, 125, 183, 231, 240
Sasson, Victor   228, 240, 245, 252, 273, 275
Saur, Markus   102, 109
Schalit, Abraham   280, 281
Schilman, Bettina   237
Schlottmann, K.   194–97, 201, 202, 206, 207, 209, 213–16, 220, 232, 235, 240, 241

Schlumberger, Daniel 152, 155
Schmidt, Brian B. 173, 181
Schniedewind, William M. 263, 275
Segal, J. B. 158, 170
Segert, Stanislav 72, 82
Sethe, Kurt 73, 82, 87, 91
Shaffer, Aaron 252, 274
Shanks, Hershel xiii, 241, 271, 273, 275
Shapira, Moses W. 217
Shapira, Wilhelm M. 203, 241
Shiloh, Yigal 48, 57, 102, 109
Shoham, Yair 22, 26–28, 33
Simian-Yofre, H. 253, 275
Singer-Avitz, L. 5, 18, 102, 109
Sirat, Colette 222, 241
Sivan, Daniel 262, 275
Smend, Rupolf 213, 241
Socin, Albert 196–98, 200, 204–8, 211–14, 216, 232, 238, 241
Sokoloff, Michael 112, 126, 157, 166, 170, 257, 275
Spenser, Jeffrey 75, 76, 82
Sperber, Alexander 264, 275
Stadhouders, Henry 40, 55
Stager, Lawrence E. 5, 18
Stark, Jürgen K. 151, 155
Steiner, Richard C. 87, 91
Stern, Menahem 279, 281
Strack, Hermann L. 220, 241
Strassmaier, J. N. (Nbk) 124
Strawn, Brent A. 173, 181
Strommenger, Eva 120, 128
Tadmor, Hayim 45, 57, 249, 250, 273
Talshir, David 252, 253, 255, 260, 262, 275
Tappy, Ron E. 5, 20
Tarelko, Michael 167, 170
Tawil, Hayim 259, 275
Teeter, Emily 76, 80
Teixidor, Javier 151, 155
Thareani-Sussely, Yifat 101, 102, 109
Thompson, J. A. 226, 241
Török, László 77, 82
Torrey, Charles C. 38, 57
Tropper, Josef 72, 82, 173, 182
Tushingham, A. Douglas 77, 82
Tyborowski, Witold 121, 128
Tyrwhitt Drake, C. F. 199, 200
Unger, Eckhard 233, 241
Ussishkin, David 46, 57
Van Beek, Gus W. 130, 136
Van Driel, G. 117, 128
Van de Mieroop, Marc 130, 136
Vanderhooft, David S. 99, 109
Vaughn, Andrew G. 25–27, 33, 49, 50, 52, 57, **183-91**
Veen, Peter G. van der 21, 24, 25, 28, 32, 33
Verbrugghe, Gerald P. 125, 128
Vita, Juan-Pablo 1, 20
Vlaardingerbroek, Johannes 250, 275
Volkwein, Bruno 226, 241, 254, 275, 276
Von Soden, Wilfram (*AHw*) 247, 254
Von Wickede, Alwo 120, 128
Von Wissmann, Hermann 96, 101, 105, 110
Walker, C. B. F. 132, 134, 136
Walsh, Jerome T. 85, 87, 91
Ward, William A. 89, 91
Watterson, Barbara 89, 91
Weidner, Ernst F. 96, 99, 109
Weil, Gerald E. 271, 276
Weinfeld, Moshe 272, 274
Weiss, Johann 226, 227, 241
Wenig, Steffen 75, 82
Weser, Hermann 197, 200, 202–4, 241
Westendorf, Wolfhart 73, 82
Wetzstein, Johann G. 207, 241
Wickersham, John M. 125
Wiedemann, Alfred 75, 82
Wildberger, Hans 250, 276
Wimmer, Stefan J. 4, 20, 60, 67, 231, 241
Wimmer-Dweikat, S. 4, 20
Wiseman, D. J. 98, 99, 109, 110, 131
Wright, Paul H. 131, 136, 146
Wuthnow, Heinz 13
Yadin, Yigael 73

INDEX OF AUTHORS

Yahuda, Abraham S.	84, 91, 217, 220, 241	Zaidel, Mosheh	70, 82
Yamauchi, Edwin	157, 168, 170	Zamora Lopez, José Àngel	1, 20
Yardeni, Ada	6, 9, 237	Zettler, Richad	120, 128
Yeivin, Israel	248, 249, 276	Zimhoni, Orna	26, 33
Yon, Jean-Baptiste	153	Zuckerman, Bruce	5
Younger, K. Lawson, Jr.	173	Zukerman, Alexander	4
Zadok, Ran	97, 99, 110		

www.ingramcontent.com/pod-product-compliance
Lightning Source LLC
Chambersburg PA
CBHW020640300426
44112CB00007B/179